All His Spies

STEPHEN ALFORD

All His Spies
The Secret World of Robert Cecil

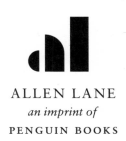

ALLEN LANE
an imprint of
PENGUIN BOOKS

ALLEN LANE

UK | USA | Canada | Ireland | Australia
India | New Zealand | South Africa

Allen Lane is part of the Penguin Random House group of companies
whose addresses can be found at global.penguinrandomhouse.com

Penguin
Random House
UK

First published 2024
002

Copyright © Stephen Alford, 2024

The moral right of the author has been asserted

Set in 10.5/14pt Sabon LT Std
Typeset by Jouve (UK), Milton Keynes
Printed and bound in Great Britain by Clays Ltd, Elcograf S.p.A.

The authorized representative in the EEA is Penguin Random House Ireland,
Morrison Chambers, 32 Nassau Street, Dublin DO2 YH68

A CIP catalogue record for this book is available from the British Library

ISBN: 978–0–241–42347–9

Death! I dare tell him so; and all his Spies.
                    Ben Jonson, Sejanus, His Fall *(1605)*

To John Guy

The heart is more devious than any other thing,
it is perverse; who can pierce its secrets?

Jeremiah 17:9

Trustworthy words
Are not Beautiful,
Beautiful words
Are not to be Trusted

Lao-Tzu, Tao Te Ching, *chapter 81,*
translated by John Minford

I may have had my frailties as all the sons of Adam.
Robert Cecil to Patrick, master of Gray, 1603

Contents

CONTENTS

List of Illustrations

Photographic acknowledgements are given in parentheses.

1. Sir Robert Cecil, c.1602, by John de Critz the Elder. Hatfield House, Hertfordshire. (Bridgeman Images)
2. William Cecil, 1st Baron of Burghley, 1587, by Marcus Gheeraerts the Younger. Bodleian Library, University of Oxford. (World History Archive/Alamy)
3. Mildred, Lady Burghley, c.1570–74, attributed to Hans Eworth. Hatfield House, Hertfordshire. (Bridgeman Images)
4. Bird's-eye view of Antwerp, from *Civitates Orbis Terrarum*, c.1572, by Georg Braun and Frans Hogenburg, (Metropolitan Museum of Art, New York)
5. Sir Christopher Hatton, probably a seventeenth-century copy of a portrait of 1589, by an unknown artist. National Portrait Gallery, London. (Art Collection 3/Alamy)
6. The 'Rainbow Portrait' of Queen Elizabeth I, c.1600, by Isaac Oliver. Hatfield House, Hertfordshire. (Bridgeman Images)
7. King James VI of Scotland c.1595, attributed to Adrian Vanson. Scottish National Portrait Gallery. (incamerastock/Alamy)
8. Title-page of William Allen's *A True Sincere and Modest Defence of English Catholiques That Suffer for Their Faith*, 1585, with handwritten notes by Richard Topcliffe. Cambridge University Library, shelf-mark F.15.24.(Reproduced by kind permission of the Syndics of Cambridge University Library)
9. A raid on a Catholic house, illustration from Richard Verstegan's *Theatre of the Cruelties of the Heretics of Our Time*, 1592. Cambridge University Library, shelf-mark U.*.4.41. (Reproduced by kind permission of the Syndics of Cambridge University Library)
10. Instructions set out by the spy Michael Moody for secret communications with Sir Robert Cecil from Antwerp, 1591. Hatfield

Principal Characters

Robert CECIL, principal secretary to Queen Elizabeth I and King James I, and later lord treasurer, created by James BARON CECIL of Essendon, Viscount CRANBORNE and 1st earl of SALISBURY.

Queen ELIZABETH I of England and Ireland, daughter of King Henry VIII and Queen Anne Boleyn; reigned 1558–1603.
King JAMES VI of Scotland (reigned 1567–1625), James I of England, Scotland and Ireland (reigned 1603–25).

William Cecil, Lord BURGHLEY, Queen Elizabeth's lord treasurer, Robert Cecil's father, and husband of MILDRED, Lady Burghley.
Lady Elizabeth Cecil (BESS), Robert Cecil's wife.
William Cecil, Viscount CRANBORNE, later 2nd earl of Salisbury, son of Bess and Robert Cecil.

Robert Devereux, 2nd earl of ESSEX, courtier and favourite of Queen Elizabeth, Robert Cecil's rival.
Francis BACON, Robert Cecil's maternal first cousin, suitor, lawyer and follower of Robert, earl of Essex.

William WADE, clerk of Queen Elizabeth's Privy Council and in the reign of James I lieutenant of the Tower of London.
Thomas PHELIPPES, decipherer and intelligencer.

Michael HICKES, Lord Burghley's patronage secretary and Robert Cecil's friend 'Master Michael'.
Henry MAYNARD, Lord Burghley's private secretary.
Roger HOUGHTON, Robert Cecil's steward.
Simon WILLIS, Robert Cecil's first private secretary.
Levinus MUNCK, one of Robert Cecil's later private secretaries.

The British Isles

N

St Albans ● — ○ Hatfield House
● Cheshunt
Theobalds ○
Pymmes ●
● Wanstead
LONDON
Southwark ● Deptford ●
Mortlake ● ○ Greenwich Palace
○ Richmond Palace
○ Hampton Court

Falkland Palace ○

Edinburgh ○
Holyrood Palace ● ● Berwick-upon-Tweed

North Sea

● Morpeth
● Newcastle-on-Tyne

ULSTER

Yellow Ford ○

● York

Bellaclynthe Ford ○

Irish Sea

Dublin ●

Stamford ○
Burghley House ○
Fotheringhay ●
● Cambridge

Cork ●

Windsor Castle ●
Bristol ●
Bath ● Marlborough ● ○ Nonsuch Palace Canterbury ●
○ Loseley Park Dover ●
○ Cowdray Castle

Isle of Wight

Dartmouth ●

English Channel

0 ———————————— 100 miles
0 ———————————— 100 kms

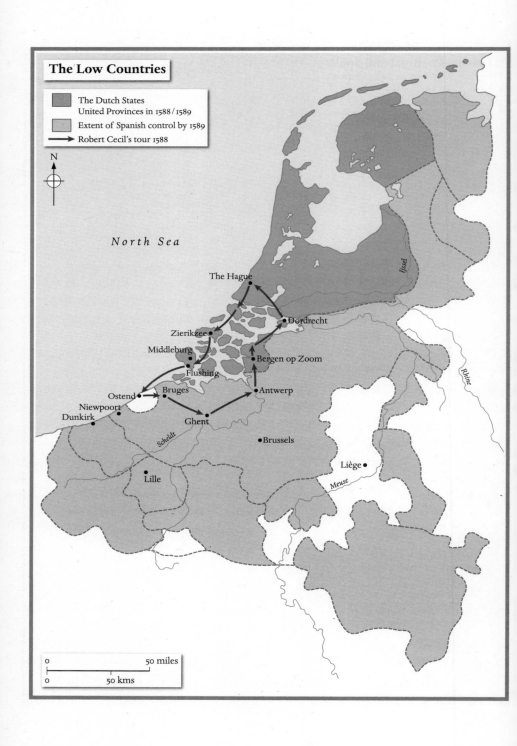

The Low Countries

- The Dutch States
  United Provinces in 1588/1589
- Extent of Spanish control by 1589
- → Robert Cecil's tour 1588

N

North Sea

The Hague

Dordrecht

IJssel

Zierikzee

Middleburg

Bergen op Zoom

Flushing

Antwerp

Ostend

Bruges

Niewpoort

Dunkirk

Ghent

Scheldt

Brussels

Rhine

Liège

Lille

Meuse

| 0 | | 50 miles |
| 0 | | 50 kms |

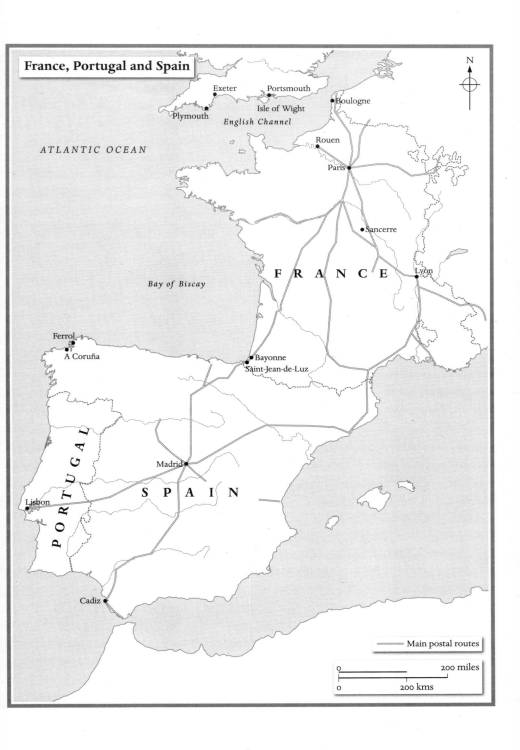

France, Portugal and Spain

N

Exeter
Portsmouth
Plymouth
Isle of Wight
Boulogne
English Channel

ATLANTIC OCEAN

Rouen
Paris

Sancerre

Bay of Biscay

F R A N C E
Lyon

Ferrol
A Coruña

Bayonne
Saint-Jean-de-Luz

P O R T U G A L

Madrid

S P A I N

Lisbon

Cadiz

Main postal routes

0   200 miles
0   200 kms

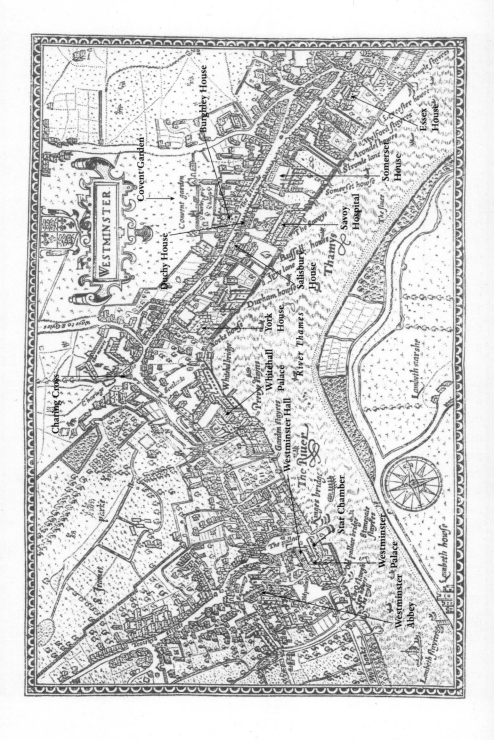

To the Reader

Some portraits get hold of you straight away. Robert Cecil's is unlikely to be one of them.

Those of Charles de Solier, sieur de Morette and Robert Cheseman, for example, both painted by Hans Holbein the Younger in an earlier time, grip you fast. These men have presence and power. They can look at and even straight through you, as the great ones often do. They are in charge and are not to be crossed. Yet all the virtuosity of the Flemish artist John de Critz couldn't do this for Cecil. He looks pallid by comparison.

And so the first impression. A middle-aged man in a sober business suit of black, with a long face and high forehead, hair combed back, a trimmed reddish beard and delicately expressive hands. Most certainly not a courtier glittering in full Technicolor or a man who dominates. More scholar than politician, we might think, though probably we'd guess a quietly ambitious one. A man who sits for an artist out of duty and for form's sake, who only tolerates the scrutiny, who would rather be somewhere else. Decorating the portrait is a motto, *Sero, sed serio*, whose clever Latin wordplay can't hide the whisper of an apology – 'Late, but in earnest'.

Resist this first impression – it is the mask Robert Cecil presented to the world, the mask this book tries to get behind.

Why should you want to read a long book about Cecil? It is a fair question to ask. I hope what follows gives you an answer and persuades you to turn its pages through to the end.

He was the most accomplished and formidable politician of his generation. No one had power quite like his – not in England, not perhaps in Europe. He was close adviser to two monarchs, Queen Elizabeth I and King James I. He manoeuvred his country through and beyond the death of Elizabeth, stage-managing the trickiest change of ruling family in a century. Some admired his political arts. Many feared him. By the end of his life some people – from political rivals, frustrated suitors and poets to ordinary Elizabethans and Jacobeans grumbling in taverns about their betters – detested him for his riches and his influence. He was the object of conspiracy theories, the subject of slanders and libels. Not many mourned his death at the age of forty-eight.

His world was full of shadows and evasions, ambition and secrecy, deceptions and betrayal. You'll soon discover that things were often not as they seemed to be. Many of the fine Elizabethan words and phrases which are quoted in this book have all the substance of smoke; friendships seem more like enmities; loyalties quickly dissolve. In the furnace of the royal court hopes and disappointments were super-heated to sometimes explosive temperatures. Unforgiving competition for patronage made courtiers struggle for the promotions, lands and offices that were in the gift of the monarch. They frequently struggled against each other. And then there was politics.

For a minister like Robert Cecil, serving the ruling prince was everything. Anticipating the wishes and navigating the moods and whims of any monarch kept advisers dancing uncomfortably on their toes. The monarch was absolute, blessed by God. She or he was also fallibly human, as ministers knew very well, even though they couldn't say it. The superlative adviser – this is what Robert Cecil drove himself so hard to be – had to wrap himself around the will of his prince. And he needed to survive. 'You good men which frequent the court, your life, and the way wherein you walk, is very slippery: ... Wherefore you ought to be very circumspect, and to stay yourselves well, lest you fall.' So wrote one of the great scholars of sixteenth-century Europe, a student of princes' power, Justus Lipsius. He was quite right. Many failed at court. But no one was more circumspect than Cecil; no one was better trained for political life. He was engineered to serve.[1]

There are lots of things we know about Robert Cecil and lots that we don't. His life has to be dug out of the mountain of paper he left behind, most of which survives today in the archives of the extra-ordinary statement house he built (but didn't live long enough to occupy), Hatfield House in Hertfordshire, and in the collections of the National Archives (mainly the State Papers of the old Public Record Office) and in the British Library in London. So vast is this collection of material that any historian or biographer, for the sake of their readers' patience and their own sanity, has to choose a path through it. Selection is necessary: a multi-volume epic that tried to include and do everything would be unreadable. There is only so much bureaucratic detail about day-to-day government that any sensible person would want to know about.

What I have endeavoured to do above all, powered by some narrative energy, is to try to get to the heart of Robert Cecil – or at the very least to give us a fuller, richer Cecil than the rather bloodless bureaucrat we find lurking on the edges of popular Tudor history. My emphases are on power and politics, state security and secrecy, and the royal succession following Queen Elizabeth. The greater weight of the book is Elizabethan, though, undoubtedly, we get close to the core of Robert Cecil in the years either side of the Gunpowder Plot of 1605.

Collecting paper was a compulsion for two Elizabethan generations of the Cecil family. Robert's father, William Cecil, 1st baron of Burghley, was the longest-serving and most influential of Elizabeth's ministers. As Burghley's obedient son and apprentice, Robert was for years in his shadow. There is no way of telling Cecil's story up to the age of thirty-five, when his father died, without Burghley.

Nothing much survives of Robert's childhood – only a few disparate sources. At eighteen he begins to come into focus, at twenty-one even more so. We can follow him properly and fully from his visit to Paris in 1584, but our best early meeting with him – where we really begin to hear the richness of Robert's voice for the first time – is on his tour of the war-torn Netherlands in 1588 aged twenty-four, a few months before King Philip II of Spain launched his Armada against England. By 1591, the year Cecil turned twenty-eight, when Queen Elizabeth appointed him to her Privy Council, he is completely present. From too few sources, we have from this time on so many, thanks to his family's habit of hoarding documents and to the long reach and depth of their power.

Where the Cecils served, they also dominated. What they dominated was government – it is a connecting thread of this book.

In some ways the corridors of power have changed very little in four hundred years: we might very easily imagine a contemporary setting for Robert Cecil's story. There are aspects to human politics and rivalry which feel eternal. Yet Elizabeth's government functioned quite differently from most governments in our age, even where there are names and institutions – Parliament, Privy Council, the Exchequer – which are still with us today. Understanding the royal court, the council, the role of the monarch's secretary, parliaments and the problem of Ireland may help you to situate Robert Cecil and his career. What follows is a very brief guide.

The Tudor and early Stuart monarchs moved (or 'removed') between their palaces; their courts were peripatetic. The great royal palaces were mainly situated along the course of the River Thames, along which it was straightforward to move by boat and barge: these were Greenwich, Hampton Court, Nonsuch, Richmond, St James's, White-hall and others. Elizabeth in particular regularly went on late spring and late summer progresses to visit her courtiers' and officials' private houses and estates, where grand entertainments were laid on to welcome her. These progresses were efficient ways of keeping contact with her elite, of meeting her people, of escaping disease-ridden London and Westminster, and (always important for the parsimonious queen) of keeping her costs down, by getting her hosts to pay handsomely for the privilege of housing the whole royal court – which, with courtiers and servants, could number about 1,700 people. Access to the monarch's private rooms, especially the Privy Chamber, was strictly controlled. Proximity to the queen or king mattered for those families at court who wanted to maintain their own high position or hoped for further favour. That Lord Burghley and Robert Cecil had so much access to Elizabeth – that in fact she needed them close by her to conduct routine business – tells us something very significant about their power and influence at court and in government.

Thronging the court and queueing outside the chambers of courtiers were suitors. Tudor and early Stuart courts and governments ran on the fuel of patronage – offices, lands and estates, privileges and preferments, in government and in the Church, all in the hands of the Crown. Those suitors who spoke loudest and petitioned most were sometimes successful in getting the patronage they wanted, putting themselves on the promotional ladder. Often jobs in royal government were 'in reversion', that is, they were passed from known successor to known successor, sometimes in the same families. It was a sort of queueing system that used contacts and connections, involved shameless lobbying, and was often lubricated by gifts and favours. Probably nothing caused more anxiety for suitors than patrons at court who might deny them what they were desperate to have. It was no wonder that flattery, self-abasement and kow-towing to powerful courtiers was so much a part of the language and life of the court.

Government followed monarch and court: the monarch *was* government, absolute in his or her power, though not a tyrant. A queen or king governed according to laws and customs, took advice and counsel and was answerable with their soul ultimately to God. She or he was aided by ministers; councillors swore to the monarch an oath of personal loyalty and secrecy. The late Elizabethan Privy Council was small: sixteen councillors in spring 1590, thirteen by December of the same year, eleven in 1598. There were occasional injections of new blood, but Elizabeth became with age ever more hesitant and conservative in her appointments. Her councillors were all from long-established families at court – earls, barons and knights, all of the nobility, knights of the Order of the Garter, and most holding the various great offices of state or roles within the queen's household, for which there was a fixed hierarchy. From the archbishop of Canterbury (the only cleric) at the top, to the lord chancellor (or sometimes a lord keeper of the great seal), the lord treasurer, the lord admiral, the lord chamberlain, the lord steward, the treasurer, comptroller and vice chamberlain of the household, the principal secretary, all the way down to the chancellor of the Exchequer and chancellor of the Duchy of Lancaster. The council met nearly every day, including Sundays, usually first thing in the morning, to discuss the routine business of government and administration. It sent out instructions to officials and noblemen all over the kingdom, for which a team of expert clerks kept register books of letters and memoranda. Every royal palace had a council chamber. What the clerks didn't record were political discussions on sensitive matters of policy, which sometimes Elizabeth would host in her own private rooms.

Low down in the council's hierarchy was the monarch's principal secretary, the central co-ordinator and planner for the whole government machine. Every piece of paper on every subject under the sun, from Church appointments to military planning, to law and justice, to economic reform, crossed the secretary's desk. This was the Cecils' métier, where Robert Cecil and, before him, Lord Burghley flourished in the great tradition of Thomas Cromwell and William Paget in earlier Tudor reigns (the latter was Burghley's model and mentor). As we will see, the secretary had to be a skilled technician of policy and detail. But he was no robotic technocrat. Everyone knew that a good secretary had to be the keenest student of human nature and a deft courtier, superbly attuned to mood and atmosphere. As one clerk of the council advised in working for Elizabeth,

> Learn before your access her Majesty's disposition by some in the Privy Chamber with whom you must keep credit, for that will stand you in much stead, and yet yield not too much to their importunity for suits, for so you may be blamed, nevertheless pleasure them when conveniently you may.

In other words, know everything about what was happening with and all around the queen, every moment, every day – your career depends on it. A secretary had to have lightning-sharp political reflexes.[2]

All privy councillors sat in parliaments, the archbishop, earls and barons (with the other bishops and the rest of the nobility) in the House of Lords, and knights and other gentlemen in the House of Commons. Parliaments met in the old Westminster Palace (most of this, except for Westminster Hall, into which were packed the Tudor and Stuart courts of law, burned down in a great fire in 1834). 'The most high and absolute power of the realm of England consisteth in the parliament. For as in war, where the king himself in person, the nobility, the rest of the gentility, and the yeomanry are, is the force and power of England', as one distinguished writer put it early in Elizabeth's reign. By passing statutes, debated as bills in and between Lords and Commons and willed into law by the monarch, parliament could in theory deal with anything, from weights and measures and the affairs of towns and cities to the greatest matters of Church and State. But Elizabethan and Jacobean parliaments were complicated. First, they were parliaments, plural; they were events, summoned when the monarch wanted them to meet, usually to raise money through taxation. It was a long-established principle that the Crown's subjects could not be taxed without their own consent and a parliament represented the voice of the whole kingdom (even though the Elizabethan electorate of property-holders was tiny). So, parliaments were important, but they didn't sit all the time, and years might pass between one parliament and the next.[3]

In addition, parliaments were not meant to be political, at least not for Elizabeth who valued their compliance, silence and generosity: when they met she wanted money, not debate. She refused to let any parliament discuss issues which she felt trespassed on her absolute powers as monarch – so-called prerogative matters such as any proposed marriage or the royal succession. Parliaments frequently flouted this limitation, however – sometimes because members of the Commons, especially, felt, in loyalty, that there were urgent issues that had to be talked about and acted upon; sometimes because the queen's ministers tried occasionally to use parliaments to galvanize her into action on matters of state like the succession. This kind of pressure she both resisted and resented, and it provoked some of the finest speeches of her reign – brilliant examples of her haughtiest 'Who's Queen?' mode of keeping subjects in their place. Robert Cecil saw for himself such complicated political theatre in the first parliament he sat in, in 1584 and 1585, when his father and Elizabeth's then principal secretary, Sir Francis Walsingham, tried to draft emergency legislation for the queen's safety and for the security of the kingdom. They even went so far as to lay out the mechanisms for an interregnum government should Elizabeth be assassinated; this she refused to accept. Robert Cecil would one day have his own struggles with parliaments, caught painfully between Lords and Commons and the monarch.

Security both from outside attack and from enemies within was always a heavy preoccupation of Elizabeth's and James's ministers. England was a small Protestant kingdom facing many powerful Catholic enemies, principally Philip II of Spain. There were a few Protestant allies: in Scotland, in France (when its kings were Protestants), in the northern Netherlands, in Denmark, and in some of the German states. But mostly the regime felt itself vulnerable both abroad and at home – especially from those less easily governed parts of northern England and Wales, a long way from Westminster and London.

Most viscerally of all, the regime felt its weakness in Ireland, the single greatest territorial problem for Elizabeth. She was its queen. It was her second kingdom, an old inheritance settled centuries before by the Anglo-Norman nobility and, more recently, by English Protestant landowners. This made Ireland a delicate, often fractious, cultural melange of Gaelic-speaking indigenous Irish, old established settlers and new, as well as a fortress-strong bastion of the old Catholic faith, which resisted the kingdom's Protestantization from the 1540s. This was a programme of Reformation insisted on by Westminster and implemented by the English government based in Dublin. But the anglicized territory around Dublin, known as the Pale, was very different from the rest of Ireland. Over the whole island Elizabethan officials laboured with great difficulty to extend their control. They either recruited the support of Anglo-Irish noblemen, or isolated those landowners who got in the way of English government. In addition, by the 1570s, they tried using Ireland as a laboratory for the colonial settlements later taken to North America. These Protestant settler outposts were justified by the supposed lawlessness and wildness of the Irish and by the need to impose order and civility on them. Gradually English officials, in trying to extend their power by placing their own clients and supporters as landholders, pushed Gaelic chieftains into open revolt.

By the 1590s Ireland was becoming a fantastic drain on English money and military resources. Armies were sent by Elizabeth but they were unable to establish English rule and order. There were brutal massacres. The Exchequer in Westminster felt the weight of an impossible financial burden: the rebellion that began in 1593 was calculated in 1603 to have consumed about two million pounds, nearly twenty times the cost of repelling the Spanish Armada in 1588, and a sum even greater than that expended on the longer war against Spain. In this book we will see one career definitively ended by a failure of leadership in Ireland – that of Robert Cecil's rival Robert Devereux, 2nd earl of Essex.

*

This book keeps Cecil moving forward at a brisk pace. In it I have tried to take you behind the arras to hear the process, as Shakespeare says in *Hamlet* – to observe Elizabethan and early Jacobean politics from the inside, as we hide ourselves away, listening to conversations, making sense of the actors at close quarters.

There are still gaps, still evasions, still bits of the story that don't quite fit together – all of these you are bound to see or sense at some point. Lives are rarely as tidy as we might want them to be. Cecil himself wasn't a static character, was never fixed in one place; he adapted himself to people and situations. The bureaucrat of paper and process, which is how we might at first make sense of the de Critz portrait, is a thin caricature. If we look more closely we begin to find the courtier, highly intelligent, perceptive, commanding and supple in his reasoning. Perhaps there was a negative energy also. 'There's power in me and will to dominate / Which I must exercise, they hurt me else', are lines from Robert Browning's poem 'Bishop Blougram's Apology' that I have kept returning to in the few years of writing this book, for it always seems to me that there was something very strongly suppressed – perhaps repressed – about Cecil. He held himself under an extraordinary and unyielding self-discipline; he rarely let slip an unguarded word; he measured and planned everything. His powers to dissimulate, to be secret, to hide motives and political moves were considerable. They were necessary too. Justus Lipsius again: 'The court is full of danger.'

There were also, I think, other Robert Cecils: Cecil as friend, Cecil as husband and father. It can't be simply an accident of de Critz's composition that Robert Cecil's wedding ring, to which I always find my own eye drawn, is almost at the geographical centre of the portrait. Yet these identities, too, he kept tightly under lock and key, giving away only so much.

He grew up late in a century fractured by religious division, war and bitter dynastic rivalry. Sixteenth-century Europe was comprised of kingdoms, provinces and small states under the authority of local or foreign princes. Rebellion or dissatisfaction expressed against overlords was common: we have some sense of this already from the case of Ireland.

As monarchies, England, Scotland and France were relatively straightforward. Scotland had a king, and for a time a queen, though the country was under the influence of France until the beginning of Elizabeth's reign (King James V, who died in 1542, twice married French princesses); France, a kingdom of power and wealth, had for centuries been England's rival. Much of the rest of the Continent was a disordered patchwork of dynastic accretions, the complexity and diversity of which can leave us dazed, used as we are today to big states with clear boundaries and (more or less) unitary systems of government. The Low Countries (roughly modern-day Belgium and the Netherlands) were provinces ruled by the Spanish Habsburgs; the German states of the Holy Roman Empire had all kinds of rulers (Rhinegraves, margraves, dukes, bishops). Italy was not unified, but was composed of city states and small kingdoms (Naples, for example, was another Spanish territory), and the pope was a head of state as well as a religious leader.

So much was shaped in Europe by the accidents and happenstances of dynasty. Royal families mattered: their births, their marriages, their deaths, their rivalries with one another. In some ways we could write the history of sixteenth-century Europe through the commanding residences these rulers built, all the way from the palaces of Falkland and Holyrood in Scotland to the royal chateaux of the Loire, from the Coudenberg Palace in Brussels south to the monastery-palace of El Escorial in Spain. All ruling families had histories, sometimes distinguished, occasionally infamous. Generation shaped generation; reputations mattered. The disposition of the first of the two monarchs we will get to know very well in this book, Elizabeth I, was described by her godson as sweet and refreshing as a westerly breeze on a summer's morning. But sometimes there was a sharp change in the weather: Elizabeth 'could put forth such alterations, when obedience was lacking, as left no doubting whose daughter she was'. Sir John Harington meant here King Henry VIII, though for Catholic Europe it was Elizabeth's mother who mattered most: Anne Boleyn, the woman for whom Henry had rejected his first wife Katherine of Aragon, precipitating the break with the Church of Rome. This action further fractured a Christendom already challenged by Martin Luther and other reformers, shattered England's faith and remapped its foreign diplomacy. These were memories still vivid in Elizabeth's reign. To her Catholic foes across Europe, she was no queen at all, simply the bastard daughter of Henry's courtesan, a heretic offspring of a heretic woman. This is one of the reasons why Elizabeth's ministers believed to their core that her throne was under constant attack from enemies overt and covert.[4]

The most powerful of Elizabeth's rivals – indeed the most powerful of all Europe's monarchs – was the Spanish Habsburg King Philip II, the 'Most Catholic King' as his official title ran, who cast himself as the great defender of Catholic Europe against heresy, against the Ottomans and Islam. Elizabeth's government believed Philip to be plotting against her at every turn and opportunity, a fear to which there was a strand of truth – the Spanish Armada of 1588 is the obvious illustration. His monarchy was multinational and highly bureaucratic, as well as very expensive to maintain and defend. It stretched from Spain and Portugal east to Italy and north to the Spanish Netherlands. It was global too, extending out to the Americas and the East Indies. Philip had very much more than Protestant England to worry about.

From 1568 he faced a rebellion by his provinces in the Netherlands provoked by complaints about heavy taxation and the high-handedness of his local governors. Two years earlier Dutch Calvinists, Protestants influenced by the teaching of the French reformer Jean Calvin, had risen in religious revolt. There was open warfare and Philip deployed troops. During the 1570s England supported the Dutch with money and mercenaries, and in 1585 agreed a treaty with the new independent 'States' of the northern Netherlands to send an army to the Low Countries. One part of this agreement was the English garrisoning of three Dutch ports. Elizabeth's ministers explained this provocative third-party involvement in a foreign rebellion as legitimate self-defence: Lord Burghley wrote that the queen could no longer 'suffer the King of Spain to grow to the full height of his designs and conquests'. They were sure that should the Dutch be defeated, Philip would invade England. Elizabeth's war against Spain lasted until 1604.[5]

Moreover, it wasn't only Spain that seemed to threaten England. For decades, the queen's ministers saw danger and division all about them. In France, divided from the 1560s all the way into the 1590s by a religious civil war with noble families, both Catholic and

Protestant, fighting for dominance, its throne contested by two dynasties, Angoulême and Bourbon. (So much hung in France – and elsewhere in Europe – on the deaths of kings.) In Scotland, where in 1567 Elizabeth's blood cousin Mary Stuart was deposed and Mary's baby son James made king. This fragile royal minority was merely one punctuation mark in decades of Scottish political infighting and instability. This is our James, the sixth of Scotland, the first of Great Britain and Ireland.

There were also deep domestic challenges. Elizabeth's Protestant Church of England drove English Catholics either underground or into exile. This provoked an international mission to recover England to the true Catholic faith, a mission that Elizabeth's government saw as treason and subversion. The queen herself, unmarried, childless and with no obvious heir, staunchly refused to name a successor. England faced its own dynastic emergency.

This, then, was the Cecils' business over four decades. Every paper on every one of these dangers crossed Lord Burghley's desk. They became Robert Cecil's concern too as he learned his trade as Elizabeth's minister.

Which takes us to the town of Antwerp on the Scheldt river a few months before the Spanish Armada sailed into the English Channel.

Prelude

Taking the Air

In March 1588 a foreign visitor arrived in Antwerp from Ghent. Keen and attentive, a privileged Englishman in enemy territory, he was twenty-four years old. So far on his journey he had shivered with ambassadors and diplomats in Ostend and had slogged his way through filthy weather from Bruges. Now on his own, his optimism was undiminished. He liked Antwerp. The young man had an appraising eye; he was an observer who missed little.

Over thirty years before, one of the artists of Antwerp's golden years, Frans Floris, had painted a great triptych of the defeat of Satan by a heavenly army commanded by the archangel Michael. The twelfth chapter of Revelation in the New Testament, as a good Protestant Elizabethan would find it in the Geneva Bible, described it so: 'And there was a battle in heaven. Michael and his angels fought against the dragon, and the dragon fought and his angels . . . And the great dragon, that old serpent, called the devil and Satan, was cast out . . . he was even cast into the earth, and his angels were cast out with him.' The triptych's vast central panel, six-and-a-half feet by ten, shows Michael and his forces striking down the monstrous rebels with scimitars and rapiers. In early spring 1588 the great painting was hanging where our visitor could not have missed it, in the half-light of the Church of Our Lady, which towered over Antwerp's market square.[1]

Antwerp and its citizens knew all about rebellion and religious violence. In 1566 Floris's masterpiece had had to be hidden away when Protestant iconoclasts had ransacked Antwerp's churches, defacing the Catholic devotional art they hated as idolatry. There followed within a few years the Dutch Revolt, the decades-long war against Spanish rule in the Netherlands.

Antwerp, which for many years had been the financial and cultural powerhouse of western Europe, suffered the humiliations and privations of war. Governed in turn by both sides – pro-Spanish Catholics, then scouring Calvinists – the town had at last surrendered in August 1585 to King Philip's brilliant general, the duke of Parma, who was received into Antwerp with bonfires and bells. Antwerp's fall was yet another defeat for the beleaguered forces of Protestant Europe in their resistance to the might of Catholic Spain. And it was a particular blow to England, whose soldiers were soon to become fully engaged in the Dutch struggle against Philip II, a commitment of men and treasure that Queen Elizabeth's government could ill afford. Antwerp's experience was a stark reminder for Elizabethans of the power of the enemy. Their Protestant kingdom was vulnerable, their world fragile.[2]

Yet, for all this the battered town was in 1588 still a sight to stir a receptive traveller eager to be impressed. The young English gentleman wrote: 'This town is one of the pleasantest cities that I ever saw for situation and building.'[3]

His name was Robert Cecil. He was in Antwerp just for a few days, with neither fuss nor fanfare. True, he carried Parma's passport; he had privilege and access; he was shown all the sights. But there again he was, after all, the son of Elizabeth's most influential minister, William Cecil, Lord Burghley. He travelled simply. With him on his short tour of the Low Countries was a middle-aged manservant whom he had known since his own boyhood. Master Cecil and Roger Houghton: the perfect gentleman and – a fact confirmed by his discreet invisibility – the perfect servant.[4]

Robert Cecil's journey to the Low Countries had begun with an invitation to join an embassy to the duke of Parma led by Henry, earl of Derby. Robert had jumped at the opportunity. He was desperate to travel, to breathe fresh new air, to see in a new light the arts of power that were his own inheritance and future.

Lady Burghley thought at first that her son was too fragile to make the journey: Robert himself acknowledged his own 'not strongest constitution'. Derby offered the young gentleman shelter from the blunt early February cold of the road to Dover, and in his lordship's coach they passed the hours in companionable conversation. Robert travelled simply, taking only a horse and two servants, Houghton and a boy. He wanted to improve himself. He promised his father that he would use his time studying books of civil law. His mind needed activity.[5]

Contrary winds kept them in Dover for about a fortnight. Each morning for exercise, Robert climbed steeply to the top of its castle to enjoy taking into his lungs the dry, cold seaside air. He felt fit and well and he was in high favour. The queen herself had sent him a message, addressing him with what Robert called 'her sporting name of Pygmy', asking after his health and looking to hear from him by letter. 'Pygmy' was a reference to his stature, for Robert was small and his spine curved by scoliosis. He squeezed out of this rare mark of favour all the dignity he could: 'I may not find fault with the name she gives me, yet seem I only not to mislike it because she gives it.' Her Majesty's letter was, he said, 'interlaced with many fairer words' than he felt he was worthy of. Robert sent his reply to Elizabeth first to his father, unsealed. The apprentice consulted the master. To a courtier every word – each stroke of the pen – mattered.[6]

At last they were able to set sail on the *Merlin*. It was an overnight voyage, and he woke to the crowing of the ship's cockerel early on Sunday 25 February, an hour before Dunkirk came into view on the broad side. Robert was quickly ashore, borrowing paper and ink for a letter to his father.[7]

The travellers' destination was Ostend, a town in allied hands. The atmosphere there was tense and the conditions grim. Though surrounded by walls and moats the town was poorly defended. The English troops garrisoning it were mutinous and had been for two years. The war was not far away; its front line was roughly marked by the course of the Scheldt twenty or so miles to the north-east. With constant fears of Spanish attack, Ostend was neither comfortable nor safe.

Robert was thrilled by it. He embraced his own heroism, relishing the discomforts of camp life, thinking of home and of his elder sister Anne as he sat (so he wrote to his father) in poor lodgings heated by smouldering turf and being smoked 'pale and wan as ashes'. In the freezing weather he was jealous of Lord Burghley's porter, sitting in his lodge all day before a fire of sea coal. To a friend – Michael Hickes, one of Burghley's team of private secretaries – Robert wrote that he and others lived 'too in safety and pleasure, both which I never wanted till now'. He himself wanted to learn what it was like to be a soldier. But really Robert was a dyed-in-the-wool civilian. To Hickes he quoted from Lord Burghley's favourite work of the Roman classics, Cicero's *De Officiis* (*On Duties*): *Cedant arma togae* – 'Let arms yield to the toga'. He concluded his letter to Hickes with a last reflection on life in Ostend: 'Not a fair woman nor an honest.'[8]

This was no idle journey for Robert Cecil. He was always in training for future office, always had to prove himself to his father. From Valentine Dale and John Rogers, the earl of Derby's diplomats in these tentative negotiations for an Anglo-Spanish peace, Cecil borrowed learned works on the law of international treaties. To Burghley he offered himself as a pupil to be disciplined. His letters from Ostend were like school exercises for correction. 'I cannot hide my defects every way,' Robert wrote to Burghley, 'though of your lordship's fatherly goodness you have been still pleased to wipe them out of your remembrance.' Others saw his quick intelligence and sharpness. Derby praised the 'many good parts in the young gentleman which do much content me'. 'Vivat [long live] the good earl of Derby', Robert wrote to Michael Hickes.[9]

In early March young Master Cecil left allied Ostend to travel out across no man's land into enemy-held Spanish Flanders. He set out with Valentine Dale for an interview with the duke of Parma in Ghent, nearly forty miles away. Lord Burghley sent Robert a cipher alphabet should any information in his letters need to be kept secret. In it, Parma had the code number 50. Burghley was Cor, 'heart' in Latin, from his motto *Cor unum, via una*, 'One heart, one way'. Robert himself was 15. The codeword for peace was Larums (from the battlefield cry 'To arms!'), that for war Spinia (in Latin 'thorn' or 'spine'). Parma potentially held the key to either one.[10]

So, Robert prepared to meet one of the most powerful princes in Europe.

They stayed in Bruges for a night. Robert slept in the same chamber of the same inn his father had occupied on a visit to the Netherlands over thirty years earlier. Robert had found William Cecil's name scratched into the chimney breast.

Dale and Robert left at 7 a.m. the following morning, Friday 8 March. Their journey was arduous, nine hours on horseback through rain and mud, along lanes and through woods where they were shadowed by anti-Spanish freebooters, criminal gangs looking for easy targets. They arrived safely in Ghent at 5 p.m.

The two men met Parma the next day. 'His Altesse' – his Highness: Robert was always scrupulous in his address – received them in the intimate surroundings of his bedchamber. This was a great honour. Parma was all friendliness and conviviality. He acknowledged with a nod what he called 'the question' that lay between his Majesty of Spain and her Majesty of England – he meant a war on land and at sea. He assured Dale and Cecil that there was no prince in the world – other than of course his own – whom he desired more to serve, of whose perfection he had heard so much. On the Dutch rebels Parma was blunt. He was wearied by a people who had brought misery upon themselves by their own folly.

Parma spoke directly to Robert, 'son to him who served always his sovereign with unfeigned sincerity'. He would, he said, 'leave no courtesy unperformed' that Robert should have need of. Master Cecil accepted that courtesy with a speech in reply. He knew that Queen Elizabeth esteemed Parma as a prince of great honour and virtue. He would himself do his Altesse service in anything he could, so long as he preserved the integrity of his loyal duty to his most gracious sovereign the queen.[11]

It was masterful diplomacy. So much was said, and so little: words soared above substance. The duke of Parma, Doctor Valentine Dale, Master Robert Cecil, all were courtesy, correctness and honour. Yet behind the manoeuvres and dissimulations, behind the duke's smile and the ambassador's politeness, there lay a formidable struggle: for Spain's mastery in western Europe and Queen Elizabeth's survival.

His Altesse, in Ghent the model of grace and sincerity, was after all preparing an army to invade England, to be supported by the fleet we call the Spanish Armada.

A few days later Doctor Dale went back to Ostend and Robert Cecil was in Spanish-held Antwerp. He visited its great citadel, the forbidding pentagon of moats and bastions that dominated town and river whose governor was the octogenarian Spanish general Cristóbal de Mondragón. Robert knew that had he not been carrying Parma's passport, Mondragón would have happily laid his authority upon an enemy Englishman. Protected and favoured, however, Robert inspected the fortress he understood to be the strongest in Europe.[12]

Robert Cecil was no ordinary sightseer – his father had seen to that. He was trained to observe, to count and to describe, all with precision. So, when he left Antwerp for allied Holland he did not miss the fleet of warships in the Scheldt. He kept his ears open to rumours and reports. 'The speech of the armado of Spain continueth still', though its preparation was being held up by lack of supplies of food as well as sailors – so he wrote to Elizabeth's then secretary, Sir Francis Walsingham, when he was back in the safe allied outpost of Ostend. He put little store in the likely success of Lord Derby's peace conference, predicting that 'immediately upon the breaking of this long-protracted colloquy' Parma would push his forces further north into the Dutch territory of Zeeland. The young man who had used honeyed words to the duke wrote here as a clear-eyed analyst.[13]

From Antwerp he travelled by boat along the front line of the Scheldt. The river was in places so narrow that from the forts of Lillo (held by the Dutch) and Liefkenshoek (held by the Spanish) the two sides regularly shot at each other across the water. He went north, deeper into the territory held by Elizabeth's Dutch allies: to Bergen op Zoom, Dordrecht, The Hague and Flushing (Vlissingen) by way of Maassluis and Brielle. As Lord Burghley's son Robert was welcomed everywhere he visited. In Flanders the duke of Parma's passport kept him safe, helped by a six days' bodyguard of twenty musketeers on the final boat trip from Flushing back to Ostend. It was nineteen days of travel, full of adventure, with plenty of delays because of the stormy equinoctial weather. Cecil was back in Ostend on 30 March, determined to witness the peace talks. He had missed nothing. Full negotiations had not even begun. Busy preparing his army for the Spanish Armada, Parma was – quite deliberately – dragging his heels.[14]

Robert Cecil was an incongruous presence in a war zone. Small and unsoldierly, he might have been a model courtier were it not for his curved back, his physical vulnerability. He didn't warm to garrison life but he was, in his own civilian way, supremely determined, even intrepid. He was a young man noting every experience, learning all the time. He watched and noticed; he wrote. Schooled in precision – for his father there were no short cuts – he kept a 'calendary journal' for his own private exercise 'and remembrance', a practice long encouraged by Lord Burghley. And his father's precepts were always to be followed to the letter.[15]

On 11 April 1588, three months before Philip launched his invincible Armada against England, Elizabeth's and Parma's commissioners met to begin to discuss peace on neutral ground in a temporary village of tents in the no man's land between Ostend and Nieuwpoort. Robert described the gathering for his father; he saw and heard everything. His own mission was complete. Later that same day Lord Cobham, the second ranking of Elizabeth's commissioners and one of the Cecil family's closest allies at court, wrote to Burghley: 'my friend Master Cecil is desirous to return with that which was passed this day at our meeting.'[16]

Robert left Ostend carrying three dispatches for Burghley. Valentine Dale's was effusive: 'Touching Master Cecil I cannot write anything but . . . he is assured I love and like him and your lordship hath great cause to rejoice in him.' Dale predicted a great future for the young man, ranking him with some of the past heavyweights of Tudor diplomacy: 'For I see but few that are furnished like to serve in such things hereafter.' On to those slight shoulders were loaded already some great expectations.[17]

And so the journey was over. Robert Cecil had taken the air. Earnest Laertes returned to grave Polonius, and with a stock of experience he was never likely to forget. Traveller and observer, diplomat and courtier, he said he wanted to serve. As he had written on 30 March to Secretary Walsingham:

I beseech you, sir, favour me so much, as only herein to regard my willing mind to show the interest you have in my poor service, and for the substance of my letter, value it at that favourable rate, which you have always esteemed my devotion to serve you, as your many favours have often assured me.[18]

Self-deprecating, alert, tactful, energetic, ambitious: here was a gentleman who looked to older men for advice, correction and validation, his eye already on a future prize that was assumed, if not yet spoken of plainly. Lord Burghley was training him for rule, an apprenticeship of son to father unique in the sixteenth century. Robert was a legacy project – he was the future, to be built piece by piece, experience by experience, into Queen Elizabeth's minister.

The young traveller was grateful for those precious few weeks in the Low Countries. 'I not a little glad,' Robert wrote to his father, 'that God hath been pleased to grant me good and perfect health, to see so many places both worth the sight, and observing, and that in a time very short.'[19]

I

Trees of Paradise

Robert Cecil was three days old when Archbishop Parker of Canterbury wrote to his father, Sir William Cecil, the future Lord Burghley: 'I wish your honour of much joy of God's good gift of late sent to you to cheer your family.' He quoted the fourth verse of Psalm 128 in the Latin of the Vulgate Bible. *Ecce sic benedicetur homo qui timet Dominum*: 'Lo, surely thus shall the man be blessed, that feareth the Lord'.[1]

Robert was born on Tuesday, 1 June 1563, and baptized on Trinity Sunday in the Church of St Clement Danes in Westminster. The sacrament of baptism washed away his sin; it was a promise of resurrection and eternal life. The old fallen Adam in him was buried, the new man raised up. At six days old Robert Cecil was a fresh recruit to the kingdom of heaven.[2]

St Clement Danes was close to his father's new mansion in Westminster, just across the street from the Savoy, the former palace given by Henry VII as a hospital for the poor of London. The fields of Covent Garden lay over the perimeter wall from William Cecil's gardens, the Thames ran nearby for commuting by boat up or down river, and Whitehall Palace was a few minutes away. This was the Strand, the axis of London and Westminster, from Temple Bar to Charing Cross.

Sir William Cecil was Queen Elizabeth's principal secretary. At the heart of her government, he was never off duty. He was her Majesty's voice on paper, and the adviser who in audience gave her good news as well as bad. He wrote in his own hand thousands of words a day of letters and papers. His opinion was always heard and always mattered, and he exercised power with easy authority. He became as the years went on a kind of official remembrancer for the reign: he had lived the Elizabethan story from the beginning. His commitment was absolute, his focus intense. 'Serve God by serving of the Queen,' he would write to Robert in 1598, 'for all other service is indeed bondage to the devil.'[3]

The strains of work were heavy. 'So pestered with business' is a typical Cecilian phrase. Once, allowed a precious few days' leave from court, Sir William said that he felt like a bird freed from its cage. He was still working, though. Crises and panics at home and abroad occurred with near-metronomic regularity. Elizabeth would make decisions but then change her mind, often changing it back again. Colleagues fell out with one another. Sir William's own health suffered. But he never rested, for still urgent papers piled ever higher on his desk, still hopeful suitors for favour and patronage clogged the corridors outside his suites of rooms at home and court. There was no choice. The show had to go on.[4]

William Cecil saw himself as the embodiment of the highest standards of royal service. He was the touchstone of all sound counsel. A planner, an organizer, a formidable processor of information and data, a theoretician and thinker, he was above all a pragmatist. In his endless policy papers and memoranda, he considered every fact, every angle, every consequence of action and inaction. Delay and procrastination offended his instincts and his experience. He conceived of his service to Elizabeth as a kind of sacrament: he called it 'divinity'. In policy he knew that reality fell a long way short of perfection; too much was rushed and left only half done. An ounce of advice was better acted upon in good time than when danger threatened, he wrote to a colleague a little after Robert's fifth birthday. 'But as long as I have served the Queen's Majesty, Epimetheus [afterthought] hath had more to do than Prometheus [forethought].'[5]

Service to God was service to the queen. Christ's 'greatest commandment' was also William Cecil's: 'Hear, O Israel, the Lord thy God is one God, and thou shalt love the Lord thy God with all thy heart, and with all thy soul, and with all thy mind, and with all thy strength.' Every day began with private devotion, the Lord's Prayer and the Creed, and close attentiveness to the will of God. Sir William believed, and he did so with an implacable sense of mission in a Europe riven by wars of faith. Some things were certain. He knew as a fact that Elizabeth's was a chosen kingdom specially blessed: no other, he felt, was better 'established by laws in good policy to remain in freedom from the tyranny of Rome, and in constancy and conformity of true doctrine, as England is'.[6]

He was one of the principal architects of the Elizabethan Church of England. Avowedly Protestant in its Christianity, the Church was comfortingly conservative in its structure, unchanged since the break with Catholic Christendom engineered by Elizabeth's father, Henry VIII. It sat on the foundations of two laws passed by the first of Elizabeth's parliaments in 1559. The first was royal supremacy: the queen alone had the title of supreme governor of her Church, a role she took very seriously. The second was uniformity of worship. The Church had one Book of Common Prayer, which every one of Elizabeth's subjects had to accept and use for worship. Anyone who refused or resisted – especially those who still believed in the Catholic faith or were loyal to the pope – found themselves subject to penalties that became tougher over the years. For some there were fines to pay; others found themselves in prison. For William Cecil this kind of harsh enforcement made true equality for all: not one of Elizabeth's subjects was 'by law admitted to profess openly the contrary without punishment'. God's truth and the English Church were indivisible and indistinguishable. Church and State were fused together: loyalty to one was loyalty to both.[7]

With Elizabeth's denouncement by Pope Pius V in 1570 as the pretended queen of England, her ministers felt her kingdoms of England and Ireland to be under assault – and with good reason. They knew that enemies plotted at home and gathered their forces abroad. Some of these enemies hated Elizabeth because she was a woman, others because they believed the true ruler of England should be Elizabeth's Catholic cousin, Mary Queen of Scots, and all because she was a heretic schismatic from the True Faith and Church of Rome. So it was that popes, the king of Spain, the French Catholic noble house of Guise, the Scottish queen, the Jesuits and English Catholic exiles and émigrés plotted and schemed.

It felt to Elizabeth's advisers like a war for survival, as well as a war of faith (which had been going on for half a century, since Martin Luther's challenge to pope and Church). For pious Elizabethans, the wars and rebellions that they saw paralysing Europe were nothing less than a portent of apocalypse. Preachers quoted from the Revelation of St John the Divine, crying out 'It is fallen, it is fallen, Babylon the great city.' They felt that God was calling time on his corrupt creation, the clock was ticking, winding down to the End of Days.[8]

In this cosmic struggle Sir William Cecil knew which side he was on. He raised Robert Cecil to know it too. As the most loyal and hardworking servants of Queen Elizabeth, they were soldiers for heaven in the last phase of a struggle that had begun with the fall of Satan's rebel angels. They were for Christ against the Antichrist and his Catholic armies. They were vigilant in defending God and queen.[9]

So, what was to be done in those final days? William Cecil was clear: 'The first and last comforter for her Majesty to take hold on is the Lord of Hosts.' Isolated, embattled, but defiant for the truth, he put his trust in God.[10]

William Cecil's generation looked first to heaven, but how they wrote and behaved was shaped too by the histories and literature of ancient Greece and Rome. Unflinching in their duty to service and public life, framed by the beauties of Ciceronian oratory, Elizabeth's councillors bound themselves to a ministerial code they took from the classical world. They were honest, unafraid of hard work, modest, imperturbable to a fault, senatorial in their rank and bearing. Or so they believed themselves to be.

Robert Cecil saw from his earliest years a father whose sense of vocation was fixed and unyielding, and for whom service and self-sacrifice meant the same thing. In his business suit of black, the queen's secretary observed, listened and spoke. Authority was his, and deep experience of when to give and when to press. His skill was to read the fluctuations of the queen's mood and mind. He was her guide and her minister. Perhaps, at times, he was her conscience. Lord Burghley obeyed the queen, 'presuming that she being God's chief minister here it shall be God's will to have her commandments obeyed, after that I have performed my duty as a counsellor.' That duty was to speak truth to power.[11]

Sir William Cecil was always more than simply a bureaucrat. He owed his political longevity to his talents as a courtier, once describing the queen's court as a kind of Eden, where could be found the trees of paradise which gave knowledge of good and evil. Some flourished at court. Some failed.[12]

The Cecils – intelligent, gifted and connected – thrived.

To tell Robert Cecil's story fully and properly involves, naturally, his family and the careers of others we will meet in these early chapters. The family: William and Mildred Cecil; Robert's very much older brother from an earlier marriage, Thomas; and Robert's sisters Anne and Elizabeth. Our first two gentlemen without whom it would be impossible to understand Robert's life and career: his maternal first cousin Francis Bacon; and Robert Devereux, 2nd earl of Essex.

Robert Cecil was his parents' middle child: his sister Anne was seven years older, Elizabeth thirteen months younger. He was the only boy – which, in a society governed by the passing of property from fathers to sons, helps to explain Archbishop Parker's reference to baby Robert as God's good gift.

Burghley's family was complicated. Thomas Cecil, Anne's, Robert's and Elizabeth's half-brother, was a generation older than his younger siblings. So, he was their father's primary heir, and would one day inherit his father's barony and the Cecils' ancestral home at Burghley near Stamford, not far from Peterborough in the English midlands. But Robert's place in his family was always going to be special.

Thomas's mother, Mary Cheke, William Cecil's first wife, had died in 1543, and William had remarried two years later. His new wife was Mildred, the daughter of a scholarly and politically well-connected courtier called Sir Anthony Cooke. When Mildred died in 1589, William Cecil celebrated her selfless Christian charity and patronage of learning and education, much of which she had kept secret even from him. He called her a 'matchless mother, by whose tender and godly care' Robert, Anne and Elizabeth were shaped and formed. Two portraits from the early 1560s show her sumptuously dressed and bejewelled. In the later picture she is heavily pregnant with either Robert or Elizabeth, the year either 1563 or 1564. Red haired and pale, she looks serious and rather worn; the skin is stretched tightly over her cheekbones, her temples are indented. Lady Mildred's face is lean and shrewd. This was the face her son inherited, the shape of her chin and nose, the note of high intelligence.[13]

Francis Bacon, whose career ran in parallel with Robert Cecil's, was the son of Mildred's younger sister Anne. By 1553 Anne Cooke had married a clever and ambitious lawyer about eighteen years her senior, Nicholas Bacon. They had two sons: Anthony, born in 1558, and Francis in 1561. The Cecil and Bacon families moved effortlessly in the highest circles of power and influence, and when she became queen in 1558 Elizabeth appointed both Sir Nicholas and Sir William to her Privy Council. They aspired to Roman virtue, holding themselves to the most demanding standards of public service. Bacon especially was drawn to the Stoic philosophers. He was a formidable orator; Elizabethan gentlemen so admired Sir Nicholas's great speeches, especially in parliament, that they kept copies of them in their commonplace books.

Bacon's sons were highly intelligent although constitutionally a little fragile. Anthony had a taste for travel and espionage and a talent for trouble. Francis was, by his late teens, ambitious for promotion. He hoped that his uncle Burghley would help him up the administrative ladder. Uncle Burghley, as we will see, had no intention of doing that.

The Bacon brothers studied together at Cambridge. In April 1573 they went off to Trinity College, Anthony was fourteen, Francis twelve by only a few months. Taken under the wing of their tutor, John Whitgift, the master of Trinity, they were spared the usual spartan austerity of university life. Their bills and accounts show that they had a weakness for high fashion and that they were often ill.[14]

Doctor Whitgift was quick to order the boys' books: Livy's *History of Rome*, Caesar's *Commentaries*, Homer's *Iliad* and the *Orations* of Demosthenes, along with Aristotle, Plato, Cicero, Sallust, Hermogenes and Xenophon, grammars for reference, and a Latin Bible. All standard undergraduate reading, stretching and edifying, and all works familiar, though he was schooled at home, to their cousin Robert.[15]

Francis Bacon was marked out early on as a high-flyer. Late in 1576, at the age of fifteen, he went to Paris with the new ambassador to the French court, Sir Amias Paulet. The experience was intended by his father to broaden his horizons and deepen his education. Francis Bacon and Paulet made a lasting friendship. Returning to England in March 1579 he carried a letter from Sir Amias to the queen: 'this bearer Master

Francis Bacon is of great hope, endowed with many good and singular parts, and if God give him life, will prove a very able and sufficient subject to do your Highness good and acceptable service.'[16]

In these same years there was no university or foreign travel for Robert Cecil. His father and mother kept him close by.

Robert would have begun his Latin exercises at the age of five or six, though we don't know the name of his teacher. As master of the Court of Wards, Sir William Cecil educated at Cecil House on the Strand some of the most blue-blooded of the queen's wards – boys too young to inherit estates their families held from the Crown. Edward, earl of Oxford, a poet and eventually the husband of Robert's sister Anne, was one such ward. Cecil expected these young men to work hard for their nobility, whether they liked it or not. Robert most likely joined them for their lessons, at least for some of the time.

But the decisive factor in Robert's education was his mother, whose 'singular knowledge of the Greek and Latin tongues' (as William Cecil himself put it) came from a deep learning Mildred shared with her husband. He himself had been taught in Cambridge in the 1530s by the leading English university scholars of a golden generation of classicists.[17]

Classical tags and quotations adorn Robert Cecil's later letters. But his learning was more than a surface show. Schooled in his father's household, he was shaped by all the resources offered by Cecil House and Theobalds, the modest Hertfordshire manor house thirteen miles north of Westminster on which William Cecil spent a fortune, transforming it into a palace which would one day be Robert's inheritance. These were the instruments of Master Cecil's education: his father's library of books, his portraits of the leaders of contemporary Europe, his great collection of maps and atlases and genealogies of English and foreign royal families and nobilities, coins and antiquities, as well as the potential for conversations at table with the family's guests and unrivalled access to Elizabeth's court. It was a conscious process of formation, but also an organic one. Robert – intelligent, alert, receptive – could not help but learn. Quietly, discreetly, surely, he was made and built for royal service.

*

Thomas Bellot, the steward of Lord Burghley, kept a book for the 1570s in which he recorded food served and diners present at his lordship's table at Theobalds. Lord Burghley watched his household accounts like one of his own hawks watched its prey. Bellot's eyes were as sharp as his master's: they had to be.

In Master Bellot's accounts, Robert is in the background: one of 'the children', with his sister Elizabeth, who ate dinner and supper most commonly with Lady Burghley and their sister Anne. Anne was, by then, married to the immaculately noble earl of Oxford, the graduate of Cecil House, who was travelling in Italy, apparently indefinitely. Day in, day out, Lord Burghley was anywhere between Westminster, Hertfordshire and the court, his coach daily rumbling along the London Road to and from Theobalds. Sometimes he ate with his family, sometimes he had working suppers alone or with colleagues. Often there were guests at his table, whether he was present or not: friends, neighbours, courtiers, bureaucrats, scholars, churchmen – the whole upper crust of Elizabethan officialdom.

In February 1577 Robert Cecil met at his father's table another boy who shared his Christian name, Robert Devereux, the earl of Essex. Rivals and collaborators, their relationship would one day shape the architecture of late Elizabethan politics. All of that was to come, however. That day, 28 February, a Thursday in sparse Lent, Essex joined the Cecil family for dinner. He was eleven years old. Robert Cecil was thirteen.[18]

Earl of Essex and Eu, Viscount Hereford and Bourchier, Lord Ferrers of Chartley, Bourchier and Lovaine – a string of grand titles sat on slight shoulders and no real inheritance. Young Essex's coat of arms may have been packed with the quarterings of his ancestors going back centuries, but his father had left him and his younger siblings more or less destitute. By the queen's prerogative Essex was a ward of the Crown. What lay ahead for him would be determined by others. Burghley was one of the boy's guardians.

Essex's father, Walter Devereux, had thrown his money into colonizing Ulster. It was the latest of so many failed efforts to pacify and govern by plantation and settlement the Tudor kingdom of Ireland. The long counter-insurgency of the Irish chieftains who resisted English rule consumed vast sums of courtiers' money and wrecked promising careers. Walter Devereux's was one of them. At first there was optimism. 'With help of others, I have again set afoot the enterprise of Ulster,' Burghley wrote to Sir Francis Walsingham in April 1575, 'and her Majesty doth by her letters greatly commend, thank, and comfort the Earl of Essex. God send him as good speed, as if he were mine own son.' Then came the reality – complete failure.[19]

Walter lost everything on his Irish adventures, leaving his progeny financially ruined. His heir Robert would have to rely for a decent future on others' kindness. Dying of dysentery in late September 1576, Walter appealed personally to Elizabeth: 'Mine eldest son, upon whom the continuation of my house remaineth, shall lead a life far unworthy his calling and most obscurely, if it be not holpen by your Majesty's bounty and favour': otherwise there was left 'little or nothing towards the reputation of an earl's estate'. Robert's education Walter entrusted to Burghley, hoping to bind the boy 'with perpetual friendship to you and your house'. Burghley would be the new earl of Essex's guide and mentor: 'So might he also reverence your lordship for your wisdom and gravity, and lay up your counsels and advises in the treasury of his heart.'[20]

In November 1576 Earl Walter's former secretary, Edward Waterhouse, was at Chartley, the Essex family's house in Staffordshire. Walter had been dead for two months, and Waterhouse was now Lord Burghley's emissary. He carried letters from Burghley to the new earl of Essex.

Delicate, handsome, clever, conversant in Latin and French, the boy replied to Burghley without any help from Waterhouse, writing a decent scholar's hand.

> I think myself bound to your lordship both for your counsel and precepts, and I hope that my life shall be according to your prescriptions. And since my lord and father commended me to your lordship on his deathbed for your lordship's wisdom, I hope to institute my life according to your lordship's precepts.[21]

Essex was spared the bitterly cold journey to faraway Carmarthen for his father's funeral, staying at Chartley until the second week of January 1577. It was a postponement only. Then he went to court.

He lodged first at Somerset House and visited Hampton Court. He was short on clothes, and so his tutor, Robert Wright, saw to the buying of apparel: a felt hat lined with velvet from Ludgate Hill, shirts and handkerchiefs from Cheapside, socks from Fleet Bridge. After his first dinner at Theobalds on 28 February, the earl stayed with the Cecils for ten weeks, their guest for twenty-five family meals. In April Essex and Lady Burghley went to court four times. On Tuesday 30 April they dined together at Greenwich Palace.[22]

Earl Walter had hoped that Lord Burghley would do for his son what Burghley had done for other noble wards of the Crown: 'I have wished his education to be in your household.' That was not the plan now made for Essex, whose future was fixed in March and April. By spring, Essex was preparing for a noble scholar's life at the University of Cambridge.[23]

He left the Cecils on 3 May, the day Anne, countess of Oxford and Robert and Elizabeth Cecil set out from London for Theobalds. Essex moved into the Whitehall apartments of Thomas Heneage, treasurer of the queen's chamber, where he stayed for eight days. The young earl had dinner with Lord Burghley on Friday 10 May. His bags had already been taken from Cecil House to the Bull inn on Bishopsgate on the road from London to Cambridge. The following day he set out for Trinity College with two servants in newly bought Essex livery. Robert Wright had twenty pounds in his purse. The young earl was kept from the beginning on a tight budget.[24]

On Monday 13 May Essex wrote to Burghley from Trinity. 'I am not only to give your lordship thanks for your goodness towards me in your lordship's house, whereby I am bound in duty to your lordship, but also for your lordship's great care of placing me here in the university.'[25]

Master Wright saw to the earl's books, another servant to the proper furnishing of his chambers, and Essex himself to a new life.

Robert Cecil was not thrown out into the wider world. Travels and adventures would come: the briefest of visits to Cambridge, Paris, the Low Countries. But not yet.

The poet and spy Henry Lok later wrote of and to Robert:

> Your agèd youth so weaned from vain delights,
> Your growing judgment far beyond your years . . .[26]

A serious boy, Lok was saying, just like his father. This was in 1597 when Lok was a desperately hopeful suitor. He was telling Robert what he thought his patron wanted to hear, which is significant in itself. The way Lord Burghley lived his life – the way he worked, the way he served; indeed, what he was to the core of his being – came to be utterly formative for his son. As Robert Cecil later wrote to Essex (both of them by then in their thirties, circling one another as rivals), Burghley was always 'the staff' of his 'poor fortune'. And Burghley had little time for vain delights.[27]

Robert Cecil was bred up for power. He was not alone. Much was also expected of others. Brilliant in Paris, Francis Bacon was surely a star of the future. And with his intelligence and education, the earl of Essex promised to outshine his ancestors.[28]

What glories, distinctions and failures lay ahead for all three.

2

The Ambassadors' Men

Paris, 1578: the house of Queen Elizabeth's ambassador to the king of France on a Sunday in June. An unremarkable sort of day on the diplomatic front line in the war for God and England.

Diplomacy is laborious. So many words and so much paper; audiences and interviews; conversations with friends and enemies; letters and reports. Everything to be recorded and sifted, all to be measured and weighed, for the ambassador should miss nothing in dispatches home. There can be a world of meaning behind a word and a gesture. In dangerous times the devil is so often in the detail.

For Elizabethan ambassadors the clock was always ticking. The queen and her ministers were impatient for news. Even the post, the official courier waiting politely outside the door, was the ambassador's tormentor as well as his friend. After all, he had a schedule to keep to. His was the familiar road north through Clermont, Amiens and Montreuil to Calais. With a fair wind the Channel could be crossed in five or six hours. In June 1578 the queen was at Greenwich Palace. If fortune and providence were on the courier's side, it was a journey of four days from Paris to Elizabeth's court.

Sir Amias Paulet, her Majesty's ambassador on this particular Sunday in Paris, was a gentleman in his mid-fifties, steely and unflinching, a conscientious resident in difficult times. France as Paulet knew it was a kingdom painfully divided, volatile and incendiary, and vulnerable to periodic outbreaks of a religious war that had occasionally descended into civil butchery. Dissimulation was the currency, Anglo-French diplomacy complicated. 'So many factions in so factious a country' was how Paulet put it.[1]

An ambassador's dispatch was always a masterpiece of long-distance co-ordination. A single report might be re-written several times, amplified or edited, each iteration containing tiny differences of emphasis for individual readers. Private letters to ministers had often a frankness that was smoothed over just a little in those written for the queen's ears. On this Sunday the letter on the writing desk of Paulet's secretary was to Lord Burghley, thanking his lordship for his favour, a debt of gratitude so great that Paulet feared he might never be able to repay it. Even tough Sir Amias knew how to write like a courtier.

The letter was not sent until at least the following day, when, knowing that Burghley was away from court, Paulet enclosed with it a copy of his much longer and fuller dispatch to the queen's two secretaries, Sir Francis Walsingham and Doctor Thomas Wilson. Paulet's secretary did his job with steady efficiency: the controlled penmanship on the watermarked folio paper, the folding of the sheets three times horizontally to form the packet, Sir Amias's personal seal applied to close it up securely. Pen, ink and paper, a signet stamp and hot wax – the day-to-day tools and instruments of routine diplomatic correspondence.[2]

What happened next was on trust. The governments of Europe, Elizabeth's included, respected the honour and dignity of ambassadors yet cheerfully intercepted and read their letters when they could, for no chance of learning the enemy's intentions was missed. In what he called 'this tickle [insecure or precarious] and dangerous time' Paulet could be suspicious even of couriers warmly recommended to him. The packet for Lord Burghley Sir Amias or his secretary handed to a gentleman, Master Wroth, who was on his way back to England. The Wroths were regular table guests of the Burghleys.[3]

Sir Amias Paulet was a hawk who knew that he was surrounded by still-more formidable predators. August 1572, when on the feast of St Bartholomew thousands of Protestants had been murdered in Paris and across France, had left lasting scars. The organized brutality of those mass killings had shaken even Queen Elizabeth's ministers. Lord Burghley had seen in them the work of the devil; the 'lamentable tragedy' of Paris, wrote Robert, earl of Leicester, made all true Christians look for just revenge at God's hands. Six years later the fear and distrust were present still. As Paulet wrote to Walsingham and Wilson: 'We stand upon our guard of every side, and nothing keepeth us from open factions, but that faith and fidelity are banished out of this country, so as no man can tell whom he may trust.' To Lord Burghley he reflected on the danger presented by Spain: 'God deliver her Majesty from the malice and cruelty of that barbarous nation.'[4]

Now, on a summer's day in Paris, Sir Amias felt for a familiar aphorism: 'The subtle malice of this time doth give us just cause to fear rather too much than too little.'[5]

Two Englishmen worked in France in these dangerous years. Thomas Phelippes and William Wade will each play a role in this book; each would become, in different ways, a citizen of Robert Cecil's secret world. They were an elusive pair, for whom we have to piece together such facts as we have. So just for a few years – let's say between 1578 and 1583 – we will stay in and around Paris, watching and noting, holding somewhere else in our mind the teenaged Robert Cecil in Westminster or at Theobalds, and Robert Essex at court or in Cambridge.

In late June 1578 'young Philippes', one of Walsingham's servants, was sent out to Paulet. The order came, most probably, from Secretary Wilson. Walsingham himself was in the Low Countries on a special embassy, leaving Greenwich Palace on 15 June. He was in Flanders by the 24th. On the 30th Wilson wrote to Sir Francis: 'your servant young Philippes . . . is now at Paris, and attendeth upon our ambassador there.'[6]

Sometimes he spelled his own surname Phelipp, sometimes Phelippes. Such fine-tunings make very little difference. 'Young Philippes' was the son of Joane and William Philipp, a merchant and customs official of the port of London who had a house on Leadenhall Street in the city, a coat of arms and some estates in the country. Thomas's age in 1586 was estimated at thirty, which, if close, means that he was about twenty-two on his posting to Paris.[7]

A Thomas Philips graduated bachelor of arts from Trinity College, Cambridge in 1574 and commenced as master of arts in 1577. He may have been our Phelippes: if he was, he happened to be an exact contemporary at Trinity of Anthony and Francis Bacon, though he would himself have been a few years older than the brothers. Thomas Phelippes and Francis Bacon would almost certainly have encountered each other in Sir Amias Paulet's house in Paris. But the only fact we can be sure of is that our Thomas Phelippes makes his first documented appearance in the summer of 1578.[8]

In Paris he was on the edges of embassy life. But why was he sent in the first place? Months earlier, in January 1578, Paulet had written to Walsingham asking for the help of a 'sufficient man' to act as a kind of policy adviser. If Phelippes was that man, he was late: and Sir Amias was after someone of rank and standing. More likely Phelippes was an embassy factotum, a helpful additional pair of hands. His brain was sharp: highly intelligent, confidential by instinct, skilled in languages, an easy traveller, Phelippes was a useful man for an overworked ambassador to have on his staff.[9]

And then there was his particular expertise in an aspect of embassy work Sir Amias Paulet, like every other ambassador or diplomat, found tedious and burdensome, and about which he complained regularly – his secret communications with the queen's ministers. In 1577 and 1578 Sir Amias was struggling with at least three unique cipher alphabets for Burghley, the earl of Leicester and Secretary Walsingham. It just so happened – we can guess to Paulet's relief – that Thomas Phelippes was brilliant with codes and ciphers. By the early 1580s 'Phelippes the decipherer' was a familiar and recurring phrase in diplomatic letters. Skilled especially at breaking enemy cryptograms, he was one of two men Walsingham and other ministers called on for their talents in mathematics and languages and their sheer dogged patience. The second was John Somers (or Somer), a clerk of the royal signet office and about fifty years old.[10]

William Wade was older than Thomas Phelippes and he had known Paris for longer. Recorded visits he made to the city may indicate longer stays there: September 1574, October 1575, June to August 1576. It was in late 1576 that Wade, then forty, met Sir Amias Paulet for the first time, a few weeks into the new embassy. Wade was Lord Burghley's man, bound to the Cecils by old ties of family and loyalty, and he called Burghley his patron and protector. On those terms he now offered his services to Paulet.[11]

Wade too was a godsend for Sir Amias, thrown as he was into the difficulties and duplicities of Anglo-French politics and diplomacy.

The fraught affairs of the whole of Europe – Spain, the Holy Roman Empire, the pope's court, the Italian states – ran through Paris. Easily wrongfooted by delays in instructions or by the ambitions of court-iers, Paulet needed eyes and ears everywhere. Wade's skills and contacts were invaluable to an ambassador finding his feet. Within a few weeks of their first meeting, Paulet was able to claim a 'little acquaintance' with Burghley's old client. Coming to a quick appreciation of his hon-esty and discretion, Sir Amias took Wade with him on the French king's progress to Blois. Wade was soon in the thick of things. 'Now late', Paulet wrote to Burghley on 3 January 1577, 'for the discovery of some things [I] have sent him to confer with some of my friends and do trust that his voyage will not be unprofitable.'[12]

Paulet wanted as early as February 1577 to turn his employment of Wade into a fixed arrangement, for which he knew he would need Lord Burghley's consent. It was to be a secret, both in Paris and Eng-land. And so Sir Amias petitioned Burghley as Wade's 'good lord and master' to 'bind both him and me' for her Majesty's service. Paulet was in good credit at court, Wade was a useful man, and Burghley gave his blessing – as well as some advice, for which Wade was grate-ful: 'I shall, God giving me grace the more earnestly embrace and religiously follow your directions.' William Wade soon had access to Paulet's special fund for paying spies.[13]

Both Phelippes and Wade preferred to work in the shadows and on their own terms. They knew and served two ambassadors to the king of France, first Sir Amias Paulet and then, from November 1579, his successor Sir Henry Cobham. Wade and Phelippes never, so far as we can tell, worked with each other. When Wade was in Paris he tended to stay close to the embassy, though occasionally he was given mis-sions further afield: he went to Protestant Strasbourg, an Imperial city, at least twice, in February 1580 and again in May 1583. Phelippes was Walsingham's servant cum courier cum decipherer. Sir Francis gave him considerable latitude and discretion.

There are some patterns to their comings and goings, and some continuity to the roles they performed. Sir Henry Cobham recognized, as Paulet had done, Wade's talent for gathering intelligence and he valued his advice. Theirs was a subtle relationship which suggested a kind of equality: in a letter to Walsingham of March 1580 Sir Henry rather coyly referred to his enjoyment of Master Wade's company. A month later Phelippes was on courier duty, carrying packets from Cobham to Sir Francis. All this time Wade's credit was growing with Sir Henry. In June Cobham asked Elizabeth herself for the assistance of 'some . . . person as is known to be confident, secret, and assured to you'. William Wade, then briefly at the queen's court, was the individual he had in mind. Over two days Sir Henry framed letters to the queen, Burghley and to Walsingham, all to secure his man. 'I beseech your honour that Master Wade may be returned with the first dispatch,' he wrote to Walsingham, 'if it so like you.'[14]

Every so often Cobham was able to pick up packets of secret Spanish correspondence and it was Phelippes who cracked the cryptograms. In August 1581 Sir Henry intercepted three original letters that had been written on consecutive days exactly a month earlier by the Spanish ambassador in Paris, Juan Bautista de Tassis, to Philip II. Cobham sent them to Burghley, who gave them to Phelippes. His deciphers and translations were documents of beauty, all set out in his tiny handwriting, perfectly spaced and presented. Only a very few highly privileged individuals – the queen, Burghley, Walsingham, some chosen privy councillors – ever saw his work.[15]

A later description of Thomas Phelippes noted that his face was scarred by 'small pocks', and it was in this summer of 1581 that he had a short sharp illness, though whether it was smallpox we can't know for sure. 'Sickness in some extremity' was how Walsingham described it, who in July had had to put John Somers on cipher duty. But Phelippes was well enough recovered by late August to travel, and when Secretary Walsingham was in Paris on a special embassy in the second half of the month, his chief decipherer – his most discreet of servants – wasn't far away.

With travel money of thirteen pounds, six shillings and eightpence in his purse, signed off by Burghley, Phelippes and his servant left Greenwich Palace on 27 August with letters for Sir Francis on her Majesty's affairs. Four days later they were in Paris. Walsingham wrote to Burghley from the French court on the 31st: 'Even as this bearer was ready to depart my servant Phelippes arrived.'[16]

*

After 1581 Wade and Phelippes went for a time in different directions. Wade steadily made his way up the ladder of career preferment. Phelippes was likewise thriving, though keeping a little more to the shadows.

In August 1582 Wade played a Rosencrantz or a Guildenstern at Elsinore Castle, as a junior member of an embassy to convey the Order of the Garter to King Frederick II of Denmark. His big promotion came two years later. Sometime around midsummer 1584 he was appointed a clerk of the Privy Council, one of the most senior positions in the royal bureaucracy and an office for life with an annual salary of fifty pounds. The clerk's oath emphasized the highest standards of discretion and loyalty: 'You shall keep secret all matters committed and revealed unto you, or that shall be treated of secretly . . . You shall to your uttermost bear faith and true allegiance to the Queen's Majesty, her heirs and lawful successors.' Master Wade had long shown himself to be a man who could be trusted to get things done and to keep his own counsel. He had very good friends at court: no one got even a sniff of a job like the clerkship of the Privy Council without powerful supporters.[17]

As Wade made his way to Denmark in the summer of 1582, Phelippes was in France, stationed at Bourges in Berry for reasons he, Walsingham and Sir Henry Cobham (who knew he was there) kept to themselves. He was his master's loyal servant, trusted to do his job. This may have been one simply of reconnaissance, or even perhaps of making tactical interceptions of letters going up and down the French post roads. In July Walsingham sent him one of the most challenging ciphers Phelippes had ever encountered. Admitting that he was at first foxed by the writer's dreadful Latin (was this deliberate?), in Bourges Phelippes cracked it, winning it (as he wrote to Walsingham) 'as it were out of the hard rock'.[18]

After Bourges Phelippes went to Sancerre on the main road from Lyons to Paris, where he stayed for a few weeks. He was in Paris in early March 1583, playing up the mystery: he had, he said, kept himself 'close' – that is, secret, concealed and hidden – in part because of plague. His confidence in Sir Francis is striking: 'But assuring myself of your honour's gracious interpretation of all mine actions I persuade myself it shall be needless for to use many words in the way of

excuse.' Valued and skilled, Master Phelippes was not a man to under-
estimate his own abilities.[19]

He stayed in the city for three months. At the beginning of May he
wanted to go home. On the 3rd, Cobham wrote to Walsingham that
Phelippes 'doth importune me for his going hence, desirous to be in
England', but he wouldn't let him go until he had a letter to send
home. When he did at last give Phelippes permission to leave Paris,
Cobham's gentleman courier should have been one Captain Sassetti.
However, Sassetti was hobbled by gout. So it was that on Saturday 11
May Thomas Phelippes and his servant set out for England.[20]

On 16 May Phelippes arrived at Greenwich Palace. Four days later
Master Secretary Walsingham signed a warrant to cover his charges.[21]

Paris was a haven for English Catholic émigré dissidents, who were
safe to live, work and study in the city. They were safe also to plot, and
for any resident English ambassador at the French court they were a
constant worry. Sir Henry Cobham, in April 1580, did his best to make
a census of them. He counted 367 English and Irish gentlemen, aca-
demics, lawyers, students and friars who could be classified as 'papists',
those who acknowledged in matters of faith only the authority of the
pope, not Queen Elizabeth, supreme governor of her Church of England. Most of these outcasts were in Paris, but some – Sir Henry
admitted that he didn't know precisely how many – were in Rouen,
Rheims, Orleans and other towns. Even for Paris he estimated that
there were about one hundred papists 'or rather more . . . which living
secretly and disquieted, as they do, cannot so readily be known'. Eleven
of the identifiable English and Irish Catholics were separately cat-
egorized by Sir Henry as 'great practisers' – the principal conspirators – of
whom the most dangerous was Thomas Morgan, chief intelligence
officer to Mary Queen of Scots. Mary was then under secure house
arrest in England, but for many Catholics she was the rightful queen
of her cousin Elizabeth's kingdoms.[22]

Here in Cobham's dossier – in those 367 names – was expressed the
painful price of loyalty to Elizabeth I, the strains of obedience and
conscience in balancing faith against queen.

The émigré groups were fallow ground for espionage; with some

27

ingenuity the enemy could be turned. In March 1581 William Wade found in Paris an Englishman calling himself Fowler, described by Wade as 'a lewd fellow and of a perilous wit'. Making out he was a Spaniard, this Fowler worked in brokerage and shipping, and Wade thought he might be a useful source on Spanish naval preparations: 'I have found the means to be acquainted with him, and he doth offer himself to do any service he shall be able here, in Spain or in Portugal.'

Was Fowler a willing volunteer for secret work or had he been leaned on by Wade? Either means of recruitment is possible. However it was done, Wade promised Fowler that he would 'be rewarded according to his deserving'. Both men knew that information had its market price. And Fowler was not alone: all kinds of suspicious individuals knocked on the doors of the embassy seeking admission and refuge. But who in uncertain times knew whom to trust?[23]

Those who lived and worked in this looking-glass world understood that the greatest danger was 'security': for Elizabethans the word meant carelessness, overconfidence, complacency. As Sir Amias Paulet once wrote to Lord Burghley: 'Nothing is more dangerous than security in these bad days, when ambition and dissimulation have so great place in the hearts of princes.'[24]

As Paulet, Cobham, Wade and Phelippes well knew – and as Robert Cecil would learn – the only defence against security was unrelenting vigilance.

3
Gathering Fruit

In July 1581, a month after his eighteenth birthday, Robert Cecil went to Cambridge for the commencement of new masters of arts. Part academic exercise, part festival, this was the university on its annual full-dress parade. He went to sermons and disputations, sat on high tables, and, so Vice Chancellor Perne assured Chancellor Burghley, behaved himself impeccably. The thought had crossed Doctor Perne's mind to make Robert himself a master of arts, but he hadn't dared to proceed without Lord Burghley's say-so. He hoped instead that his lordship would send his son back to Cambridge at some later date for the edification of its scholars. Perne wrote and signed his letter to Burghley on Sunday 9 July. Robert himself carried it back to his father.[1]

In 1581 the academic honours in Cambridge went to John Harington of King's College, a precocious godson of the queen, who came first in the ranked list of MAs. Harington was a young man of court pedigree and supple high intelligence; he was a poet and a satirist, all charm and elegance. But the shining star of this commencement was Robert, earl of Essex, of Trinity College, now also a master of arts (though one too grand to appear in the ordinary academic ranking). The fifteen-year-old earl appeared in tawny velvet hose, a cloak 'laid on with flames of fiery gold' and a satin doublet. His pantofles – heeled, cork-soled shoes – brought to dully provincial Cambridge a bracingly expensive dash of Italian and Spanish fashion. Essex was developing a taste for luxury he couldn't afford, some months later admitting to Lord Burghley that 'through want of experience' he had 'in some sort passed the bounds of frugality'. The noble penitent blamed his own youth and asked for the courtesy of Burghley's pardon. 'I do beseech your good lordship . . . still to continue a loving friend unto me'; Essex hoped, in other words, that Burghley would keep paying his bills.[2]

Nothing in Robert Cecil's early life was ever a coincidence: his father was too compulsive a strategist for that. It so happened that in early June 1581, a month before commencement, Lady Burghley gifted to her husband's old college, St John's, a valuable Bible whose eight volumes Robert may very well have taken with him to Cambridge. More significant is that on 30 June an indenture was agreed between St John's and Lord Burghley, Robert Cecil and his half-brother Thomas for the endowment of twenty-four scholarships, supported by a considerable sum of Burghley's money. So, Robert visited a university freshly aglow with his family's generous patronage. As a grateful Doctor Perne wrote to Burghley: 'we do greatly rejoice in ... your lordship's good will toward the advancement of learning to St John's [sent] by your honour's loving son Master Robert.' Like all good senior academic administrators communicating with higher powers, Doctor Perne knew precisely when to turn on the charm.[3]

While in July 1581 Robert Cecil went to Cambridge, sixteen months later Cambridge came to Theobalds – or at least one of its best scholars did. He was a Yorkshireman whose name was William Wilkinson, a fellow of St John's College.

He was a recruit, headhunted for the position of Robert's tutor. By the time Wilkinson arrived at Theobalds for an interview in late November 1582, various soundings had been taken at St John's. He had been the highest college performer of his two graduating years as bachelor and master, coming an outstanding second in the list of eighty-five MAs. But the new job was no easy sinecure. Wilkinson must have known that he would be grilled by Lord Burghley, for his lordship, in matters of scholarship as much as in politics, took no prisoners. On Wilkinson's side was the letter he carried from the master of St John's, Richard Howland, which praised to the skies Wilkinson's abilities and character. Not only was he diligent and able, Doctor Howland wrote, but also quiet, staid, honest and of a good nature – something, Howland added, very hard to promise for any man.

Master Wilkinson passed the test: he seems to have stayed with Robert for the next six years. His task was, as Howland put it, 'to read unto' his pupil, putting him seriously through his paces, sharpening Robert's mind to its keenest edge, preparing him for his future.[4]

Robert Cecil came of age in a decade of emergency. Hostile powers planned the invasion of England and Ireland and plotters conspired to murder the queen. English Catholic priests, trained in foreign seminaries, were infiltrated into England and Protestant Scotland. When captured, they said that they were on a spiritual mission, but the government treated them as political agents and traitors. Most dangerous of all, given the sheer reach of her influence across Europe, was Mary of Scotland, held in England under protective custody and house arrest since 1568. Mary's cause animated a ragbag of spies and fantasists in France and England. Elizabeth's ministers saw all about them a spidery web of conspirators and conspiracy. They believed they were battling for their kingdom's survival. This was why ambassadors in Paris like Sir Amias Paulet and Sir Henry Cobham were so alert to the activities of the émigré dissidents, why Thomas Phelippes and William Wade were kept so busy.

Faith was everything, conformity to the Elizabethan settlement of religion the greatest test of loyalty. Supremacy and uniformity were the two absolute principles of the Elizabethan state: the queen as supreme governor of her Church, one prayer book for common worship. Both were non-negotiable, both were enforceable at law. Some Catholic dissidents, or 'recusants', refused to comply with the 1559 Act of Uniformity. Caught between private conscience and the law they were fined and imprisoned. The government believed them to be the spiritual enemy within. The prominent Protestant preacher Gervase Babington knew for a fact that 'our recusants ... that is our refusing papists to come to church' would one day boil, body and soul, in the heat of the unquenchable fire of divine judgement.[5]

The fundamental assumption of Elizabeth's government was that no English Catholic could ever quite be trusted. The authorities believed that even the most submissive recusants were prey to those Catholic priests covertly at work in the kingdom and denounced by Lord Burghley in his passionate pamphlet defence of the Elizabethan regime, *The Execution of Justice*, printed in late 1583. True, he admitted, priests were not in open warfare against England; they did not carry weapons. They were traitors nevertheless, more dangerous because they hid their treason. 'But if they will deny, that none are traitors that are not armed, they will make Judas no traitor, that came to Christ without armour, colouring his treason with a kiss.'[6]

One such recusant was John Towneley, a rich and influential gentleman from the religiously conservative county of Lancashire. Towneley, so removed from the world of Robert Cecil in his early twenties, played an unlikely role in Cecil's arrival at Elizabeth's court. The connection was Towneley's half-brother, Doctor Alexander Nowell, dean of St Paul's Cathedral, who was a friend and spiritual adviser to Robert's mother Lady Burghley.

Towneley was a serial church non-attender right from the beginning of Elizabeth's reign, time and again brought before the authorities and punished for his recusancy. Fines turned into long-term imprisonment. Doctor Nowell, even though he was a senior Elizabethan churchman on the front line of the long hard battle for souls, used what influence he had to make life as comfortable for his brother as it was ever likely to be.

The authorities were usually lenient on Towneley, within limits. Kept in 1581 a 'close prisoner' in the Gatehouse in Westminster, the Privy Council permitted him the freedom to walk in the prison garden. Two years later, then in Manchester, he was given a short period of liberty for matters of family business. He had enough of a fortune left to be able to offer substantial financial bonds for his good behaviour. This was never seriously in doubt: 'the said Towneley (his religion excepted) doth carry himself dutifully and quietly.'[7]

By February 1584 John Towneley was sick and brother Nowell was petitioning to have him moved from the New Fleet prison in Manchester to a gaol in London. On 28 February Robert Cecil wrote to Sir Francis Walsingham on Towneley's behalf, 'by the importunity of a good friend of mine' – presumably this was Alexander Nowell.[8]

His letter was short – a third of a side of folio paper – and something of a presentation piece, neatly written, precise and controlled, in a rounder and more fluid italic hand than some of the older copybooks prescribed. Cecil's model was the master Italian penman Giovanni

Francesco Cresci, whose *Il Perfetto Scrittore* was first published in Rome when Robert was seven. Cresci kicked against the older authority of Giambattista Palatino, whose style he felt was too slow and heavy. Cresci's technique – the pen kept upright to improve speed, always an eye for innovation especially in the joining of letters – suited Robert's temperament. There was nothing here of his father's narrow-nibbed angularity, where every word was pared back by abbreviation to a kind of spiky telegraphic shorthand. Lord Burghley's handwriting had its own precision and rhythm. But Robert's hand, heavier than his father's, flowed. He enjoyed words, using plenty of ink to form them.[9]

Robert knew that the framing of his address to Secretary Walsingham had to be perfect. 'I beseech your honour to pardon me both in my presumption of writing and the matter ... I shall offer to your favourable consideration.' It was the most careful of opening lines: he was traversing sensitive territory. Already he had a courtier's talent for caveats and excuses. He was 'credibly informed' that Towneley was 'in some extremity'; he himself had no direct knowledge of this. He had chosen not to take up the matter with his lordship his father 'knowing not how unworthy the man [Towneley] be of favour'. He merely offered the case to Sir Francis's 'honourable consideration'. Walsingham would of course know best.

Robert was here trying his hand in a wider sense, tentative in exercising just a little independence and agency as a courtier. It was a gentle entrée, the smallest glimpse of the future. The 'Robert Cecill' at the foot of the letter is the earliest surviving dated example of his signature. Robert's 'Cecill' – always the two l's – was a careful facsimile of his father's old signature before William Cecil got his barony, down to its last and smallest flourish. Robert must have practised it to perfection.

To the real purpose of Robert Cecil's letter John Towneley's fate is almost incidental. Robert wrote 'From the court' on Friday 28 February. The following Tuesday Alexander Nowell himself communicated with Walsingham, asking Sir Francis 'to be a mean' not for Towneley's liberty (Nowell couldn't possibly expect that) but that his brother might 'be appointed to some other prison' than the New Fleet. Three weeks later the Privy Council, at the earnest suit of 'our loving friend and Dean of Paul's', directed that Master Towneley should be brought south: 'at his coming, we mind to take further order what shall be done with him.'[10]

Robert Cecil went to France in the summer of 1584. He was twenty-one years old and it was his first journey out of England.[11]

France was at a dynastic crisis. Francis, duke of Anjou, brother of King Henry III and heir to his throne, died of natural causes at the beginning of June. The news was known at Elizabeth's court within ten days, and the queen took it badly: Anjou was an ally and had been a long-term suitor for her hand (the marriage negotiations having drained the energies of ministers and diplomats in 1579 and 1580). Now in 1584 one seasoned former diplomat had heard that the French king's health was poor and that his and Anjou's once utterly dominant mother, Catherine de' Medici, long the power behind the throne, was 'almost witless, for her senses (as we hear) begin to fail'. In France some 'noble alteration' was surely coming.[12]

More shocking was the assassination a month later of William of Nassau, prince of Orange, the leader of the Dutch independence struggle against Spain. His killer, one Balthasar Gérard, had infiltrated himself into Orange's household and, with grim irony, had earlier that same day informed William of Anjou's death. Gérard, tempted by the price Philip II of Spain had put on Orange's head, was himself killed.

News of the assassination arrived at Elizabeth's court on Sunday 5 July. Even veteran ministers were stunned by it. They now had to face the reality of a substantially weakened international Protestant cause in Europe, the crown of France perilously uncertain, Nassau dead and a Spanish army in the Low Countries pressing further north.[13]

Three weeks later Robert crossed the English Channel to Boulogne.

Robert was welcomed into Paris on 1 August by the latest of Elizabeth's ambassadors to the court of France, Sir Edward Stafford, a suave and accomplished courtier in his early thirties who, unlike his predecessors Paulet and Cobham, was an unapologetic Francophile. Stafford's family were friends of the Cecils, and yet each one of Sir Edward's letters to Burghley in the few weeks that followed is pricked with anxiety. Robert was precious cargo. He chose not to lodge in

Stafford's house near the Seine, preferring (as Sir Edward put it) 'to be somewhat the more in French company and out of hearing of English'. He wanted to immerse himself in the language.[14]

Even for a young man born in Westminster, Paris was on a scale of its own. At about 300,000 souls it was three times the size of London in terms of population, and geographically much larger too, with four principal areas – the Cité, the Ville, the Université and the faubourgs, with the cathedral of Notre Dame on the Île de la Cité at its spiritual centre.

Sir Edward promised Lord Burghley that he would show Master Robert everything worth seeing in Paris: 'Assure your lordship that he shall not want anything where I have any credit.' Stafford was especially keen that they visit the house near Fontainebleau of Henri Clausse, sieur de Marchaumont, a member of the late duke of Anjou's household who had been in England a couple of times in the 1580s, when the teenaged Robert may very well have met him. More than this, 'When the King cometh', Sir Edward wrote, 'he shall see him and as much as may be.' On Robert's command of etiquette Stafford paid Burghley the expected compliment: 'for his government of himself he is so well that way that he shall not need of my counsel'.[15]

A little over a week later they were preparing for the visit to Fontainebleau. Robert and Stafford went on horseback 'to take the air', as Sir Edward put it. They saw Marchaumont's house, and by the time Sir Edward reported that Robert was safely back in Paris, on 24 August, the young man had seen 'all that is to see in those quarters'.[16]

There were times when even Robert Cecil was just a little bored by Paris. 'It was never so dead in the town, in all men's opinion, as now it is,' he wrote at the end of the month. He wasn't particularly inclined to write letters home, other than of course to his father.[17]

Nevertheless, Robert kept himself busy, going every day to hear scholarly disputations at the Sorbonne. The University of Paris, made up of about fifty constituent colleges, made Cambridge look very small. Student life in Paris was boisterous, and the intellectual pulse of the Latin Quarter beat strongly because of the printers, book sellers and book binders whose shops were packed in around the colleges – there were two hundred on the rue Saint-Jacques alone. And beyond Paris there was so much more to explore: Robert was hoping before his return to England to visit Orleans, Tours and Blois. Even the quietness of Paris in summer couldn't blunt the bigger experience: 'I never liked country better, nor of all persons of quality received better usage.'

These words he wrote to a friend, William Parry, a Welshman and possessor of a doctorate in law from the University of Orleans, then in England but a familiar figure in Paris, who had struck up an easy relationship with Robert. Sir Edward Stafford knew and liked Parry, who for a few years had played – indeed increasingly overplayed – the credit he possessed with Lord Burghley. To Parry Robert opened up; in his letter he was witty, open, settled and contented, with little of that controlled formality he had to show to powerful men. Parry had even briefed Robert on what Robert called 'the choice of pretty novelties of this town' – not the kind of phrase that would ever appear in one of his letters to his father.[18]

William Parry was plausible on paper and in person, a clever and ambitious social climber skilled at attaching himself to impressionable young gentlemen of rank and fortune. Robert Cecil in Paris in August 1584 called him 'my loving friend Master Doctor Parry'. But there was something about his friend he didn't yet know. William Parry had sold himself to the Catholic enemy. From late 1583 he was plotting to kill Queen Elizabeth.[19]

At this time the familiar propaganda war, Catholic against Protestant, was hotter than ever and the Paris printing presses were busy. In September 1584 Stafford picked up a pamphlet celebrating 'the new martyr' who had assassinated the prince of Orange, as well as some fragments of a book justifying the rightful claim of Mary Queen of Scots to the throne of England. He had a theory, too, about the identity of the writer of an anonymous published response to Lord Burghley's *The Execution of Justice*. What Burghley defended as the lawful prosecution of traitor priests fomenting rebellion against Elizabeth was seen instead by Catholics as a persecution of priests and recusants as vicious as imperial Rome's destruction of the first Christians. The author of this latest excoriating attack on Elizabeth's government was, Stafford believed, Doctor William Allen, a Lancashire man educated at Oxford, for many years an exile from his homeland and a polemicist who wrote with punch. Sir Edward was sharing this highly sensitive material ('these be yet closely enough kept') with Robert. Indeed, Stafford assumed that the pamphlet on Balthasar Gérard's murder of Orange had already been sent by Robert to his father.[20]

By late September Robert was busy compiling information on France, its nobility, its government and its key officers. This wasn't secret material – much of it he copied. But Robert was learning his trade, as well as practising his written French, which was very good but not faultless. He signed and dated his compilations from Paris on 30 September and 3 October. They were, in a sense, final assignments that did something to rebalance the holiday feeling. Leisure without purpose was not the Cecils' way.[21]

Robert's key piece of analytical work was an essay commissioned by Sir Francis Walsingham. Its subject was the future of the French royal succession. Like any keen Elizabethan courtier taking on such a task, Robert bewailed his own ignorance and turned up the rhetoric. As unworthy as he was, he wrote to Walsingham that he would nevertheless have a go at it: 'Yet notwithstanding am I rather content by following your commandment herein to bewray [reveal or make known] my ignorance than not to obey him whom I have vowed to serve during life.' The result was a close reading, full of detail, on the intense and often secret politicking of families and factions over the Protestant Henry of Navarre's claim to the throne. Here at work was the observer of a court and its courtiers, though the optimism of a twenty-one-year-old was in contrast to the native pessimism of so hardened a political veteran as Walsingham. Robert saw the likelihood of Navarre's eventual accession even in the teeth of Catholic efforts to thwart him, for Henry had God and right on his side. Robert beseeched Sir Francis to take in good part 'these unripe gathered fruits' of two months' hard work.[22]

Robert wrote to Walsingham on 18 September 'stilo novo', according to the 'new style' calendar introduced to Catholic Europe by Pope Gregory XIII in 1582. Here Robert was being daringly modern, for his father stuck resolutely to the old-style Julian calendar and insisted that any ambassador abroad should use it, refusing to accept the mathematical calculations which now gave ten days' difference between France and England. But whether it was 18 September or (as Secretary Walsingham and Lord Burghley calculated it) 8 September, Robert Cecil's sojourn in Paris was almost over. That same day he also wrote to his friend Michael Hickes. He was in good health and looked forward to telling Hickes and his other friends all about his journey. Robert left Paris fully briefed by Sir Edward Stafford.[23]

Lord Burghley knew by 27 October that his son was coming home. He wrote from his mansion on the Strand to his friend and political ally Lord Cobham: 'I think there will come to your house by way homewards out of France a fugitive that cometh home for lack of money to continue longer abroad. He is your lordship's poor servant, whose name I leave to be guessed, to be merry with your lordship.'[24]

The parliament that assembled in Westminster in November 1584, Elizabeth's fifth, looked to the queen's safety in dangerous times. An ambitious bill for her Majesty's 'surety' set out mechanisms to be activated in the emergency circumstances of invasion or of any attempt on Elizabeth's life. Always conscious that the queen had no obvious Protestant successor, privy councillors and other lords and MPs were haunted by the murder of William of Nassau. Another bill exposed those Jesuits and priests being infiltrated into England to stringent penalties. It was the toughest of crackdowns on England's enemies without and within.

Robert was a member of this House of Commons for the constituency of Westminster. It was a first natural step, a rite of passage, though MPs for urban boroughs like Westminster had not the social cachet of those gentlemen elected for the rural counties. Robert played no part in business, or at least any business that was recorded. By contrast, however, his loving friend Doctor Parry, also an MP (thanks to one of the well-born young gentlemen he had taken under his wing, Edward Hoby, Robert's first cousin by Lady Burghley's sister Elizabeth), made rather more of a splash in the Commons chamber. Thursday 17 December was meant to be a routine day in the House, with a third and final reading of the Jesuits bill. But Parry made an extraordinary intervention. This bill, he was reported as saying, 'carried nothing with it but blood, danger, terror, despair [and] confiscation'. It was a shocking breach of convention, and he was hauled out of the chamber and sent to the Privy Council to explain himself. Parry apologized, and for a few weeks at least he behaved himself. Or so it seemed.[25]

In February 1585 Parry and a co-conspirator, his kinsman Edmund Nevylle, were arrested for plotting to assassinate the queen; Nevylle, as hopeless a plotter as Parry, had given himself up and confessed. The plan was formulated, Parry said, in Paris with Thomas Morgan, the Scottish queen's secret eyes and ears in France, and with various shady Jesuits. Was Doctor Parry here Lord Burghley's brave double agent – as he had claimed to Burghley himself – or a traitor in collusion with the Catholic enemy whose supposed loyalty to queen and minister was merely a ruse? Probably he himself didn't know. Both he and Nevylle were amateurs, far out of their depth, and Parry was intoxicated by his own vanity. But the horror of their conspiracy, such as it was, spoke to anxious times. William Parry was executed in Westminster Palace Yard on Monday 2 March. On St Valentine's Day he had written to the queen herself of 'the dangerous fruits of a discontented mind'. He had led a double life, a disappointed narcissist who felt that he should have had more recognition than he ever received, too dazzled by his own cleverness and brought down by hubris.[26]

This lesson in treason showed all too clearly how deeply some secrets had to be buried. A few days after Parry's execution, when some of London's printers were getting ready to go to press with their own accounts of this most horrible of crimes, Lord Burghley convened at his mansion on the Strand a special meeting of privy councillors to decide what could and could not be printed about Doctor Parry's treason. They gathered together Parry's papers and confessions, which Burghley assiduously redacted. Much was suppressed – Parry had been too close to the Cecil family. His friendship with Robert Cecil, the many letters he had written over the years to Lord Burghley, his offers of secret service to the queen – all of this was buried. The pamphlet that appeared, under Burghley's control, told only a selected fragment of the full story.[27]

4
R. C.

Of Robert Cecil's reaction to William Parry's treason there is no record. His relationship with Doctor Parry was too delicate and exposing to be very easily articulated. Much better a discreet silence.

Was it so difficult to believe what Parry had done? The 1580s was a decade more febrile, more anxious, more obsessed with conspiracy than most; loyalties were tested until they broke. Parry confessed that he had been inspired in his plotting by *A True, Sincere and Modest Defence of English Catholics* (1584), William Allen's brilliantly pungent response to Burghley's *Execution of Justice*, and the dangerous book whose authorship Sir Edward Stafford in Paris was trying so hard to fix with certainty. Only a handful of copies of Allen's *Defence* were kept in England, under strict control, for the purpose of answering the enemy. Printed on its title page was a verse from the Psalms: 'Thy mouth hath abounded in malice, and thy tongue hath cunningly framed lies.' But who in this twisted age spoke the truth?[1]

That such a world of deception and dissimulation existed could have been for Robert by now no surprise at all. In Paris he came to know something of the secret byways of diplomacy. Being his father's son gave him privileges, for in matters of secrecy birth and rank mattered. This was Doctor Parry's problem. As Burghley made plain in the pamphlet on Parry's treasons, never trust a low-born upstart who is too clever by half.

Robert Cecil had left Paris with a confidential message for Sir Francis Walsingham from Stafford. An Englishman travelling under an assumed name had visited the Spanish ambassador's house in the city. This secret individual was sent off to Rouen, a familiar bolthole for English

Catholic dissidents, but was expected again in Paris. Sir Edward was doing his best to find out more.[2]

There was nothing unusual here. In France, and elsewhere, conspirators plotted against Queen Elizabeth and her government, practisers great and small.

The issue of the future line of succession to the crown of England, which had no clarity after the death of Elizabeth, haunted two generations of the queen's ministers. Until 1587, a few months before Robert Cecil's twenty-fourth birthday, that deep anxiety was focused on one woman – until her execution. For Queen Elizabeth, Mary Queen of Scots was the most potent reminder of the fragility of the English crown and the coming extinction of the Tudor dynasty.

Late in 1586, the year of reckoning for Mary and Elizabeth, Cecil took an important step in moving from a privileged court insider to being a participant in affairs of state. He played a small role in the downfall of the Scottish queen. To explain how this came about, and the significance of Mary Stuart, we have to go back to the early decades of the sixteenth century.

In 1503 the Tudor King Henry VII's daughter Margaret had married the Stuart King James IV of Scotland. Their son James was born in 1512. This James V married Mary of Lorraine, also known by her family name of Mary of Guise, and in 1542 they had a daughter, Mary. She was just a week old when James died and Mary succeeded to the throne.

Ambitious to unite the two kingdoms of England and Scotland into one Great Britain under his own military and imperial dominance, Margaret's younger brother Henry VIII proposed the marriage of baby Mary to his own young son and heir Prince Edward, later Edward VI. England and Scotland had been at war and the betrothal of Edward and Mary was part of a peace treaty agreed between the two kingdoms in 1543. The Scots quickly renounced it, looking instead to French military aid against King Henry. So the war resumed. And thus began too Henry's single-minded effort to exclude the heirs and successors of James V from any hope of inheriting through their

Tudor blood the crowns of England and Ireland. This Henry made crystal clear in an act of succession in 1544, confirmed in his last will and testament in 1546: anyone but the Stuarts.

In 1548 the child Mary was sent to France, where her ultra-Catholic grandfather and uncles, the dukes of Guise, were powers to be reckoned with. She was betrothed to the French king's son, the dauphin Francis, and they married in April 1558: he was then fourteen, she sixteen. Had Francis not died just over two years later, in December 1560, Mary might have been only the smallest footnote in the history of England. As it was, in 1561 she returned to Scotland a nineteen-year-old widow to rule as queen in her own right and name. In 1567 she found herself deposed from the Scottish throne by her enemies and a year later in England a supplicant for her cousin Queen Elizabeth's hospitality. For Mary Queen of Scots there followed nineteen years of effective house arrest.

Stuart, Guise, Tudor: these were her families. And this is why, as she herself put it in 1584, she was 'come of the blood and noble progeny of England', thanks to her grandmother Queen Margaret and her great-grandfather Henry VII. This fact was also potentially a claim to rule and power, now or in the future. Of this Elizabeth did not need to be reminded.[3]

Mary became supremely skilled at playing on her imprisoned isolation. Her faith mattered deeply. Catholic Europe's hatred of Queen Elizabeth found in Catholic Mary a symbol of resistance, and Elizabeth's government knew it. Sir Edward Stafford in Paris, as Robert Cecil had seen for himself, sent to London books and genealogies printed in the city demonstrating the Stuarts' supposed royal claim to England and Ireland. European support for the Queen of Scots was not always enthusiastic or unstinting – for King Philip of Spain it was sometimes nominal and, frankly, begrudged. But this hardly mattered. Mary's confinement in England was all the better for her cause; it was a role she embraced quite as much as she resisted.

Mary entertained hopes of rehabilitation and freedom. Now and then, there were conferences; every few years Elizabeth dispatched deputations of privy councillors and officials to Mary for discreet talks. Once, in late 1584, Mary's secretary came to court for private meetings with the queen and Privy Council. Expectations flourished for a time and then disappeared. There was no chance that Mary would ever be put back on the throne of Scotland, for that was occupied by her son James VI, who had been placed there by her opponents. James was raised a Protestant and, more importantly, as a boy king he could be steered and shaped – one might say manipulated and used – by the most powerful noblemen in Scotland. Really Mary's imprisonment in England was for Elizabeth the least worst of very few options. But could it really go on indefinitely? In 1584 Sir Ralph Sadler, then Mary's gaoler, expressed the logic of her situation in binary terms: 'For there must be an end of this matter, either by the death of this Lady, or by some honourable composition.'[4]

It was deception that sent Mary eventually to the executioner's block: her own, her servants', above all Sir Francis Walsingham's and Thomas Phelippes's. The 'young Philippes' who had gone to Sir Amias Paulet in Paris in 1578 was, eight years later, deciphering Mary's secret correspondence with her supporters in Europe: by early 1586 he controlled the couriers that Mary and her secretaries thought were theirs. Phelippes also infiltrated those of her adherents in London who were putting together plans to free Mary from her detention as well as to murder Elizabeth, though this second element of their conspiracy was the least formed. The young Catholic gentleman who emerged as the leader of this group was Anthony Babington.

By a careful reading of Mary's letters, as well as by the breathtaking forgery of her own cipher, Walsingham and Phelippes believed by late summer 1586 that they had proof of the Scottish queen's complicity in the murder plot against her royal cousin. Walsingham had for weeks been briefing Elizabeth on the activities of Babington and his associates. When they made public the plot in early August, Thomas Phelippes worked furiously to assemble the evidence that was necessary to hold Mary to account: the piles of secret letters he had deciphered, the plotters' examinations and confessions, every piece of paper available on Mary's contacts abroad. With Walsingham sick and immobile at his country house at this time, it was Master Phelippes who became his master's voice at court. In August and September Elizabeth got to know Phelippes very well.

Elizabeth agonized over Mary, not out of sympathy for her cousin, but from her own deepest instincts as a monarch who wanted to hold on to her throne. She did not want to condemn Mary, but she knew that she might have to and knew the reasons why. The case against the Scottish queen was unique. There were all kinds of legal uncertainties, and Elizabeth prevaricated from the beginning. But eventually it was agreed that Mary would be tried at Fotheringhay Castle in Northamptonshire. The noblemen chosen to hear the evidence against her met there in October.

It was a month or so before Robert Cecil would find himself playing a role in the last act of the Scottish queen's life. For most of 1586 he, like his cousin Francis Bacon, was preoccupied by patronage, the currency of life and careers at court.

How similar yet how different these young men were. Both were clever, both driven to please and impress. For half a decade Bacon had been in chambers at Gray's Inn, the lawyers' society in which his father and uncle Burghley had been major forces a generation earlier. There he waited and hoped for a preferment, which always seemed to be just out of reach. He pressed Lord and Lady Burghley with suits. Hopes were raised and Bacon had his supporters. Sir Christopher Hatton, one of Elizabeth's most favoured courtiers, promised to help; Bacon heard nothing more. When Francis wrote to his uncle in early May 1586 that all he desired was 'an ease' in making his way up the legal ladder, 'not any extraordinary singular note of favour', he was worried that Burghley had received misreports of his character. 'I find also that such persons as are of nature bashful (as myself is), whereby they want [lack] that plausible familiarity which others have, are often mistaken for proud.' Hopeful suitors like Bacon were always on tenterhooks. Lord Burghley kept his own counsel. Francis had to wait for his moment – if it should ever come.[5]

Cousin Robert, on the other hand, was fine-tuning his skills as a courtier – not for him the disappointments of the importunate suitor, at least not yet. In June, weeks after Bacon's letter to Burghley, Robert promoted a suit to the queen on behalf of his brother-in-law, Edward, earl of Oxford. The purity of Oxford's noble blood was easily matched by his arrogance, but his lordship was trying – at least on this occasion – to behave himself, believing, thanks to Walsingham's support, that he was 'almost at a point to taste that good which her Majesty shall determine'. Almost there, but not quite – hence a begging letter to Burghley. The earl was, as he put it himself, like one trying to capture a fort who has to call off the siege for lack of munitions; put simply, he was short of money. Bridling his customary petulance, Oxford framed as polite a letter to his father-in-law as he could manage. The effort was worth the cash. Burghley took up his pen and wrote on the back of the letter: 'Earl of Oxford to borrow £200 whereof I lent him £100.'[6]

Just enough, but not too much.

On Sunday, 23 October 1586 Robert Cecil was in his father's apartments at Windsor Castle. If Burghley followed his planned itinerary, he was resting up in Westminster after the journey from Fotheringhay by way of Burghley House and Theobalds, readying himself for the final meeting of the commission on Mary Queen of Scots in Star Chamber on the following Tuesday. At Windsor that night Robert met Thomas Danett, a hopeful candidate for a precious clerkship of the Privy Council. Master Cecil was deputizing for his father in a matter of high patronage.

Danett grabbed his chance. He pressed as hard as he could. Surprised even to be named as a candidate for a clerkship, he cultivated the support of three privy councillors. One of these was a new second secretary to Walsingham, the gifted William Davison, only a few months in office. But Burghley mattered most of all, and what Robert had to say that evening at Windsor did not fill Danett with confidence. But what did Robert say? Danett failed to make complete sense of Master Cecil's blizzard of words.

Robert told Danett that his rival for the clerkship was William Herle, an old hand at the court game, an intelligencer of twenty years' standing and a man whose political connections (to the earl of Leicester, to Burghley, to many others) were impeccable. So why did Robert tell Danett this? Master Cecil seemed sympathetic enough to Danett, but he seemed to be holding back: Robert 'told me' (this is Danett's account to Secretary Davison) 'that he thought he should neither do you nor me pleasure in this cause'. Did Burghley really want Herle as clerk, Danett wondered? Or was Master Cecil talking up Herle's chances as a means of emphasizing how hard his father was having to work on Danett's behalf? Danett himself honestly didn't know – but like any suitor he hoped for success.[7]

Playing the patronage game was like navigating a labyrinth. It helped if one had the privileges and connections of Robert Cecil. At twenty-three he already knew this game. He was treating Thomas Danett kindly, gently pointing out the difficulties that lay ahead in his suit, how delicate it all was. But though words might mean something at Elizabeth's court, they might also signify nothing at all.

Tuesday, 25 October. A busy and decisive day in Star Chamber.

In his career Robert Cecil would come to know Star Chamber very well. Deep in the great tangle of ancient buildings that made up the old Palace of Westminster, the queen's privy councillors and judges met there to hear certain kinds of legal cases. In Star Chamber they exercised on Elizabeth's behalf the fullest prerogative powers of a monarch who answered only to God.

On this Tuesday the commissioners who had been at Fotheringhay met to satisfy themselves of the evidence which had been submitted against the Scottish queen. At her trial in Northamptonshire Mary had appeared only briefly, before withdrawing, refusing to acknowledge the tribunal. Her accusers had carried on without her. They did so now.

Mary was guilty: 'all the commissioners present (except Lord Zouche) pronounced that the Scottish Queen ... had compassed, practised and imagined the death of her Majesty our sovereign Lady.' Thirty-year-old Edward Lord Zouche knew his own mind. Accepting that Mary was privy to the conspiracies, he was not persuaded that she was herself an active conspirator. The distinction – and Zouche's scruple – made no difference at all. It was now up to Elizabeth to declare Mary's guilt and bring her to the justice she deserved.[8]

After the judgment Lord Burghley wrote one of his familiar position papers. He laid out the choice: to keep Mary in prison or to put her to death. He himself strongly favoured the second course of action.[9]

Sir Christopher Hatton, Elizabeth's vice chamberlain, had all the gifts of the courtier. He wrote to her days before Fotheringhay: 'God in heaven bless your Majesty and grant me no longer life than that my faith and love may ever be found inviolable and spotless to so royal and peerless a prince.'[10]

On Thursday 3 November Hatton was in a very different mode. It was the first business day of a new parliament, Elizabeth's sixth, Robert Cecil once again the member for Westminster in the House of Commons. Opening debate in the Commons Sir Christopher made a ferocious attack on the Scottish queen's conspiracies and papistry. Other privy councillors supported him; it was a co-ordinated effort. The destruction of the Scottish queen would be an act of God in defence of the true faith.[11]

Parliament agreed that the case for justice had to be made urgently to Elizabeth. The day following Hatton's blistering opening barrage, the Commons appointed a committee to draft, with the Lords, a petition to be made to Elizabeth in the name of the whole parliament; the group was chaired by the speaker of the Commons, John Puckering, a serjeant-at-law who had led the prosecution at Fotheringhay. The real power in the petition committee was (a surprise to no one) Lord Burghley. Behind the scenes Robert Cecil's father applied to his queen as much political and rhetorical pressure as he could.

Robert was still just in the wings.

On Saturday 12 November Speaker Puckering went to Richmond Palace with the petition. Received by Elizabeth in her Chamber of Estate – the big reception room just outside her private apartments – he began by rehearsing Old Testament histories of kings and princes whose persons and kingdoms suffered because they had spared the wicked. This was an exhortation and warning: act, or else. God demanded justice. Heaven was watching, the queen's people waiting.[12]

Given two days' notice of what parliament's petition contained, Elizabeth was ready at Richmond with her response to Speaker Puckering.

She spoke with extraordinary self-control. She began by acknowledging the goodness of God, the 'bottomless graces and immeasurable benefits bestowed upon me by the Almighty'. Reflecting upon the vicissitudes of rule and power, she emphasized her own commitment to justice, honour and fair dealing: she needed above all to establish clearly and plainly her own blamelessness, feeling that she had been strong-armed into a situation she had so long resisted. She knew that all eyes were on her: 'for we princes, I tell you, are set on stages, in the sight and view of all the world duly observed'. A blemish on the spotless garment of monarchy would be quickly noted.[13]

She must have known that her speech was no kind of conclusion. She was delaying. A second deputation from parliament arrived on 24 November. Again Elizabeth responded, but in her own time. A month after the judgment against the Scottish queen in Star Chamber she had still not made her public proclamation of Mary's guilt, as the law required her to do. Elizabeth was maximizing what little room for manoeuvre she had left. And she was controlling her own words, preparing to make public her two speeches, revising them in the cat-scratch italic scrawl – frenetic, angular, intense – she called her 'skrating hand'. Always a scrupulous writer who wrestled to make her meaning clear, she was also implacable in policing her own authority. Here was Elizabeth now at the age of fifty-three, monarch for twenty-nine years, a graduate of (as she wrote) 'the school of experience'. She would have her say.[14]

The decision to print and publicize her speeches in a pamphlet must have been her own. Always her instinct was to stay silent, but if it had to be done she would control the process herself. She used the royal printer, the long-experienced Christopher Barker. And she needed a facilitator – a link between court and Barker's workshop – she could trust. This person was Robert Cecil.

For Robert it was a unique opportunity. It was also an extraordinarily delicate operation. He wasn't the queen's editor as such. Certainly, both he and his father handled Elizabeth's revised texts of her speeches; Robert made a small note on the manuscript. Each read with care her meditations on power and rule. They saw in her own handwriting the queen's struggle with privacy and openness, her conscience at war with a self-protective pragmatism. But the words belonged to her: Robert brought to them the gentlest touch. The twenty-three-year-old courtier knew his place.

Christopher Barker printed Robert's name simply as 'R. C.' The pamphlet was dedicated to Robert, earl of Leicester. Just home from his command of Elizabeth's army in the Netherlands, Leicester's return coincided to the day with the second of parliament's two deputations to the queen. The earl was quickly pressing Elizabeth for decisive action on the execution of justice against Mary. This was the editor's and printer's way in. Cecil and Barker offered all the speeches – Speaker Puckering's and the queen's – as a briefing dossier for Leicester. It was most probably printed in the first week of December when – at last – Elizabeth made her proclamation of Mary's guilt.[15]

Robert played the editorial lightness of touch to his own advantage. He presented himself as a keeper of record, a simple reporter. Who, after all, could hope to aspire to the queen's own words? Yet the pamphlet was deftly arranged. It captured something subtle and significant, articulating brilliantly the fraught complexity of the moment, those anxious days before Elizabeth had to see through to their conclusion the unyielding mechanisms of the emergency law parliament had passed – with her assent – weeks after the revelations over William Parry in early 1585. Thanks to this Act for the Queen's Surety, Elizabeth had to proclaim the Scottish queen's guilt when it was clear by legal process that she was guilty – hence parliament's urgings after Fotheringhay and Star Chamber. On that statute Elizabeth had written the usual formula for acts of parliament to which she gave her royal assent: 'La Royne le veult'. But though the queen had willed it, she did not want it – not then, and most certainly not at this moment in late autumn when Mary's life was now in her hands.[16]

In all this was Robert Cecil's challenge. His pamphlet had to satisfy both Elizabeth and those – parliament, Speaker Puckering, the queen's ministers (especially his own father) – who were pressing her forcefully on Mary. No one who read it could escape the fact that the Scottish queen was guilty of monstrous crimes against Elizabeth. But transparent also was Elizabeth's agony in trying to reconcile two duties, the one to a fellow prince and cousin, the other to her own security and the safety of her people. She wanted it to be plain to everyone that she was being compelled to act against the grain of her character, yet she was not naive: 'I am not so void of judgement, as not to see mine own peril: nor yet so ignorant, as not to know it were in nature a foolish course, to cherish a sword to cut mine own throat.'[17]

A parliament's uncompromising position on the Scottish queen justified, Mary denounced and condemned, Elizabeth pristine in her own conscience, a record for other princes, a statement before God: this was no easy balance to achieve in the pamphlet. It took some skilful and intelligent arrangement by a bright and energetic young courtier.

Like Lord Burghley, the earl of Leicester was a veteran in the fight against the queen's enemies. 'Your lordship and I were very good motes in the traitors' eyes', as Burghley had written to the earl a month before Fotheringhay.[18]

Robert Cecil's dedicatory letter to Leicester was more than decoration. It began with Robert acknowledging to the earl 'the honour you first vouchsafed me from beyond my cradle'. He was suggesting here a personal relationship which makes sense for the years of the 1560s when Lord Robert Dudley (as Leicester had then been) and Sir William Cecil were coming to terms with each other's power and influence at court: Leicester was Robert's godfather. The Christian name they shared is a further clue – this by tradition was a gift from a godparent to a godchild.

Robert used R. C.'s letter to tell something of his own story. He explained that he had wanted to go with Leicester and his army to fight with the Dutch against the Spanish in the Netherlands. His father and mother had refused: he had been 'letted [prevented] by the over-much tendering of me by my parents'. Robert's authentic voice just breaks through the veneer: the young man in his mid-twenties wanted adventure. In the pamphlet he revealed something of himself to the world beyond the court.[19]

He excused himself to Leicester for not setting the scene for Elizabeth's words more fully and richly:

I have but slenderly portrayed the lineaments, without expressing to life the external ornaments of her royal speech, accompanied with all princely and graceful accomplements: yet doubt I not but your lordship will easily find her inward virtues, whereof it is impossible for me to make the least adumbration.[20]

Robert Cecil was for the first time on the public stage. But a wise courtier knew that the show began and ended with Elizabeth. R. C.

had made his mark. Discretion was the better part of service – a lesson for life.

The manuscript ready, the final decisions about words and presentation made, Christopher Barker went to press in his workshop near Foster Lane in London, just off Cheapside.

The formal proclamation of Mary's guilt in plotting against Elizabeth was read across London and Westminster on Tuesday 6 December. It was done. All that now remained was to execute justice.

That same week the queen was in a sardonic mood. On 10 December she sent to Thomas Phelippes a secret paper for him to decipher. Thinking he must now be idle, she sensed he might need the mental exercise. This was Elizabeth's familiar gallows humour. She knew how efficient he had been in breaking the Scottish queen's ciphers. She recognized the energy with which he had prepared the dossier against Mary before Fotheringhay. It was a compliment of sorts.[21]

Christmas and New Year were fraught. Thomas Phelippes wasn't idle for very long. In early January 1587 he, Vice Chamberlain Hatton and Secretary Davison were unpicking yet another suspected plot to kill Elizabeth, this time linked to the household of the ambassador of the king of France, Monsieur de Bellièvre. The putative assassin was an Irish gentleman called Michael Moody – an individual we will meet properly in later chapters. William Wade, the Paris embassy veteran of the late 1570s and early 1580s, now in 1587 busily at work as a clerk of the Privy Council, was sent by Elizabeth to France to protest at this 'new intended conspiracy against our person'. His leave of absence from his duties as clerk was recorded with a flourish in the council's register book.[22]

The necessary paperwork for the execution of the Scottish queen was ready: nearly eight hundred words composed by Lord Burghley, needing only Elizabeth's sign manual and the great seal of England. The queen did nothing. Lord Burghley watched and waited.

The day of action was Wednesday, 1 February 1587, the eve of the feast of Candlemas. The court was at Greenwich Palace. The Privy

Council met as usual, the only absentee Secretary Walsingham, sick at his house on Seething Lane near the Tower of London. Sometime during that day the queen asked Secretary Davison for the death warrant. She was resigned. Signing the paper, she commented to Davison that the news would aid Walsingham's recovery.[23]

When Burghley discovered from Vice Chamberlain Hatton that the queen had signed and released the warrant, he acted with speed and secrecy. He called the Privy Council into his chambers where together they decided that the warrant and the executioner would be sent to Fotheringhay. Hours after she signed the warrant, Elizabeth changed her mind and recalled it. But she was by then too late – the warrant was already travelling north. On Wednesday 8 February Mary was beheaded, a fact Elizabeth found out the following day.

Part fury, part necessary political theatre, Elizabeth's response was extreme. Only a few escaped her anger, most notably and surprisingly Leicester and Hatton. Within hours of convening the council, Lord Burghley, knowing that Elizabeth held him primarily responsible for Mary's death, was writing long papers of self-justification. Secretary Davison was unluckier still. He found himself before too long in the Tower.

Burghley was in disgrace with Elizabeth, and for his family winter and early spring 1587 were hard months, perhaps especially for Robert who must have previously felt the honour of putting Elizabeth's words into print. The queen now cut Robert's father out of her life as much as was possible. Burghley's response was agonized bafflement. Leicester counselled patience and time: as he wrote to his old comrade, God would in the end remind Elizabeth of her lord treasurer's 'long approved painful and faithful service'. Like Burghley he knew what had had to be done out of necessity for the safety of queen and kingdom: 'Some folks are not yet of like filled enough with the continual perils and dangers we daily saw her in.' When Burghley wrote to the queen to justify himself, Sir Christopher Hatton, with a courtier's discretion, neglected to give the letter to her. It was William Killigrew, a gentleman servant of Elizabeth's privy chamber who eventually did. She refused to acknowledge it.[24]

*

In April Elizabeth was still wearing mourning dress for Mary Queen of Scots. She was unhappy and discontented. And she was still rebuffing Burghley.

It was fortunate for him that he had good friends at court. Frances, Lady Cobham, one of the women closest to Elizabeth in her private chambers, offered herself as a means of reconciliation with the queen. She told Burghley that she and her husband 'have been beholding to you and to no councillor else . . . I do beseech your lordship to hasten your coming hither.' Burghley wrote on the back of the letter: 'The Lady Cobham, offer of her friendship.'[25]

By mid-April it was time for Burghley – and his family, including Robert – to come in from the cold.

Sir Christopher Hatton would be a stalwart supporter of Robert Cecil's ambitions to get a seat on the Privy Council. That was a little way in the future. But the Hatton factor was significant in the spring of 1587.

At the end of April Hatton was promoted. As the Queen's vice chamberlain, sandwiched in the council's order of precedence between Secretary Walsingham below and the lord president of Wales above, his appointment as Elizabeth's lord chancellor after the death of Sir Thomas Bromley gave him rank even over Lord Treasurer Burghley. Vice chamberlain was a key role: few privy councillors were closer to the queen in her private rooms. But the chancellorship mattered. Only Archbishop Whitgift of Canterbury, an irregular attender in the council chamber, pushed the lord chancellor into second place in the hierarchy.

The Cecils were prompt to send their congratulations to Sir Christopher. Hatton was installed as lord chancellor on Saturday 29 April. The following day Robert Cecil was dispatched by his mother to visit his new lordship. It is one of those rare moments when we see Lady Burghley at work, where we sense her finely developed political instincts. Like her close friend Lady Cobham, she knew the ways of the court quite as well as her husband.

Scrupulous to a fault, Robert wrote to his father with a full report on his meeting with Sir Christopher. All that he had said was to the point; everything had a purpose; Robert was pitch-perfect. He communicated his mother's congratulations, and reminded Sir Christopher of his father's support for Hatton's candidacy. And then there was of course himself: 'I added besides a particular declaration of the love and duty I always had borne him, with an earnest desire now to be protected with his favour and good opinion hereafter.' Robert noted that Hatton had now changed his usual hat and feather for a flat velvet cap just like Burghley's – the fashionably flamboyant courtier was now the serious minister.[26]

Hatton's first meeting of the Privy Council as lord chancellor was on Tuesday 2 May at Nonsuch Palace. Burghley was there too, and his friend Lord Cobham, Robert's future father-in-law.

Spring 1587 was a season of calm. Summer brought favour. Robert Cecil, now twenty-four years old, flourished.

Robert's future was Theobalds, and fixing him as a gentleman of Hertfordshire was an early phase of Burghley's longer-term planning. But the queen's favour was everything. By August she was ready, granting to Robert the reversion of Lord Burghley's offices and duties in Hertfordshire. One day he would succeed his father as the most important landowner in the county.

Burghley's letter with this news was handed to Robert soon after 9 p.m. on Thursday 24 August: Robert called it 'the advertisement of her Majesty's conclusion of that she promised me'. We should note that last pronoun: the queen had at some point talked to him about his future. Up until then there had been an understanding, an intimation of what was to come. But one never knew with Elizabeth until it happened.

To his father he owed so much; Burghley was 'the whole stay of my good fortune', as Robert put it. Yet one other supporter was Robert Devereux, earl of Essex, who a few months earlier was reported to be inseparable from the queen. This was the time of Essex's effortless rise to influence: the star-lit courtier of twenty-one, playing cards with the queen most of the night, going to bed with the birds' dawn chorus. Burghley told Robert just what he owed to Essex, who had argued Master Cecil's cause with Elizabeth.

On Friday morning Robert replied with thanks for Burghley's sound and fatherly direction. He was just then leaving London for Theobalds.[27]

5

Enemies and Friends

Cecil's first big adventure was his journey in February 1588 to the Low Countries with Henry, earl of Derby. He took the bracing air in Dover. He froze in Ostend. He saw Bruges, Ghent, Antwerp and the northern Netherlands. Robert pushed himself to his physical limits, beyond what Lady Burghley imagined him capable of. He saw the courteous dissimulations of his Altesse the duke of Parma and polished up his own diplomatic skills, at least as an observer. He was on his best behaviour, so conscious of whose son he was. He was determined to impress.

The queen continued to call Robert her 'Pygmy', a familiar name which spoke to his physique. Pygmies were believed to be a race of Ethiopian or Indian dwarves, so very different from the courtly ideal of elegant physicality for the gentleman. Elizabeth liked to keep her most favoured courtiers on their toes; it was high favour with a seasoning of malice – the monarch with a chip of ice in the heart. Robert accepted her name with a courtier's grace and a courtier's resignation: he had little choice. But at least the Pygmy was noticed. Better that than to be ignored.

From Ostend to Ghent Robert saw the grim effects of war. This was Spanish-controlled territory, but land fought over between the Dutch and the Spaniards. The country around Antwerp had suffered less: there were populated villages and tilled fields, and no marauding freebooters, all thanks to the efforts of the local Spanish governor. Robert came to Antwerp in mid-March on his own, and against his initial resolution to visit the town only in the company of Valentine Dale or one of the other English diplomats in the earl of Derby's entourage. Adventure had trumped prudence. Robert had Parma's passport, and he liked

Antwerp. Most of the merchants were gone, except for the Italians, fellow countrymen of Parma. One of these merchants – and one of the richest – took Robert into his own house. He wrote to his father that he and the merchant had fallen into company together, but their meeting was no accident: 'he gave me all manner of good entertainment, affirming that his Altesse had so appointed him.' The merchant, in other words, was his minder. The authorities in Antwerp gave Master Cecil all the freedoms he needed to be able to explore the town. Its burgomaster was the son of the late Emperor Charles V's ambassador to the court of King Edward VI. Even in enemy territory Robert had fallen on his feet.

On his mind in Antwerp was the duke of Parma, and for his father Robert tried some analysis of the positions of both the duke and his master the king of Spain. The duke was rich; he had more than enough money to maintain the dignity of a prince. Indeed, Spaniards said privately that the Dutch wars had left him richer. The resources of Philip of Spain, on the other hand, were being heavily drained by maintaining soldiers and garrisons – Cecil's host estimated the sum to be more than four hundred thousand crowns each month. They were preparing a military action. But what was it? An invasion of England? Or a push further north beyond the Scheldt into the northern Dutch provinces? The view of the Italian merchants in Antwerp was that Philip was unlikely to risk 'a war with so mighty a nation as ours'. So Robert put it, his patriotism temporarily ignoring Spain's formidable war machine.

Robert volunteered to be his father's eyes. Under Parma's protection in Spanish-held territory, he would cross the front line and travel from Antwerp to Bergen op Zoom (lightly garrisoned by English cavalry and infantry) and see the ships for himself. He could look both ways, north to the Dutch United Provinces, south to Spanish Flanders: the Scheldt estuary and the rivers Maas and Waal together formed a watery barrier between the two. He would report what he heard. He wanted to be precise and accurate. 'These speeches that I have here reported, are as they delivered them, the judgement whereof is left to your lordship as it please you, whom I beseech God with her Majesty's other most honourable council still to direct with the light of his understanding.' He added that Parma's advisers were either

Burgundians or Italians and his partiality towards them annoyed the Spaniards, 'from whose glorious insolency and inveterate malice to our nation I hope God will save us to their confusion'.

All of this he wrote on Thursday 14 March in a letter of two pages and three sides, a restless balance between the competing priorities of beauty, accuracy and economy. Robert wrote at speed. His handwriting was neat enough, but he wasn't afraid to correct his own words, scratching out some, adding others. Thanks to the arrival of a ship just in port from Italy, Robert sent his letter to Burghley with a gift of the best seeds he could find in Antwerp. Burghley's gardens were one of his lordship's innocent pleasures.[1]

In Antwerp Robert encountered two other Englishmen. They were Catholics, and outcasts. One he was prepared to interview; the other he refused to meet. He made sure to give Secretary Walsingham a full account of his dealings with the queen's enemies – even the credit of Elizabeth's Pygmy stretched only so far. Four years earlier he had written to Sir Francis on behalf of the recusant Catholic John Towneley. Now he was on more dangerous ground.

The dissident he met was one Wiseman, a gentleman from Essex who had been in the service of the king of Spain, who now wanted to come home and to redeem what Robert called his lost and misspent years. Cecil made no promises: he simply passed the message to Walsingham. Master Tresham, one of a large family of defiantly dissident Catholics, was trickier to handle. 'Tresham would have spoken with me,' Robert wrote, 'but it fitted not my poor fortune to deal with persons so disloyal without a warrant.' It was a wise choice for him to make. By May, Walsingham had information through Thomas Phelippes that this Tresham was trying to build up a party of émigré English Catholic support for the duke of Parma.[2]

By the first week of April Robert was back in Ostend and only a few days away from returning to England. He was wrestling with the unlikely diplomacy of procuring English hunting dogs for the duke of Parma, who had approached Robert with the request through an intermediary. It turned out – a surprise to Robert who thought it would be a surprise to his father – that Parma was extraordinarily fond of English dogs. When Valentine Dale and Robert had had an audience with Parma in Ghent, the duke had taken a fancy to one of the dogs with them and begged it for himself. Robert felt he couldn't with good manners refuse the request. He thought that his friends in England would be able to procure more hounds; he hoped the gift would cause no offence at home. The tokens of esteem from Parma's negotiators kept arriving: a couple of hawks for Robert, and three for Lord Cobham, along with hares, pheasants and oysters.

Parma was, in reality, preparing an army for the invasion of England and the peace talks, which the duke strung along for as long as he was able in order to divide and confound Elizabeth's commissioners, continued to achieve nothing. England was beset by enemies. When Burghley received his son's letter from the front line of negotiations that meant peace or war, he wrote on the back of it: 'Robert Cecil. A line hound and a brace of greyhounds.'[3]

In his letter to Secretary Walsingham from Ostend, Robert had offered his opinion of the negotiations with Parma. He was diffident but plain:

> Of the peace those who understand it I know will best inform your honour, whose honourable place challengeth all such advertisements; for mine own part, I see it not begun yet and therefore believe it cannot so soon receive any perfect end. If it do, either may we thank the King of Spain's weakness, or fear the consequence.

In other words, it would be at best a paper peace.[4]

On Wednesday, 12 June 1588 Lord Burghley received in the diplomatic post from the Netherlands a book whose author called himself 'the Cardinal of England'. Burghley opened it straight away, and by the time he finished reading he was furious. The book had to be forbidden; even to possess it without passing it to a privy councillor should be an act of treason. He wanted it to be answered and refuted. He sent the book to Secretary Walsingham, so livid that even Burghley, usually a master of self-control, doubted the balance of his own judgement.

William Allen's *Admonition to the Nobility and People of England and Ireland* was the most incendiary attack on Elizabeth ever to be set in type, an astonishingly personal assault on the queen herself, even by the flammable standards of Catholic polemic. Elizabeth, daughter of that infamous courtesan Anne Boleyn, had usurped with 'Luciferian pride' the ecclesiastical government of the kingdom. She was a bastard who had intruded herself into the possession of the English crown. She was guilty of perjury and impiety. She was a persecutor of the Catholic religion and a corrupt tyrant. The earl of Essex, her amorous minion, she had advanced to high office and excessive wealth. With him and with others she had abused her own body, working through them to overthrow the ancient nobility of the kingdom. Machiavellian, godless and conscienceless, there was no foulness the queen had not herself perpetrated. The slaughter of the Scottish queen was merely a single example of 'her open enormities': there were 'other her secret wickedness hidden from us'. But this was not simply polemical abuse for its own sake. Allen's *Admonition* was a call to arms and resistance.

Just before the cardinal ended his text from his lodging in St Peter's palace in Rome, he commended the strenuous efforts of the pope and King Philip to rescue England. Allen trusted that he would himself be home very shortly. The end of tyranny was near: help was at hand.[5]

Just over three weeks later, Valentine Dale had an audience in Bruges with the duke of Parma. No one from Lord Derby's entourage knew he was there, other than the earl himself and Lord Cobham. Derby's embassy was still in Ostend, a peace with Spain still notionally on the table. But trust and patience were wearing thin. Doctor Dale had received his instructions from the queen on 1 July. On the 7th he arrived in Bruges, and the following morning he met Parma.

Burghley had been told that Allen's *Admonition* was printed in Antwerp with Parma's encouragement. To add to the outrage, Allen had written a condensed version of his book which was printed to look like an official condemnation of Elizabeth by Pope Sixtus V. Walsingham had informed Burghley in the last week of June that twelve thousand copies of what Burghley called this 'roaring hellish bull' were being printed also in Antwerp. Back in England, the solicitor general was drafting a proclamation to suppress it. This was published on the day

Doctor Dale in Ostend received the instructions for his secret mission. Dale's task was to confront Parma with the facts and to hear what the duke had to say.[6]

Valentine Dale described for Parma both the *Admonition* and the bull. He wanted from the duke's own mouth an explanation for them, concluding his speech thus: 'Therefore her Majesty would be satisfied from your Altesse in that point and would take satisfaction from none other.'

Parma was unruffled. He said that he had neither read nor even seen the book. He had nothing to do with it, and had no control over what men chose to write or print. He was only, he said, at the commandment of his master the king. Parma chose to say nothing about the bull.

Dale's reply was undiplomatically frank: 'if it were so there were a war purposely taken in hand at the instance of the Pope, this treaty were but vain.' In this situation, Elizabeth would have to recall her commissioners, expecting them to enjoy the benefits of safe conduct.

'Yea, God forbid else', Parma replied. He told Doctor Dale 'that he did not know nor esteem what bull the Pope had set forth nor did undertake anything for him'. Perhaps – just perhaps – Valentine Dale believed him.[7]

A few weeks later King Philip's invincible Armada set sail.

Robert Cecil saw for himself the Spanish Armada, at least from a distance. But he got as close to it as he was able.

On Thursday 25 July (by the English calendar), a day that Robert was at court, Elizabeth's navy under the command of her lord admiral, Charles Howard, had met a formidable Spanish fleet in the English Channel. For forty-eight hours already Lord Burghley had been supervising the mobilization of a force of lancers and light horsemen to attend the queen. Robert's brother Sir Thomas Cecil was named as colonel of nearly three thousand men to be raised from the counties of Kent and Surrey.[8]

Robert understood as much as anyone at court – and that was a considerable amount: regular bulletins were arriving. He knew that Howard had kept the advantage of wind and had followed the Armada up the Channel from Plymouth as far as Portsmouth, shooting at them from long range. The Spaniards barely returned fire: they were waiting to join up with the ground forces prepared in the Low Countries by Parma. Early indications were positive for England. Robert wrote: 'It hath pleased God yet to give us the first sign of victory.' The Spanish vice admiral, unable to keep up with the main fleet, had been taken prisoner by Sir Francis Drake. Drake had captured a great Spanish argosy, and the seized men – four hundred of them, a quarter of whom were gentlemen – were taken to Weymouth and would soon be brought up to London. Their leader's name was Don Pedro de Valdéz. 'This is all that yet hath happened, for which good beginning God's name be praised.' They hoped that night to hear from the lord admiral.

Robert wanted to see the action. The fighting between the fleets would be done in the narrow seas between Dunkirk on the French coast and Margate in Kent. He would ride down there and see if he could 'take a ship a little way into the sea without danger, as many gentlemen did upon the western coast' when the Armada had first been sighted.

At Richmond that Thursday he was unstinting in his praise of Elizabeth:

> It is comfort to see how great magnanimity her Majesty shows, who is not a whit dismayed herewith, as I hope in God she shall have no cause, seeing they missed firing of our ships and that they cannot take us suddenly, but their fleet is of no small strength.[9]

On Saturday 27 July the ships of Lord Henry Seymour and Lord Admiral Howard met off Calais, close to the Spanish fleet. At 11 p.m. that night the admiral sent seven fireships towards the Armada. Burning with pitch and tar, they did their work: within hours the Spanish ships had either to cut or let slip their anchors. One contemporary account relates how Howard took the fullest advantage of the fireships' effect.

> In this pursuit of the fire wrought by our folks, the Lord Admiral in fight spoiled a great number of them, sunk three forthwith, and drove

four or five to the shore, so as at that instant it was assured that they had lost at the least sixteen of their best ships.[10]

Charles Howard wrote to Walsingham from his flagship *Ark Royal* on Monday 29 July. The Spanish fleet was in distress, but victory was not yet certain. 'Sir, I will not write unto her Majesty before more be done. Their force is wonderful great and strong and yet we pluck their feathers by little and little. I pray to God that the forces on the land be strong enough to answer so puissant a force.'[11]

Watching Howard's slow plucking of the invincible armada from his vantage point in Dover that same Monday was Master Robert Cecil.

Cecil finished a letter to his father at 12 noon on Tuesday 30 July. He sealed and addressed it himself. He was still in Dover but was setting out soon for London. That is where the court would be, and an army too, commanded by the Queen's lord chamberlain, sixty-two-year-old Lord Hunsdon, her first cousin: the men from the nearest counties to London first, the rest to be in the city by 6 August. Should Spanish troops land they would have to be fought on the coast and London protected. Burghley had laid out the plan.

In Dover Robert watched and reported. The gunpowder sent by his father had arrived safely and had been taken out to the fleet on Sir Walter Raleigh's *Roebuck*. Prisoners were being questioned: they blamed Parma for not shipping his troops in time to join up properly with the main fleet, which would have waited off Calais and Gravelines had not Lord Admiral Howard deployed what Robert called 'the device of the fireworks'. So far as Robert understood, those crack Spanish veterans had still not embarked. He had heard nothing about the earl of Derby and his fellow peace commissioners.[12]

On 1 August Derby was still in Calais. He knew that the Spanish fleet had sailed on but was otherwise in the dark. 'Being most desirous to hear of the good success of her Majesty's navy (the which I rest not to pray that God may prosper),' he wrote to Walsingham, 'I am therefore bold to desire a few lines from you by this bearer, for we hear little in these parts.'[13]

Derby arrived at Dover on the evening of 7 August. Peace

negotiations with Spain were definitively over. Although Parma had outmanoeuvred Elizabeth's commissioners diplomatically, the Spanish fleet would be driven in the following days into the North Sea and broken into pieces on the coasts of Scotland and Ireland. Philip II had committed about one hundred and fifty ships to the invasion of England. Accident, battle and weather meant that only about sixty-five returned to Lisbon.

In London the queen gave thanks to God that her naval commanders had had heavenly assistance in scattering her enemies.[14]

In Robert Cecil's letters to his good friend Michael Hickes, Burghley's busy patronage secretary, we hear one of his other selves: not the earnest obedient son, Polonius's apprentice, but a voice of easy and teasing familiarity, where poor Master Michael's baldness was an old theme. In a jumble of letters from 1589 and 1590 – notes quickly written, full of in-jokes and practically all undated – Robert would invite Hickes to share dinners with him, often standing his boat fare on the River Thames or paying the courier who carried their letters. Business often lurked in the background: Robert was by now a broker of court patronage, a maker of deals on the side. Scribbled notes expressed the warmth of a bond between two men with twenty years' difference in their ages. Once Robert wrote: 'I must needs confess with acknowledgement [of] your kindness, knowing that letters are the means for friends' correspondence, and so cause the absence to be the less grievous.' It was a sentiment as conventional as a verse in a modern-day greetings card, taken from the Roman poet Turpilius. But Robert meant it: 'To tell you I love you still, were but to remember you of that you are I hope assured of.' In the toughness of court life superficial professions of love and friendship often signalled danger – it was quite the opposite for Master Robert and Master Michael.[15]

Robert spent time when he could with family and old friends. There was his 'sweet sister' Anne and her daughter Lady Elizabeth, the teenaged earl of Southampton (Henry Wriothesley, later Shakespeare's patron), Master Arundel, 'my good knave Tom Speed' (one of Lord Burghley's gentleman servants), Burghley's private secretary Henry Maynard and, of course, Michael Hickes. Robert's letters to Master

Michael's mother, Juliana Penne, were buoyantly convivial. He was the model of thoughtfulness and generosity, offering in October 1588 to act as discreet middleman in securing for Mistress Penne 'a pretty silver bell' – an Armada memento which had belonged to Don Pedro Valdéz. He was adept at these transactions, the gifts and favours that lubricated high society. As Robert wrote to Mistress Penne: 'If I may pleasure you or yours I will be more ready. And thus wishing you health and long life for my friend's good your eldest son I commit you to God.'[16]

Robert Cecil was well used to the company of women. He wrote as easily and fluently to Juliana Penne as he did to the grandest knight of the Garter. In his letters from the Low Countries he had always conveyed his compliments to his mother and sisters. He had a special soft spot for Anne, as did their father.

Both of Robert's sisters died young; Elizabeth in 1583 at the age of eighteen, Anne at thirty-one, five days after Robert's twenty-fifth birthday. Anne's marriage to the impeccably noble 17th earl of Oxford, Edward de Vere, should have been one of the great adornments of the Cecil family. It wasn't. Their marriage was strained and unhappy and Burghley stoically salvaged out of the situation as much dignity as he was able. From June 1588 Robert was the only surviving sibling, and the sixty-seven-year-old lord treasurer of England became guardian to his three Oxford granddaughters, Lady Elizabeth, Lady Bridget and Lady Susan.

In 1588 both Anne and Burghley's mother, Jane, died. In 1589 it was Lady Burghley. Her death hit Lord Burghley hard. Her husband wrote: 'There is no cogitation to be used with an intent to recover that which never can be had again, that is to have my dear wife to live again in her mortal body.' One of the foundations of Burghley's life had been pulled away. He celebrated her piety and charity and her role as the 'matchless mother, by whose tender and godly care' her children were raised.[17]

When Robert had proposed his journey to the Low Countries with the earl of Derby, Lady Burghley had made plain her opposition. She didn't forbid it – that was a decision for her husband to make – but she did expect Robert to take upon himself its consequences. As he had written to his father at the time:

My lady my mother hath imparted unto me that she did send up to your lordship ... that ... it was not a journey that she would have chosen out for me in respect both of the unpleasantness of the country and mine own not strongest constitution, yet [she] ... would in no sort hinder it, only adding this that if any harm came to me I should thank myself.

Robert had humbly thanked her ladyship for her care.[18]

Her funeral at Westminster Abbey in April 1589 was so grand that Burghley felt he had to justify its scale. It was not, he emphasized, 'done for any vain pomp of the world, but for civil duty towards her body' – an appropriate tribute to her family and its noble connections, as well as a testimony of his love. Burghley himself choreographed the great procession. Robert helped, making two additions to Burghley's list of mourners – two women, as it happened, the wife of Burghley's secretary Henry Maynard and that of another old family servant, Bernard Dewhurst, though Anne Dewhurst was family too. She was Burghley's niece by his first marriage to Mary Cheke. Robert's family antennae were as well-tuned as his father's.

The most prominent of the mourners were Lady Burghley's sister Lady Russell, her eldest granddaughter Lady Elizabeth de Vere and Lady Burghley's old friend Lady Cobham, who had been chief mourner to Anne Oxford only ten months earlier. Robert Cecil was first assistant to the corpse, one of the most visible people in the cortège: Burghley put his son at the head of all the others of the Cecils, their relations and servants. Cousin Francis Bacon carried one of the banderoles, a pennant showing the coats of arms of his late aunt's extended family.[19]

Lord Burghley commissioned for Lady Oxford and Lady Burghley a grand tomb in the abbey's chapel of St Nicholas. He wrote the epitaphs himself, emphasizing his wife's deep learning and charity and Anne's faithfulness to her husband and submissiveness to her parents. The model wife, daughter and sister, both dead. The senior male weeper on the tomb is Robert Cecil, his effigy carved very much from life.[20]

Even with family still in mourning after Lady Burghley's death, it was time to mark a change in Robert Cecil's life. He became a landed gentleman in his own right. Not Theobalds, of course, but the first step on that journey: a house and land in Middlesex, Pymmes, which Burghley had bought in 1582. It lay between the villages of Tottenham and Edmonton on the main road out of London. Robert, as boy and man journeying from Westminster to Theobalds and back again, had passed by it hundreds of times.[21]

Naturally it was part of a plan. For Robert that plan was marriage, the most strategic of all decisions for a court family. It was never rushed; negotiations were entered into, the pieces put carefully into place; weaknesses were tested, and alliances were formed or perhaps broken. When Robert was a small boy, he had nearly had as a brother-in-law the poet Philip Sidney, but the putative match between Philip and Anne Cecil hadn't passed the necessary tests and conditions between Sir William Cecil and Sir Henry Sidney: Anne's unhappy future was the egregious Oxford.

Robert's in-laws would be Lord and Lady Cobham, his wife their daughter Elizabeth Brooke. Quite apart from the Cobhams' impeccable standing at court – one foot in the Privy Council, the other in the queen's Privy Chamber – Robert knew Lord Cobham very well. It was at his house that Robert was expected when he returned to England from Paris in October 1584, and Cobham who kept an eye on Robert at Ostend in spring 1588, writing to ask 'whether my friend Master Cecil be safely come unto you and in health'. Lady Cobham had been Lord Burghley's supporter in that slow thawing of Elizabeth's coldness after the Scottish queen's execution. Robert and Elizabeth celebrated their wedding on Sunday, 31 August 1589.[22]

Elizabeth Cecil, like Mildred Burghley, is rather a mystery, which is at once frustrating and oddly fitting. A goddaughter to the queen, she served in Elizabeth's most private chambers. Like mother, like daughter, Elizabeth Cecil shared with Lady Cobham a talent for both discretion and anonymity. She was happier in the background. In letters Robert called her Bess: he described his marriage as 'The dearest bond that ever I was tied in'.[23]

She even shared her husband's sense of humour. 'Poor Bess Cecil will know you, she saith, for a cosiner in leaving her your poll pate instead of a French crown', Robert wrote to Michael Hickes early in the marriage. Friends and servants, a typical in-joke, and all at poor

Hickes's expense – devious Master Michael's only gift in making a visit to them was his bald head, and nothing as useful as money.[24]

Late summer 1589: Robert Cecil the established married gentleman, the new sheriff of Hertfordshire, with his own house and small estate at the half-way point on the road from London to Theobalds. The last a plain fact of geography and a metaphor for his journey to power.

Behind the scenes Bess Cecil became her husband's greatest supporter.

6

Hermit, Gardener, Molecatcher

At Greenwich Palace on Monday, 6 April 1590, William Wade and Daniel Rogers – scholar, poet and the latest appointee as clerk of the Privy Council – opened a new council register book. It was the usual hefty volume that was needed every year or so, a repository for office copies of outgoing letters, bought for six shillings and eightpence by the official, one Randoll Bellyn, who looked after the chest in which the council's papers were carried from palace to palace. The clerks often broke in a new book by doodling on the first page: this time it was with some practice signatures, a few Latin and Italian mottoes, even some lines in Greek from Plato. By convention each book began with a full list of the councillors and their offices, signed at the bottom by Wade and on this day by Rogers, whose pen had been busiest on the page. This time, too, Lord Burghley checked the list and corrected an inaccuracy that had caught his eye, where Rogers had mistaken the under treasurer of the Exchequer for its treasurer. All routine, all proper, with councillors named in strict order of precedence.

Today was different. Within hours of the ink drying on the page, one of the councillors was dead. Rogers appended a note to the thirteenth name on the list: 'Sir Francis Walsingham, knight, Principal Secretary to her Majesty, and Chancellor of the Duchy of Lancaster; departed the same day about eleven of the clock in the night.'[1]

The queen now had no secretary, and sixty-nine-year-old Lord Treasurer Burghley would soon have more work than ever piled on his desk.

It was Burghley himself who had made the queen's principal secretary the workhorse of her government. For fourteen years William Cecil was a secretary both single and singular: putting to one side twenty years of inherited practice he worked on his own and bore the whole burden himself. He wrote early in Elizabeth's reign that some of his predecessors had made the secretaryship a '[work]shop for cunning men'. He, however, as he liked to believe himself as much as he needed to tell others, was better than that. When Elizabeth made him lord treasurer in 1572, the secretary's portfolio was once again divided between two privy councillors. Walsingham's poor health and frequent absences from court in the later 1580s made this more necessary than ever. For a few months Walsingham had a highly talented second secretary, William Davison. But Davison's dismissal and disgrace for his role in Mary Queen of Scots's execution in 1587 – he had no choice but to take the blame for the councillors' dispatch of her death warrant, putting him briefly in the Tower – pushed the secretariat to breaking point. Davison kept his salary, but his humiliation left him embittered and resentful.[2]

Thus from spring 1590 the lord treasurer was also acting secretary. By May Burghley's omnipresent secretary, Henry Maynard, who every day when he was on duty – this was most of the time – took down so many thousands of words of his master's dictation, was making entries in the book once kept in Walsingham's office which recorded payments made under the Queen's privy seal, kept by the principal secretary and the means by which Walsingham had been able to authorize discreet payments for anything from armies to spies. Now, Burghley as both secretary and lord treasurer drove the engine of Elizabeth's government.[3]

Burghley moved the levers of power by both deep instinct and long practice. But he was an old man, working beyond his own formidable physical limits. Now there was no rest, no remission from paperwork, no peace from suitors, little of a private life. He was more smothered by business than ever.

In late October Burghley was gathering together Walsingham's papers. He sent Doctor John James to Walsingham House on Seething Lane. James – a physician, linguist and an occasional censor of books – had the task of packing up those books and files still there that now properly belonged in the new secretariat in Westminster.[4]

The most sensitive documents of all, concerning espionage and secret diplomacy, were kept secure. Two of Sir Francis's private cabinets, with their keys, were put into the safe custody of Elizabeth's recently appointed vice chamberlain, Sir Thomas Heneage, one of which Heneage gave to Burghley, who kept it in his chambers. On Elizabeth's instructions, Sir Thomas held on to what he described as 'a little black box', where the papers for each country were distinguished from one another only by letter. Out of this Doctor James had already removed Walsingham's secret ciphers and given them to Burghley.[5]

Burghley wanted this to be a temporary arrangement. He expected Elizabeth to appoint a new secretary as quickly as possible. Or so he hoped – he knew from long experience the time it could take the queen to make any decision. He had at court a useful agent of persuasion, a former servant many years before in his own household by the name of Thomas Windebank, a clerk of the signet office. By 1590 Windebank was almost permanently on duty in Elizabeth's private rooms. He read letters to the Queen, took her dictation and acted as a day-to-day adviser and confidant, liaising with her minsters. He was always the model of tact and reassurance. And he always made full reports to Burghley, to whom the old ties of obligation were as strong as ever.

On Thursday 22 October, two days after Burghley had signed a warrant to pay Doctor James the sum of twenty pounds for his work at Walsingham House, Windebank and Elizabeth were discussing ambassadorial appointments. He saw the opportunity to raise with the queen the subject of the secretaryship. He told Elizabeth (so he reported to Burghley that same evening) 'how greatly her favour should be extended to your lordship by easing you of the burden she layeth upon you through want of a Secretary'. Windebank wrote: 'She confessed as much as I said.' But she made no promise, no commitment.[6]

Lord Burghley needed to plan for the future. Elizabeth needed a new secretary she – and he – could trust.

For men much younger than Burghley and Windebank it was the season for ambition, and for all the travails that invariably attend it.

At the beginning of October Robert, earl of Essex, as yet a long

way off from establishing his own power base in Elizabeth's government, had adopted the cause of former secretary William Davison.
This was a potential investment with prospects. For a courtier as
ambitious as Essex was, to be responsible for Davison's rehabilitation would be a coup.

Davison was a thoroughbred retired well before his prime. In the
weeks before his humiliation in the Tower and trial in Star Chamber,
Burghley himself had lauded Davison as the best of all principal secretaries. That was praise indeed. But on former Secretary Davison
Elizabeth was, even after three years, grimly resistant, for she had a
long memory for others' misdeeds. Essex, however, was tenacious. He
described for Elizabeth what he called Davison's sufferings and his
patience in bearing them. He had faced poverty, imprisonment and
disgrace with faith and humility. The queen replied that Davison's
presumption had been intolerable. She could not forget it. She refused
to meet him.[7]

But Essex kept pressing. 'What you will have me do for your suit I
will as far as my credit is anything worth', he wrote to Davison. 'I
have told most of the Council of my manner of dealing with the
Queen. My Lord Chancellor [Hatton] tells me he hath dealt for you
also.'

All the councillors wished as he did, the earl wrote to Davison, 'but
in this world that is not enough'.[8]

Robert Cecil also had his eye on the secretaryship, though he was too
coy to name it directly. He also was courting Lord Chancellor Hatton
and building up a cadre of supporters.

It was an ambitious hope – too ambitious in reality, and on some
level Robert must have known that. He was twenty-seven years old.
The queen liked him. He had done small favours for powerful men,
and he had been abroad once as an observer at a peace conference. He
was praised. And, most important of all, he was Burghley's son. With
a couple of foreign embassies under his belt and another ten years'
experience of court and government, perhaps. He had great potential.
But late 1590 was too early for a new Secretary Cecil.

His father, too, was holding back – or at least so he said. Robert
wrote to Hatton in November 1590 that it was 'so far from my lord's

[Burghley's] own thoughts to hold me worthy the nomination and so much farther from his mind ever to have pursued it directly or indirectly'. It was Hatton's intercession that made the difference and raised Robert's hopes. Burghley wasn't pushing. At least not yet.

To the lord chancellor Robert professed love and duty. The letter he sent to Sir Christopher was, as he put it, his poor sacrifice, his promise of service.[9]

A fortnight later there were tremors at court that Elizabeth would appoint her new secretary. There appeared to be two candidates. One was Robert Cecil, the other Thomas Wilkes, a clerk of the Privy Council who had been educated at All Souls, Oxford, in the early 1570s and was an experienced diplomat. Davison was not on the short list. One courtier described both contenders: 'the one in respect of the great helps he shall have from his father, himself being a towardly personage; the other a well experimental [experienced] gentleman, and of good understanding, and great dispatch, and no less courage.' The first, of course, was Robert, the junior hopeful: 'towardly' was the kind of adjective used for a promising and willing young man. It was Wilkes who had the necessary weight for the job, however.[10]

One of the many undated notes sent by Robert to Michael Hickes may belong to this day, Tuesday 24 November. Expecting his father home from court, Robert was on tenterhooks, waiting for news of 'the election, creation, suspension or confusion o[f] her Majesty's Principal Secretary'.

Waiting with him was Bess Cecil. She too signed the letter to her friend Master Michael, her 'Cecill' a careful facsimile of Robert's signature – a mark of wifely obedience, a show of solidarity.[11]

There was no decision – there rarely was with Queen Elizabeth. As autumn turned to winter Burghley was busier than ever, and Robert Cecil found himself in the new and uncomfortable role of importunate suitor. He was hopeful, he was frustrated. It was a life of treading on eggshells.

He clung to Hatton's favour and support. His letters to Sir Christopher gushed with courtly courtesies. He wrote in mid-February 1591 'that your lordship, being my only oracle, may not be unacquainted with the proceedings of your poor follower'. He reverenced Hatton as his second father; he was ever Sir Christopher's creature. Robert was feeling the cost and discomforts of high ambition. 'After the quick apprehension that the world conceived of my preferment', he wrote to Hatton, he was 'loath to appear ambitious' by coming to court to try for a place which he knew he would only achieve through what he called the queen's goodness. As Robert knew, only Elizabeth mattered. 'Let him [the aspirant minister] be as the moon, and attribute all the brightness of his glory to that sun', as one of the greatest European classical scholars of the day, Justus Lipsius, put it. And Lipsius counselled prudence and circumspection, for royal courts were dangerous: 'You good men which frequent the court, your life, and the way wherein you walk, is very slippery.' Robert Cecil was beginning now to experience that for himself.[12]

Yet he put his confidence in Hatton, finishing up his letter careless (as he put it) of others' envy because he enjoyed the lord chancellor's favour. Bess, too, was in touch with Hatton, a key link between her husband, the lord chancellor and the queen's inner circle, though in what she did and said she was characteristically mysterious, always discreetly in the background.[13]

To Michael Hickes Robert wrote of the silence at court. He felt gloomy. 'Of the matter you wrote to me yesternight, did my lordship's [Burghley's] letter today only speak, of mine own nothing more ... I believe worse in it ...'[14]

Robert, by early spring 1591, was both expectant suitor and expectant father. Bess Cecil was pregnant. On 10 March Robert invited Michael Hickes to join 'two of your friends'. He had already paid the post and would settle Master Michael's boat fare. Through Hickes Lord Cobham had sent his compliments to Robert: Robert returned them, promising his love and service. He was looking forward to making Lady Cobham a grandmother. Of his suit at court there was no news. 'My lord [Burghley] writ to me yesterday which today I received ... that he heard no more of my matter yet.'[15]

Their son was born at Westminster on Palm Sunday, 28 March. He was a new William Cecil, one of a number already in the wider family.

But only he was Mildred Burghley's grandson, Robert's heir. As Burghley's motto expressed it, 'One heart, one way'.[16]

In the days following his grandson's arrival Burghley was at court at Greenwich. Robert was still fretting about his suit to the queen; still there was silence. On Wednesday 7 April he wrote to Sir Christopher Hatton with his 'private tedious causes' but hoping, as ever, for the lord chancellor's direct intervention. He bemoaned his poor fortune, feeling his case – his suit – tossed around like a tennis ball. He said that his service to the queen was dearer to him than life. He was at her sacred pleasure.[17]

Robert had known Theobalds since boyhood. Over decades his father spent many thousands of pounds turning a modest, moated manor house into one of the great palaces of the kingdom. It was a celebration of the Cecils' family roots and of their calling as the queen's servants and ministers. It was built, too, as an education for Robert, full of portraits, statues and books that gave him a panorama of the Europe of his time, a kind of laboratory of power, a foundation for his inheritance and the promise of his career. To Burghley it was a labour of love. The plans and sketches of his architects are full of his annotations, evidence of his usual sharp eye for detail.

When enemies criticized its luxury, Burghley defended himself. He had built and expanded it not so much for himself as for Elizabeth. 'My house at Theobalds was begun by me with a mean measure,' he once wrote, 'but increased by occasions of her Majesty's often coming, whom to please I never would omit to strain myself to more charges than building is, and yet not without some special direction of her Majesty.' Indeed, Elizabeth was a frequent, almost an annual, visitor on her early and late summer progresses. And she wasn't shy in making plain to her courtiers what she expected of them in terms of their hospitality and her comfort.[18]

Such a visit was preoccupying Burghley in spring 1591. On Monday 3 May the busiest of the queen's ministers, moving between Greenwich, the Strand and Star Chamber, was trying in a characteristic memorandum to face down the logistical hydra that was a ten-day royal progress to Theobalds. Beds and hangings had to be brought from court, along with more beds from London; there were tapestries to be transported; there were squadrons of household servants to deploy. Visiting courtiers would include Robert's in-laws the Cobhams, his friend and supporter from his Low Countries adventure, Henry, earl of Derby, and the hero of the Armada's defeat, Lord Admiral Howard. So much work, no detail left to chance: Lord Cobham, Burghley noted, needed a better chamber. And for the lord treasurer of England, who counted halfpennies, there was so much expense.

All royal visits mattered, but this one more than most. It was Burghley's opportunity to communicate to Elizabeth a statement on his own service in front of the queen and her whole court. It was his chance to recommend to her the young man to whom he was entrusting his legacy.

One small detail of Burghley's planning is easy to miss. Camouflaged by the busy scribblings over so many domestic arrangements, Burghley made on his paper a small note to order from the storeroom of the queen's Office of the Revels the costume of a hermit.[19]

Even at Theobalds, with its three central great courts and outbuildings, it was a squeeze to accommodate Elizabeth's court. The sheer numbers of officials and servants who had to be able to work was dizzying, from the queen's maids and the esquires of the body to the gentlemen ushers, the grooms of the privy chamber, Elizabeth's physicians, surgeon and apothecary, her waiters and groom porters, the wardrobe of the beds, her equerries and chaplains, the grooms and pages of the chamber and the staff of the Privy Council chamber. Not to be forgotten – they were in daily attendance – were three of the queen's favourite lutenists and singers.

Elizabeth had first visited Theobalds in 1564 for the christening of Robert's sister Elizabeth. Over the following years, on six royal progresses, she saw the house transformed. In 1591 she lodged as usual on the south of the second court, with a view across Burghley's fabulous gardens. A privy chamber, a withdrawing chamber, her bedchamber, two inner rooms for her chamber servants and a gallery with more accommodation for staff. Lord Admiral Howard was given four rooms above her privy chamber, and the earl of Essex, as master of the queen's horse, was assigned chambers at the southern end of her gallery, with two or three additional rooms on the floor below. Burghley gave over his own chambers, gallery and book room to Lord Chancellor Hatton, at the end of whose apartment would be the Privy Council's chamber. Every other room available was packed with courtiers and privy councillors.[20]

Hatton was honoured with Burghley's private rooms. He would play his own indirect part in the show that Burghley was about to stage for the court. What unfolded over the coming days was carefully choreographed.

Burghley set out from Westminster for Theobalds in the late morning of Thursday 6 May. It was an overnight stay only: we can assume he wanted to inspect the preparations with his superlative steward, Thomas Bellot. On Friday he was busy in Star Chamber and Henry Maynard attended him at Burghley House on the Strand, where that evening Burghley had requested a meeting with the king of Scots's ambassador. The weekend was as busy. On Saturday he was still dictating letters to Maynard and on Sunday he sat in Privy Council. The court was by then at the house of Sir Rowland Hayward at Hackney, a third of the way on the journey from London to Theobalds. On Monday, 10 May, the queen had lunch in Tottenham before she and her entourage travelled up London Way, at one point within hailing distance of Robert Cecil's house at Pymmes. She was at Theobalds in time for supper.

Courtiers with long memories might have remembered a great show put on in the hall of Whitehall Palace in April 1581 for a party of French ambassadors, who were in London for marriage negotiations between Elizabeth and Francis, duke of Anjou. One of them was Monsieur de Marchaumont, whose house near Fontainebleau Robert Cecil visited with Sir Edward Stafford, and perhaps at Whitehall in 1581 seventeen-year-old Robert had seen for himself the show and spectacle. Burghley had laid on the grandest of dinners for the French visitors at his Strand mansion, at which Francis Bacon, then twenty, and Michael Hickes were two of a team of in-house translators. The Whitehall entertainment had cost the Office of the Revels the better part of three hundred pounds to stage. It had included a mount with a castle whose sides fell down, a dragon and fireworks, a tree hung with shields, a chariot, some savages and an enchanter – and a hermitage with its hermit.[21]

Ten years and a month later it was a hermit, perhaps dressed in that very costume (little in the revels office was ever thrown away), who welcomed Elizabeth to Theobalds:

> My sovereign lady and most gracious Queen
> be not displeased that one so meanly clad
> presumes to stand thus boldly in the way
> that leads into this house accounted yours.

Then in a speech to which Robert Cecil may have contributed – in the manuscript there is just the suspicion of the presence of his handwriting – the hermit told his sorry tale.

Turned out of his cave by the owner of Theobalds, who had been grieving for two years over the losses first of his mother, then his daughter and most recently his wife, the hermit had been called by Burghley to take up the government of the house and its family. But the hermit wanted peace, to live a contemplative life, and he wanted his hermitage back. He had gone up into the lantern of the great hall of Theobalds and had seen a vision of a lady in white, a holy prophetess, who had spoken to the hermit of a maiden queen, a princely paragon. Hearing the rumour of Elizabeth's visit, Burghley, who was occupying the hermitage, instructed the hermit to prepare for it. But the hermit replied that there were others who could take up the task. He looked also to the future: there was a new baby, Burghley's younger son's son, his grandfather's namesake, another William Cecil.

It was at this point – before the hermit went on to praise Lord Admiral Howard's victory over the supposedly invincible Spanish navy and gave a cue to Lord Chancellor Hatton – that he came to his principal message:

> Therefore I wish for my good founder's sake
> that he [Robert] may live with this his firstborn son,
> long time to serve your sacred Majesty
> as his [William Cecil's] grandfather faithfully hath done.

The hermit was pointing to those who should now take charge: not himself, not Burghley, but Robert Cecil and, eventually, his son, with Theobalds as their seat.[22]

The hermit's nod to Hatton was to 'award a writ', a mock charter drawn up by the Chancery ordering the restoration of 'Sir Hermit' to his hermitage, commanding him back to his old cave at Theobalds, which was 'too good for the forsaken [hermit], too bad for our worthily beloved councillor'.[23]

The pitch for Robert's promotion was driven home with rustic vigour in a further entertainment, a dialogue between a gardener and a molecatcher. The words of the gardener's speech survive in a copy made by Simon Willis, Robert Cecil's new private secretary. In the dialogue, the gardener took Elizabeth and her courtiers imaginatively to Pymmes just a few miles away, where the ordering of Robert's new garden there was a metaphor of his service to the queen. Formerly a wilderness of thistles and molehills, now, thanks to Robert, it had been tamed and planted with virtues. Prominent was a maze and an arbour of eglantine, a symbol of virginity, planted by the gardener on Robert's advice so deeply that its smell was sweeter, its greenness able to resist even the hottest Spanish sun.

And then the molecatcher told his story. He had travelled to Greenwich to be told that the queen was gone from the palace. And so he had tried Hackney, to find that the court had already gone into the country. 'I thought to have made hue and cry thinking that he who stole fire from heaven had stolen our heaven from the earth.' But at last the molecatcher met a courier who told him that Elizabeth was at Theobalds, and he was glad for the queen, for he honoured Lord Burghley as the owner of that house, wishing his virtues might double his years and treble Elizabeth's.

Quite what the court made of all these heavy and earnest orations is impossible to know. But the message they communicated was clear even to the slowest mind. Robert Cecil was the future.

Elizabeth was too much a battle-hardened veteran of her courtiers' efforts to persuade and woo her to give them what they desired when they wanted it. She knew from long experience that the more she resisted, the harder they tried – and the more they gave. She waved no magic wand; courtiers sometimes had to go on hoping, as Robert

Cecil was learning. Retirement or retreat for Burghley, moreover, was a self-indulgent fantasy: he hadn't stopped working, even at Theobalds. Two council meetings, always paperwork to sign, ever more letters for Henry Maynard to read and to write. Rest for the lord treasurer was out of the question, at least for the time being. For the sake of the show, Elizabeth permitted Sir Hermit to go home to his cave. When a week-and-a-half later she left Theobalds, Lord Burghley went back to the Strand where he and Maynard were busy the next day with long and intricate diplomatic correspondence.

For Robert there was no appointment as secretary – no promotion to the Privy Council, no taking of the oaths with his patrons looking on, no neat conclusion to months of fretful waiting. But there was a knighthood. Before Elizabeth and her court removed from Theobalds after breakfast, he became Sir Robert. Thomas Wilkes, who had been on duty in the council chamber, made a wry comment on the honour given to Cecil in the light of 'the expectation of his advancement to the secretaryship: so it is (as we say in court) that the knighthood must serve for both.'[24]

Were those ten days at Theobalds a disappointment for Burghley and his son? Perhaps. But the secretaryship was always a long shot for Robert Cecil, and Burghley never wanted for a moment to leave Elizabeth's service, which for him was a lifetime's commitment. Was the visit then a failure, thousands of pounds spent by Burghley for no tangible result? Not at all, for Elizabeth's Pygmy had been honoured, his credit at court was strong. The Cecils knew how to play the long game.

Certainly Robert Cecil was in favour. Within months Elizabeth would indeed appoint him to her Privy Council.

7

Spies

Spies were woven deep into the fabric of Robert Cecil's career. Some served for a short time, others for many years. Every one of them was useful, up to a point. None was ever fully trusted. In the year of his knighthood, he began to learn the trade of espionage.

A month before Elizabeth and her court visited Theobalds, Thomas Phelippes was at his father's house on Leadenhall Street in London. The old outer framework of his life had changed. By the spring of 1591 he was a year without a master: Sir Francis Walsingham, who had died confident in the mercy of Jesus Christ his saviour and redeemer, was waiting for the Day of Judgement in his tomb in St Paul's Cathedral. Dead also was Thomas's father. William Philipp had left his wife with a life interest in his property and his eldest son with a library of books, a signet ring engraved with their coat of arms, and the reversion of his office of collector of her Majesty's small customs outwards (that is, on exports) in the port of London – a new day job for Phelippes in the city's customs house. Thomas's secret world remained intact, more or less, even without Walsingham to anchor it. With the queen's knowledge he continued to run a spy against the Catholic enemy. Now he paid his agent out of his own purse.[1]

The spy was Thomas Barnes, once upon a time courier for Mary Queen of Scots, who in 1588 had made an offer of service to Walsingham to bring to light 'any of their treacherous intents towards the state hereafter which be fugitives and traitors at home or abroad'. He had made and signed a full confession, which Phelippes noted and filed. From that point onwards Barnes was on the books, and before long was showing himself to be clever, versatile, elusive and apparently trusted by those he spied on in France and the Low Countries.[2]

They had settled quickly into a routine. Phelippes prepared newsletters that Barnes would communicate to his Catholic friends. They survive as Phelippes's own drafts, doubling as copies, all in his tiny script, all scrupulously done. Full of information about happenings at court and in government, they were broadly neutral in tone, but carefully phrased and edited so as to nourish émigré prejudices. This was a subtle and intricate double game.

Generally Barnes did well. He was brisk, businesslike and secret: in letters to Phelippes 'the place accustomed' and 'yours whom you know' were sufficient, and his reports were filed without name. Phelippes had his own archive of secret papers – his own little black box.

Just occasionally Barnes found himself in trouble. Three weeks before Walsingham's death he was surprised by the queen's officers carrying the archbishop of Canterbury's warrant for the arrest of a dangerous Catholic. This was a tribute to Barnes's cover, though it gave him an evil few hours at the Saracen's Head tavern on Carter Lane near St Paul's; he called on Phelippes for help. A few months later, in quite different circumstances, Barnes fell ill through eating (as he put it) a surfeit of cherries. Thinking he was going to die he had consulted a physician, whose fee he couldn't pay. To Phelippes he uttered the familiar *cri de cœur* of the Elizabethan spy, the shabby gentleman short of money. 'Not ... so well furnished at this instant of money as my present case requireth', Barnes hoped that Phelippes would lend him five or six pounds until he could be given proper financial support.[3]

The day after Elizabeth left Theobalds, Friday, 21 May 1591, Phelippes gave Barnes the briefest summary of the royal visit to Burghley's house. Spanish ships had been sighted off the Cornish coast. When this news had reached the court, the queen was upset by it: she was 'very melancholy at my Lord Treasurer's ... his son not being yet Secretary'. English dissident Catholics liked to hear about the Cecils being snubbed. Burghley was the man they hated most; he was England's ruin.[4]

When Lord Burghley returned to the Strand from Theobalds he found two prisoners waiting for him, brought up from the south coast. They had been captured in the English Channel aboard the *Adulphe*, a ship under the command of a Flemish skipper that had set out from Portugal bound for Amsterdam. Their names were John Cecil and John Fixer. They were using false identities: Cecil called himself John Snowden, Fixer Thomas Wilson. If Cecil was any kinsman of Burghley's it was by a very distant route, but perhaps his surname – that frisson of connection – helped in some way to save the men's lives. For as well as having in common both age (the prisoners were in their early thirties) and education (they had been contemporaries at Trinity College, Oxford), John Cecil and John Fixer were Catholic priests.[5]

That same day John Cecil made his first written confession, which Burghley annotated carefully. Plain from the beginning was that he was close to Cardinal William Allen, the polemical firebrand, director of Catholic Europe's efforts to rescue England from the abomination of heresy and author of the blistering personal attack on Queen Elizabeth in 1588, the *Admonition to the Nobility and People of England and Ireland*. The young priest was, then, potentially valuable. Most significant of all was his task of assessing the likely reception in England of an invading Spanish army.

But handling John Cecil was not straightforward: that was clear early on. He was plausible but evasive; he didn't easily give up the truth. Burghley pressed him hard. Kept busy with their pens, for the next week both Cecil and Fixer wrote and re-wrote statement after statement: the more they wrote, the less time they had to invent or misdirect. They knew that their lives were now in Burghley's gift.

Whether to trust a volunteer for secret service was always the question. It was an especially tricky one when that volunteer had made what reputation he possessed in a conspiracy to murder the queen. Such a man was Michael Moody.

When there had been a panic in January 1587 over suspicious activities in the household of the French ambassador, Monsieur de Bellièvre, the investigations of Sir Christopher Hatton, Secretary Davison and Thomas Phelippes had exposed the part played in the plan by Moody, who in Paris had had a dubious record of corresponding with émigré dissident English Catholics. Those early weeks of 1587 were strained, as Elizabeth's pen hovered uncertainly over the Scottish queen's death warrant. But it was in reality a mirage of a conspiracy, and Michael Moody survived it. After a spell in the Tower he lived in France, at least for a time, before returning to England. By late 1590 he needed a patron and a job. In December of that year Moody wrote to Vice Chamberlain Heneage, appealing to his 'great clemency to all distressed persons' and 'great and fatherly care of her Majesty's service'. He asked for what he called 'foreign employment' either in France or Spain.[6]

It was an ebullient Moody who wrote the following May to Lord Burghley when the court was at Theobalds being entertained by the hermit, molecatcher and gardener. 'Your honour is desirous to know what grounds I can set down to do her Majesty service.' And so he explained: he would 'set down unto you a means whereby Master Robert Cecil, your honour's son, shall have more intelligences from abroad than either her Majesty, your honour and all the rest of her Majesty's Council besides can have'. Writing in the same week that Burghley's carefully choreographed entertainments put Robert in the vanguard of the Cecils' continuing and future service to the queen, Moody timed his moment perfectly.[7]

Just over a week later he wrote again to Burghley. Moody was ready that day to leave England: Charles Paget, one of the most influential and dangerous dissidents in France, was expecting his arrival. Moody was trying to discover for Burghley the truth about some Jesuits who had been sent secretly into England: 'what their intent is you shall shortly know by this bearer from a friend of mine, with whom if your honour do deal well, you shall have very good service performed by him'. It seems unlikely that Moody knew about Father John Cecil: his lodging at the Strand was known only to Burghley, to Sir Robert Cecil and to a handful of close household servants. His lordship was happy to use Moody, but he was too old a hand to trust him.

Moody was by now wrapped up in his plans, directing his small band of secret actors: a priest in prison, willing to serve Burghley; Moody's messenger; another friend unnamed. He was busy composing the cipher he would use to communicate with Cecil, along with an impressively convoluted system for posting his letters. He wanted – and needed – to convince Burghley of how well he could serve, how

much he could give. He asked for half an hour of his lordship's time
before he left England.[8]

On Thursday 27 May, Burghley authorized the payment of money
from Vice Chamberlain Heneage's chamber accounts to 'Michael
Moody, gentleman, upon a warrant . . . for carrying of letters for her
Majesty's service beyond the seas and for other service to be done
there.'[9]

Whether or not Moody got his interview, his purse was fuller by ten
pounds.

By the beginning of the following week Burghley had decided to employ
John Cecil as a spy. Robert arranged the practicalities: the priest's brief-
ing and preparation, the passport which would get him safely out of
England, the means of secret communication he would use.

The transition for Father John from the queen's enemy to double
agent against those who had sent him secretly to England gave him
moments of conscientious agony. He worried that his betrayals would
put Catholics' lives in danger. Robert Cecil told him that Lord Burghley could neither overrule nor dispense with any law, just as he could
never openly support Father John or any other Catholic, however
well-meaning. John Cecil's only assurance was that if he worked reasonably with reasonable people, then Burghley would always be an
intercessor with a merciful queen.

The truth was that John Cecil had no choice but to spy on Lord
Burghley's terms. He was being set free on the condition that he
provided information. This, Robert Cecil told him, reminding
Father John of just how fortunate he was: 'you must bring forth
good fruit with profitable correspondency for her Majesty's service
and your country's good, which is the true end of your enlargement,
and cause of this extraordinary favour which many others do thirst
for.'[10]

The wording of the passport was everything. Father John drafted
his own preferred form of words: 'You shall let the bearer hereof pass
without trouble or vexation, for that the knowledge and examination
of his cause and person I have reserved to myself for divers occasions.'

Burghley's signature on the document would tell any inquisitive English official to mind his own business.[11]

But the priest's passport would be authorized only by Sir Robert Cecil.

At the end of June Sir Robert Cecil was working in Burghley's office handling routine diplomatic correspondence. To the resident ambassador in Scotland, he wrote: 'My lord my father's business at this time makes him command me to answer your letters which he hath lately received.' It was a small taste of the job he coveted.[12]

The business preoccupying Lord Burghley was that of sending an expeditionary force of English troops to France. There the Protestant King Henry IV was caught between Philip of Spain's forces that had landed in Brittany and Henry's internal enemy, the French Catholic League in Normandy, where they held the town of Rouen. Queen Elizabeth was always a reluctant interventionist. She detested the frequent military miscommunications of adventures abroad, their almost inevitable diplomatic tangles and, above all, their crippling expense. Yet given the frequency after 1588 of armada scares and invasion panics, and the recognition by her ministers of how dangerous it would be both to allow Spain any more of a grip on western Europe and to leave Henry IV unsupported, Elizabeth bowed to necessity – which didn't mean that she would accept it with good grace.

By spring 1591 the political and diplomatic momentum was building. In April letters arrived at court almost daily from English diplomats and soldiers on the French coast. At Theobalds in May, Elizabeth dined with King Henry's ambassador in Burghley's magnificent gardens. The contract for the English expeditionary force was sealed at Greenwich Palace on Tuesday 15 June by the ambassador and all thirteen of Elizabeth's privy councillors. Three weeks later another of King Henry's diplomats, Monsieur de Reau, left Dover for Dieppe, by which time Lord Treasurer Burghley and the Privy Council were mobilizing an army of four thousand troops to be shipped over to Normandy.[13]

The general appointed to lead the expedition was Robert, earl of Essex.

For Father John Cecil, hidden away in Lord Burghley's mansion on the Strand and busily exchanging letters with Sir Robert, there was no quick and easy start to his new career as a double agent.

On the evening of Saturday 19 June Father John and Burghley met for what turned out to be a fractious private interview. Sir Robert Cecil was not present: he heard about it from the Jesuit the following day.

Burghley was blunt. He had been checking the priest's story, which had taken time –John Cecil's books and papers had had to be recovered from the ship which had brought him from Portugal, the *Adulphe*, which was by now in Amsterdam. These papers contained the substance of his secret mission to England on behalf of his Jesuit superiors and proof of what information he knew about Catholic invasion plans. Burghley, however, was unimpressed by them. He told Cecil that he was merely peddling 'vulgar and trivial intelligences and to no great purpose'. Feeling provoked, the priest hit back, though the following day he was contrite. He wrote to Sir Robert that he revered Burghley, 'esteeming all things that proceed from his mouth as oracles'.[14]

The squall passed. Perhaps it had been a necessary release of nerves for John Cecil before leaving the protection of Burghley House, for within a few days he was ready. He and Sir Robert Cecil had agreed the mission. They had worked out how the priest would send his reports back to Cecil in England from Saint-Jean-de-Luz, about ten miles south-west of Biarritz on the Atlantic coast of southern France. What those reports would contain was up to Father John to decide, with some occasional direction by Sir Robert.[15]

John Cecil was Robert Cecil's first spy. They planned to meet again, though in July 1591 neither man knew for sure that they would. It was a journey into the unknown for them both.

With the English army that embarked for Normandy went a new ambassador to King Henry IV. Sir Henry Unton was from a long-distinguished Berkshire gentry family, a graduate of the University of Oxford, a member of the lawyers' society of the Middle Temple, and in his youth a European traveller, polished and accomplished. In short, he was the perfect gentleman. Unton's best friend and ally at Elizabeth's court, just a handful of years younger than himself, was Robert Cecil.

Elizabethan ambassadors fretted about money for their embassies. This was often difficult to squeeze out of the queen. Sir Henry was fortunate however, and thanks to Lord Burghley's intervention, Elizabeth was feeling generous. Unton was unembarrassed to write to his friend Robert Cecil to secure the money – he knew that Burghley was 'full of weighty affairs'. (This was true enough, though Burghley was probably no busier than usual at a weekend: that particular Saturday he had drafted the instructions to the earl of Essex for his command of the expeditionary force, and on Sunday morning he sat in Privy Council at Greenwich.) Unton had the necessary paperwork ready, with just the sum of money to be filled in. He was hoping for six hundred pounds.[16]

For nearly half a decade, Robert Cecil had been a route to his father's favour, as Unton knew. Like so many others, he petitioned hard and apologized for doing so – it was the courtier's familiar routine. 'Thus you see my boldness to trouble you,' Unton wrote to Cecil,

> which I rather choose than to fail in due respects to my lord your father and to importune his lordship . . . If my poor love or fortune may yield requital, you have power to command, and your lord and mine shall never fail of my due service and true thankfulness.[17]

A week later, on 19 July, Essex assembled his cavalry in the fields of Covent Garden. 'The earl of Essex mustered his troops afore the Queen at my house at Westminster', Burghley noted. The army was scheduled to be shipped the following day, and on the 22nd Essex received his commission at Greenwich. He and Sir Henry Unton left for Dover on Tuesday 27 July, but they were then delayed by summer storms in the Channel. When they did finally set sail, the fleet took three nights and three days to make the crossing to Dieppe.[18]

Unton's evident relief in getting safely to France was quickly replaced by the familiar tremor of anxiety for any courtier a long way from

Elizabeth. This was especially the case with ambassadors. What would the queen think of his service? Who at court was on his side? Unton appealed to Robert Cecil as his confidant and adviser and the surest route to Burghley's favour. Cecil was the ambassador's friend at court – a manager, a mediator, a smoother of ruffled feathers.[19]

Before Henry Unton had left Dover he knew that something was stirring at court for Robert Cecil. Lord Burghley had told him so. The rumour was that Cecil was about to be appointed by the queen to her Privy Council.[20]

He swore the councillor's oath at Nonsuch Palace on Monday 2 August. William Wade inscribed into the clerks' register book the following note: 'This day Sir Robert Cecil, knight, second son to the Lord Burghley, Lord High Treasurer of England, was sworn of her Majesty's Privy Council.' The event had almost not happened. Elizabeth was in an especially indecisive mood, and it was thanks only to the intervention of the lord chancellor, Sir Christopher Hatton, that late that Monday morning the queen had met her council and then sent for Cecil. Robert wrote to Unton that he owed everything to Hatton, his honoured patron.[21]

The rumour at court was that Elizabeth might even appoint a principal secretary – perhaps even two. Robert wrote to Unton that they were all expecting Sir Edward Stafford – the former ambassador in Paris who had introduced the twenty-one-year-old Master Cecil to the French court – to take an oath that Monday, at least as a privy councillor and probably also as secretary. Stafford did not, however, receive the call.

This made Robert's promotion all the more precious. 'I was sworn alone [by] his lordship's own only favour': he kept going back to Hatton, by whom he was more star-struck than ever. On a day when the queen had otherwise teased her courtiers with the familiar mirage of decision, for Cecil the lord chancellor had worked his magic.

Elizabeth announced that she had decided to do nothing about the role of secretary until at least the middle of August, exercising again that most potent of all her royal powers – the prerogative of procrastination.[22]

8

Progress

Sir Robert Cecil basked in the pleasant warmth of his promotion. From the beginning he was a diligent attender of council meetings and an energetic rapporteur of court events for Hatton, busy in Chancery. He barraged the lord chancellor with letters, excusing their roughness and lack of form with a courtier's apology. Yet not a single word was ever out of place; each letter was a masterpiece of deferential collegiality. Sir Robert could hardly believe his good fortune. Six days after his oath-taking at Nonsuch, when the court was on progress in Surrey, Cecil wrote to Hatton glad that his 'poor mite' was acceptable to his lordship: 'this your extraordinary favour to me hath taken such deep impression in my heart'.[1]

So here was the right honourable Sir Robert Cecil, the now assiduous privy councillor, his father's son, Sir Christopher Hatton's client and colleague, above all the servant of the queen. There were thirteen councillors, and in the order of precedence Cecil sat below Vice Chamberlain Heneage but outranked two others – John Wolley, Latin secretary and chancellor of the Order of the Garter, and John Fortescue, master of the great wardrobe and under treasurer of the Exchequer. In the council's register book he was simply 'Sir Robert Cecil, knight': no office or portfolio yet. It was a comfortable-enough spot, a modest start. For the time being.[2]

There was one small change in Sir Robert which is easy to miss. From the day he was appointed to the Privy Council, he wrote the 'e' of his surname in the style of the Greek letter epsilon – ε – something he had never done before. It was a simple movement of the pen, a private significance lost to us.

*

For the first full weekend of August Queen Elizabeth's host was Sir William More. The court was at Loseley Park in Surrey, a house rebuilt and improved by Sir William in the grandest style over twenty years. It was the first leg of the late summer progress. This year the objective was the Hampshire coast – as good a spot as any to be able to receive news efficiently from the expeditionary army in Normandy.

Across the English Channel the earl of Essex was feeling his way into his new command, and Sir Henry Unton carried on his shoulders the painful weight of ambassadorial responsibility for a mission he knew mattered. The earl's early letters to Elizabeth from France were effusive; the one constant with Essex was that he never undersold himself. Presuming the constancy of the queen's favour, he promised to 'forsake himself and all the world besides'. Unton was already in a very different frame of mind, writing privately to his friend Cecil to bemoan what he was calling his 'banishment'. Quickly established was a familiar pattern for what remained of the summer of 1591: tangible favour for Cecil, Essex's easy presumption of it, and the almost constant anxiety of Unton. What the earl was or wasn't doing with his army overshadowed the summer progress, with consequences for him and Unton and for those around the queen – Burghley and Cecil especially. They had to navigate her swings of mood and temper, which came and went like storms in the English Channel.[3]

At Loseley Park even the usually unshakeable Henry Maynard was feeling dispirited by the mounting piles of Lord Burghley's paperwork. Life in the office was going to get only busier. It looked to Maynard unlikely that Elizabeth would appoint a principal secretary any time soon, and he knew that much of the work would fall on Sir Robert Cecil. On Saturday 8th, from Bess Cecil's chamber, he wrote to Michael Hickes: 'At this time there is no speech of any Secretary, nor no man urgeth it as I see.' Their honourable friend – he meant of course Robert – would have to take up the burden.[4]

Moreover, from their honourable friend there were no complaints, simply the ambition to serve. Where at Theobalds three months earlier Sir Hermit had made his case directly to the queen, and the gardener and molecatcher had discussed the promise of Master Cecil's garden at Pymmes, Lord Burghley, a few days after Maynard's letter to Hickes, used an ecclesiastical metaphor. Writing to Lord Chancellor Hatton, Burghley likened himself to a vicar hoping for retirement, and Robert to a young curate, keen for a chance to take up his responsibilities but temporarily parked where he was: 'able for no greater cure, but I hope he will in some behalf discharge me of my cure'. Cecil's future was mapped if not yet travelled.[5]

Michael Moody had promised Robert Cecil secret intelligence of unparalleled richness and value. Moody was always persuasive and charming; he emitted a kind of energy which was impossible to resist entirely. Whether he could be trusted was quite another thing.

Having left court for the Continent in late May with Burghley's blessing, Moody was now, in early August, back with secret papers from Brussels. Closeted away on Friday 6 August with Vice Chamberlain Heneage, Moody had done enough to earn himself a further twenty pounds in travelling expenses. But one man suspected that Moody had already colluded with the enemy. This was John Ricroft of London. He shared his suspicions with Robert Cecil.[6]

Who John Ricroft was isn't clear. He called himself Moody's kinsman, though for Elizabethans that term was very elastic. Perhaps he really did believe that Moody was giving Heneage false intelligence, or perhaps Ricroft simply wanted to impress Sir Robert Cecil, hoping to get a reward or find employment. But this was a delicate business. Ricroft knew that Heneage believed Moody, and the vice chamberlain was a privy councillor of weight and substance. So Ricroft took his time. He watched and waited; he noted Moody's comings and goings; he sent letters to Cecil.[7]

Cecil took Ricroft's reports on Michael Moody seriously enough to write his own assessment of Moody's alleged betrayal. He took time over this paper, covering two-and-half folio sides in his best handwriting – the familiar shape and rhythm, the careful organization, the eye for order, a tidiness often lacking in letters written quickly, all method and care.

Ricroft claimed that on arriving in Brussels Moody had gone straight to the secretary of the governor of the Spanish Netherlands, the duke of Parma. He had surrendered the secrets of his mission, handed over his cipher and revealed the identities of two English spies, one in Brussels, one in Calais. Ricroft wanted to confirm Moody's treachery by encouraging him in a new plot on which (so Ricroft claimed) Moody was already working – to betray to the Spanish the English garrison town of Bergen op Zoom.

Cecil knew what Michael Moody's defence would be: 'He will allege that this which Ricroft accuseth him of without witness is merely false.' To which Cecil had ready a response: that Moody was plotting so earnestly and secretly with Ricroft that he, Moody, was more likely to be a traitor than not.

Cecil sent John Ricroft a reward for his information. But he only watched and waited, holding back from any conclusion. Knowing who to trust was the most difficult judgement of all.[8]

All this time Elizabeth's court was enjoying the dazzling six-day entertainment given by Lord Montague at Cowdray Castle in Sussex. It began on Saturday 14 August at about 8 p.m. when Elizabeth had arrived to music and a speech of welcome which praised her to the skies: 'O miracle of time, Nature's glory, Fortune's empress, the world's wonder!' The entertainments were elaborate, the hunting good. The queen and her courtiers walked in the gardens and listened to music. All was peace and harmony. Or so it appeared on the surface.[9]

Elizabeth had spent the following Wednesday at Cowdray waiting for long-delayed letters from Essex and Unton in France. With each passing hour her impatience at the silences of her general and ambassador had moved on a rising scale from irritation to anger. She knew that Unton hadn't yet presented himself to King Henry. She knew that she had an army in France apparently doing nothing but eating up time and money. She snapped at Burghley, blaming him for dispatching Unton too hastily before everything was properly in place for his embassy. As he wrote to Unton, not everything could be planned for or anticipated.

Unton's letters arrived five days later. Within forty-eight hours of their delivery to the queen, the same courier was making his way back to Dieppe carrying her stern instructions to get her army to Rouen. Elizabeth was already losing patience with the French king. Unless

Henry IV brought in more troops himself, she would order her forces to withdraw.[10]

Unton, it turned out, had been bedridden in Dieppe with a high fever and jaundice. On 22 August Sir Robert Cecil also scribbled a short letter of news to his friend: 'My heart thirsteth for good news of your health, which if I hear I doubt nothing else.'[11]

'This progress grows wearisome, though it will not be confessed', as Cecil wrote to Lord Chancellor Hatton on 23 August. Burghley was struggling with his gout. Elizabeth had once again delayed making a decision on the secretaryship until after the progress. But within a few days the heaviness began to lift a little. The queen instructed Cecil to write to Unton 'with princely care and kindness', glad of his recovery and even praising him for his embassy. As the court moved nearer to the Hampshire coast Elizabeth was in good spirits – 'merry', as Cecil described her mood to his friend Michael Hickes, though he noted how pestered she had been by suitors. Conscious that he was stuck at his desk, both Robert and his wife Bess wanted Hickes to come to court.[12]

Cecil was travelling a little ahead of the queen. She arrived in Portsmouth on Thursday evening, 26 August at 8 p.m., just as he was concluding a letter of news to Lord Chancellor Hatton. Cecil reported that the queen was happy and well, if 'somewhat disquieted' by news from France, where Essex and his army seemed still to be doing very little. But in terms of her health and mind, Robert wrote, 'I saw it not better these seven years, praised be God'.[13]

'These seven years': it was a conscious span of time measurable to this late-summer evening in Portsmouth from the letter to Secretary Walsingham Robert Cecil wrote in 1584 as a twenty-one-year-old. How carefully and neatly then he had written those three words, full of significance: 'From the court'. How proud he had been of that address. How well he knew it now.

Of course, his career was still a work in progress: the curate was understudy to his vicar apparently indefinitely. Lord Treasurer Burghley was still working, whether he liked it or not – and Burghley would always find it difficult to give up control and power. But by 1591 the first phase of Robert Cecil's apprenticeship had been served.

In the middle years of the 1580s he had kept copies of speeches, letters and policy papers in what looks at first sight like a conventional gentleman's commonplace book – all quite formally done, written out for him by a servant or scrivener. Though it begins, as many Elizabethan commonplace books do, with the widely admired speeches of his uncle Sir Nicholas Bacon, 'Master Robert Cecil's book' shows the privileges of being an insider. It is an interesting compilation. There are early letters of his cousin Francis Bacon to Lord and Lady Burghley; some sensitive policy papers copied from his father's archive; material on the most urgent and testing political questions of the 1580s which had circulated in Robert's early parliaments – on the Scottish queen, on the emergency responses to fears of Elizabeth's assassination. This was some of the formative architecture of his political consciousness. English verse by his friend Fulke Greville and by George Peele, along with some Latin word-games, speak to the young man who ribbed Michael Hickes and, when away from home, asked after his friends, feeling at a distance the warmth and generosity of their companionship. The two sides of Robert Cecil, in other words. The adept student of power, serious and earnest, looking forward to his future; and the traveller and observer, from those years when he visited Paris, corresponded with the traitor William Parry, travelled the Low Countries and saw from a distance the invincible Armada.[14]

All of this had been a preparation for his career as a privy councillor, seven years of Robert Cecil watching and observing, absorbing and learning – from his father, from Elizabeth herself, from experience and practice. There was a single objective in everything he had written, said or done in his years at court: to serve the queen. The Elizabeth he had come to know by this key year of 1591 was vain, imperious and irascible, as generous as she was querulous, both perceptive and obtuse, guarded and elusive. She kept control of these aspects of her personality by fusing deep instinct with sheer intelligence; she practised remarkable self-discipline.

There was so much that ran deep below the surface froth of court gossip and flattery, the flare-ups and calming-downs. Elizabeth acknowledged the union in her own person of divine authority and human frailty, a kind of fault line between two modes of existence so at odds with each other. In the most intimate of her writings – her prayers and collects and the translations she made from classical literature – she revealed, if only to herself and a few intimates, her struggle to reconcile the duties and costs of rule. Just occasionally she let down her guard, and there were moments of soliloquy. Putting into her own idiosyncratic English the famous *Consolations* of the late Roman philosopher and minister Boëthius, she wrote: 'What then is power, that cannot chase bites of care, nor shun the stings of fear? . . . Dost thou think him strong that fills his sides with guards, that whom he affrights, himself doth fear?' Elizabeth understood power from the inside. She felt its burden. She knew how fragile it was.

She was drawn to history, especially (like so many other late Elizabethans) to that of Tacitus, the best of all analysts of imperial Rome: pungent, unsentimental and unsparing in his studies of power politics. To Justus Lipsius, Tacitus was a 'sharp writer, my God, and a prudent one'. In writing about the past he spoke powerfully to the present. Lipsius wrote: 'You will find here adulations and accusations under tyranny, evils not unknown to this age: nothing genuine, nothing sincere, and no sure faith among friends.'[15]

By the early 1590s Elizabeth had translated the first book of Tacitus' *Annals*, on the earliest Roman emperors. She captured in her own way the terseness of his prose. In her Englishing of his complex Latin she was often elusive and sometimes colloquial. She cut her words back to a kind of verbal skeleton, all bones and no flesh. Her translation was so very different from the orotund flatteries of her court – and perhaps closer to her private self, that inner steel, the internal struggle.

In 1591 the scholar Henry Savile of Oxford, in his own translation of Tacitus, praised Elizabeth's work on the history for the reason that she knew what she was writing about. When princes translated histories, he argued, they improved the originals, 'the writers being persons of like degree and of proportionable conceits with the doers'. In other words, Elizabeth had more in common with the characters of Tacitus' history than she did with Tacitus himself. Savile didn't mean this as any kind of backhanded compliment: quite the opposite, in fact, for he wrote it in the dedication 'To her sacred Majesty' of Tacitus' account of the convulsive years following the death of Nero – he couldn't equal the quality of her work. It seems likely that Savile had Burghley's support in getting his book printed, perhaps too in securing the permission for that all-important dedication. Burghley noted in his papers the date that Savile's publisher received his licence from the stationers' company (this was a few days after the Theobalds entertainments), and in the Cecils' papers (whether Burghley's or Sir Robert's isn't clear) there survives a pristine manuscript copy of a portion of the translation.[16]

Tacitus was blunt on the costs of misrule by princes and their advisers. There is something of this in Savile's final paragraph on the last leaf of his manuscript, a reflection on the failures of the Emperor Galba. For a man in public office there was no escape from responsibility. How easily it could all go wrong:

> To private men it is sufficient, if themselves do no wrong: a prince must provide, that none do it about him: or else he may look, when the first occasion is offered against him, to be charged with all the whole reckoning together. To him that suffereth the injury it matters not much who made the motion, when he feeleth the hand that is heavy upon him.

Complacency was a sin which in sovereigns and councillors was impossible to forgive – yet how easily one might go off the straight and narrow path. These were words of warning and instruction for an earnest young privy councillor like Robert Cecil, a minister to the queen still learning his trade.[17]

In early September 1591 the court still waited for delayed news from France. When at last it arrived the response was swift – the dispatch of letters by Elizabeth and her council remonstrating with Essex to stick to his orders. He had taken his army away from Rouen, where it was supposed to be engaged, with the earl preferring to follow King Henry. Sir Henry Unton was caught in the middle of queen and general. Unton's urgent request to Essex – 'in the mean season to vouchsafe me the favour to let me know how your lordship doth dispose of yourself' – must go down as one of the most elegant pieces of diplomatic understatement of his century. The queen preferred bracingly Tacitean plainness. 'Her Majesty', Cecil explained to Lord Chancellor Hatton, 'will in no wise yield to have her troops thus wander and be employed upon petty towns and fortresses, there to be consumed and wasted.' So she had written sharply to the earl, 'reproving his negligence in advertising and his looseness in being more pliable to a strange king's demands than to his sovereign's instructions': the words, again, are Robert Cecil's.[18]

A couple of days later the queen came down with a cold. Finding herself not well disposed (as Cecil put it) the court turned towards home. Gloom had returned.[19]

Elizabeth was at Oatlands Palace in Surrey by Michaelmas, 29 September, and a couple of days after that removed to Richmond. Sir Robert Cecil was busy with her correspondence, though he had time on 3 October to instruct Sir Henry Unton in the art of a courtier's self-promotion. With more conscientious editing, Unton's letters to Cecil might be shown to the queen; as it was, Cecil was holding them back from her. They expressed, he said, too much of the closeness between friends: put less elegantly, Unton was too frank about the realities of the situation in which he found himself. Cecil wrote: 'You know me and I you; from henceforth touch in your letters our true loves no more so largely [fully].'

Five days later Elizabeth had again taken a heavy cold and was, 'to us that any time she vouchsafeth to speak withal, very melancholy and indisposed'; so Cecil reported to Hatton.[20]

'To us': he was by now one of the chosen few.

In that same first week of October Michael Moody presented himself to the governor of the town of Flushing, Sir Robert Sidney. Moody was a long way from London and the suspicions of John Ricroft. He was in Zeeland on the Western Scheldt, just across the water from Spanish Flanders.

Sidney thought he was meeting a Scottish merchant called Robert Cranston before Moody – who found it hard to resist a dramatic revelation – told Sidney his real name. He said that he had travelled to Flushing from Antwerp, confessed that he had once been a prisoner in the Tower of London for his alleged part in a plot to kill Elizabeth – here he anticipated Sidney, who recognized the name Moody for that very reason – but claimed now to be on a secret mission for Lord Burghley and some other privy councillors. He told Sidney that he had important information to send to England and asked for the services of a clerk and the use of Sidney's diplomatic bag.

Sidney was convinced by Moody's performance: 'The man I never knew before but for that little that I have been able to see in him methinks he wants not wit nor ableness to do the Queen service in those parts where he is.' Nevertheless, the governor knew he would have to watch Moody carefully.[21]

To Vice Chamberlain Heneage Moody promised loyalty: 'The duty that I owe to her Majesty [and] the promise I made to your honour doth bind me to endeavour to do you all the service I can.' But Burghley didn't trust him, and he told Heneage so. There was no mention of John Ricroft's suspicions in Burghley's letter to the vice chamberlain, but really Burghley couldn't have been plainer. Moody's so-called intelligence was simply common news from the Low Countries. He wasn't even trying to keep his espionage secret. Moody had offered his secrets to Sir Christopher Hatton and to Lord Admiral Howard. Even the queen had been told that in Brussels Moody had said openly that he was working in her service, which made it likely that he would be recruited by the enemy.

Yet Michael Moody might still be useful: 'I am not of opinion to reject his service', as Burghley wrote to Heneage.[22]

So, returning to Antwerp, Moody continued to spy.

As autumn 1591 turned to winter, Robert Cecil attended Elizabeth. 'I read both your letters to the Queen,' he wrote to Henry Unton on 9 November, 'being long and to good purpose.' He was in an impish mood, even risking a joke: 'The manner of your apology being such as you need not fear the Tower for your punishment.' Knowing that she loved a good tale, Cecil told her that when Unton had met the king of France he had impressed Henry by taking fifty of his own horsemen.

'The Queen speaks of it, and tells everybody. She troweth she hath sent no fool nor no beggar, with much more in your commendations.' Proud of Unton one day, furious with her ambassador the next: Cecil saw the squalls come and go and steered around them accordingly.[23]

Lord Burghley was sick for a fortnight, closeted away in Westminster, his secretary Henry Maynard never far away from him. He couldn't travel, even to nearby Whitehall Palace. And so the Privy Council came to Burghley's mansion on the Strand. One absentee at the councillors' meeting that day, Saturday 14 November, was Lord Chancellor Hatton, who had last been seen at the council table a week earlier at Richmond. His health was failing and quickly.[24]

Saturday 20 November was, on the surface, a day like any other. The court was now at Whitehall Palace; there were the usual stacks of paperwork for the council and for Burghley and Maynard. Near Rouen, where he was at last preparing for siege warfare against the forces of the Catholic League, the earl of Essex had that day an early morning meeting with Henry IV, Sir Henry Unton close by. Nothing ever stopped; the tremors of even profound change might at first be hardly felt. This Saturday in Westminster Sir Robert's patron and protector, his second father, died. Hatton, so long a presence and a force at court and in government, was gone. Vice Chamberlain Heneage reassured Unton, 'though you have lost a dear and honourable good friend of my late Lord Chancellor, you shall find me ever faithful, ready, and careful for your good'. Robert Cecil stuck close to the queen.[25]

Not everyone gushed over Sir Christopher Hatton. One of Essex's circle, recently arrived in Westminster with letters from Rouen, wrote acidly to the earl's secretary Edward Reynolds: 'Here is little news but for certain my Lord Chancellor is dead, whose greatness is descended from his heaven here in earth, but whither he is gone I cannot make a report, nor the devil himself.'[26]

Christmases were always celebrated at Whitehall. As well as the music and masques there were letters and warrants to sign. The Privy Council was back to its routine on the feast day of St Stephen.

It was the season for indecision. Over the festive weeks the queen blew hot and cold on whether to recall Essex and his army, even though they were now outside Rouen. In late November Essex had made a surprise visit to Whitehall. A month later he was fighting in the trenches. On 23 December the earl wrote to Cecil: 'If I die, pity me not, for I shall die with more pleasure than I live with.' On Christmas Eve Essex and his men stormed and captured an enemy counterscarp in Rouen's defences, while at Whitehall Elizabeth decided that there was no point to his continuing in France 'to so small purpose to the needless hazard of all such as are with you there in our service'. Again, the Tacitean plainness. She was cutting her losses. Within days she had once more changed her mind back again: Essex and his army *should* stay in Normandy.[27]

The earl wrote to Sir Robert on 29 December from that same counterscarp. It was no fit place to write a letter; Essex knew that. The servant who brought his lordship pen and ink was too scared to think straight. 'We will now keep it or be as well beaten as ever men were.' Essex was digging in for defence.[28]

Two Roberts, each ambitious, each keen to impress. One either at his desk or in audience with the queen, the other in a trench on the bloody front line of her service. Theirs were two careers, impossible now to disentangle – and two rivals who needed each other.

9
Fox and Cub

Michael Moody collected his secret letters from Sir Robert Cecil at a free school on the rue de Saint-Esprit in Antwerp. It was a poste restante arrangement. Packets for one Monsieur Cranston were kept by Monsieur Fabritius, the schoolmaster. The courier would be paid, the letters collected. Fabritius may have believed that they really were for a Scottish merchant called Robert Cranston.

Because he used the ordinary London couriers who travelled into the Low Countries, Moody was careful to protect himself. Sensitive material in his reports he put into cipher. Usually, he ended letters with a special mark that Robert Cecil knew was his, though occasionally he used false names such as John Heath or John Bristowe. Moody wanted to avoid any letters arriving in Antwerp secured with a seal that might be traced back to Cecil; post couriers and others had sharp eyes. He sealed his own packets with a small signet of an orb and he used only a dark red wax. The presence of a different seal would show that a letter had been opened by someone else. Moody addressed Cecil or Burghley as Robert or William White, and made sure that packets were sent to one of Lord Burghley's officials in the Palace of Westminster, a Master Marmaduke, who would hand them personally to Cecil.

Michael Moody loved playing secret games with powerful men. In this he never undersold his own talents, the limitless potential of his service. 'I assure you,' he wrote to Cecil, 'if I have so good means as others have, and have had, in this place, and in this kind, you shall be as well served as ever was any. And so I refer myself wholly to your directions.'[1]

Or almost. For all of his secret manoeuvres and his love for the technique of spycraft, Moody couldn't quite keep himself bound to a single patron. In autumn 1591, for example, he found for sale in Antwerp two tapestries of the finest quality, one depicting the ancient Persian King Cyrus, conqueror of Greeks and Babylonians, and the other a study of beasts, birds and trees. Moody had seen no other hangings of their quality even in Brussels. Yet he thought, not of Robert Cecil, but of Robert Devereux, earl of Essex, and it was to the earl he wrote – Elizabeth's general in France, for whom martial Cyrus was so appropriate. Moody doubled as dealer and middleman: luxury procurement, like intelligence, was a money game. He had negotiated a price for the tapestries, which would be held for him for a month. Moody asked Essex to reply to a second of his discreet addresses in Antwerp, this one on Black Sisters Street, in the sailors' quarter near the Scheldt. Names and languages changed from employer to employer. On the rue de Saint-Esprit Moody as Cranston the Scottish merchant used French; on Zwartzusterssstraat, as Jacques Luytens or Jan Janson, Flemish.

Michael Moody ended his letter to Essex: 'Thus leaving to trouble you, I wish you much happiness.' He sealed up the packet in just the same way he used for his reports to the mysterious 'Master White' – that is, Robert Cecil. He pressed his signet ring into warm red wax; the orb left a clear impression, inverted as one read the address.[2]

Moody was everyone's servant, always with something to offer.

A few months later, in spring 1592, he was trying to find copies of a book, recently printed. Moody knew that trouble was on the way. He wrote from Antwerp to Cecil at the end of March: 'There is new answer to the proclamation coming forth. I wish you had them all in your hands, for that the substance doth much concern the Lord Treasurer.' He put the last two words into cipher. This was sensitive ground.[3]

The proclamation by Queen Elizabeth Moody was referring to, issued the previous October, was an effort to strike hard at what it called the 'secret infection of treason in the bowels of our realm'. New local commissions employing tough prosecutorial methods would hunt down and capture Catholic priests illegally in England, pulling to pieces the underground networks of recusants which hid and supported them. The full power of the Elizabethan state, such as it was,

was directed at breaking the Catholic mission: the queen and her ministers, with truth on their side, were fighting back. Dissident émigré Catholics weren't surprised. To them the proclamation showed how rotten England was. They called the new commissions inquisitions.[4]

Moody had heard in January the first rumours of a published Catholic response to the proclamation. In late March this new book was imminent: when he wrote to Cecil the printer's ink was still drying on its pages. The book might as well have been printed in vitriol; its seventy-seven pages of scalding polemic were directed exclusively at the Cecils. When Burghley or Cecil received a copy isn't clear, but probably by mid-April they had in their possession a full handwritten transcript of it.[5]

Its title was typically Elizabethan – stodgy and over-long, more like that of a dense committee report: *A Declaration of the True Causes of the Great Troubles, presupposed to be intended against the Realm of England*. But it is hard to image an angrier work: it was driven by a holy rage. On its title page were the words 'Seen and allowed', used for official pamphlets in England and a formula long mocked by Catholic writers. The irony here was deliberate and bitter. The anger showed soon enough. Quickly *True Causes* revealed itself. Its target was Lord Burghley, who had established himself as England's dictator in perpetuity. The book identified Robert Cecil as a leading member of this corrupt regime. *True Causes* was a dystopian fantasy of tyranny and corruption, soaked in blood and despair.

The book advertised no writer and no printer. There was no attempt even to fabricate an author – or even a couple of initials – for its introductory epistle. It most likely came off the press of Antwerp's Joachim Trognesius, or Trogney, publisher in the late 1580s of other English Catholic émigré attacks on Elizabeth's government. The author proved to be Richard Verstegan, born in London as Richard Rowlands, the son of a cooper, educated at Oxford, who was now in his late forties and one of the dissidents so feared by the queen's ministers. He adopted the surname of his paternal grandfather, who once upon a time had come as a refugee to England from Gelderland, changing his name to Rowlands. Richard had made a kind of return journey, to Paris, Rome, Rheims and finally to Antwerp, where he settled in 1587 as a writer, an engraver of copperplates, and a gatherer and distributor of news out of and into England; the notes he included in *True Causes* show how closely he monitored the London presses. He was a lynchpin of his fellow émigrés' efforts to rescue their homeland from heresy and criminality. He guided the books and pamphlets of Robert Persons, the leading English Jesuit, through the presses of Antwerp's printers. He was also an accomplished smuggler of such banned works into England.

Passionate and partisan, Verstegan's prose was flint-sharp. He was a gifted and ruthless polemicist. Though safe in Antwerp, with its tidy red-brick houses and crow-stepped gables, all under the protection of a Spanish garrison, Verstegan lived imaginatively in the ruins of England as a soldier on God's side in a holy war. He saw in his mind's eye and felt in his soul the persecution of the true faithful by murderous heretics. This was the dominating theme of his work and had been for some years: in his first year in Antwerp he had published under his own name a collection of copperplate engravings which gave visual form to his native country's misery. Here each image was a scene of pain, an appeal to heaven. Sacred images torn down, smashed and burned; innocent Catholics' houses ransacked for profit; the faithful imprisoned. Priests tortured; martyrs' heads removed; bodies eviscerated at the gallows. *Theatre of the Cruelties of the Heretics of Our Time* became a multi-edition European bestseller. To Verstegan the persecution that so wounded his soul was a calamity almost beyond endurance. It gave him an unbending sense of mission. It made him hate Lord Burghley with the most intense of spiritual passions.

Verstegan's thesis in *True Causes* was that early in Elizabeth's reign a man of humble birth, wily and ruthlessly ambitious, had set about satisfying his insatiable desire for personal greatness by setting up in the kingdom a false church and religion. Promoting his own wider family (Francis Bacon's father Sir Nicholas was also one of Verstegan's guilty men) he set about destroying the ancient nobility – the guardians of order and true faith – and had at last made himself dictator. This sinister figure was a surname only, Cecil, who ruled England, Scotland and Ireland. He governed from his own stately palaces and exercised power through monopoly and bribery. Queen Elizabeth was under his control, though Cecil – Burghley – was himself neither accepted at court nor loved by the country, a friend to no one but for his own profit. He resembled 'a storm in the air which all creatures do fear and shun, and none do love or desire'. 'And albeit that he now in his altitude doth manifest in himself the very nature and condition of a tyrant, whose vile and abject courage is to murther and butcher such as innocently live under his jurisdiction.' His victims' blood called for vengeance. Burghley the tyrant would answer to God.[6]

The writer who copied out *True Causes* for the Cecils called the manuscript a 'slanderous and defamatory libel'. The book was most certainly that. Verstegan maintained that one of Burghley's means of domination was Elizabeth's promotion of Robert Cecil to her council, 'which of wise men is much marvelled at . . . in the choice of so ill-shapen and crooked a councillor (having neither wisdom nor experience)'. Cecil's physical frame, his scoliosis, was already an easy and predictable line of attack for his critics and enemies in public and private: he was Monsieur Bossu (Master Hunchback), or the dwarf-like hunchback 'Microgibbus'. And there was a deeper layer of criticism, too, carefully disguised by other anti-establishment writers like the poet Edmund Spenser as beast fables. This was a literary assault on the Cecils' power through satire and insinuation: Burghley the false fox, Robert his crooked cub, or the fox and the ape.[7]

There was one especially vulnerable spot for Elizabeth's government, which Verstegan hit so precisely that even he may not have recognized the deadly accuracy of his aim. Elizabeth had no named successor, which everyone knew. There were a number of candidates, of whom James VI of Scotland, son of Mary Queen of Scots, was only one – and James in 1592 was a very long way from being any kind of clear front-runner. Verstegan reminded his readers of the long turmoil of civil war in England of the fifteenth century, of the cost in blood of competition for the crown. So far, so obvious. But *True Causes* named the nightmare that had beset two generations of Elizabeth's councillors – the threat of interregnal anarchy and war. 'And what authority, or any dissolved council, shall prohibit any of the competitors to attempt the same upon the decease of the Queen?' This was the horror.[8]

When in June Robert Cecil wrote to Moody about *True Causes* he had one particular passage on his mind. Perhaps he was still using the manuscript copy, for it was Moody who, in his reply, gave the correct pages of the book itself – fifty-five to fifty-six. It was Verstegan's claim

that Burghley planned to marry his grandson William to Lady Arabella Stuart, the sixteen-year-old cousin of King James VI, born and
brought up in England and on the outer edges of the royal succession.
Her name had been rumbling around émigré circles for months,
thanks in part to the calculated stirrings and provocations abroad of
Thomas Phelippes's agent Thomas Barnes. Verstegan prodded in this
passage at Burghley's high dignity by pointing to his father Richard
Cecil's career at the court of Henry VIII; Richard had been an official
in the king's wardrobe, an important but below-stairs role. Verstegan
wrote that a family marriage to Arabella would be the means 'Whereby
England may happen to have a King Cecil the first, that is suddenly
metamorphosed from a groom of the wardrobe, to the wearing of the
best robe within the wardrobe.'[9]

True Causes was Richard Verstegan's fight back, a polemical hand
grenade lobbed at the heretic enemy. Strange to think that for three
days four years earlier, mid-March 1588, with Robert Cecil in Antwerp, Cecil and Verstegan had shared the same streets around the
Church of Our Lady, the Grote Markte and the bourse.

It wasn't surprising that in spring 1592, at the time when he was communicating with Michael Moody, Robert Cecil was quick to respond
to the discovery of cargoes of banned works being smuggled from the
Low Countries into the south of England. These seditious works were
being brought into the kingdom in vast numbers. To Elizabeth's government they were poison.

One such shipment had been opened near Sandwich in Kent: 'divers
books of sedition and divers letters to Catholics'. One of these bun-
dles of papers contained secret letters mainly for Sir Thomas Heneage,
Elizabeth's vice chamberlain, and for Lord Burghley from Michael
Moody. Robert Cecil made sure they got safely to his father.[10]

In September 1592 came Sir Robert Cecil's first special mission as a
privy councillor. That month Cecil and his father were moving with
Elizabeth's court from Gloucester to Oxfordshire. Because his fingers
were less supple than they had been for a few months, the daily
entries Burghley made in his almanac were scratchier than normal.

'7 [September]. The carrack came into Dartmouth at night . . . 16 [September]. Robert Cecil to Dartmouth.'[11]

In late summer a small fleet of English ships – including *Dainty*, *Dragon*, *Foresight*, *Samson*, *Teager*, *Prudence*, *Phoenix* and their flagship, Sir John Burrough's *Roebuck* – had been lurking off the islands of the Azores in the hope of picking off any Spanish ships they came across. On 2 and 3 August Burrough's fleet had been fortunate to encounter two carracks – vast merchant galleons, fitted out for war, three or four times the size of the privateers' own ships – sailing from the Portuguese East Indies back to Europe, each carrying a queen's ransom of merchandise, jewels, spices and books. The first carrack they had captured, but it was heavily damaged by fire. The second, following some hours behind it, was the *Madre de Deus*, which became better known in England under its Spanish name *Madre de Dios* ('Mother of God'). This, too, they had taken in a savage and bloody fight, Burrough's fleet eventually overpowering what was in effect a kind of floating fortress with a crew of about eight hundred Spanish and Portuguese sailors. The riches they had discovered in the carrack were spectacular, Spanish wealth from the Indies which could only make Elizabethans envious: 'goods valued by the Spaniards' own reports to be above seventeen hundred tons, and in value, as they thought, many thousand pounds'. A month after the sea battle, the great carrack was sitting in the port of Dartmouth on the Devonshire coast.[12]

Behind this privateering expedition (one of so many in the 1580s and 1590s) had been the organizing brain of Sir Walter Raleigh – soldier, sailor, favoured courtier and poet, now in his late forties – and a consortium of investors that included the earl of Cumberland (an experienced naval commander and general), various merchants in the City of London and the queen herself. The division of these investors' financial interests in the cargo of the *Madre de Deus* was a complication that Robert Cecil had to begin to unpick when he travelled to Dartmouth. The ship and some of its cargo had been damaged in the battle to take it. The investors and Raleigh's commanders were squabbling over the damage and the division of the profits from the carrack.

A second complication was the status of Raleigh himself, who was in deep disgrace with Elizabeth. Months before the capture of the *Madre de Deus*, his secret marriage to one of the queen's maids of honour, Bess Throckmorton, became known at court. To add to the offence, Bess was pregnant. In late May 1592 Raleigh was put into the custody of Robert Cecil. A month later he was sent to the Tower of London.

Raleigh had communicated to Cecil his sorrow and misfortune in a letter, a courtier-poet's lament, dramatic and overblown yet heartfelt nevertheless. He praised Elizabeth to the skies:

> I that was to behold her riding like Alexander, hunting like Diana, walking like Venus, the gentle wind blowing her fair hair about her pure cheeks like a nymph, sometime sitting in the shade like a goddess, sometime singing like an angel, sometime playing like Orpheus: behold the sorrow of this world, once amiss hath bereaved me of all.

Feeling fully sorry for himself, he signed the letter to Cecil 'Yours not worthy any name or title'.[13]

Raleigh's disgrace and the disagreements over its riches were going to make tricky any effort to resolve the problem of the *Madre de Deus*. But there was more. When the great carrack arrived in Dartmouth, much of its cargo had been looted: one eyewitness likened the free-for-all to Bartholomew Fair, London's famously busy and rowdy annual market. Commissioners appointed to oversee the ship's unlading – Sir Francis Drake and William Killigrew, a gentleman of the queen's privy chamber – had not prevented the looting. Jewels and spices were found weeks later for sale in London. By mid-September it was clear that a new commissioner was needed to recover what had been taken and to preserve and make a proper account of what was left.[14]

As that new commissioner, this was Robert Cecil's opportunity to impress the queen. His most important task would be to make sure that Elizabeth received every penny of her investment in Raleigh's expedition. This fact made Cecil's mission to Dartmouth a risk too, for when it came to her money Elizabeth was unforgiving. As Cecil knew from Raleigh's situation, no courtier, however elevated, was immune from disfavour.

Cecil took with him a commission drafted with great care by his father and signed by Elizabeth. Supplementary instructions gave him wide powers to act, with her Majesty's full authority, 'for finding out of all . . . precious things'. Cecil sat in Privy Council at Burford, about fifteen miles west of Oxford, on Saturday 16 September. Two days later he was in Exeter.[15]

The smell of the carrack hung in the air: Sir Robert wrote that he could detect its perfumes and spices on every bag or cloak within seven miles of Dartmouth and Plymouth. So he came down hard. Within twenty-four hours of arriving in Exeter Cecil had sent two innkeepers to prison and established a line of inquiry which connected a Londoner's shop with bags of pearls, rich fabrics (damasks, cypresses and calicos) and a great pot of musk, all of which had been pilfered from the carrack. He set up searches of every bag coming up from the coast. By what he called his 'rough dealing' he had shocked the local authorities. He was a privy councillor on a mission: 'my sending down here hath made many stagger', he wrote to his father. The people were stubborn, and the weather was foul: yet there was progress – the lack of which so far, in his estimate, had cost the queen twenty thousand pounds in a week. 'My lord,' he wrote to Burghley, 'there was never such spoil.'[16]

At 10 a.m. on Tuesday morning, 19 September, he was ready to ride to Dartmouth. He boarded the carrack at 1 p.m. the following day. Half an hour later Raleigh himself arrived under escort, miserable and disconsolate, furious at how the *Madre de Deus* had been stripped of its cargo but greeted by the sailors as a hero. When someone congratulated him on his freedom, he responded by saying: 'No, I am still the Queen of England's poor captive.' At this Sir Robert squirmed. He wrote to Vice Chamberlain Heneage:

> I wished him to conceal it because here it diminisheth his credit, which
> I do vow unto you before God is greater amongst the mariners than I
> thought, for I do grace him as much as I may, for I find him marvellous

ready to do anything to recover conceit of his brutish offence [i.e., Raleigh's secret marriage and Bess Throckmorton's pregnancy].

A few years earlier Robert Cecil had shivered in Ostend before a lukewarm fire of peat, reminding his friends by letter of their home comforts. That was in 1588. Now in 1592 he was enjoying the hardships of Dartmouth. 'We have rats white and black, drink like smoke in taste, and, as God help me, I brought so little provision for long tarrying.' To Heneage there was humour: 'Give me leave to be merry with you for if I were whipped I must with my friends be bold.' He asked the vice chamberlain to be good to Bess Cecil.[17]

In Dartmouth the queen's bloodhound was on the scent, his private secretary Simon Willis never far away. 'I pray you hear my servant Willis herein, whom I have acquainted with all my mind', Cecil wrote on one paper. On 27 September he asked to return home – with Burghley's sanction.[18]

Perhaps Cecil had been touched by Raleigh's muse. He praised Queen Elizabeth, to Heneage reflecting on 'her ... whose angelical quality works strange influences' in her servants' hearts. He wrote to God's 'celestial creature' herself: 'It is the property of the Creator to accept the labour of men from the abundance of his affection without measure of their ability to perform any actions acceptable to divine worthiness.'

Simon Willis made a copy of his master's letter to Elizabeth and sent it to Lord Burghley. His lordship read the letter. He noted and filed it.[19]

Raleigh was impressed by Cecil's energy and focus in Dartmouth. He had checked every inch of Raleigh's great prize, forensic in searching the *Madre de Deus*. Raleigh wrote to Burghley: 'I dare give the Queen ten thousand pounds, for that which is gained by Sir Robert Cecil coming down, which I speak without all affection or partiality, for (God is my judge) he hath more rifled my ship than all the rest.'[20]

Leaving others in Dartmouth to carry on the work, Sir Robert returned to Privy Council on 10 October. It was plague time in London, sharp and ferocious. Two days later Hampton Court, where the queen was residing, was closed to all outsiders. Burghley was ill. He was bled and purged and took a sweat: it was enough to get him to Westminster and then to find some little refuge at Theobalds. By November he was recovered, his coach rumbling up and down the roads of Hertford- shire and Surrey. Backwards and forwards – and always business.[21]

The accounts for the *Madre de Deus* took months to tie up. Cecil was still busy in London 'about the carrack' in December. The queen was pressing Burghley on the portions of the profits for the earl of Cumberland and Sir Walter Raleigh. Burghley passed her questions to his son: 'Now I am desirous to have these points answered.' At last, in early 1593, senior officials in the City of London and the London cus- toms house determined what seemed to be a fair division of money between the investors. Thomas Phelippes, himself a London customs officer, made his own calculations: of the cargo remaining and recov- ered, valued at £150,000, Cumberland would receive £37,000, Raleigh £24,000, the City of London £12,000, and other miscelleneous inves- tors about £7,000, with £10,000 used to pay the expedition's sailors. That left Elizabeth herself with £60,000, though Phelippes later reported that the carrack's vast stock of £80,000-worth of pepper – in Europe a spice of immense value – belonged to the queen. The longer- term value to Robert Cecil's career was impossible to work out, though it was most certainly proportionable to the material rewards of this remarkable example of state-sponsored piracy.[22]

Stripped and bare, the *Madre de Deus* sat in Dartmouth harbour. Nobody quite knew what to do with it. It was still there in 1594.[23]

The business of the great carrack had been long and complicated. But Robert Cecil had succeeded in his commission. Though for Burghley, the expectations were clear – the father gave orders, the son obeyed them – Cecil was settling in as a privy councillor, finding both his place and his voice.

'And so I pray God bless with his grace to direct you and fear him,' Burghley wrote to Robert in December 1592, 'remembering *melius est obedire Deo quam hominibus.*' It is better to obey God than men. Cecil knew that his place was to obey father, queen and God.[24]

IO

The Bear's Whelp

In early 1593 Elizabeth visited Sir Robert Cecil, her youngest privy councillor. It was an overnight stay, 31 January to the eve of Candlemas, 1 February. Either it was at his apartments next to his father's house on the Strand, a stone's throw from Whitehall Palace, or out beyond London on his estate at Pymmes, where the court would have had more room to spread out. Wherever it was, the visit was an honour – a mark of recognition. Westminster knew it too: the bells of the Church of St Martin-in-the-Fields rang out, as they always did when Elizabeth passed by.[1]

The court was at Burghley's Westminster mansion a week later, though those six days on the Strand were more a necessity for the old lord treasurer than a pleasure. Burghley's health was fragile, business punishing: warrants, diplomatic correspondence, the ongoing military campaign in France to manage, a new parliament only days away.

Elizabeth removed down the street to Somerset House on Saturday 17 February. Two days later she made the short river journey up the Thames to Westminster Palace for the opening of her eighth parliament.

That Monday was a day of fuss and jostle. Members of the new House of Commons were marshalled into the Court of Requests to take the oath of supremacy from a privy councillor. There was a slip of protocol when the lord keeper of the great seal, Sir John Puckering, began his first speech, so important in laying out the parliamentary agenda, before MPs had even come into the Lords' chamber.

At nearly fifty, Lord Keeper Puckering was a no-nonsense lawyer, a veteran of the emergency years of the 1580s. He had led the prosecution of Queen Mary at Fotheringhay Castle, and as speaker of the Commons a month later he had pressed Elizabeth, at Richmond Palace, on the urgency of Mary's execution. Robert Cecil had edited Puckering's words, and the queen's in response, for the printing press. Now, nearly seven years later, Puckering was as robust: 'The great malice of the King of Spain set forth which he had towards this realm, and that he showed by sundry instances.' England's war against Spain, which had only intensified after the defeat of the great Armada in 1588, had entered a new and dangerous phase. Elizabeth's realms were in danger.[2]

In facing this threat to the kingdom, money in taxation, to which the Commons had to assent, was everything. Every Elizabethan gentleman knew his Cicero: *Nervos belli, pecuniam infinitam.* 'The sinews of war, unlimited money.' But when that money was coming out of their own purses, it was, as Sir Robert Cecil would soon find out, conservatively finite.

Lord Burghley was a master of the set piece *tour d'horizon*, the great speech which took in the long history of Elizabeth's reign. Before the trial of the Scottish queen, in 1586, he had told the commissioners her story from the beginning. He had lived it all, seen it, directed it. His words had weight and substance. Now, with the help of his private secretary Henry Maynard, he prepared to speak to the House of Lords facts, truths and imperatives.

Maynard did most of the writing for the speech, but Burghley was in absolute control. He knew what had to be said. He was weary, he was ancient, and he excused himself to the Lords, thanking them for their 'patience in suffering an old man, besides his years decayed in his spirits with sickness'. But the hand in which he drafted parts of his speech was strong, his intellectual grip as firm as ever.[3]

Spain still menaced England. Philip II was preparing a new armada. Religious civil war, Catholic against Protestant Huguenot, continued to paralyse the kingdom of France. English Catholic dissidents abroad conspired against Elizabeth and the Jesuits were busy infiltrating both England and Scotland. The young Scottish king, twenty-six-year-old James VI, was particularly vulnerable to Catholic plots. As recently as December 1592 three Scottish earls – Huntly, Errol and Angus – had been discovered trying to open negotiations with Philip of Spain for an invasion of Scotland. If Scotland fell, England would be next.

Not surprisingly, father and son co-ordinated efforts in the Lords and Commons. On Robert Cecil the pressure must have been considerable. Burghley was a veteran speaker in parliaments, but this was Cecil's first major speech, and it could not have mattered more. He, like Burghley, was laying out the justifications for raising taxes to continue fighting the war.

Cecil's speech, which he gave on Monday 26 February, was framed as precisely as his father's had been. He wrote it to achieve just the right effect: he was earnest, diffident and attentive. He wanted to make a good impression. He needed to convince his fellow members of the Commons – after all, it was they who would be asked to put their hands into their purses to pay for ships and soldiers. The first thing he had to do was to explain his silence in parliaments so far: 'I have not determined to say anything in those assemblies further than my cogitations should concur with my conscience in saying bare aye or no.' In asking for pardon, he quoted from an apothegm of Dionysius Cato, one of those bitesize pieces of conventional morality that helped generations of Tudor schoolboys learn their Latin: *Nec te collaudes nec te vituperes ipse*, 'Neither praise nor blame thyself.' His audience would have known what came next in the distich, as familiar to them as a proverb: fools make mistakes when they are stirred by vain hopes of glory.[4]

Here was a beginning for Sir Robert Cecil, his first proper introduction of himself. Nothing too clever, nothing too unconventional – a bright young councillor taking it carefully, given the wings to fly, but fully intending not to get too close to the sun.

He explained that the most important thing was to protect the queen and her kingdoms. She and they were threatened by the forces of Spain as well as by the Antichrist of Rome (by which Cecil meant the Pope) and the combined power and menace of Catholic Europe. The danger was immediate. England was threatened. It was time to act, and Sir Robert Cecil asked Speaker Sir Edward Coke to appoint a committee of 'the sufficientest and wisest men' to consider what needed to be done.[5]

The day before Cecil's speech to the Commons, Robert Devereux, earl of Essex, had joined Lord Keeper Puckering, Lord Treasurer Burghley, the earl of Derby, Lord Admiral Howard, Lord Buckhurst, Sir Robert Cecil and Sir John Wolley in the Privy Council chamber at St James's

Palace. At 4 p.m. that Sunday Essex swore the oath of supremacy and the oath of a privy councillor.[6]

This was the latest of many parts Essex had played over the years, and would continue to play: courtier and favourite, the great patron, the general of the queen's armies, and now the serious councillor and minister. He never attempted anything by half: the conservative restraint of Dionysius Cato's apothegm on the dangers of seeking glory didn't suit Essex's temperament. The Normandy campaign of 1591 had been for him a failure. His younger brother Walter was killed in a skirmish near Rouen in early September, and Essex spent the autumn months fighting Elizabeth as well as laying unsuccessful siege to the French Catholic League. He had sought from the queen operational freedom as her general, and he had not got it; two visits back to court and a number of absences from his army left his troops demoralized. He had returned to England in January 1592.

Being appointed by Elizabeth to her Privy Council was a fresh start. The earl sought now to impress his colleagues with his seriousness and sagacity. One of his followers, an old friend from Cambridge, wrote: 'His lordship is become a new man, clear forsaking all his former youthful tricks, carrying himself with very honourable gravity and singularly liked of both in parliament and at the Council board, for his speeches and judgement.'[7]

At last Essex had the place and respect he knew he deserved.

The eighth parliament was not as straightforward as Cecil perhaps expected it to be. To be convinced by an argument, especially when it has to do with the defence of queen and country, is one thing; to agree to be taxed out of your pocket to fund military adventures is quite another. So began in the House of Commons weeks of wrangles and tussles and debates and bad temper over the tax bills.

The first week of March was especially testy. Sitting in all the committees, taking part in every conference with the House of Lords, Sir Robert Cecil negotiated and persuaded. He was thrown quickly into frontline action; and diffident speeches seasoned by schoolboy apothegms took him only so far. Managing a restive and fractious Commons bickering over money was quite different from handling the queen in audience, sitting at a desk on the Strand, or pouncing as her Majesty's commissioner on the lax authorities in Exeter and Dartmouth. Suave manners and administrative acuity were not enough. In the Commons and in committee he lost his temper and he made mistakes, finding himself wrongfooted and challenged. For the first time in his career events outpaced him.[8]

There was a long debate on the tax bill on Wednesday 7 March. Grandees and courtiers queued to speak: Vice Chamberlain Heneage, Robert's brother Sir Thomas Cecil, Sir Walter Raleigh, Sir Henry Unton, Sir Henry Stafford, Sir Francis Drake, Sir John Fortescue and Francis Bacon. Cecil found himself uttering the cry of a minister who wanted confusion brought into order, who couldn't abide loose ends:

> And my desire is that the sentence [that] hath had so many parentheses might now be brought to a period, and the bear's whelp that had been so many times licked over might now be made somewhat. For that is always the most honourable conclusion which having received many contradictions is in the end concluded.

His metaphor was a familiar proverb: Cecil of course knew the work of Pliny the Elder, the Roman writer and scientist who, in his *Natural History*, explained how bear cubs were born as mere lumps of flesh and had to be slowly licked into shape by their mothers.[9]

The bear's whelp: William Shakespeare, ten months younger than Robert Cecil, knew his Pliny too. In the twelfth scene of the play he probably co-wrote with Christopher Marlowe, *3 Henry VI* (1590/91, revised by Shakespeare in about 1594), there is a verbal resonance with Cecil's speech to the Commons. It connects the proverb to what everyone, friend and enemy, knew about Robert Cecil – his scoliosis, the shape of his back.

In the play Richard, duke of Gloucester says in soliloquy:

> Why, love forswore me in my mother's womb:
> And, for I should not deal in her soft laws,
> She did corrupt frail nature with some bribe
> To shrink mine arm up like a withered shrub,
> To make an envious mountain on my back
> Where sits deformity to mock my body,

To shape my legs of an unequal size,
To disproportion me in every part,
Like to a chaos, or an unlicked bear-whelp
That carries no impression like the dam. [Scene 12, ll. 153–62]

Gloucester explains the deformity of his back by saying that he was not licked into proper shape by his mother: as a consequence he is an aberration, a chaos unformed, barely human.

Therefore he is evil too, and in his speech he lays out his sinister ambitions, giving Shakespeare the opportunity, in some chilling verse, to show the familiar association Elizabethans assumed there to be between crookedness of body and wickedness in morality:

I'll drown more sailors than the mermaid shall,
I'll slay more gazers than the basilisk,
I'll play the orator as well as Nestor,
Deceive more slyly than Ulysses could,
And, like a Sinon, take another Troy.
I can add colours to the chameleon,
Change shapes with Proteus for advantages,
And set the murderous Machiavel to school.
Can I do this, and cannot get a crown?
Tut, were it farther off, I'll pluck it down. [Scene 12, ll. 186–95]

Sinon was the Greek who persuaded the Trojans to take the wooden horse into Troy. Everyone knew Machiavelli, and shuddered at his name: he spoke the Prologue to Marlowe's *The Jew of Malta*. Such men were ruthless and power-hungry. And their characters were used by writers like Richard Verstegan to condemn the tyranny and oppression of the ambitious Cecil family. In his pamphlet *True Causes*, Verstegan wondered why the queen hadn't promoted Master Cecil to a humble clerkship, given that 'he was fittest for such purpose, for that he carried his desk on his back'.[10]

Though so rarely spoken of other than in terms of the delicacy of his health, the young privy councillor who spoke and worked so hard in the House of Commons in the spring of 1593 was physically different, visibly set apart from others, and everyone saw it.

*

Ten days after Cecil's speech, a secret Catholic report on events in England was written from London and sent to Verstegan in Antwerp. 'The Lord Treasurer is recovered of his sickness, as lusty as ever, more potent than ever. He in the Upper House, and his son, Sir Robert, in the Lower House, make what laws they list.'[11]

Burghley thought that spring that he was dying. He was taking quicksilver – liquid mercury – as a treatment. The headaches he suffered as a result were excruciating, especially at night. He was finding it difficult to walk. He told Robert on 26 May that it was time to prepare for death: 'I find myself so decaying in strength as I find it more needful for me to be occupied about my last will and other establishments for my children.'[12]

Ferried around Westminster by coach or litter, he knew that Elizabeth wanted to see him.

> I am weak, and uncertain how I shall be able to come to the court. Yet I am in mind to come tomorrow to the court with opinion that [in] one or two days her Majesty will license me to return to seek my amendment or to take my journey to follow *universam viam carnis* ['the way of all flesh']. You must allow me to be in this humour, for I find no other taste of any other thing.

He had little privacy and no peace. 'Until this dinnertime I have had neither kin, nor inward friend to see me or salute me, but multitude of suitors that only come for their own causes.'

Only death offered Lord Burghley an escape from service and business, though he wrote that even in heaven he would counsel God on Elizabeth's behalf.[13]

At court at Nonsuch Palace, in Surrey, in the first week of June the earl of Essex wrote to Sir Henry Unton, Elizabeth's now former ambassador to Henry IV of France: 'They which are most in appetite are not yet satisfied, whereof there is great discontentment. If it stand at this stay a while longer they will despair. For their chief hour glass hath little sand left in it and doth run out still.' Essex's 'they' were the Cecils and their clients; their chief hourglass the septuagenarian minister being carried around Westminster in a litter. He believed that Burghley would soon die. Essex was now so tantalizingly close to the prize of a brilliant career – pre-eminence in Elizabeth's government. Surely time and mortality were on his side.[14]

The growing friction between Unton and Robert Cecil was one of the sharpest stings of the eighth parliament. The diplomacy of Unton's embassy to Henry IV mirrored Essex's lacklustre military command in Normandy. His relationship with the king of France was strained and the embassy had been ruinously expensive for him. Elizabeth, however, showed neither understanding nor sympathy for his predicament, so Unton returned to England desperate for office, preferment and rehabilitation. During his posting in France there had been an ever-widening gap between what Unton wanted in terms of favour at court and what Cecil was either able or willing to give him. This pushed him in the direction of Essex instead. The mutual love Unton and Cecil expressed for each other in the early months of Unton's embassy was burned down to the end of its wick.

In the House of Commons Unton had accused an unnamed minister of preparing for the queen a list of troublemakers over the tax bill. It was a step too far. To Cecil, Elizabeth's favour outranked loving friendship. Unton knew the game as well as Robert did. Cecil fought back and he had Elizabeth on his side. Essex wrote to Unton of the queen: 'She startles at your name, chargeth you with popularity, and hath every particular of your speeches in parliament without book.' She was keeping record, Robert Cecil was in favour, and Henry Unton was warned.[15]

In October 1593 Elizabeth and her court visited Theobalds. Lord Burghley, tied as ever to business and beset by suitors, found himself checking inventories of domestic furniture and scrutinizing lists of linen again.[16]

The character of the hermit of Theobalds had made his first appearance before the queen and her court in May 1591. Now he made his second: he, like Lord Burghley, was an old man: he, like the lord treasurer, wanted the kind of relief that could only come by a prince's favour. The hermit petitioned Elizabeth on his master's behalf, Burghley's 'body being laden with years, oppressed with sickness, having spent his strength for public service, desireth to be rid of worldly cares by ending his days, your Majesty, with a bond of princely care'.

Sir Robert Cecil was ready to serve, even if he couldn't match the abilities of the great Lord Burghley – so the hermit had learned from the people round about. The self-deprecation was expected: the obedient son could never outshine Burghley. 'I hear it of all the country folks I meet with, that your Majesty doth use him in your service as in former time have done his father my founder . . . although his experience and judgement be no way comparable.'[17]

Autumn 1593 was for Queen Elizabeth a season of introspection. Providence gave her challenges for which she had to draw on her deepest resources. She needed to make sense of messy human realities under the aspect of eternity.

She knew that princes suffered. They were put under stresses and strains that no one else felt. They made mistakes, they clung on to kingdoms. In Scotland King James VI had faced open rebellion and the revelation of the three Catholic earls' plans for a Spanish invasion. The security of Scotland mattered, for its strength was England's too, and its vulnerability Elizabeth's. This made especially significant the fact that by October 1593 Burghley had given his son the oversight of Anglo-Scottish diplomacy, a big step up in Cecil's responsibilities. Now his secretary, Simon Willis, kept the entry book of letters to and from ambassadors at James's court. But on a personal level, Elizabeth struggled with James, whose mother – a mother he had never really known – she had executed six years earlier. The queen worried that the Scottish king would compromise with rebels, that he was too weak to bring them to justice. In her letters to James she lectured him as a subordinate. This James resented.[18]

On Sunday 7 October Elizabeth wrote to him. 'My dear brother, if the variableness of Scottish affairs had not inured me with too old a custom, I should never leave wondering at such strange and uncouth actions.' The rebel earls might argue that the intervention of a foreign power would strengthen the king and his kingdom. She knew better: 'O how wicked sirens which in first show please, in end ruin and destroy.' Elizabeth concluded with a prayer for James's deliverance from betrayal and deceit.[19]

Hers was the voice of experience, the position of seniority.

Elizabeth worked in these mid-autumn weeks on a translation of *De Consolatione Philosophiae* (*On the Consolations of Philosophy*) by the sixth-century Roman minister Anicius Boethius. It was a classic and well-known text in the sixteenth century: William Caxton had printed Geoffrey Chaucer's edition of it, and from 1556 there was a serviceable translation in print. Elizabeth's work on Boethius was for her own private meditations. She worked at speed in October and November, dictating Boethius' prose to amanuenses – one was Thomas Windebank, an old familiar of her privy chamber. Boethius' verse she scratched out in her skrating hand, her spelling as opaque as ever, her syntax experimental and often baffling. The sprinting pace at which she translated *Consolations* meant that her English almost bounced off Boethius' Latin.

Through these idiosyncrasies Elizabeth made *Consolations* her own. Boethius, condemned to die, explored in his work the transitory and fragile nature of life, human folly, the justice of God. All of this was relevant to Elizabeth. She knew better than anyone that, as King Lear puts it, a prince might live in a walled prison. When she was twenty years old, back in 1554 in the reign of her sister Mary I, implicated in a plot against the queen, she had spent some weeks in the Tower of London. In 1587 she had signed the warrant which, by its circuitous route, had killed another Mary – James of Scotland's mother and Elizabeth's cousin, a monarch tarnished but a monarch still. As queen, Elizabeth had in theory absolute power. Yet she found herself so often constrained and limited by accidents and failures, or simply by the grind of daily business. She was getting older, having turned sixty in September. Though touched by the divine, she was mortal. And one day – who knew when? – she would answer before God at Judgement Day.

Yet there *was* hope and meaning: redemption, reconciliation, providence. In book five of *Consolations* Boethius put his confidence in

God, in whom all is explained. The verse of Elizabeth's final portion of her translation sparkles with clarity (especially when we modernize her spelling):

> There lasteth also a viewer of us all the foreknowing God, whose ever-present eternity of sight agreeth with the following property of our actions. And so dispenseth to good reward, to ill their deserts, neither in vain do we put trust in God, neither of small price our prayers, which being truly made, can never fall in vain. Avoid vice therefore, praise virtue, your minds lift up to true hopes, and settle your humble prayers in highest place.

This was Elizabeth's consolation – her certainty – as she began the seventh decade of her life.[20]

Lord Burghley in early December was in as playful a mood with Robert as health and business would allow. His son was his voice at court, his intermediary with the queen: it was essential for him to maintain the connection. He joked that he was surprised that Elizabeth was allowing his absence from court given that she used not to give audience in cloudy or foul weather, and now there was plenty of that. Robert Cecil read the letter to the queen.[21]

11

Desperate Treason

Robert Cecil was by now a courtier, a minister and a perhaps slightly bruised parliamentarian. With Elizabeth I he had, by 1594, a growing relationship of mutual trust and understanding. He was taking up something of his father's vast workload, with a special responsibility for Scotland. He knew, of course, the darker side of Elizabethan court politics. He had employed spies like Michael Moody and Father John Cecil; they came and went. He understood the rivalries and collaborations of courtiers. He saw, as everyone did, that the earl of Essex was ambitious for power. But Robert Cecil's fullest initiation into the brutality of Elizabethan politics – an episode that neither he nor anyone would forget – happened at this point in his career: the so-called Lopez Plot, when one of the queen's physicians, a Portuguese named Ruy (or Roderigo) Lopez, was accused of plotting to poison Elizabeth.

The story has several strands. Each is important, each is a little tangled, but this was characteristic of late-sixteenth-century Portuguese politics. The most important elements, for us at least, are these.

The death in 1580 of Portugal's ruler, the childless Henry the Cardinal, had precipitated a crisis of succession in his kingdom. There were two claimants for the throne. One was Dom António (Elizabethans called him 'Don Anthony'), the prior of Crato and nephew of Henry the Cardinal. The other was the most powerful monarch in Europe, and king of Portugal's neighbour Spain, Philip II. Philip won the contest, leaving Dom António to take up the unhappy career of itinerant pretender, begging foreign powers for aid and followed by a clientele of supporters whose loyalties could never quite be trusted – many after 1580 were tempted by Spanish money and power.

To Dom António Queen Elizabeth was polite but non-committal; he was after all an enemy of her enemy, Philip of Spain. By the early 1590s the pretender was living in England, where he had one prominent loyalist at the queen's court – Doctor Lopez, one of Elizabeth's team of physicians. Lopez, by this point in his mid-seventies, came from a family of Portuguese *conversos* – in other words, from a family of Jews who in 1497 had become Christian either by choice or compulsion. Born in about 1517, the son of a physician to the king of Portugal, Lopez was a graduate of the University of Coimbra. He became a skilled and talented doctor, who in middle age moved to England. Resident in London by 1559, he built up a distinguished medical practice, treating patients as grand as Robert Dudley, earl of Leicester and Sir Francis Walsingham. Recognizing his doctor's political connections in Portugal, Secretary Walsingham in the 1580s employed Lopez as a diplomat and spy.

Another of Dom António's supporters in the early 1590s was Manuel Luis Tinoco, a much humbler character than the eminent Doctor Lopez, employed mainly as a letter courier and familiar with London and Brussels. In December 1593, after turning up unannounced at the Calais home of an English merchant in the town, Tinoco insisted that Lord Burghley should be given a message. There was a dangerous plot against Elizabeth that he, Tinoco, knew all about: as the merchant put it, 'he hath discovered great matter pretend[ed] by the enemy which he will declare unto her Majesty or your honour. He saith it must be foreseen with speed.' Accordingly with speed, Tinoco received from Burghley a passport that guaranteed him safe passage to Dover and on to court.[1]

So it was that at seven o'clock on the morning of Friday, 11 January 1594 Manuel Luis Tinoco found himself waiting outside Sir Robert Cecil's chamber at Hampton Court. He sat there for three hours before meeting Cecil.[2]

Tinoco's revelation over the following few days, which he began to set out on paper, was that King Philip had recruited a priest of Galicia, in north-west Spain, to murder Elizabeth with 'a device of fire' (presumably gunpowder) on a feast day at court. The assassin, he wrote, would arrive on the north-east coast of England not far from Newcastle upon

Tyne, where he would receive help from a secret network of Jesuit priests. Unconnected to this plot, Tinoco explained that those Portuguese working for the king of Spain were keen to recruit Doctor Lopez. We can understand Tinoco's discomfort when after a few days he realized that Cecil was using Lopez himself to translate Tinoco's various confessions and papers.

Manuel Luis Tinoco was not the first Portuguese to come to Elizabeth and Burghley with allegations of various plots and conspiracies being engineered by Philip II. To these Burghley always brought a practised scepticism: he treated them as he handled Michael Moody – even rogues might have their uses. But the new factor in 1594 was the earl of Essex, who was quick to question Tinoco himself. This was no coincidence: for some months Essex, with the help of other privy councillors, had been following the letters and movements of those of Dom António's supposed followers who had been plotting with Spain. In October 1593 the queen had instructed Essex to apprehend in London Estevão Ferreira da Gama, another former supporter of the pretender, who had conspired to betray Dom António's sons to Philip, as well as to negotiate with Elizabeth's government a false Anglo-Spanish peace. Tinoco had been a courier of da Gama's letters and so he was, not surprisingly, a person of interest to Essex. In Calais Tinoco had asked for complete discretion – he must communicate only with Burghley and Elizabeth. Now he was under 'secret examination' by Essex, 'not a little encumbered' (as he complained to Robert Cecil) 'by the cunning demands of my lord the earl, wherein I seemed to falter'. In other words, Essex had interrogated him hard and Tinoco had wilted under its intensity.[3]

Here we see the network of associations which came to matter so much. Tinoco led Cecil and Essex to Estevão Ferreira da Gama who, as one of Dom António's household in London, had for a time lodged with Doctor Lopez. Lopez, too, was suddenly in focus: by Monday 21 January, only six days after Tinoco's first statements, there was a change in the atmosphere, an intimation, the first suggestion of a possibility. Could Lopez himself be trusted?

This was the question being wrestled with all that Monday afternoon, Essex closeted away in conference with Lord Buckhurst and

Cecil at the earl's house on the Strand. They met again for the whole of Tuesday morning, and Essex and Cecil talked later in the day at Hampton Court. On Wednesday, 23 January, Tinoco was interrogated again, when he spoke about a jewel that Philip of Spain had sent as a gift to Doctor Lopez. Tinoco was very careful not to make a direct accusation of treason against Lopez – he played on circumstantial and suggestive details. In Brussels, Tinoco said, he had been told about this jewel. And now he revealed that da Gama had written letters identifying Lopez as 'his Majesty's [King Philip's] friend and that he could do him great service'.[4]

Tinoco was being pushed and squeezed – he was trying to divert attention away from himself. But this was now the allegation: Doctor Lopez had indeed been lured into the service of Spain. Or perhaps he had pretended to be, which is what a letter from Burghley to Cecil, written that Wednesday, appears to suggest – a letter censored, with key words inked out by a pen nib thick enough to be Cecil's. Burghley wrote: 'In — folly I see no point of treason intend[ed] to the Q[ueen] but a readiness to make some gain to the hurt of —.' The first word crossed out begins with the letter R, the other with L, with a p half-way through it.[5]

Whose folly Burghley thought it was isn't clear. But Doctor Lopez was now exposed. Essex was swift to appreciate this, able to make connections. Lopez made a plausible traitor; he fitted the model. He had for years been entangled in Portuguese and Spanish secret politics. He was a Jew, against whom there was deep prejudice. He was a man who had been named ten years earlier as a poisoner in a particularly scurrilous and well-known Catholic libel called *Leicester's Commonwealth*, whose main target had been the queen's then favourite, the earl of Leicester. This was the material that Essex had to play with: circumstantial facts, loose associations, prejudice. And play with them he did.[6]

At Hampton Court on Thursday 24 January the earl was again deep in conference with Cecil, with Lord Admiral Howard joining them. In the evening he spoke to the queen. It was perhaps the audience at which she declared herself sceptical of the charge being made against her doctor, allegedly calling Essex a 'rash and temerous [foolhardy] youth' – words calculated to get under the skin of a

twenty-eight-year-old minister both driven and ambitious. The following day the council sat in Star Chamber but Burghley, Essex and
Sir Robert Cecil were absent; busy instead, at the queen's direction,
questioning Lopez at Burghley's mansion on the Strand. On that
Friday Essex didn't get what he wanted, at least if the manner of his
return to court is significant. At 4 p.m. he stormed into his chambers
and in a temper shut himself away.[7]

Forty-eight hours' reflection turned Essex's anger and frustration to
cold resolution. He became the convert who finds an unshakeable
truth. On Monday 28 January he wrote to his ever-loyal follower
Anthony Bacon (like his younger brother Francis, a stalwart supporter of Essex):

> I have discovered a most dangerous and desperate treason. The point of
> conspiracy was her Majesty's death. The executioner should have been
> Doctor Lopez. The manner by poison. This I have so followed that I
> will make it appear as clear as the noon day.[8]

On Wednesday 30 January Star Chamber heard the case of the forgery of a will and other legal documents. Six privy councillors, the
chief justice and the chief baron of the Exchequer sat through the
whole session. Two councillors arrived late. They were Essex and
Cecil, busy in conference elsewhere.[9]

Over January and February a number of Portuguese living in
London were rounded up for questioning. The most important of
these was Estevão Ferreira da Gama. Tinoco and da Gama were
now the two most important witnesses. William Wade of the Privy
Council office, who in a few months' time would write the official
account of the Lopez investigation, described their confessions as 'a
fortress with trenches and many defences, as it seemed invincible.
But by continual labour, sapping and mining, and hewing out of
hard rock, and approaching by little, all their defences were away
and a breach was made.'[10]

Essex became possessed of the inquisitor's irresistible energy. Wade's
military metaphor was fitting. Whether in hand-to-hand fighting outside Rouen or by the interrogation of prisoners at his house on the

Strand, it was in the bloody trenches of service that Essex was at his most focused. In sacrificing others he sacrificed himself; he hardly rested. At one point, he wrote, he was 'so tired with examinations as I had scarce leisure to eat'. Wade himself worked on the prisoners, a critical link in the communications between Essex, Burghley and Cecil.[11]

What followed in February and March 1594 could in different circumstances have been something like this. Recognizing the thinness of the case against Lopez, the Cecils went into battle on his behalf. Burghley knew the facts about him, as Secretary Walsingham too had known and employed him: the doctor may have played a secret game with and against Spain, but he was no traitor. After the touch-and-go months of Burghley's sickness in late 1593, this was the Cecils' opportunity to hold back the earl of Essex's aggressive play for pre-eminence in the Privy Council and at court. Common sense and balance – and Elizabeth's instinctive caution – would prevail.

But this is not what happened. The most plausible explanation for the pattern of events that followed is that Cecil fully co-operated with Essex in destroying Doctor Lopez. Perhaps he came to believe in Lopez's treason. Perhaps he recognized as true the evidence that Essex squeezed with menaces from the prisoners in February. Perhaps.

A complicating factor by February was the discovery of yet another putative conspiracy to murder the queen. The origin of this plot was the rogue regiment of Irish Catholics fighting for King Philip commanded by Sir William Stanley. Stanley had been one of the most trusted officers in the army sent by Elizabeth to help the Dutch in 1586 under the generalship of Robert Dudley, earl of Leicester. A year later Stanley had made a shocking defection to Spain by surrendering up to the enemy the town of Deventer. By the early 1590s his regiment of Catholic recruits looked, to Elizabeth's government, like a band of fanatical commando assassins – a very long way from their chaotic ragbag reality.

Some of Stanley's Irishmen were in London by December 1593, supposedly there to kill the queen: 'come into the realm with full purpose, by procurement of the devil and his ministers, her Majesty's enemies,

SERO, SED SERIO

Sir Robert Cecil in c. 1602 by John de Critz the Elder: the queen's minister and secretary,
ate, but in earnest'.

2. Robert Cecil's father, William Cecil, 1st baron of Burghley, by Marcus Gheeraerts the Younger: Queen Elizabeth's lord treasurer and minister and his son's model and mentor.

3. Robert Cecil's mother, Mildred, Lady Burghley, attributed to Hans Eworth: distinguished classical scholar, courtier and matriarch.

4. Spanish-held Antwerp on the Scheldt river, shown here as Robert Cecil would have known and explored it in March 1588, months before the Spanish Armada set sail.

5. The Rainbow Portrait of a Jacobean-styled Queen Elizabeth I, commissioned by Robert Cecil at the very end of her reign, decorated with the motto *Non sine sole iris*, 'No rainbow without the sun'.

r Christopher Hatton, Cecil's early orter and patron at court: 'my only oracle', obert addressed Hatton in 1591.

7. King James VI of Scotland in 1595, in a portrait attributed to Adrian Vanson: for years wary of each other, from 1601 Robert Cecil and the king worked together to ensure James's eventual succession to Queen Elizabeth's throne.

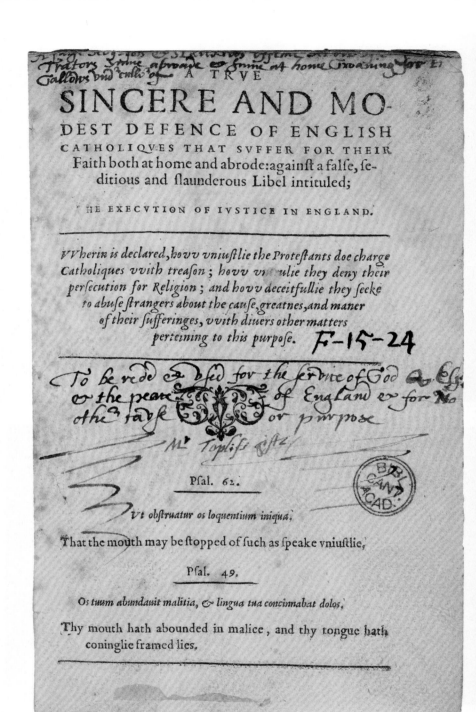

A TRVE

SINCERE AND MO-
DEST DEFENCE OF ENGLISH
CATHOLIQVES THAT SVFFER FOR THEIR
Faith both at home and abrode: againſt a falſe, ſe-
ditious and ſlaunderous Libel intituled;

THE EXECVTION OF IVSTICE IN ENGLAND.

*VVherin is declared, hovv vniuſtlie the Proteſtants doe charge
Catholiques vvith treaſon; hovv vn ulie they deny their
perſecution for Religion; and hovv deceitfullie they ſeeke
to abuſe ſtrangers about the cauſe, greatnes, and maner
of their ſufferinges, vvith diuers other matters
perteining to this purpoſe.*

Pſal. 62.

Vt obſtruatur os loquentium iniqua,

That the mouth may be ſtopped of ſuch as ſpeake vniuſtlie,

Pſal. 49.

Os tuum abundauit malitia, & lingua tua concinnabat dolos,

Thy mouth hath abounded in malice, and thy tongue hath
coninglie framed lies.

8. A Catholic view of Elizabeth's persecution of the true Catholic faith, by William Allen, printed in 1585: the handwritten notes are by Richard Topcliffe, one of the foremost hunters and interrogators of Catholics.

9. One of the milder scenes from Richard Verstegan's *Theatre of the Cruelties of the Heretics of Our Time*, showing a raid on a Catholic house, with the priest, a gentlewoman and other worshippers led off to prison.

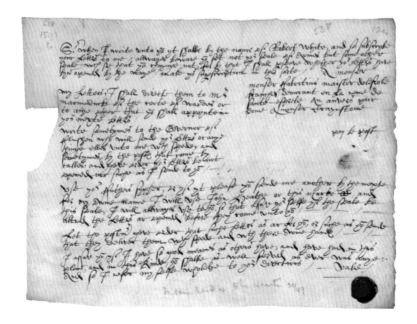

10. Instructions set out by the spy Michael Moody for secret communications with Sir Robert Cecil from Antwerp, 1591: 'I assure you, yf I have so good meanes as others have ... in this place ... you shalbe as well served as ever was anye.'

11. Courtier, favourite, minister, soldier, self-styled hero of Protestant Europe, and Robert Cecil's rival: Robert Devereux, 2nd earl of Essex, from a miniature by Isaac Oliver *c.*1596.

12. Sir Edward Hoby, a maternal cousin to Robert Cecil and a close friend of Robert's wife Elizabeth.

13. The tomb in Westminster Abbey of Lady Elizabeth Cecil, always known as Bess to her husband Robert, her friends and close family.

14. The contents page to the most secret work of reference in Secretary Cecil's office, 'The names of the Intelligencers' posted across Europe, begun by Cecil's private secretary Simon Willis, and originally containing papers on spies' salaries and ciphers.

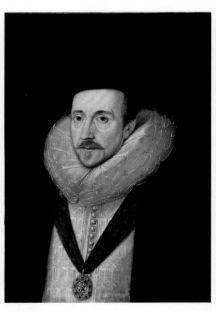

15. Charles Howard, Lord Howard of Effingham and earl of Nottingham: Elizabeth I's lord admiral who commanded the navy that faced the Spanish Armada in 1588.

16. Lord Henry Howard, made earl of Northampton by King James VI and I: one of the secret correspondents with James between 1601 and 1603, referred to by Cecil in the code numbers they used as 'My friend 3'.

17. Alessandro Farnese, prince and duke of Parma, King Philip II's general and governor of the Spanish Netherlands: Robert Cecil met Parma in Ghent in 1588.

18. Johan van Oldenbarnevelt, the leading politician of the Dutch States which resisted Spanish rule: as Queen Elizabeth's ambassador to King Henry IV of France, Cecil negotiated with Oldenbarnevelt in 1598.

and rebels on the other side the sea, to endanger her Majesty's noble person', as the public proclamation to apprehend them put it. Over the weeks of Christmas and New Year 1594 snippets of reports on Stanley and his regiment had featured in Burghley's letters to Cecil. Now Stanley's soldiers took on an arresting significance. Their supposed plottings were coming into clearer view. They caused a panic. They also gave Burghley the opportunity and initiative to expose other plots against the queen – Essex was not the only councillor who worked tirelessly to protect Elizabeth. By February, a few days before the above proclamation, Burghley ordered strict security measures limiting access to court – it was in effect a lockdown.[12]

Stanley's soldiers in England were said to be aided and encouraged by a cadre of extremist Jesuits who were urging Elizabeth's assassination. There was a plan, supposedly, to blow up the Tower of London using its own stocks of brimstone and gunpowder. Behind this operation was a familiar name, that of Michael Moody, the former, highly questionable employee of the Cecils – and indeed of any other privy councillor receptive to his persuasive skills. It is impossible to know whether Moody was a real plotter or was trying his hand as an agent provocateur, once again trying to impress Lord Burghley. What is certain is that every resource was thrown at questioning and re-questioning three of Stanley's Irishmen arrested in London. The attorney general, the solicitor general, William Wade and other investigators interrogated the prisoners.

The Irish revelations and the supposed Iberian conspiracies could, by making certain assumptions, be connected together. Manuel Luis Tinoco – perhaps voluntarily, but probably under the threat of torture – continued to give the evidence he had encountered of the conspiracies of Doctor Lopez. One of the Irish suspects, John Annyas, admitted to knowing Tinoco (though 'not very well') and writing him a letter in Calais in January 1594. Annyas offered a significant nugget of information: he referred to 'the principal man' in whom one of the putative assassins 'reposeth his great trust in the court in England', 'a man of great calling about the queen: of this man he hath heard speech about five months past at Brussels'. Another prisoner, unconnected with Stanley's regiment, confessed to knowledge of secret letters that had been sent to Doctor Lopez by a merchant in Calais and claimed that he had witnessed a conference back in May 1593 between Lopez and a known Catholic agent provocateur. All these separate pieces fitted together only loosely, but in the circumstances of emergency that hardly seemed to matter. The imaginative glue that held them together was highly elastic.[13]

In that first week of February 1594 Father John Cecil – Robert Cecil's first spy – was captured by Sir Francis Drake on board ship in the English Channel. Drake, with his colleague Piers Edgcumbe, made a brisk report to the Privy Council. Their letter went to Simon Willis in Cecil's office. The response was immediate.

Drake managed to keep John Cecil's identity a secret, treating him as a 'mere Scotsman' and holding him in seclusion near Plymouth. At the priest's request, Sir Francis produced safe conducts that would get him to Scotland or Calais if he needed to. Within days the order was made to send him to Sir Robert Cecil as safely and secretly as possible. Father John set out on his journey from Devon to Westminster with one of Drake's servants.[14]

John Cecil was nervous. He fretted that he had given too much of himself away to Edgcumbe's servant. He worried, too, that Sir Robert would get the wrong idea about Drake's passports, that he was planning to disappear. He wrote to Cecil on Thursday 14 February: 'If you had not sent for me, Sir Francis Drake ... know[s] I was resolved privately to have come up for certain especial points which I would not commit to paper.'[15]

John Cecil was potentially a star agent. He had left England in July 1591 with the paperwork prepared for him by Robert Cecil. He seems to have been in Madrid in 1592 and involved there in discussions about a Spanish invasion of Scotland and England. After that he worked in Scotland, where the Jesuits established a covert base. Cecil was close to Cardinal William Allen (in Rome) and Father Robert Persons (in Spain), both of them at the heart of the English Catholic mission. From Robert Cecil's perspective, John Cecil was able to see the enemy's planning from the inside.[16]

But John Cecil may have been compromised right from the

beginning of his career as Cecil's spy. It seems that he and his companion and fellow priest John Fixer had been noticed in Westminster and London in the spring and summer of 1591, in the weeks following their capture at sea and seclusion and debriefing at Burghley's mansion on the Strand. As early as January 1592 Cardinal Allen, then living in a modest house next to the English College on the Via Monserrato in Rome, wrote to Persons:

> Two companions ... were with the [Lord] Treasurer, and were suspected to have discovered [revealed] all they knew, and more than they knew, since which the former of them hath been here ... But now we are further advertised that they have betrayed all indeed.[17]

But perhaps, too, the Cecils knew that their spy was known to Cardinal Allen. In August 1592 another Catholic priest captured in England confessed to Lord Burghley that Cardinal Allen kept John Fixer close within his circle precisely because he knew of Fixer's own secret communications with the lord treasurer. If Burghley believed this confession, then Robert Cecil knew he was playing a delicate game with his agent.[18]

John Cecil stayed quietly in London in late winter and early spring 1594. He appears to have put nothing down on paper: we might assume he gave his reports and took his instructions in private interviews. There is a single fragment of evidence which hints at his whereabouts. On Tuesday 12 March William Wade, clerk of the Privy Council, was at his house on Wood Street, the bustling city street that led from the Eleanor Cross on Cheapside up to Cripplegate. Wade wrote to Sir Robert: 'I have discharged my guest and given him twenty pound in gold as he desired to have it. Your honour shall hear from him so soon as he shall be on the other side. I sent one of my servants to bear him company to Gravesend.'[19]

The mysterious career of John Cecil shows how complex were the manoeuvres between the Cecils and the leaders of dissident English Catholics abroad. Father John may have been compromised; perhaps he was working for Allen and Persons; probably he was trusted by neither side. Was he agent, double agent or even triple agent? It is impossible to know for sure; and it seems likely that Father John himself was not wholly conscious of how he was being used by Robert Cecil, a small piece in a game being played to anticipate the moves of the queen's enemies.

After 22 February 1594 events moved quickly in the Lopez investigation. Manuel Luis Tinoco had broken. He was starting to remember all kinds of details that until now he had forgotten. He made three new confessions in quick succession, 'calling many matters to memory', as he wrote to Robert Cecil from his prison cell. He wanted the allegations of treason to be put to Doctor Lopez's face.[20]

That same day Lord Burghley was struggling with 'continual melancholy cogitations both night and day' over the queen's business. He communicated to his son that he was feeling ill and weak. He did not mention Doctor Lopez.[21]

On 26 February Tinoco confessed that he himself was complicit in Lopez's treason. Tinoco had written a letter to Estevão Ferreira da Gama using as cover a communication about precious stones and their value. It was code for the treason: Lopez's murder of Elizabeth had been sanctioned by King Philip's officials in Brussels. 'The letters which I wrote ... which speaketh of pearls and the price of them was to give him [da Gama] to understand ... how that the Doctor would kill the Queen.' The doctor himself wrote the same day to Robert Cecil. He wanted to see both Essex and Cecil, desperate to save himself by volunteering as their spy, offering himself to queen and state. It was not enough to save his life, for by now Essex and Cecil were perfectly in step. Doctor Lopez's arraignment was two days away. The earl wrote to Cecil that he would tie up any remaining business with Elizabeth. He would see Cecil very soon: 'I wish you all happiness and rest.'[22]

On the morning of 28 February Essex and Cecil went hawking together. A few hours later Doctor Lopez was brought before a jury at the Guildhall in London, the most public of possible courtrooms – this was a moment for maximum publicity.

Lord Burghley had his own copy of the indictment. Cecil was present in the Guildhall to see justice done. The evidence of Lopez's treason as outlined by the attorney general and the solicitor general – his plot to poison Elizabeth, agreed with his Spanish controllers in February 1593, for which he was to receive a substantial reward from King Philip – was, for those who knew the evidence, convincingly watertight. His guilt was beyond doubt. Everyone knew it, most especially Robert Cecil.

Cecil was home at his apartment on the Strand by 4 p.m. He wrote to Thomas Windebank at court.

> The villain confessed all the day, that he had indeed spoken of this matter and promised it but all forsooth to cozen [deceive] the King of Spain but when he saw both his intent and overt fact were apparent, the vile Jew said that he did confess indeed to us that he had talk of it, but not he must tell true; he did belie himself and did it only to save himself from racking which the Lord knoweth our souls witness to be most untrue . . . , and the most substantial jury that I have seen have found him guilty in the highest degree of all treasons and judgment passed against him with an applause of all the world.

Lopez had claimed that his secret communications with Spanish agents – which he did not deny – had had the purpose of deceiving them into believing that his plot was real. But Cecil's point was that it was a double deception: Lopez really had intended to murder Elizabeth.

This was a day to remember and to mark. A great horror had been averted. That evening Cecil stayed up with Essex till after midnight.[23]

Thomas Windebank read Sir Robert's letter to the queen as soon as she was out of bed the next morning. Essex was tired but in a buoyant mood. 'You may be assured that you are wished all happiness,' he wrote to Cecil. He signed as 'Your affectionate friend, Essex'.[24]

In the middle of March Manuel Luis Tinoco wanted to return to mainland Europe. He asked William Wade about the protections promised him by Burghley in the safe conduct his lordship had sent to him in

Calais back in December. There were none: here Wade did not waste words. 'For it is only for his repair hither,' he wrote to Cecil, 'and with this clause to serve him for his return, if it shall be thought meet he should be returned back; how far he is from deserving that favour he himself doth confess, and I did satisfy him in that point of his passport before my Lord of Essex.' Burghley had drafted the safe conduct in such a way as to guarantee a return journey to Calais 'if he shall be sent back again from hence'. That *if* was life or death for Tinoco.[25]

Wade, of course, knew all about characters like Tinoco: 'For ever I took him to be a most excellent varlet.'[26]

A few weeks later both Manuel Luis Tinoco and Estevão Ferreira da Gama were tried for their parts, as they themselves had confessed, in the Lopez treason. On 18 February, before the earl of Essex and William Wade, da Gama had admitted that he knew all about the plot: he believed that Lopez would have poisoned the queen as soon as Philip II sent the money he had promised. Tinoco, too, admitted his part in the secret correspondence.[27]

At the London Guildhall on Thursday 14 March da Gama pleaded not guilty, but on being presented with convincing evidence of his conspiracies he confessed and was convicted of treason. Tinoco heard the evidence against him through a Portuguese interpreter. He accepted each charge. He acknowledged his faults and asked for mercy. Both men were returned to the Tower of London to await execution.

At about the time of Doctor Lopez's arraignment, Lord Burghley instructed William Wade to prepare a report on the plot: 'a short narration of the treasons of Doctor Lopez', as Wade himself called it. He wrote it at home on Wood Street during the time he entertained his secret houseguest, John Cecil. He didn't waste any time in getting to work. As well as the complex task of drawing together a tangle of intercepted letters and confessions, he felt a head cold coming on.[28]

The first attempt to frame a public account of the Lopez treason never made it to the printing press. The initiative was Burghley's. He did it in a characteristically elliptical way, taking the trial papers of the solicitor general, Coke, adding some commentary – here his private secretary Henry Maynard did most of the drafting – before passing the manuscripts to Francis Bacon, Robert Cecil's cousin, always eager to impress. In the early weeks of March Bacon was busy at work.[29]

Bacon's account of the plot was a lively piece of reportage seasoned with erudite references to classical history and literature. (This may have been why it was never published – Bacon enjoyed the words and drama too much.) One strong theme of his narrative was the timely intervention of divine providence. He brought some of his characters powerfully to life. The most compelling – the most evil too – was Lopez himself, a Jew affable and pleasing, mercenary and corrupt, 'subtle of himself, as one trained in practice; and besides, as wily as fear and covetousness could make him'. The queen, by contrast, is a model of integrity and honesty. At one point in Bacon's story Lopez asks the queen the question 'Whether a deceiver might not be deceived?' The line and scene belonged on the stage: the scheming poisoner toying with his innocent victim.[30]

It was on the stage on Tuesday 26 February – the day that a desperate Doctor Lopez had offered to Robert Cecil his service as a spy – that the earl of Derby's company of actors performed at the Rose theatre in Southwark a play that had been in and out of performance for a few years. It was *The Jew of Malta* by Christopher Marlowe.

Barabas, the play's protagonist, is a Jew of immense wealth and influence who seems, on the surface, to have adapted himself comfortably to Christian society. The secret reality is very different. Barabas reveals in the play his long career of evil and calculated betrayal, plotting the deaths of enemies and friends, practising usury and extortion, poisoning wells. In his young manhood he had been a student of medicine who had contrived to kill his patients.

The resonances with the Lopez treason were irresistible: the Rose's owner and impresario, Philip Henslowe, counted on that. As Ferneze, the governor of Malta, says in the play (or at least in the mid-seventeenth-century text which has come down to us):

> O fatal day, to fall into the hands
> Of such a traitor and unhallow'd Jew!
> What greater misery could heaven inflict? [5.2.14]

That Tuesday Henslowe took fifty shillings from the playgoers in the galleries. The audience was in the hundreds, about the same as for a performance of Shakespeare's *Titus Andronicus* in the same month. *The Jew of Malta* ran every ten days to a fortnight well into June.[31]

At about 3 p.m. on Wednesday 17 April the lieutenant of the Tower of London, Sir Michael Blount, received from the attorney general a warrant to deliver Lopez, da Gama and Tinoco to the gallows the following day. Hours later Elizabeth, caught in a moment of indecision, ordered a stay of execution; it was Sir Robert Cecil who informed Blount. By Thursday Blount, not sure how to proceed, was expecting a visit to the Tower by Cecil and Sir Thomas Heneage. The clock was ticking, as Cecil well knew. The warrant stood; the stay of execution was temporary. Without a decision by 6 p.m. the prisoners would have to die the following morning. Londoners, eager to see Lopez and his confederates on the gallows, were getting restive.[32]

Barabas died that day; Lopez, da Gama and Tinoco did not – their executions were postponed. The playgoers who crowded into the Rose theatre for *The Jew of Malta* added to Philip Henslowe's accounts the respectable sum of forty-eight shillings and sixpence.[33]

12

Credo in Deum

In early 1594 Francis Bacon, by now thirty-two years old, was as ambitious as ever. He wanted office and advancement. He wanted to impress. He hoped to attract a patron.

In February Bacon argued a challenging case in the Court of Exchequer. He did well; promotion looked almost certain. 'All is as well as words can make it,' wrote one expert observer, 'and if it please her Majesty to add deeds, the bacon may be too hard for the cook.' The pun, impossible to resist, was a sly reference to the queen's solicitor general, forty-two-year-old Edward Coke of Inner Temple, brilliant and ambitious, against whom Francis measured his own career.[1]

In April the queen appointed Sir Thomas Egerton master of the rolls and Coke replaced him as attorney general. In a patronage system that abhorred a vacuum, clients and patrons pressed to fill the solicitorship. As early as March, with foreknowledge of the promotions of Egerton and Coke, Bacon lobbied Egerton for the vacancy. Cousin Robert supported him.[2]

In the letter Robert Cecil wrote to Egerton from the Strand on Wednesday 27 March there are no obvious hesitations, no caveats, no half compliments, no evasions. Cecil praised Egerton's wisdom in having let Bacon make his case. Cecil and Bacon were family.

This I do assure you, that I have no kinsman living (my brother excepted) whom I hold so dear; neither do I think that you or any other can confer any good turn upon any gentleman (though I say it to you in private) likelier for his own worth to deserve it ... Sir, I could write more if I spake not in manner for myself, for so I assure you (in measure of love and affection) he stands unto me.[3]

Bacon was also an energetic lobbyist on his own behalf. As well as Egerton and Cecil, he approached Lord Keeper Puckering, Vice Chamberlain Heneage and, most important of them all, the earl of Essex. It was now Essex, the great patron, who pushed hardest. Where the destruction of Doctor Lopez had shown the earl to be vigilant in protecting the queen, now securing the solicitorship for Bacon would demonstrate his skill in influencing and persuading her. By late April Essex was co-ordinating his efforts at court with Heneage, keeping Bacon informed of progress with notes that were of necessity brisk: 'This I write in haste, because I would have no opportunity omitted in this matter of access [to Elizabeth].'[4]

With Essex there were always ups and downs. In May he was languishing once again in the doldrums. He felt he had a sickness coming on. But more than this his energy had stalled, his mood soured. He was for a time no longer the unconquerable hero but instead his shadow, the frustrated courtier and discontented councillor, side-lined and beset. Rebuffed on an issue in Privy Council and taking it personally, he went on a leave of absence to his house at Wanstead in rural Essex. On 3 May he explained himself to Cecil, writing late that Friday night: 'It becomes me not to censure the resolution of her Majesty and her Council. But I am glad I was not so much as present at it. If it do succeed well I am glad of it ... My absence is both forced by own business and warranted by her Majesty's leave.' Two days later he pressed Sir Robert to emphasize to Elizabeth Bacon's brilliance as the only qualified and suitable candidate for solicitor general.[5]

Bacon was already seeing any hope of office slipping away, and he was desperate to present himself at court. Closeted at Gray's Inn, he asked for Robert's help. Cecil wrote a short paragraph on the letter itself and returned it. He gave a rapier-sharp analysis of Bacon's situation. The problem was Essex. 'Cousin, I do think nothing cut the throat more of your present access than the earl's being somewhat troubled at this time. For the delaying, I think it not hard, neither shall there want my best endeavour to make it easy.'[6]

The waters calmed a little when Essex returned to court a couple of weeks later. On 13 May the earl spoke to the queen. He wasn't fully recovered: his head ached painfully. Yet he was earnest in pressing Bacon's candidacy, mentioning that during his leave of absence he had written on Bacon's behalf to Cecil. Elizabeth refused to talk to him about the suit; she made a joke of it. 'Her answer in playing jest', he wrote to Bacon of Elizabeth, 'was that she came not to me for that; I should talk of those things when I came to her, not when she came to me.' He wanted to reply, but the queen wouldn't let him: 'She stopped my mouth.'[7]

Essex spent the whole day and evening of 17 May walking the queen's private galleries. He took Elizabeth at her word. He went to her about Bacon's suit, again making his pitch, by now so well-rehearsed. And this time she responded, though with a coolness that was likely to have made Bacon shiver when Essex next day sent him an account of the audience. She told the earl that Bacon's powerful friends – Elizabeth mentioned Burghley and Essex himself – made men give a more favourable estimate of Bacon than they would otherwise do, hoping to impress her. She acknowledged Bacon's wit and gifts of speech and learning. But in matters of law she thought that he was better at impressing with the range of his knowledge than showing its depth, and here at least one other agreed – a close professional observer of Bacon who noted the 'unusual words wherewith he . . . spangled his speech' and the obscurity of his references. Elizabeth told Essex that the more he had pushed on Bacon, the more inclined she had been to resist him. One of them had to give way: it was not going to be the queen.[8]

The earl knew Elizabeth's methods. On the solicitorship she would stall and procrastinate. 'She did in this as she useth in all; went from a denial to a delay.' The queen told him that when the Privy Council was at court she would think about it; there was no need to rush to a decision. Essex replied that his sad heart had need of hasty comfort.[9]

In spring 1594 King James VI of Scotland sent two ambassadors to Elizabeth. Sir James Colville of Easter Wemyss and Edward Bruce had their first audience with the queen at Greenwich Palace on Saturday 4 May. A few days later they had a private meeting with Lord Burghley, Lord Admiral Howard, Lord Buckhurst and Sir Robert Cecil.[10]

The ambassadors' mission was a delicate one. Elizabeth was furious that James had not yet, so far as she was concerned, sufficiently

punished the three Scottish earls (Huntly, Errol and Angus) whose invasion plottings with Spain had been exposed in December 1592 and had
panicked her eighth parliament a couple of months later – hence Cecil's
bruising effort to squeeze tax bills out of a reluctant House of Commons in the spring of 1593. Back then Elizabeth had lectured James by
letter on his duties as king. She knew – as she was not afraid to tell
him – that his passivity and inaction in Scotland at facing their common
enemy put her kingdoms in danger. James resented her interference,
though he was careful not to risk the annual pension of four thousand
pounds that Elizabeth had been paying him since 1586. James called it
his 'gratuity'.

The two monarchs had fallen into a pattern of aggrieved misunderstanding. Elizabeth's own ambassador, sent to Edinburgh a few months
earlier, was Edward Lord Zouche. Perhaps he was chosen to make a
point: Zouche had sat on the commission to try Mary Queen of Scots,
and James was quick to take offence. 'Remember Zouche's person,' he
wrote in a memorandum, 'one of my mother's jury and enemy to my
title, being Burghley's dependar [adherent]'. James did not trust Burghley. Burghley, after all, had sent the Scottish queen to the executioner's
block.[11]

Even more provocative for James than Zouche's embassy was
Elizabeth's covert support for thirty-one-year-old Francis Stewart, earl
of Bothwell. Bothwell was a kinsman of James VI, once a companion
to the young king before the earl's ambitions led to open rebellion and
outlawry and, in July 1593, the forfeiture of his earldom. Elizabeth's
calculation – and it was a surprising one for a queen usually so conservative and averse to risk – was that the Protestant Bothwell was an
effective counterweight to a king of Scots who was refusing to face
down his rebel Catholic nobility. Naturally she disavowed all knowledge of help for Bothwell: Burghley and Cecil worked behind the
scenes to keep the earl and his supporters protected and supplied. It
was in the context of this covert aid that Cecil captured in twelve
words Elizabeth's long-practised skill at shifting responsibility away
from herself. 'The Queen', he wrote to Lord Zouche in January 1594,
'would have her ministers do that she will not avow.'[12]

James knew what was going on, even if he couldn't say so openly.
He didn't trust the Cecils, and the queen was frosty and combative.

And of course, in her view, she was always right. She wrote to James in May, haughty as ever: 'I am that prince that never can endure a menace at my enemy's hand, much less of one [James] so dearly treated.'[13]

Colville and Bruce brought with them two letters. The first was for Elizabeth; the second, as private and as delicate, for the earl of Essex. If the Cecils, father and son, were in lock-step on Scotland, then Essex had his own position and a back channel of communication with the king managed by Anthony Bacon. James was, after all, a potential candidate for Elizabeth's throne. Like all other courtiers – the Cecils included – Essex looked prudently to the future.[14]

After the conventional pleasantries of a first audience, the ambassadors got briskly to the main business. James complained bitterly about English support for Bothwell, pointing to the peril of helping rebels. Colville and Bruce expressed their monarch's feelings about Lord Zouche's high-handedness and inflexibility in negotiations. They reminded Elizabeth of the king's gratuity, thousands of pounds of which had not been paid, emphasizing the 'urgent occasions' for which James needed the money. This was the deal: the king would prosecute the rebel Catholic nobles so long as Elizabeth offered him favourable assistance.

James's own letter to Elizabeth explained all this. He went through the motions of politeness: she was his hope, his safe way between Scylla and Charybdis, and he looked to her for help and guidance. Yet near the end of the second page his tone changed when he quoted from Book VIII of *The Aeneid*: 'I trust ye will not put me in balance with such a traitorous counterpoise nor wilfully reject me, constraining me to say with Virgil *flectere si nequeo superos Acheronta movebo.*' 'If I cannot prevail upon the gods, I will stir up hell.' It sounded like a threat. Certainly Elizabeth took it as such.[15]

James's letter for the earl of Essex was also in his own handwriting – the clearest possible evidence of the king's favour. James asked Essex to support Colville and Bruce on their mission and to 'move and assist the Queen with your good advice not to suffer herself to be syled [deceived or betrayed, especially for the betrayer's own advantage] and abused any longer with such as prefer their particular and unhonest affections to the Queen's princely honour'. James meant here the Cecils.[16]

Edward Bruce, a St Andrews graduate in his mid-forties and James's trusted lawyer, a model of expert discretion, would turn out be one of the most important individuals in Robert Cecil's career. May 1594 was their first meeting. But for all his persuasive skills Bruce got nowhere with Elizabeth.

It was always meant to be a short special embassy, and by mid-May Bruce, in truth the lead negotiator, was winding it up. He met the queen on Wednesday 15 May. Two days earlier she had teased Essex over Bacon's preferment. Now she was showing her steel, refusing to budge on the question of money for James. Bruce told Elizabeth that he had heard from his king. James found it hard to believe that the queen would refuse to give him the money he needed, for which (so Bruce told Elizabeth) he was blaming his ambassador's 'evil service and indiscretion'. If Bruce's travails (real or not) were supposed to produce in the queen a softening of her position, it obviously didn't work. The ambassador wrote next day to Burghley, a little desperately, to emphasize the urgency of financial aid for James, trusting to his lordship's strong commitment to the deep friendship – the 'amity' – between Scotland and England.[17]

On 17 May Bruce had his last audience with Elizabeth and kissed her hand. He would set out north the following day, while Colville travelled on to France to the court of Henry IV. But events that Friday moved quickly.

By 2 p.m. Sir Robert had finished a letter to Robert Bowes at King James's court. In the light of Colville's and Bruce's embassy, Bowes was instructed to tell James that he, the king, had produced words, not deeds. Elizabeth would not be moved by threats: James's quotation from Virgil had angered her. Money would only follow a demonstration of 'the King's resolute course' against the Catholic earls.

Cecil told Bowes that he had written the letter because his father was too busy to attend to it himself. This was a version of the truth: Cecil did most of the writing but Burghley read the text carefully and added to the draft a paragraph of his own handwriting. This letter was too important not to receive the attention of the lord treasurer.[18]

And then, some time late in the afternoon or early evening, a courier arrived from Scotland. The situation had changed. Bowes's latest report indicated that James had at last acted against the rebels, or at least had shown a concrete willingness to do something about them: they would be punished. So a new letter had to follow the one dispatched by Cecil a few hours earlier, for Elizabeth now revised her original decision. The pension money would be delivered. But the queen wanted Bowes to make it very clear to James that it was not the king's 'sharp style in his letter' which had convinced her. 'You may see that the Queen's promise is of no particular sum, though they would have a gratuity and a portion, and I know not what.' It was just enough to keep James dangling.

Sir Robert Cecil's letter was Robert Bowes's authority to speak to James for Elizabeth: 'this shall be your warrant, which I must not deny.'

It was midnight and Cecil was still at his desk.[19]

To all of this there was a postscript, showing how quickly councillors' feathers could be ruffled. It shows too how sensitive the earl of Essex was over Scotland.

On 22 and 23 May Robert Bowes received both of Cecil's letters. The change in Elizabeth's instructions didn't make a difference: Bowes wasn't able to see James straight away. In fact, he had to wait a week, for the king was too busy preparing for a parliament – and perhaps wanting to make Bowes and Elizabeth wait. At audience on 30 May, James was garrulous as ever, telling Bowes with 'many liberal and pithy words' that he would use parliament to act with severity against the rebel Catholic earls. At last a breakthrough: this is what Elizabeth wanted, and the condition on which she would release money. When, a few days later, he received Bowes's report of the meeting, Cecil underlined this passage and wrote in the margin of the letter the opening statement of the Apostles' Creed, *Credo in Deum* – 'I believe in God'. It was a sigh of relief.[20]

But was Essex now being side-lined on Scotland, intentionally ignored by Elizabeth and Cecil? On 3 or 4 June the earl was reading letters to the queen, of which one may have been Bowes's report to Cecil of his audience with James on 30 May, annotated for commentary by a relieved Cecil. A letter on the queen's business was never entirely private: any minister might read it, just as Elizabeth might instruct any councillor to reply. But Essex was not happy: he felt something had been kept from him.

The missing link here is Essex's letter of complaint to Cecil. However, Cecil's reply to it, written on 4 June, survives intact. He tried to mollify and calm the earl. He had, he wrote, no secrets. All business was transparently open to Essex.

> My good lord, you shall not need to make ceremony with me for opening of any letters, public or private. If public, they be matters wherein your lordship hath a great partage [share or portion]. If private I dare trust you, seeing I am no loner, which humour indeed affords no company.

Cecil made sure to address the packet himself to Essex as a privy councillor and Garter knight. Sir Robert signed it on the outside. He was scrupulous in showing the earl all respect. Honour was due.[21]

Crisp, plain, simple, courteous. Robert Cecil used no spangled words. He took no refuge in rhetorical tricks. All openness, no room for misinterpretation. He addressed the earl of Essex as an equal. He was no subordinate. That was something Cecil needed to make plain.

On Friday, 7 June 1594 Doctor Lopez, Estevão Ferreira da Gama and Manuel Luis Tinoco were taken at last from the Tower by river up to Westminster. In the Court of King's Bench, they were told that they had been charged with high treason against the queen, had been tried, found guilty, and received judgment. Each was asked to say why he should not suffer death accordingly. Speaking Portuguese, da Gama and Tinoco were silenced by Attorney General Coke: Tinoco spoke for too long, da Gama tried in a prepared written statement to challenge the evidence against him. Lopez said in English that he had never meant to harm the queen.

The three prisoners were then taken on a roundabout route from Westminster Hall to the gallows: first across the Thames to King's

Bench prison in Southwark. There they were strapped to hurdles, dragged over London Bridge up to Leadenhall and so out of the city to Tyburn.

The chronicler and antiquary John Stow described what happened next. 'There [they were] hanged, cut down alive, holden down by strength of men, dismembered, bowelled, headed and quartered, their quarters set on the gates of the city.'[22]

Elizabeth stayed at Theobalds in the middle of June. A month later she visited Robert Cecil's house to have a conference with his father. The high summer weeks were taken up for Burghley by medicinal bathing: 'Sleep not too much, to cool baths go' was the advice in his almanac for July. Between treatments he entertained the earl of Essex, Lord Admiral Howard and Lord Hunsdon, the lord chamberlain.[23]

Burghley wrote to Robert on 21 July:

> I can affirm nothing of my amendment, but yet if hereafter my attendance shall be earnestly required, I shall be content to wear out my time at the court as I do here. I pray you in all your letters, certify me of the Queen's Majesty's health. For she being well, my sickness will not discomfort me.[24]

By the beginning of October Burghley had finished the first draft of the official narrative of the Lopez plot. He knew it needed further work.

Fifteen ninety-four had been a busy year for conspiracy, and over the summer the plots of Sir William Stanley's Irishmen had moved from interrogation chamber to courtroom. There had been the revelations, too, of a Jesuit priest, Henry Walpole, captured on the coast of Yorkshire, one of whose inquisitors in London was Francis Bacon, keen as ever to show his skills in service of the state. It was time by early autumn to make the connections across all the plots, to lay out publicly in print the skeins of conspiracy.

The acknowledged expert on the Lopez case was William Wade who, from his house on Wood Street on Monday 7 October, began a letter to Burghley with a courtier's humble apology for doing the job he had been instructed to undertake. He had read Burghley's discourse, adding to it here and there, amending some of the details. He was, he wrote, careful in his fact-checking: 'And because the whole course of proceeding in that cause is perfectly known to me, as my memory did serve me, I have noted the same that it may in all points agree with the truth.'[25]

Burghley emphasized Philip of Spain's hatred for Elizabeth.

It shall manifestly appear to the world, how unjust and dishonourable the King of Spain and his ministers' actions are against the Queen of England contrary to all warlike, princely, manlike, and Christian examples in any war, or other contentions by attempting to take the Queen of England's life not by arms or other warlike actions but secretly sundry ways by murders hateful to God and man . . . thereby to follow his long intended insatiable and so ambitious and earnest enterprise to conquer her kingdoms and countries.[26]

Robert Cecil read his father's final manuscript in October. He made one or two alterations more – a couple of facts restated, some points of emphasis. He explained the queen's right, in the context of Spanish hostility, to take any action that was necessary to protect herself. He explained the time it had taken to publish Lopez's treason in terms of necessary secrecy. He knew by instinct the minister's classic defence of 'need to know'.[27]

And so the plot was explained:

Lopez the physician . . . was of late years allured to do service secretly to the King of Spain . . . [He] did secretly advertise the King of Spain divers times of such occurrents of the Queen's Majesty's actions as he could by reason of his place attain unto: and afterward upon sundry motions made to him, he assented to take away the Queen's life by poisoning, upon a reward promised to him of fifty thousand crowns.

Da Gama and Tinoco had aided Lopez in his planning.[28]

Burghley was vague on who had first discovered Doctor Lopez's 'abominable conspiracy'. He mentioned no names, something typical of government pamphlets: officialdom was well hidden behind a veil of discretion. In the case of Lopez, God had revealed the plot to 'one of the lords of her Majesty's Council'. Was this privy councillor Lord Burghley himself? After all, it was he who had brought Tinoco over to England, so beginning the unravelling of the plot. Or was it Robert Cecil, the first investigator of Tinoco's espionage? Or the earl of Essex, who had pushed and strained so hard to bring down Lopez? Burghley's politic silence offered a kind of mirror in which each of these ministers might see his own reflection.[29]

It was Henry Maynard who, as ever, did most of the penwork: all he ever needed was a fresh quire of watermarked paper, his pen and ink. On Friday 1 November he wrote to his friend and colleague Michael Hickes about some patronage business. 'I could have little speech with Sir Robert Cecil, who only told me the matter was dispatched being in the midst of Lopez's treasons, which I hope is now brought to some pass, having written the same twice out containing sixteen leaves.' It was as near as Maynard ever came to complaining about his workload.[30]

A true report of the sundry horrible conspiracies to have taken away the life of the Queen's Majesty was produced by Charles Yetsweirt, a small-scale printer of legal textbooks whose workshop was at Temple Bar on Fleet Street, near to Middle Temple. 'For the more manifest proof of the matters' contained in the report, Yetsweirt printed an annex of key documents. For so complex and tangled a plot, it looks rather thin. The annex contained two confessions by Tinoco, one by da Gama and a single letter from the former to the latter. And absolutely nothing by the dangerous Doctor Lopez himself.[31]

13

Assured Friends

Both Robert Cecil and the earl of Essex had been in Cambridge for the commencement of the university's masters of arts in 1581. Cecil had then been eighteen, Essex, the new MA graduate with a taste for fashionable clothes and a talent for spending money he didn't have, fifteen. In February 1595 both men were in Cambridge again, this time for that year's commencement of the bachelors. The teenagers of 1581 were, fourteen years later, now privy councillors and ministers.

One senses that for Cecil it was something of a last-minute arrangement. Only days before commencement, the master of St John's College, William Whitaker, sent him a flustered letter offering Cecil the hospitality of his own chambers. 'My lodging is but mean: but the best I have, and all that I have, I most humbly and most willingly offer your honour: and if other things be wanting, yet I trust to provide them that you shall have quiet and sufficient rooms.' Doctor Whitaker wrote that Cecil's visit to the college was a double joy: 'my Lord Treasurer your honourable father was of this college, and I his poor chaplain'.[1]

Essex, by contrast, was well prepared. He took with him to Cambridge a whole entourage of noblemen and gentlemen. They were given honorary degrees, and it was Essex himself who set the questions for the BA scholars' competitive disputations. He and his followers saw plays at Trinity College and Queens' College. Doctor Whitaker preached before the earl. All this was the kind of show for which Essex had a gift. Was he promoting himself as an alternative patron to Burghley, the university's long-serving chancellor? A few years earlier, stuck in the military camp outside Rouen, he had grumbled at being snubbed (at least as he saw it) for high office at the University of Oxford. To make such a splash in the Cecils' Cambridge may have been irresistible. This was his time, 1595 his year.[2]

Essex loved followers, and his clientele, which he carefully cultivated, possessed rank and elegance. But they weren't all for show. The earl maintained within his household and following a kind of foreign policy think tank, of whom Francis Bacon and (particularly) his elder brother Anthony were founding members. Another recruit was the unapologetically disreputable Antonio Pérez, a defector from Spanish service, indeed, a former secretary to King Philip. In Cambridge in early 1595 Essex was on a new recruitment drive for talent, just as he was in Oxford.[3]

Essex's followers felt the frustrations of a system of court patronage in which the earl was so frequently blocked. That at least was how it felt, especially to Francis Bacon, who in 1595 was still stretched painfully out on tenterhooks over the vacant solicitor generalship: Elizabeth had not budged on making an appointment. At court Essex continued to press Bacon's suit while the queen gently rebuffed him. In January Bacon withdrew to his country retreat at Twickenham Park – a gift from Essex – to play the tormented courtier. Elizabeth wanted him back at court and sent Robert Cecil to find his cousin – this was just a few weeks before the Cambridge commencement. By March 1595 Bacon was back in London in his chambers at Gray's Inn, from where he wrote to his uncle Burghley, calling himself 'a tired sea-sick suitor' (he took the metaphor from the Roman poet Ovid), explaining his time in Twickenham: he wished to 'be out of eye, I absented myself'. His suit he left to his friends to pursue for him and the queen to decide on.[4]

Bacon called cousin Robert his 'right honourable kinsman and good friend'. This was necessary politeness, and a nod to the fact that Cecil had the kind of credit with Elizabeth of which Bacon could only dream. Behind the facade it was different. To many in Essex's circle it seemed that the Cecils preferred over all others their own unexceptional clients: dull mediocrity suppressed (their own) flair and brilliance. This point of view was one which could only be spoken in private, or muttered quietly in chambers and galleries, usually carefully coded, hidden away. Antonio Pérez, however, possessed no such filter. In a letter to Essex in late summer he wrote that

'Aeolus' – 'Spirit', Elizabeth's familiar name for Lord Burghley – was more favourable towards Pérez than the dwarf-like hunchback who would be better advised to stoop with his hunch than beg with his mouth. Pérez reflected that persons with misshapen bodies and souls were more agreeable when they couldn't be seen.[5]

For Lord Burghley business in 1595 was unremitting. At court Robert Cecil took up some of the strain, but his father's small memorandum book was filled every day with matters to tend to, multiplying all the time – some were crossed out as completed, many were pending. There was no peace, no rest. In July he was stuck in Exchequer and Guildhall in London, fantasizing about escape from pestering suitors – he didn't care where to. In September, with Westminster jittery about Spanish invasion plans and Burghley planning the defence of the kingdom, he ended a letter to Robert with a note that 'The misty weather creepeth in to my head through my hat and caps.' Less than a week later Cecil was ferrying his father's letters between court and Theobalds. On 8 October Burghley took physic. It didn't work. A week later he was having trouble sleeping. His head ached so badly that he could barely read. He signed a letter to Robert with the Greek name *Akepholos* – headless.[6]

In autumn the earl of Essex also attended to business, authorizing Privy Council letters with Burghley and Cecil – an unlikely but significant triumvirate. As an earl, as master of her Majesty's horse and as a knight of the Garter he signed level with the 'W. Burghley' that the lord treasurer scratched out with his painfully stiff fingers; even Henry Maynard couldn't help him here. Cecil's signature sat a little way down below. It was a small, significant reminder of Essex's superiority of rank and nobility.[7]

But things were not happy between Elizabeth and the earl. One source of court news from late September said that she was being fed 'tales of my Lord of Essex . . . which brings unquietness in the Queen and occasions the like in my lord'. His private life was and had been difficult. Five years earlier he had married in secret Secretary Walsingham's daughter Frances, the widow of the soldier and poet Sir Philip Sidney. Their separation, and the fact of Essex's numerous affairs with women at court, was frequently a source of friction with the queen: she hated sexual indiscretions. In addition, there was now a report of a book, printed in Antwerp, which put the earl under a particularly uncomfortable spotlight. *A Conference about the Next Succession to the Crown of England*, by the Jesuit Robert Persons (but issued under the pseudonym R. Doleman), explained and justified the claim of Philip II of Spain to the English throne. Out of political malice, Persons had dedicated the book to Essex, 'of an intent surely to bring him in jealousy and disgrace of it' as one of the longest-serving clerks of the Privy Council, Robert Beale, put it. As well as all this – which was really enough to be going on with – the earl's placing of Francis Bacon as solicitor general was being frustrated still.[8]

So Essex was prickly. Someone – perhaps he himself, perhaps one of his followers – said something to or about the queen he should not have done. This was in October, and Cecil, through a letter to Essex, tried to draw a line under it.

Cecil chose his words very carefully. Elizabeth and Burghley had already written to Essex; Cecil's job was to make sure his lordship understood the warning – the queen, after all, was never wrong. The business was now over, to be forgotten. But Cecil did need to emphasize one more thing, and here he was on sensitive ground. Essex's followers at court had not been helpful to their patron's cause. Professed friendship, Cecil suggested, was not always quite what it seemed.

He signed his letter as Essex's loving and assured friend.[9]

In the first week of October Burghley was ruminating over Doleman's offensive *Conference*. It was a month later, on Monday 3 November, that Elizabeth showed the book to Essex. He was unlikely to have forgotten the experience quickly. One observer noted that he left the court ashen-faced, 'being exceedingly troubled at this great piece of villainy done unto him . . . he is sick, and continues very ill'.[10]

Persons argued for Philip II's direct claim to the English throne through his fourteenth-century ancestor John of Gaunt, duke of Lancaster and son of King Edward III. The pseudonymous Doleman affected to be a loyal and long-standing supporter of the Devereux family. He honoured Essex's noble blood and dignity, and in dedicating the book to the earl, Persons delivered his full punch: 'I thought no man more fit than your honour . . . for that no man is in more high and eminent place or dignity at this day in our realm, than yourself.' Essex was of the highest nobility, in great favour with the queen and popular with the common people. No one would have 'greater part or sway' in deciding the royal succession 'when the time shall come for that determination' – in other words, when Elizabeth was either dying or dead.[11]

Whatever the queen said to Essex that November morning sent him to his chamber to nurse his bruises.

He recovered quickly from his solitary misery. Essex was in retreat for at least four days, slowly gathering himself for action. By mid-November he was in better shape than Burghley. The lord treasurer was confined to bed, with Henry Maynard and Cecil managing his visitors and suitors. On 16 November Burghley was the only great officer of state missing from the council meeting at Whitehall Palace. It was a Sunday, the eve of Accession Day.

Accession Day had been a fixture of the national calendar for decades. It celebrated the anniversary of the queen's accession, 17 November 1558, marking God's providence in protecting Elizabeth and her kingdoms, especially after the defeat of the Spanish Armada in 1588. In towns and cities there were bonfires, the ringing of church bells and sermons, and at court lavish entertainments. This year it was Essex's turn to put on the great show – a reverential entertainment for her sacred Majesty, in the Whitehall tiltyard and in the palace.

It was the fruit of a number of brains and pens within Essex's circle, of whom Francis Bacon was almost certainly one. Essex himself was the impresario, and the players in the entertainment were the same scholars from Cambridge who, in March, at the bachelors' commencement, had performed a Latin comedy called *Laelia* for the earl and his entourage.

This was the opportunity for the earl of Essex to shine.

On Accession Day morning Essex sent one of his pages to read a speech to the queen. The page returned with her glove, a sign of her favour. When Essex arrived at the tiltyard, close to the Holbein Gate at Whitehall Palace, spectators saw him greeted in dumb show by an old hermit, a secretary and a soldier, along with a squire, who was his master's – that is Essex's – servant. What happened next put Essex at the centre of things. The Hermit presented the earl with a book of meditations, the Secretary a set of political discourses, the Soldier with accounts of great battles. Soon after this a courier arrived in a great rush, riding a worn-out horse, huffing and puffing. To the character of the Secretary he delivered a packet of letters. The Secretary then handed them on to Essex.

The resonances with the entertainments at Theobalds in 1591 and 1594 were unmistakeable: no courtier would have missed them. The Hermit in particular stood out. Essex's entertainment looked like satire, a deliberate poke at the Cecils – the father portrayed as a tired old man, the son as an unscrupulous politician ambitious for power – and a positioning by Essex of himself as Elizabeth's only true supporter. The characters of the Hermit (Burghley), Secretary (Cecil) and Soldier (an old-fashioned warrior, quite unlike the dazzling hero Essex) were each introduced to Elizabeth and the audience by the Squire. The Hermit, Secretary and Soldier, he said, were followers of 'Philautia', or Self-Love.

Through his own words, the character of the Secretary revealed himself to be cynical, superficial and ruthless. 'Let him not trouble himself too laboriously to sound into any matter deeply,' he said, 'or to execute anything exactly: but let him make himself cunning rather in the humours and drifts of persons, than in the nature of business and affairs.' He succeeded only by suppressing the brilliance of others: 'Of that it sufficeth to know only so much as may make him able to make use of other men's wits, and to make again a smooth and pleasing report; let him extenuate the propositions of others.'[12]

The Squire had the last word, and what a contrast he offered to the old worn Hermit, full of wandering aphorisms and platitudes, and the self-serving Machiavellian Secretary. But the Squire's master was best of all, the only character who did not speak for himself that Monday: 'Erophilus', the Lover of Love, the earl of Essex – the queen's only true servant.[13]

Less than a week after the entertainment a courtier commented:

> The world makes many untrue constructions of these speeches, com-
> paring the [characters of the] hermit and the secretary to two of the
> lords [of the Privy Council] ... but the Queen said that if she thought
> there had been so much said of her, she would not have been there that
> night, and so went to bed.

Courtiers knew that Essex had been mocking Burghley and Cecil.[14]

They sensed, too, that Elizabeth had colluded in the satire. She had, after all, taken in the whole performance. Following the Accession Day entertainment, the queen had been elusive, irritated by the conclusion which was being drawn from the fact she had stayed on to watch the players for the rest of the evening. As usual, she kept her true thoughts to herself. She used misdirection and obfuscation – the old discipline. At the age of fourteen she had admitted that it was 'rather characteristic of my nature not only not to say in words as much as I think in my mind, but also indeed, not to say more than I think'. At sixty-two she was not so very different.[15]

The Secretary's speech was satire, and Robert Cecil – characterized as a cunning and scheming bureaucrat – its target. But the world did not fall in on itself after the Accession Day entertainment, as it was never likely to do. Life at court carried on as normal. Business, gossip, activity, change, challenge, frustration – the usual mix. Burghley, still confined more or less to the Strand, struggled through papers and business, Henry Maynard as ever his uncomplaining shadow. The earl of Essex, the great patron, dined with his friends. Robert Cecil attended his queen.[16]

'I cannot be long silent from actions.' So Cecil wrote in January 1596 to Thomas Bodley, the latest of Elizabeth's representatives on the Dutch Council of State. It was a letter in Sir Robert's own hand, brisk and to the point. He was always busy, always alert and always on call.[17]

Serving Elizabeth was an art. Anticipating her decisions took skill;

making them a reality called for creativity and suppleness of judgement. None of this was easy or straightforward. In matters of policy the queen so often went backwards and sideways – going forwards was something she found more difficult. With timing and patience, the minister nudged and influenced, opening up possibilities, quick with objections, taking the temperature of the situation, mixing gentleness and purpose. He was the alchemist who transformed base bureaucracy into the gold of service.

With Elizabeth there was a time for chat and banter, a time for hard-headed discussion. Judgement was everything. The minister had to listen carefully to the queen's words. In the right conditions he made them his own. In January 1596 clever Thomas Lake of the signet office received a draft document from Elizabeth, a routine-enough event: it was Lake's job to turn it into a fair copy. The draft was heavily corrected by Elizabeth: 'blotted and interlined' was how Cecil described it. Elizabeth, Cecil wrote to Lake, was 'curious' in expressing herself on paper: he meant careful and fastidious. Cecil gave Lake the go-ahead to get to work. He approved of the text as Elizabeth had finessed it: 'If you read all unput out, you read as much as I would have inserted.' In other words, he would have written as the queen had written. She and he, monarch and minister, were in happy synchrony.[18]

By now Robert Cecil's long-served apprenticeship was over. Probably he knew it himself. He was still, naturally, briefed and instructed by his father, who in early 1596 was kept at home by illness and winter cold. But Robert's self-confidence, his deftness and feel for command, had over half a decade grown so much. He was at last an artificer of counsels, as his father had described the job of principal secretary early in Elizabeth's reign. He was not secretary quite yet. But he didn't have so long to wait.

14

'Believe Cecil'

In the long and wearing conflict against Spain, the earl of Essex saw himself as a military strategist whose push for decisive action had to be listened to for the protection of queen and country. Other ministers might suggest defensive alliances, such as the one Lord Burghley proposed in autumn 1595. Responding to consistent intelligence reports of a forthcoming Spanish invasion of England, Burghley had suggested the idea of prodding King James VI to join Elizabeth by sending him a copy of Robert Persons's *Conference*, 'hereby to move him ... against these the King of Spain's tyrannous practices'. This played on James's dynastic self-interest as a future claimant to the kingdoms of England and Ireland: *Conference* maintained the Spanish counterclaim. Burghley asked Cecil to put the idea to Elizabeth with urgency. But Essex and his circle of advisers believed that King Philip's squeezing grip on Europe could be broken only by a superlative show of force: attack, not simply defence. By the spring of 1596 Essex was working tirelessly to put together an expedition to save Protestant Christendom.[1]

Every so often Lord Burghley liked to give Robert Cecil a distillation of his life's wisdom. His philosophy was a heavy one, filled with aphorisms of Ciceronian duty; one could never say that Burghley was blessed with a lightness of touch. But when he was in the mood, he liked to capture truth in a paradox. Saturday, 13 March 1596 was such a day. To Robert he took a few moments, in 165 words, to consider the shape and nature of his service to the queen, and her service to the highest power of all.

I do hold, and will always, this course in such matters as I differ in opinion from her Majesty, as long as I may be allowed to give advice: I will not change my opinion by affirming the contrary, for that were to offend God, to whom I am sworn first; but as a servant I will obey her Majesty's commandment, and no wise contrary the same, presuming that she be God's chief minister.

Should the councillor obey God or monarch? Obviously he should obey both. But God's will came first, to be discerned by the minister. 'You see I am in a mixture of divinity and policy, preferring in policy her Majesty afore all others on the earth and in divinity the king of heaven above all, betwixt alpha and omega.'

'This my cogitations you may use to your own good,' he told Robert, 'beseeching God to bless you.'[2]

So many years before, Burghley, as plain Sir William Cecil, had observed that most of the time Elizabeth reacted to events: there was little planning ahead. 'Epimetheus [afterthought] hath had more to do than Prometheus [forethought]', as he had put it. Events – often unexpected, sometimes disturbing – had Elizabeth's ministers doing their best to respond. Often, they felt powerless.

The news that arrived at court on Good Friday 1596, 9 April, shocked even the most experienced of them. The town of Calais, held by Elizabeth's ally King Henry IV of France, had been captured by a Spanish army; its citadel was under heavy siege. The enemy was at England's door.

The irony is that for weeks Robert Cecil had been working to assemble a military expedition against Spain to be led by the earl of Essex and Lord Admiral Howard, working out with the queen all the intricacies of their co-generalship of Elizabeth's forces. Their objective was to destroy a fleet reported to be gathering off the coast of Spain. That now had to change; there was a new, urgent priority. Over the Easter weekend Westminster and the City of London were mobilized. Within twenty-four hours of the news of Calais arriving at court, Essex was given the authority to raise and command an army of six thousand men to relieve Calais. The Spanish expedition was paused.

Burghley was certain that without Elizabeth's quick intervention, all of Calais would be lost. But already she was wavering. On 10 April he wrote to Cecil:

> I am heartily sorry to perceive her Majesty's resolution to stay this voyage, being so far forward as it is, and surely I am of opinion that the citadel being relieved the town will be regained, and if . . . it shall be lost, by judgement of the world the blame will be imputed to her.

There would be grave consequences if Calais were captured by the Spanish.[3]

That same day Essex was hoping to leave London from Tower Wharf. He was in Dover by the evening of the 12th and wrote to Cecil at 10 a.m. the following morning. The earl could hear the heavy fire of batteries of artillery from across the Channel. Eleven hours later he and Lord Howard wrote to Burghley that they desperately needed supplies which had been left behind at Tower Wharf. There was a sensation of panic, with reports of a possible Spanish fleet west of Boulogne. It felt like a fight against time.

These were difficult days for Howard, who was fuming on Tuesday 13 April that primary command of the relief force had been given to Essex. It was to Cecil that he made his protest, and so urgently that he covered the packet in 'post hastes'. He couldn't have been plainer. He wrote that his office of lord admiral counted for nothing. He wanted to be relieved of his command: he said he would prefer the Tower of London. 'My commission in being joined with the earl is an idle thing for I am used but as the drudge . . . This is far from that which her Majesty made show to me at my departure.'[4]

Even Essex was unsettled by the magnitude of Howard's anger: he saw that it might so easily compromise a mission that was hanging in the balance. Like Howard, Essex wrote to Cecil: Cecil needed to contain at court a potentially combustible situation:

> I never [saw] so afflicted a man as my Lord Admiral . . . By Christ, I am so sensible of it as I have written to the Queen in passion. I pray you, as you love either of us, or the service, get it discharged . . . I pray you

show not my Lord Admiral's letter to the Queen, for it is too passionate, and it may break all our actions, if she take him at his word.[5]

Wednesday 14 April felt like the day of reckoning. Essex at Dover had heard the enemy batteries pounding the Calais citadel since day-break. No instructions arrived from court. He feared the worst; he felt the frustration of inaction. At 6 p.m. he finished a letter to Cecil:

> I pray you think it is the greatest scorn in the world to lie here, in sight of a French king that stays but to join with us, and of a place that imports us and all our friends in these parts of Christendom so much, and to have moved an expectation of doing somewhat, and yet to have our hands tied . . . Sir, I am so full as I know not what I write . . . I pro-test before God I would redeem the infamy of it with many ounces of my blood, if bargain could be made.[6]

He was still at his desk six hours later, still stewing over Calais. He wrote to Burghley: 'I wish myself in another world, where I might not hear the complaints that through all Christendom will run upon us for losing such a place, and in such a manner as this is like to be.'[7]

As Essex was ruminating in Dover, Elizabeth was aboard the *Due Repulse*, a new warship of over forty guns. She was in a Tilbury mood, heroic and authoritative, and wrote in her own hand to General Essex. Simon Willis made copy for his master's archive.

> As distant as I am from your abode, yet my ears serves me too well to hear that terrible battery that methinks sounds for relief at my hands; wherefore, rather than for lack of timely aid it should be wholly lost, go you, in God's blessed name, as far as that place where you may soonest relieve it, with as much caution as so great a trust requires. But I charge you, without the mere loss of it, do in no wise peril so fair an army for another prince's town. God cover you under his safest wings, and let all peril go without your compass.

Here was the command to act with both decision and caution. Eliz-abeth ended with a sentence of five words: 'Believe Cecil in the rest.'[8]

It was now too late. Within hours the Calais citadel fell to the enemy. Protestant Europe was more vulnerable than ever.

The purpose of Essex's and Howard's expedition, postponed by the Calais panic, was first to destroy King Philip's new fleet and then to intercept his treasure ships returning home from the Caribbean. The English fleet would see action alongside a Dutch contingent – going to war was a multinational endeavour. No Spanish towns or cities would be occupied. In a printed pamphlet translated into Dutch, French, Italian, Spanish and Latin, Elizabeth's government publicized to Europe the fact 'that her Majesty armeth her navy only to defend herself and to offend her enemies'.[9]

Essex left court in early May on strained terms with the queen. They differed on how aggressive the mission should be. In Plymouth, where the senior commanders of the expedition were gathering, he nursed his unhappiness. A letter to Elizabeth he sent first to Cecil, expecting him to read it to her.

> This is only to protest unto your Majesty that the print of your unkind dealing (if I may presume to use that phrase) the very day of my departure doth stick very deeply in very heart and soul . . . Perhaps it had been too much for me to go with this force, by which I know we can do your Majesty exceeding great service, and to have parted with words of encouragement from your Majesty. But howsoever it pleaseth you to punish me at my going out, I know your just and royal heart will right me at my return and then I will bury my sorrows in the joy I shall receive.[10]

Essex justified himself. How much he had worked, he wrote to Cecil, how much he wanted to serve. He had asked nothing of the queen. Everything for this expedition he alone had organized, stretching himself to his limits, and all for Elizabeth.

> I am myself, I protest, engaged more than my state is worth; my friends, servants and followers have also set up their rests: my care to bring a chaos into order, and to govern every man's particular unquiet humours

possesseth my time both of recreation and of rest sometimes and yet am I so far from receiving thanks, as her Majesty keepeth the same form with me as she would do with him that through his fault or misfortune had lost her troops. I receive no[t] one word of comfort or favour by letter, message or any means whatsoever.

He said he would neither blame the queen nor justify himself. He would cast off all care of himself to serve her. And he was aggressively plain with Cecil, who was either with him or against him: 'you do wrong me and betray her service if you do not put her Majesty in mind how much she is bound in honour and justice to be protectress of me against all the world but mine own actions.'[11]

Sailing with the expedition was another of Cecil's first cousins, the son of his mother's sister Elizabeth, thirty-six-year-old Sir Edward Hoby. On 31 May, from Plymouth Sound aboard the *Ark Royal*, Hoby wrote what he hoped would not be his final letter to Robert. He owed his cousin an apology: before leaving for the coast he hadn't visited Robert's chambers to say goodbye. Most of all he regretted not seeing Bess Cecil: 'my error was before my departure not to come to the honourable lady for her favour (to whom of all the court I rest most bound) and to whom to excuse me, I most humbly beseech your honour but the remembrance of her.' Hoby began a postscript. 'If I perish in this action . . .' Quickly he recovered himself. 'But what? I mean to come home again, to play the wag once again.'[12]

That same day the flag of the red cross of St George flew on *Ark Royal* to mark the first meeting of the council of war. In the evening Anthony Ashley, the council's secretary, back on board his own ship the *Due Repulse*, reported the day's events to Cecil. Ashley, temporarily on secondment from the Privy Council office, had long been a keen student of navies and navigation.

Elizabeth wrote a prayer for the fleet which Cecil sent to Ashley. 'The devout prayer so divinely conceived by her Majesty (and sent by your last) is so thankfully and cheerfully accepted,' wrote Ashley, 'that there is no less hope of good effect thereby, than was wished at what time it was conceived in the depth of her sacred heart.' Essex and

Howard ordered the prayer to be recited by the sailors and soldiers of the expedition as an 'invocation unto the Lord, purposely indicted by his spirit in his anointed Queen, his instrument in this action'.[13]

Elizabeth asked the omnipotent Creator for his protection:

We humbly beseech thee with bended knees, prosper the work and with best fore winds guide the journey, speed the victory, and make the return the advancement of thy glory, the triumph of their fame, and surety to the realm, with the least loss of English blood. To these devout petitions, Lord, give thou thy blessed grant.[14]

Essex had left a letter for the queen to be opened only when the fleet had set sail and was beyond recall. He stated very clearly that he knew what had to be done, even if Elizabeth and those ministers who preferred to cower in fear before King Philip did not. He intended, quite deliberately, to disobey his orders. 'On the coast of Spain your troops shall possess ports unguarded, and, if you please, take towns unfortified . . . to give your Majesty great glory.'[15]

Very early in the morning of Sunday 20 June the English fleet was close to the city of Cadiz on the south-western coast of Spain, the port of Philip II's fleet. They were riding about a league offshore and the weather was poor. A squadron of large Spanish ships sailed out from the bay of Cadiz bound for the Atlantic, estimated at about forty merchantmen and nineteen or twenty galleys. The English lookouts kept careful watch over night.[16]

On Monday the conditions had improved, and Howard and Essex ordered the fleet to attack the Spanish ships. Roger Marbeck, Lord Howard's personal physician on the expedition, described the battle as 'very hot . . . very terrible, and most hideous to the beholder by the continual discharging of those roaring thundering great pieces on all sides'. The Spanish fleet broke: the galleys escaped, the merchantmen, some bound for the West Indies, others laded for Lisbon, either ran aground or were boarded.

Essex lost no time in ordering and leading an amphibious landing: 'Immediately upon this notable victory, without any further stay in the world, the lord general . . . put to shore' in a sandy bay at Puntales with about three thousand pikemen and musketeers. They were three miles or so south-west of Cadiz, on the eastern side of the narrow peninsula which was crowned by the city. The day was hot, the going hard over heavy sand. Marbeck described how a company of Spanish cavalry and infantry were waiting for them. This first fight was over in an hour, and Essex's force won it: 'the most famous earl with his valiant troops, rather running indeed in good order than marching, hastened them on with . . . unspeakable courage and celerity.' Essex's men then scaled and held the walls of Cadiz, after which the two lords general entered the city. Sir Edward Hoby carried the colours. That same day Cadiz surrendered. Howard and Essex marked their victory by knighting sixty-three noblemen and gentlemen.[17]

Cadiz was a rich and impressive city, and even Marbeck's gener-ously positive account of those intense days of fighting and victories couldn't ignore the soldiers' and mariners' pillaging for spoils as well as their general disorder. Slowly discipline was restored: the generals held governing councils between 23 and 25 June. On Sunday 27th, they heard divine service in the city's cathedral. The sermon was preached by one of Essex's chaplains. For a few hours Elizabeth's Church of England challenged in his own kingdom the pious ortho-doxy of the Most Catholic King Philip.[18]

'I am glad that I may truly direct my letters to your honour from her Majesty's city of Cadiz, not in fancy, but won and yet held by her soldiers' swords': so Sir George Carew wrote to his friend Cecil on 30 June. Carew had already sent to Lord Burghley a full report of the city's capture, so to Cecil he gave a three-page summary. Sir Anthony Ashley – the secretary to the council of war and one of those knighted – was going to be sent back to England with the news that the generals had decided (in Carew's words) 'to quit the town with as much exped-ition as they may'. They had intended to keep Cadiz but had not the supplies to hold out for any length of time. In Carew's judgement, Essex had shown extraordinary energy and courage. He had led his troops from the front and had been involved in the most perilous fighting. 'I do conclude him in my private opinion to be as worthy a subject as hath been born in England in my age, and . . . I think he will prove as gallant a commander as any in Europe.'[19]

From Cadiz Sir Edward Hoby, too, had written to his cousin Robert. Like Carew, he had sent to Burghley a longer letter. Hoby was thinking of Bess Cecil. 'I would not have troubled your honour thus far, but that none shall pass me, without remembrance of my duty unto you and my honourable lady, whose fair hands most humbly kissing I rest.'[20]

On Sunday 4 July Elizabeth's generals ordered Cadiz to be 'razed and defaced so much as they could'. Only the cathedral, churches and religious houses would be spared. Cadiz was stripped of all useful provisions and anything of value that could be carried away. Then it was torched.[21]

On Monday, with Cadiz smoking, the English fleet sailed for home. That same day, some hundreds of miles away at Greenwich Palace, Sir Robert Cecil was getting a long-desired promotion.

15

Maecenas

Robert took his oath as secretary on the afternoon of Monday 5 July. Four other ministers were in the council chamber at Greenwich: Lord Keeper Egerton, Lord Treasurer Burghley, Lord Cobham and Lord Buckhurst. In the clerks' register book William Wade noted the appointment in his best handwriting: 'This day by her Majesty's express commandment Sir Robert Cecil, knight, second son to the Lord Treasurer, was sworn Principal Secretary to her Majesty.' Then it was down to business.[1]

He was Secretary Cecil at last. Sir Francis Walsingham had died in 1590. Lord Burghley had taken up the secretary's workload, over time sharing some of it with Robert. For the Cecils, Robert's appointment was long in the planning, hoped for and expected, at least so far as anyone at Elizabeth's court could expect anything. Politics – especially with this queen – was a life full of uncertainty with high ambitions unfulfilled: and Elizabeth had procrastinated over the vacant secretaryship for years.

Cecil had been at court now for twelve years, five of them in the queen's inner circle. He was skilled at business, assiduous and stable of temperament. It was clear that his father's health was fragile. He had been Burghley's voice at court and he had the queen's trust. He was able to read her and she him; both had the measure of the other. Most recently the Calais panic, where Cecil had co-ordinated the gathering of the makeshift relief force, had shown something of his abilities. As Elizabeth herself had written to the earl of Essex only a few months earlier, 'Believe Cecil in the rest.'

He knew the scale of the job. It had made some of the early candidates for the secretaryship, all highly experienced and extraordinarily able, nervous. One essay on the secretary's responsibilities, by Robert Beale, a clerk of the Privy Council, was as long as twenty modern, closely printed pages. The secretary was the engine of the whole government: the job was complex, a mass of responsibilities all overlapping, and delicate and sensitive too. The view of Sir Francis Walsingham's private secretary, Nicholas Faunt, was that the secretaryship defied any prescribed form: the secretary had to find his own way of working.[2]

Congratulating Cecil four days after the oath-taking, Roger Lord North hoped that Cecil's 'painful and faithful service . . . will encourage you to undergo the great burden you are charged withal'. 'The Lord bless you in all your counsels and actions and assist you with his Holy Spirit that you may . . . grow more and more worthy.'[3]

It was a time of change, as Lord North himself knew, appointed treasurer of the queen's household two months after Cecil's promotion, with Cecil's father-in-law William Cobham now Elizabeth's lord chamberlain. It was a typically conservative finessing of the council. Elizabeth made her appointments, slowly, from her circle of trusted advisers.[4]

Burghley was still lord treasurer and still the weightiest of the queen's ministers. But he also wasn't slow to pass to Robert a heavy pile of papers from his own desk. On 8 July his lordship was in the country trying to escape the press of suitors. The journey from Westminster to the privacy of Theobalds had been grim – he complained that unseasonably heavy rain had made the road worse than it was in midwinter – and he had new pains in his knees and feet. He hoped they were improved before he returned. 'I have thought to put you in remembrance of these things following', he wrote. His summary of the eleven tasks he was now handing to Secretary Cecil ran to two pages. By the end of the letter Burghley's hand was aching.[5]

The lord treasurer was troubled by gout that Thursday night, but well enough the following morning, Friday, to ride his mule into the great gardens at Theobalds: it was a favourite pastime. While his master was out, Henry Maynard wrote to Sir Robert with a couple of other matters of business to add to his list. On Saturday Burghley sent another letter to his son, his hand now a little steadier. 'God bless you and give you grace to serve her Majesty with her contentation by your faithfulness, dutiful love and diligence.'[6]

Was this the hermit of Theobalds finding at last the peace and quiet of retirement, retreating to his garden walks and homely septuagenarian meditations? Not really, as Burghley's sister-in-law and Sir Robert's aunt, Anne Bacon, well knew. On 10 July she wrote to her son Anthony, a passionate partisan of the earl of Essex, with a warning. Now that Cecil was secretary – 'fully stalled in his long longed-for secretary's place' was how she phrased it – she told Anthony that he now needed 'to be more circumspect and advised in your discoursings, doings and dealings in your accustomed matters, either with or for yourself or others'. The secretary had considerable influence. Together Burghley and Cecil were as one: 'The father and son are affectionate [ambitious], joined in power and policy.'[7]

She wanted Anthony to burn the letter, which he didn't do.

On 28 July Sir Anthony Ashley was making his way to Salisbury and on to court. It had been a long journey from Spain. He arrived at Greenwich three days later, where he explained to Elizabeth and her council what Essex and Lord Admiral Howard had done, and now would do, in Cadiz. Given that Ashley had set out for England before the generals had made any final decision at their council of war on 9 July, this latter had to be a best guess.[8]

Secretary Cecil now had the letters from Sir George Carew and Sir Edward Hoby, and he knew enough about the expedition to give David Foulis, James VI's agent at Elizabeth's court, the headlines of a stunning victory. The queen's generals had confirmed the taking of Cadiz and victory over a Spanish fleet of sixty ships. Some merchantmen were captured and burned, the forty ships bound for Mexico destroyed. English losses were few, spoils many, including two galleons' worth of brass ordnance and other military hardware. The following day, Sunday 1 August, Essex's letter to Cecil of 1 July arrived in Cecil's office: 'This letter shall carry to you my best wishes and shall assure you that I desire to give you all satisfaction, since by your industry and assistance we have had the means to do her Majesty and our country service.'[9]

Yet for all this, Sir Anthony Ashley got a much colder reception at court than he expected. Within a week of arriving at Greenwich he was feeling battered and bruised. His trunks and coffers had been searched. He was being cold-shouldered. He wrote plaintively to Lord Burghley, emphasizing his duty to the queen 'in place of a poor secretary . . . in this expedition'. He adapted a line from Seneca's essay 'On anger', in Ashley's words *Iniurias ferendo et gratias de ipsis agenda* – the Roman philosopher's observation that the secret to a long life at court was accepting injuries and returning thanks for them. But Ashley couldn't quite play the Stoic, and a couple of weeks later he had to confess to Cecil that he had been 'too faulty and forward of tongue'. He was, he said, ruined: all men were shunning to have dealings with him as with the devil. He saw Cecil as his saviour: 'I know you might with a word have cut me off by the root.'[10]

One explanation for Ashley's situation on his return to England was an accusation that there was some questionable accounting in the expedition's finances. The deeper truth, however, was an eternal one: it is always easier to shoot the messenger than the sender. After initial celebration at the Cadiz victory, there followed a closer examination by Elizabeth and her councillors of how her orders for the expedition had been carried out. Ashley was on the sharp end of this. The queen had no clear idea from his briefings of what her generals proposed to do next in occupying Cadiz, when they had been clearly instructed not to capture a town or city. 'With her own mouth' she ordered the Privy Council to write to Howard and Essex.

Egerton, Burghley, Cobham, Cecil and Sir John Fortescue signed the letter to the generals at Greenwich on 7 August. They were blunt. 'Upon the coming of Sir Anthony Ashley her Majesty hath entered into divers doubts what she might expect from you since your coming from Cadiz, finding no certainty of your resolutions.' Elizabeth's irritation with Essex was that he had disobeyed her orders. Taking upon himself the authority to make decisions, he had in fact no clear idea of what to do next.[11]

A week later, Essex the hero was home. 'Our most worthy and dear earl is returned (God be thanked)', Anthony Bacon wrote from Essex House, 'with great honour and safety, and hath brought back an army victorious, hail and rich.'[12]

Essex was full of his achievements and London wanted to hear about them. One of Archbishop Whitgift's chaplains preached a celebratory sermon at Paul's Cross, praising Essex's wisdom, valour and 'noble carriage in this action, making many comparisons . . . with the chiefest generals'. The earl wanted to publish his own 'True relation of the action at Cadiz', a collaboration between Essex and his servant Henry Cuffe. Together Cuffe and the earl's private secretary, Edward Reynolds, contrived in July to get the narrative into print, working out ways to make it difficult to trace back to them – much better to disguise the pamphlet as the work of a gentleman carried away by enthusiasm at Essex's great victory. They knew that any public telling of what had happened at Cadiz, especially one which lauded Essex, was going to be sensitive. The existence of the 'True relation' was leaked to privy councillors by Ashley. On 9 August, two days after the council's letter of reprimand, Reynolds told Essex that any narrative had to be first authorized by the Privy Council. The queen herself sent an emissary to Cuffe to warn him on pain of death not to make public any account without her knowledge and permission.[13]

Essex had of course returned home to find Robert Cecil appointed secretary. He was deeply unhappy about it, 'exceedingly dejected in countenance and bitterly passionate speech'. For a year he had fought Cecil's promotion. The queen, he had believed, had promised not to make the appointment: this she confirmed in a letter Essex had received before setting sail from Plymouth for Spain. But the queen had made the appointment anyway – on her own terms, to suit only herself, and just possibly to keep Essex in his place.[14]

In September the critical stocktaking of the Cadiz expedition continued. It was not now viewed as Essex's brilliant victory. In fact, its lustre seemed to tarnish with time – even the volume of treasure brought back home seemed now to be disappointing, and some of the spoils of war had apparently been lost. At Greenwich on Tuesday 7 September – Elizabeth's sixty-third birthday – Essex was grilled by Burghley and Cecil. 'My Lord Treasurer and Sir Robert Cecil', the earl wrote to Anthony Bacon, 'did before the Queen contest with me . . . that nothing was brought home.' The following day Secretary Cecil tackled him again: 'I was more braved [challenged, provoked] by your little cousin than ever I was by any man in my life', Essex told Bacon. It seemed he was following Sir Anthony Ashley's efforts at Stoic calm:

'But I am not nor was not angry, which is all the advantage I have of him.'[15]

Yet tempers were not easy to contain, especially Elizabeth's, who a few weeks later berated Burghley for defending Essex's claim to keep at least some of the prize money from the prisoners he had taken. Burghley named Lord Buckhurst and Sir John Fortescue as witnesses that the queen had called her lord treasurer a miscreant and a coward, telling him that he seemed to regard the earl more than he regarded his queen – she didn't know whether out of fear or favour. Retreating to Theobalds to nurse his bruises – 'laden with grief for her so implacable displeasure', as he put it – Burghley then heard reports of Essex's hostility towards him. Attacked from both sides, he wanted to be as open as he could with the earl, or at least to suspend hostilities. On 22 September he wrote disarmingly to Essex with what he called a weak hand and a troubled mind.[16]

The whole Cadiz episode exposed so many sensitivities all at once – the hopes of military victory soured, Essex's petulant independence, the complexity of his relationship with the queen, the needling of his lordship by the Cecils.

In the tense weeks and months after Cadiz, Francis Bacon wrote for Essex a paper of advice on his lordship's deportment at court. Master Bacon suggested, none too subtly, that the strands of Essex's career could in the future make him vulnerable: he was 'A man of a nature not to be ruled, that hath the advantage of [the] Queen's affection and knoweth it, of an estate not grounded to his greatness, of a popular reputation, [and] of a military dependence.' Absolute self-belief and independence of action, royal favour, lack of money, popularity with the common people, military heroism – these were difficult all together to hold in balance.

Bacon's counsel could be reduced to a single piece of advice: the earl should stick to Elizabeth. It was not the first time he had told Essex this. 'I said to your lordship last time, *Martha, Martha, attendis ad plurima, unum sufficit* ['Martha, Martha, thou art careful, and troubled about many things: But one thing is needful', from Luke 10:41–2]; win the Queen: if this be not the beginning, of any other course I see no end.'[17]

*

Anthony Bacon was in a more strident frame of mind than his brother. He hadn't taken their mother's advice to guard what he put down on paper. In December he wrote to Henry Hawkyns, as fierce an Essex loyalist as Anthony. Bacon's letter had partisan bite. He reported that Robert Cecil was finding the secretaryship 'a harder province to govern than he looked for and beginneth inwardly to be as weary of it, as outwardly the world is already of him'. Antonio Pérez, one of Essex's followers, who had before characterized Cecil as a dwarf-like hunchback, was now calling the new secretary '*del Robert* [sic] *il Diabilo*'.[18]

On 23 December 1596 Secretary Cecil entertained the queen for dinner. As usual, the bells of the Church of St Martin-in-the-Fields rang as she came out of Whitehall Palace, and again as she returned there later the same day. For Cecil there was no rest from work: even on Christmas Day there was a Privy Council letter to sign.[19]

It was a time of truce at court, time for the backbiting, sniping and partisanship to stop. Cecil made the first move – even Anthony Bacon admitted that, and even he believed his cousin Robert's initiative to be genuine. Amnesty and oblivion for all past misconceits, Bacon called it. 'Misconceit' was a significant word: not a fault, not an injury, but a misunderstanding, an error of perception and judgement. Even Bacon knew that some balance and perspective needed to be restored at court.[20]

In late December Cecil wrote to Essex emphasizing his loyalty, respect and the interests they had in common. 'Your lordship is a person extraordinary in all my father's reckonings and respects, and one with whom his lordship would observe most strictly, in all things fit for him, an extraordinary good name.' The bearer of the letter to the earl was an old servant in Burghley's private chamber and Essex held the key to an office that the Cecils wanted for him. Cecil became a humble suitor on his father's behalf, Essex's 'poor friend at commandment'.

Robert Cecil called Burghley 'the staff of my poor fortune'. It was a statement of fact, a pledge of his loyalty.[21]

Early in 1597 Burghley, Essex and Cecil, along with other privy councillors and courtiers, were the subjects of sonnets composed by Henry

Lok. These, which provided an epilogue to Lok's formidable verse translation of the Book of Ecclesiastes in the Old Testament, had already been in the workshop of the printer Richard Field, at Black-friars near Ludgate, since late November.[22]

Lok was one of those gentlemen who haunted the Cecils' chambers and besieged Lord Burghley in particular, the limpet-like suitor assiduously pursuing potential patrons at court. He played this part to a T – heavy on the rhetoric, frequently saccharine in his praise of the great man, always painfully self-deprecating when it came to exposing his own faults and travails.

He had first written to Burghley in November 1590, having by then served for almost twenty years in the household of the 17th earl of Oxford, the lord treasurer's ne'er-do-well son-in-law. He had been as direct as he was strangely elliptical: '[if] that it should please God . . . to touch the heart of some honourable person with will to procure my good, which I would to God might grow by the service of my country in any honest calling for which I were accounted fit'. It was the sort of pitch Burghley had heard hundreds of times before: Lok was the familiar hopeful volunteer.[23]

In fact, he did turn out to be employable. In the early 1590s Lok lived in or near Edinburgh, close to the court of James VI: in 1591 he wrote a commendatory sonnet for a book of James's poems. Three years later Lok was one of Cecil's discreet intermediaries with the renegade earl of Bothwell. In this covert diplomacy he communicated with Cecil directly, and at least once they had a private interview. This was in July 1594 at Greenwich Palace and from it Lok understood the political and diplomatic delicacy of supporting Bothwell: 'her Majesty looketh not for any action from him prejudicial to the amity' – 'the amity' being old and familiar shorthand for the alliance between Scotland and England. In their communications Lok, and other English agents in Scotland, referred to Cecil in their letters as 'Maecenas'. The codename possessed for Lok, the poet, a particular significance. In Roman history Gaius Maecenas had been the trusted counsellor of Emperor Augustus as well as patron to the poets Virgil and Horace.[24]

In the mid-1590s Henry Lok lurked in the shadows of Anglo-Scottish diplomacy and politics. But by 1596 he was struggling: his sources of support appeared to be drying up. He was in debt, twenty or thirty pounds short of being able to pay his fines and fees to the Exchequer; pursuing suits at court was expensive. He owed money to Cecil's old friend Michael Hickes, Burghley's influential patronage secretary, a rich man and a prolific moneylender. To Hickes he wrote: 'I know ... that the borrower is a servant to the lender, and that he which is surety for another may want himself.' But being able to diagnose the situation in which Lok found himself was not the same as being able to settle his debts.[25]

June 1596 was an especially bad month. Lok wrote again to Robert Cecil. Perhaps Cecil read it: the most we can say is that his secretary Simon Willis noted and filed his letter. Lok was desperate and disappointed. There was no obvious resolution to his crisis, though he knew he was at the end. He was plaintive, he was resigned:

> As for myself, if my deserts be disparaged in court: if my sufficiency disabled for my country: if my fortune be calculated with disaster: yet I rather yield to all these (to me being unexpected, more grievous than exile or death) then to the least offensive importunacy of your heart and patient ear. If these times be not for suitors ... my means must be elsewhere.[26]

Over the following months he put his hopes in patronage and publication. His new patron and supporter was the queen's cousin Lord Hunsdon, and it was at Hunsdon's residence, Somerset House on the Strand, that Lok finished his great translation of *Ecclesiastes* and his sonnets dedicated to courtiers. The book was designed to make a splash. Two hundred pages long, with a conscious nod to Edmund Spenser's ground-breaking epic poem of 1590, *The Faerie Queene*, Lok introduced his master work ('Compendiously abridged, and also paraphrastically dilated', as it said on the title page) with a predictably elaborate letter of dedication to Queen Elizabeth.[27]

Lok celebrated Lord Burghley as the father of the queen's government and Essex as the muscular champion of European Protestantism, fighting on a grand scale the works of the devil. Here the poet was dead on target: this was Essex as his lordship saw himself. Neatly working in the victory at Cadiz months earlier – and neatly sidestepping just how problematic Cadiz had in fact been for Essex – Lok celebrated the earl's mastery of sea and land. Essex was a shield to the Church, a defence against the Antichrist.

Where Lok beheld Essex from afar as a kind of superhero, outsized, larger than life, Robert Cecil he was able to make sense of on a human scale. They had a connection of patron and artist – Cecil as a Maecenas, Lok a Virgil. Lok gave Cecil what he, Lok, thought he would want to hear. Cecil was trained for rule and service; he was serious and assiduous. Uninterested in the world's passing pleasures, Cecil's eye was on heaven:

> To you (my hopes sweet life, nurse to my muse,
>   Kind foster father of deserving sprights)
>   This Poem comes, which you will not refuse
>   (I trust) because of blessednes it wrights:
> Your aged youth so waind from vaine delights,
>   Your growing iudgment farre beyond your yeares,
>   Your painefull daies, your many watchfull nights,
>   Wherein your care of Common good appears,
> Assureth him that of your fame once hears,
>   That you some heavenly object do aspire;
>   The sweet conceit whereof your soule so chears,
>   The earths bred vanities, you not admire:
>   Such is this theame, such was first writers mind,
>   For whose sakes, I do crave, it favour find.

Lok, months earlier dispirited and broken, framed his hopes in a new way.[28]

On the title page of Lok's *Ecclesiastes* were printed two verses (3 and 4) from Psalm 144. They read:

> Lord what is man, that thou regardest him: or the son of man, that thou thinkest upon him?
> Man is like to vanity, his days like a shadow that vanisheth.

Life – Henry Lok knew it, Robert Cecil knew it – was fragile and fleeting, a passing shadow.

16

The Burial of the Dead

Of all the mysteries in Robert's life Bess Cecil is the deepest. The smallest surviving fragments we have of their life together, as occasional as Cecil's scribbled notes to his friend Michael Hickes, communicate the solidarity of their love, their affability, their sense of fun – even when they joked about Master Michael's baldness. Bess was Robert's greatest supporter from the beginning; together they had waited in 1591 for news of his hoped-for promotion. As a lady of the queen's bedchamber, Bess saw every day those two parts to Elizabeth which Robert once called the 'Queen's Majesty' and 'Elizabeth Regina' – woman and monarch. Of all this experience and observation Bess left nothing – and what stories she might have told. We know that she was a route to her husband's favour, a factor behind the scenes. We know too that she was loved by friends and family: Robert's cousin Sir Edward Hoby was never shy in saying how much.

On Sunday, 23 January 1597 Cecil was missing from the Privy Council's meeting at Whitehall. His absence was an indication of an emergency at home on the Strand. The following day Bess Cecil died in childbirth. Her baby survived, later baptized Catharine.

At court the news travelled quickly. That same Monday, Simon Willis received the first letter of condolence for his master, from Sir Walter Raleigh. Friends and family – Raleigh, Lord Admiral Howard, Robert's maternal first cousins Edward Hoby and Anthony Cooke – sent him admonitions to patience and endurance. Their letters didn't obviously penetrate his grief, at least not straight away. Over the following two days Cecil read official papers. With Willis close by, on Tuesday he dictated a short letter to the agent of James VI at Elizabeth's court. Willis wrote it, Robert signed it; his

pen was unsteady and he blotted his signature. He stayed away from
Privy Council.[1]

Cousin Hoby was one of the first to visit him. Charles Howard and
Walter Raleigh held back, though Howard wrote that he would go to
Robert at any time to offer comfort, even should his friend want him at
midnight. On the Strand Hoby, normally so fluent and easy, was over-
come and lost for words. 'I found sympathy in sorrow,' he wrote, 'though
not in so high degree as your honour, having myself lost such a friend as
in haste I may not look for the like: which upon the aspect dulled my
senses and my lips became tongueless.' Hoby offered Robert his house
on Canon Row, close to both Westminster and Whitehall palaces, as an
escape from 'the place I know you can take no great delight in'.[2]

Raleigh's was the most bracing of the letters. Sir Walter wanted to
penetrate to the heart of things. 'You should not overshadow your
wisdom with passion,' he wrote, 'but look right into things as they
are.' Bess was no longer Robert's; she was immortal and had no need
of his love or sorrow; 'she hath passed the wearisome journey of this
dark world and hath possession of her inheritance.'

> Sir, believe it that sorrows are dangerous companions, converting bad into
> evil . . . and do no other service than multiply harms. They are the treasures
> of weak hearts and of the foolish. The mind that entertaineth them is as the
> earth and dust . . . Sorrows draw not the dead to life but the living to death.

Yet even the poet's pen was, in all this, still inadequate. Raleigh
signed the letter as 'Yours ever beyond the power of words to utter'.[3]

On the evening of 27 January Sir John Stanhope was trying, but failing, to talk to the queen about the late Lady Cecil. Elizabeth was deep
in conference with her council in a privy chamber lit on a winter's late
afternoon by candlelight, working through two competing proposals
by the earls of Essex and Cumberland for a new assault on Spain;
Burghley had prepared the discussion papers. For the first time in over
five years, Sir Robert Cecil was not involved in the debate, was not
close to the queen. On Stanhope's mind was funeral protocol. He
knew that there was a precedent to bury Bess as a baroness. Sir John
planned the following day to brief Robert at home.[4]

Robert Cecil was experienced in grief. His younger sister Elizabeth had died, in 1583, at the age of eighteen. She was followed by their older sibling Anne, countess of Oxford, in 1588, and by their mother Lady Burghley in 1589. Robert had seen his father wrestle painfully with his mother's death: he had felt how for a minister private emotions and public duties could pull in opposite directions. But a Christian had to submit to the will of God, to master sorrow. There was no choice; the truth of Sir Walter Raleigh's spiritual counsel was overwhelming. And the old formalities had to be observed. Robert commissioned from an accomplished Latin scholar thirty-six elegant verses on Lady Cecil's life and virtues and made for her a place in Westminster Abbey, a discreet and compact tomb of black marble and alabaster.[5]

One of its three epitaphs is descriptive. Two go deeper and say more. Born a Brooke, Baron Cobham's daughter, her husband Cecil built her this tomb 'to prove his love did after death abide'. Nature made her wise; she had wit; she was 'silent, true and chaste'; she was full of rare virtue, valued at court in service of her sovereign. Blessed with two babies, 'the third brought her to this'.

It was in Latin that Robert found both his and Bess's voices. In paired epitaphs husband and wife speak to each other. She tells him that they had shared one love, an undivided will, one unbroken trust. He responds: her tomb and his heart witnessed with how great a love he had returned hers. But there could be no grieving while the queen was on the throne, and a greater love bound Bess now to Christ. She would enjoy blessedness in peace. He hoped, too, for heavenly peace in company with her.

A wise man left the dead to their heavenly inheritance. Calling Robert back to life was duty to the monarch Bess herself had served.

In a few days everything had changed, and nothing. On Sunday morning, 20 February, Cecil was present in the council chamber at Whitehall Palace. Elizabeth needed her secretary.[6]

A late February browser in Humphrey Hooper's bookshop at the sign of the Black Bear on Chancery Lane, deep in lawyers' London, might have noticed on display a small slim book of essays and religious meditations. Its author had chambers just a little to the north of

Chancery Lane, in the cluster of ancient buildings occupied by the barristers of the honourable society of Gray's Inn. He was thirty-six-year-old Francis Bacon, Robert Cecil's cousin, energetic suitor now turned contemplative hermit. Bacon dedicated his book to his brother Anthony.

Discovering that poor pirated manuscript copies of his essays were circulating, Bacon had rushed the book into print. Hooper of Chancery Lane was a small-scale bookseller, but the printer who produced the collection of essays for him, John Windet, was well established, with two workshops in the city. In his dedicatory epistle Francis made a private joke of his brother's long and often secret journeyings in Europe: clearly the essays wanted to escape, so who better to guide them than Anthony? 'Since they would not stay with their master, but would needs travel abroad, I have preferred them to you that are next myself, dedicating them, such as they are, to our love.' For Anthony Francis wished a life of service to the queen. He himself, installed at Gray's Inn, was better suited to scholarship and study.

Bacon's essays were products of his and Anthony's small world, where followers of great men found themselves at court chasing suits and nursing disappointments. Anthony, certainly, as a devoted loyalist of the earl of Essex, felt all the intensity of political life. Francis's aphorisms and short reflections were all conventional enough. He balanced positives and negatives: care in spending money, the pursuit of honour without envy, the dangers of political faction. Relationships at court were instrumental, means to ends: mutual need was the only foundation for decent behaviour. To Bacon, friendship was easier between superiors and inferiors than it was for two individuals equal in position and rank: only the superior and the inferior knew that they were getting something tangible out of the relationship. With some skill people could be steered and manoeuvred: 'If you would work any man, you must either know his nature and fashions, and so lead him; or his ends, and so win him; or his weaknesses or disadvantages, and so awe him; or those that have interest in him and so govern him.'[7]

Here, for the browser of books on Chancery Lane was a flavour of the courtier's life.

*

In high summer 1597 Burghley was hidden away at Theobalds. Though on 4 July his lordship's fingers were still unyielding – and though his secretary Henry Maynard was, as ever, on call – he insisted on writing a letter to his son in his own hand. Staying with their grandfather were Robert's children William and Frances Cecil, now six and four respectively, and their new sister Catharine: 'All your offspring are here merry', Burghley wrote to Robert.[8]

Secretary Cecil was at court that same Monday, though planning to have supper the following day at Cecil House. He invited Michael Hickes to join him. If Master Michael wanted to, he was welcome to stay overnight on the Strand. Cecil sent with his note a piece of venison for Hickes's dinner. He gave away a little of his own loneliness, offering his commendations to Hickes's wife Elizabeth, 'in whom I envy your good fortune, but rest for all that your loving friend'.[9]

The latest and long-debated naval attack on Spain, discussed in the privy chamber three days after Bess Cecil's death, had by summer 1597 assumed a final form. Essex would command the new expedition, with George Clifford, earl of Cumberland, in reluctant co-command. Cumberland – a highly experienced privateer now nearly thirty-nine – resented being cast as Essex's understudy, but when he complained to Elizabeth she gave him a brisk dressing-down. Essex himself had alternated over the months between lethargy and energy. In the end he got his way and his command – or at least as much as the queen and her council would allow him. His disobedience to his orders at Cadiz in 1596 was forgiven but not forgotten.

By the end of June, the fleet was assembling off the coast of Kent. Divided into three squadrons under the commands of Lord Thomas Howard, Sir Walter Raleigh and Essex, and supported by an army of four thousand conscripted soldiers, the expedition was reinforced at the end of the month by ten Dutch warships and a thousand more English troops sent over from the Netherlands. The expedition's objective was to confront the enemy fleet reportedly gathering itself off Ferrol, a town on the northern Spanish coast a few miles north-east of A Coruña. Following what had happened at Cadiz, the private instructions Essex received from the queen and her council were especially clear and precise. His first purpose was to destroy the king of Spain's armada, whether in port or at sea, and after that to set course for the Azores to intercept Philip's West Indies treasure fleet. Essex and Cumberland had to be home by winter. In essence it was a replay of what the 1596 expedition should have achieved.

Not surprisingly, Essex had proposed the taking and holding of the ports of Cadiz and Lisbon in order to cut off Spain's seaborne trade. Not surprisingly, these actions were out of the question – they would be cripplingly expensive to support and reinforce, and would probably involve a substantial loss of life. The Spanish, if such an attack were successful, could easily devote long-term resources to such an outpost, while England's already stretched military capacity would have been devoted to maintaining them to no rational purpose. Elizabeth was plain with Essex: 'you should be an author unto us of such a growing charge, such a continual peril of our subjects' lives and our honour and, shortly, such a confusion as we should repent to have given the charge, power, and trust we committed to you.'[10]

So it was that Essex's instructions were tightly drafted. Any orders he gave would require the consent of at least four out of the six senior officers in the expedition's council of war. But with Essex one never quite knew.

On 5 July Burghley, though nursing a painful foot, was in a magnanimous mood. He wished General Essex well. 'And now I do write unto him with my weak hand', he told Cecil, 'only to congratulate with him for this favour of God; I do exhort him as a Christian soldier to acknowledge the same beyond all man's power and wit.'

A few days later he had in mind a verse from the Psalms to celebrate an apparent change in the stormy weather that until then had kept Essex's fleet in port. 'God hath like a gracious father, after a few days' frowning to make his power known, hath changed his countenance into blessing.' Now it was time for the expedition to take courage and to trust in God.[11]

It was Michael Hickes who was with Lord Burghley that weekend. Still at Theobalds, his lordship ate dinner on Saturday with a former ambassador to the Russian tsar, an official in the Court of Wards, and his nephew Francis Bacon. Afterwards he read a book under a tree in his gardens, trying to keep himself awake on a hot summer's afternoon. He and Hickes waited until the day cooled to play a game of bowls.[12]

This July weekend Burghley saw all about him harmony and balance. The monarch commanded, the servant served, and Elizabeth recognized her minister's worth. 'It is my comfort that her Majesty maketh such a comparison of my simplicity with her princely worthiness,' he wrote to Robert Cecil, 'to which in very truth I think neither foreign prince nor British subject can approach.'[13]

The earl of Essex: hero, Christian soldier, privy councillor, patron, the most loving of the queen's courtiers, her most steadfast servant; larger than life, always superlative. The energy all this consumed was exhausting: no wonder the earl oscillated between ferocious overdrive and wounded retreat.

By the summer of 1597 he was also close to financial ruin. That at least was how it looked to two of his senior household servants, Henry Lindley and Edward Reynolds, when they tabulated their master's debts. These were – and there was no way to sugar-coat this – massive. Essex had borrowed heavily from foreign merchants in London. He had mortgaged away some of his estates, manors and parks. His debt that July was £10,577 and ten shillings, with £3,180 more owing to other creditors. Moreover, the earl was facing serious legal action by one of those creditors to recover the loan. Something had to be done – in days, not weeks.

For eight years Essex had been kept approximately solvent by his privilege to farm customs revenue on sweet wines. It was a piece of royal patronage that had to be renewed every four years. The renewal fell in 1597, which is why Lindley and Reynolds sent their papers on Essex's debts to Cecil, 'hoping that if it shall please you to acquaint her excellent Majesty therewith, she will be graciously moved'. Once agreed, Lindley and Reynolds would do the rest, negotiating with Essex's creditors new contracts and avoiding further forfeitures.

When Cecil went to Elizabeth with Lindley's and Reynolds' papers he held in his hand Essex's future. Yet it was just another item of business; he wrote on the paper 'This I showed to the Queen also.'[14]

Essex got his renewal.

*

The truth was that the two Roberts, Cecil and Essex, needed each other, as Lindley's and Reynolds' appeal to Cecil showed. But their co-dependence – their mutuality – went deeper than this. Each was the other's shadow self, each what the other was not. Secretary Cecil's steadiness balanced Essex's native unpredictability: the earl was too influential a courtier and patron ever to be underestimated. Essex's relationship with the queen was unique: no one else could have challenged or angered her in the way that he did and still have kept his position at court. That was as true in summer 1597 as it ever was. As late July gales kept his fleet in port, Essex exchanged warmly effusive letters with Elizabeth. Cecil's sensitive antennae picked up the signals. When the earl's uncle Sir William Knollys, comptroller of the royal household, wrote to his nephew that 'Master Secretary remaineth in all show firm to your lordship and no doubt will so long as the Queen is so well pleased with you', he wasn't perhaps so very wide of the mark.[15]

Cecil's own letters to Essex in July tingled with ambiguity. Were they friendly or frosty? Or both at the same time? He hoped for Essex's happy success, mindful of the risks he took: 'I protest I shall never but for obedience to your desires be glad of your hazarding your fortune thus continually in such a time.' 'The Queen is so disposed now to have us all love you, as she and I do every night talk like angels of you.' Was this love for the earl only by royal command? Was it a reminder that Cecil, not Essex, was cosy with Elizabeth in an intimate bubble of favour?[16]

Praise followed the whiff of dispraise, all heavy on the rhetoric. Cecil seemed to enjoy toying with Essex. The masterpiece was Cecil's letter to the earl on Friday 29 July. Essex's last letter had pleased Elizabeth 'exceedingly, for it was short and full of gracefulness'; Cecil told the earl that he would keep a copy for himself as 'monument of your virtues'. So far, so good. But in a postscript there was a sting. Cecil wrote that the queen had in fact 'said little less of your letter when I had read it and debated it, than I do write'. He was being deliberately – and we might say provocatively – unclear in his meaning. He seemed to have built Essex up only to knock him down. And that was their relationship in 1597.[17]

The weather kept Essex and his fleet idle for weeks. With autumn approaching, they were running out of time and the planned expedition looked now unlikely to sail. At the beginning of August, he and Sir Walter Raleigh went to court to propose a new plan – a surprise attack on the Spanish West Indies, abandoning Ferrol for this fighting season.

Focus and momentum had been lost. By mid-August the decision was made to stand down the land army – this was at Essex's request, who did it anyway without permission – and to support a more limited naval adventure. The earl wrote to Cecil on 11 August about his 'unconstant fortunes'.[18]

Everything about what had been planned as a great venture was now an anticlimax. The queen allowed the demobilization of the army and permitted a limited naval operation against Ferrol, which she insisted that Essex himself should not lead. There were other commanders who could do it instead; she did not want Essex to risk his life. The skeleton council travelling on the late summer progress (Lord Treasurer Burghley, Lord Admiral Howard and Secretary Cecil) told Essex that they wished with all their hearts for God's blessing on the venture – a wish with surely a hollow ring to it, at least for Essex.

Eight days later Cecil noted that Essex and Raleigh had been graciously received back at court. A small fleet had sailed, but he doubted that it would achieve very much. The Spanish armada at Ferrol would not be burned, as had been the plan; the treasure ships from the Indies were now already home. The expedition was a show to prop up Essex's self-esteem: its 'weak watery hopes', Cecil wrote, 'do but faintly nourish that noble earl['s] heart's comfort'.[19]

Both patronage and policy mattered in Elizabethan court politics. To have influence in either sphere made one a courtier to be reckoned with. To have both made a courtier – or, as in the case of the Cecils, a family – unstoppable.

Where Essex was a considerable patron with a clientele of loyal followers hoping for office and promotion, he never quite got the grip he wanted on the direction of the queen's government – Lord Burghley seemed immovable, especially now with his son in office too. Heroic expeditions to fight Philip of Spain were very much Essex's métier – if those weak watery hopes ever left port. And the Cecils were themselves formidable patrons. Lord Burghley controlled the

Court of Wards and Liveries, the most profitable patronage machine of Elizabeth's government – profitable at least for Burghley, whose questionable financial deals over the estates and futures of young wards of the Crown had made him very rich. Now in 1597 the Cecils were able to add another institution to their portfolio. On Friday 7 October, in the council chamber at Richmond Palace, Robert Cecil swore his oath as the new chancellor of the Duchy of Lancaster.[20]

The Duchy was a jurisdiction, an ancient accretion of lands and estates, mainly in the north and midlands of England, over which it ruled. The most significant of its lands were in and around Lancashire, hence the Duchy's name, from the earls, and then dukes, of Lancaster, the most famous of whom was Shakespeare's 'Old John of Gaunt, time-honoured Lancaster', son of King Edward III. The Duchy court met in Westminster Palace, where the chancellor presided from his green velvet cushion. As a well-oiled administrative machine, the Duchy of Lancaster contributed many thousands of pounds of estate revenue each year to the royal Exchequer.

For the privy councillor who held its chancellorship, the Duchy was a formidable power base. Sir Francis Walsingham had been chancellor; so, too, had been Sir Thomas Heneage, the old vice chamberlain. The chancellor was a patron: he nominated sheriffs and magistrates in Duchy territory, appointed clergy to church benefices and exercised considerable influence over parliamentary elections. The chancellor of the Duchy of Lancaster mattered.

Its headquarters was a grand house with a garden on the Strand just across the street from Burghley's own mansion: thirty-two rooms with lodgings for its chancellor and an archive and offices for its bureaucrats. Water was plumbed in from Somerset House. The chancellor's lodgings had been recently refurbished: the last incumbent, Heneage, preparing for a visit by the queen in December 1594, had spent a few hundred pounds altering staircases and making some of the chambers bigger.[21]

Three days after Robert Cecil's oath-taking at Richmond, the queen was in a sunny mood. She and Lord Admiral Howard had been talking about Burghley and the new chancellor. Howard wrote to Cecil: 'Well, father and son are blessed of God for her love to you, and the Lord continue it to the end . . . I may never hear the contrary.'[22]

17

Ways of Safety

Paolo Teobast's private interview with Secretary Cecil in late November 1597 was not a happy one. He had said something to Cecil that he shouldn't have; it was a loss of temper and control. Within hours he set to work on a letter of apology and petition. He explained that money was tight. He had a family to provide for, and the cost was high of entertaining in London the merchants and captains from the Low Countries on whom he relied for information. His lodgings were meagre, his table bare; he needed more support.

The familiar plaintive appeals of the chancers and opportunists who pestered the Cecils usually got them nowhere. Teobast was different. An Italian long-established in London, acting from the mid-1580s as a factor for various merchants from Middelburg and Amsterdam, he was first recruited for secret service by a prominent Anglo-Italian merchant called Sir Horatio Palavicino, himself a specialist in high financial diplomacy. By 1597 Teobast was one of Cecil's intelligencers responsible for the Biscay coast. He had a secret cipher and funding, and he could be trusted – he was too important to set aside after a fit of temper. A couple of weeks after their fractious encounter, Teobast met Cecil's household steward, Roger Houghton, who gave him fifteen pounds for his next mission; scrupulous with his master's money, Houghton made sure that Teobast signed a receipt for it. This wasn't a sympathy payment. The day after their difficult meeting, Teobast had given Cecil a long and detailed report on the dispositions of what was thought to be the latest fleet the king of Spain would use to menace Elizabeth's kingdoms.[1]

Power needs information. Those in charge of kingdoms had to possess the skills of secrecy, dissimulation and deception, as Justus Lipsius recognized, taking as his authority Cicero: 'They shall never govern well, who know not how to cover well.' Where private individuals might choose honesty and openness, states, said Lipsius, could not.[2]

Nearly two years into his secretaryship Cecil had a network of intelligencers like Teobast busily at work across Europe. Over nearly a decade, Cecil had known bad spies and good. They came and went: John Cecil, Michael Moody, Thomas Phelippes. Sometimes he trusted them, sometimes he didn't. But he could not function – and Elizabeth and her kingdoms could not be kept safe – without them. For all their human frailties and evasions, on balance he supposed they were worth the money he paid them. 'When I consider that those I use are but the sons of Adam, and it is not impossible but that they might be corrupted or deceived,' he would write in 1599, 'I have given way to these preparations that are made, preferring therein the ways of safety before any matter of charge.'

The most secret file in Secretary Cecil's office ran to a little over thirty folios. It was a compilation, the product of at least three individuals within his inner circle, begun in about 1596, and it was the central record of the secret ciphers of, and payments made to, his sources of information across Europe. Its contents page, mainly in the hands of his private secretary Simon Willis and William Wade, clerk of the Privy Council, but with one name written by Cecil himself, listed nineteen men. Willis entitled it 'The names of the intelligencers'.[3]

These individuals were fixed points in the bureaucratic system. Some held official or semi-official positions in government: a secretary to an embassy, for example, or a royal courier. Some were merchants, or merchants' factors, whose businesses put them in the Iberian peninsula or on the French Atlantic coast, key areas of strategic interest for spotting any Spanish naval activity. A little under half of the intelligencers were foreigners. One was a captured Catholic priest.

Overseeing Secretary Cecil's intelligencers were Willis and Wade. There was a certain amount of devolution in the system. Generally, the official, councillor or courtier who recruited an intelligencer ran him too: this might be Wade, whose particular skill was spotting turncoat priests; or Lord Admiral Howard; or Sir Horatio Palavicino.

After Secretary Walsingham's death, Burghley and Vice Chamberlain Heneage had heavily pruned back those spies then on the payroll. Many by 1590 were defunct, and some had been turned by the enemy. Now, by the late 1590s, survivors from the Walsingham days were in a minority. One was Robert Poley, who would serve Robert Cecil into the early 1600s. Poley was a veteran spy. He had played a significant role in the Babington Plot in 1586; he was elusive, dangerous and highly able – he had been one of the drinking companions of the poet and playwright Christopher Marlowe on the day Marlowe was stabbed to death in Deptford in 1593. Robin Poley was one of the busiest diplomatic couriers at court, dispatched on various missions to Denmark, Holland, Berwick-upon-Tweed, Flushing, Ostend, Brussels, Antwerp and Edinburgh: he was a resourceful traveller.

Some names on the contents page of the secret file were crossed out, but more were added. Over time – 1596, 1597, 1598 – it grew fatter. It contained no letters; those were filed elsewhere. Each intelligencer had a number – the system which had been used in Secretary Walsingham's office to keep intelligencers' identities as secret as possible, where the number was indicated by the symbol #, the key to the arrangement of tills and boxes to which the secretary kept the key.

The whole system ran on regular payments of money. In this context the name that crops up again and again in the file is that of Roger Houghton, Cecil's long-serving servant and steward, by now in his mid-fifties. Houghton had overall responsibility for the sums paid out to the intelligencers at court, aided by Richard Percival, a junior member of Cecil's expanding private secretariat. Houghton's and Percival's later accounts show that between October and December 1596 they paid four hundred pounds to fifteen intelligencers, while the total disbursement for 1597 and 1598 was somewhere near fifteen hundred pounds. In some cases, the money for intelligencers' missions might come from a recruiter or handler: in the case of Paolo Teobast, for example, it was sometimes Palavicino who gave him his funds (with Sir Horatio, if he had a rich man's talent for economy, doubtless recovering the sums from Cecil). The payments were made ad hoc but with such regularity that for the most productive intelligencers (like Teobast) they amounted more or less to a predictable salary.[4]

Secret communication in the 1590s was basic but effective enough for what it had to achieve. No cipher was wholly secure – Thomas Phelippes's powerful brain was proof enough of that – but it would slow down an enemy who got their hands on any letter. The ciphers used by Cecil's intelligencers, which were kept in Willis and Wade's secret file, relied on a simple substitution of letters for either other letters or symbols, along with codewords for places and numbers for people, and sometimes scrambled names or phrases for objects (military and naval hardware, for example) that an intelligencer might find himself reporting on. In Teobast's cipher, ships were referred to as pipes of oil, galleons as sacks of wool, horsemen as shovels. Striking in Teobast's cipher was the geographical range of any potential report he might make. Pretty much everywhere in Europe was covered, every state, every monarch, every principal political figure.[5]

Robert Cecil had received secret intelligence on Spain's naval dispositions even before he was secretary – this was part of the growing portfolio of work he shared with his father at Burghley House on the Strand. Cecil's two most important and trustworthy intelligencers on Spain were Edmund Palmer and Thomas Honiman, both of whom were merchants long established on the French Atlantic coast. Palmer was based in Saint-Jean-de-Luz, about ten miles south-west of Biarritz, and from there he had reported since the 1580s, first to Walsingham, then to Burghley. Honiman's range of operations ran from Lisbon all the way up the coast of Brittany. Honiman too was an efficient intelligencer, making early contact with Cecil in December 1594. With the help of his brother – who became a permanent fixture in his intelligence operations – Honiman fitted out a boat with a French crew which made reconnaissance voyages out of Bayonne. Honiman in 1594 enclosed with his first letter to Cecil a paper from the heart of Spanish military planning for the invasion of England – the late marquis of Santa Cruz's preparation of ships, sailors and armaments, along with a detailed financial costing. Doubting that Cecil could read Spanish, Honiman gave him a full English translation. Between October 1596 and September 1597, at the peak of the latest armada panic, he was active in gathering intelligence on the ports of Ferrol and A Coruña (both highly relevant to Essex's abortive 1597 expedition), Spanish fortifications in Brittany and enemy plans for a landing in Cornwall. In all his reports Honiman was confident, authoritative, detailed and crisp. Edmund Palmer was equally efficient and busy in autumn 1596: in November, at Richmond Palace and in London, he was given a new cipher and supplied with money by Roger Houghton.[6]

Teobast employed for Lisbon, Honiman employed for Spain, Palmer employed for Saint-Jean-de-Luz: the first three names in the secret file, the foundations of Sir Robert's espionage system.

For so very long war had shaped Queen Elizabeth's policy, in the Low Countries, in France, in Ireland. Its cost in blood and treasure was high, its diplomatic and political dislocations profound. Since the 1560s continental Europe had been convulsed by wars and rebellions and the queen found herself dragged into conflicts she wanted no part of. After a decade of supporting the Protestant Dutch with money and mercenaries, an English army went to fight in the Low Countries in 1586. Expeditions in the 1590s to aid Henry IV of France against his Catholic opponents at home and the king of Spain achieved little militarily, often because of Henry's lack of grip and consistency in fighting his enemies (so Elizabeth seemed to see it). Every army, every navy, every commitment drained the Exchequer of money it did not have. But now there was a hope – just a possibility – that 1598 would bring to Europe something like peace.

The proposal came first from the Spanish court in Brussels to France, and then from France to England. Was it real? Could the Spanish be trusted? Henry IV, it seemed, was willing to believe that it was and that they could. He had had enough of war; he felt his kingdom to be at breaking point. In December 1597 Henry sent to Elizabeth an ambassador, fifty-eight-year-old André Hurault, sieur de Maisse, to explain his willingness to negotiate a peace with Spain.

At Whitehall Monsieur de Maisse saw Burghley as the chief of the queen's ministers and detected a sharp rivalry between Essex and Cecil. He courted both Burghley and Essex. Cecil, to the ambassador's eyes physically small and unimpressive as a courtier, lurked somewhat in the background. In audience de Maisse found Elizabeth to be clever, erudite, self-absorbed and apt to run off on long (and one senses quite deliberate) conversational digressions: she performed and lectured. De Maisse met the Privy Council in the council chamber at Whitehall

Palace. At their meetings were always the same ministers: Burghley, Lord Admiral Nottingham (in October Charles Howard, still lord admiral of England, had been created earl of Nottingham), Lord Buckhurst, Secretary Cecil and Essex. The ambassador noticed that Robert Cecil was always close to the queen.

On the putative peace Monsieur de Maisse found Elizabeth and her council cautious. They wanted to know much more about the Spanish proposals, seeing as significant the fact that they had come, not from a now-failing Philip II but from Brussels, where Cardinal Andreas of Austria was the acting governor general. They were alert to the possibilities of redrawing the diplomatic map; they sensed the opportunities. King Henry believed that the boundaries of Europe would be put back to what they had been at the conclusion of the Peace of Cateau-Cambrésis in 1559 – nearly forty years of change and dislocation restored to order.

For de Maisse, the weeks ticked by. Elizabeth and her ministers were not rushing the talks, and he was quickly frustrated by lack of progress. He had been in Westminster for six weeks before he felt any serious effort by Elizabeth and her ministers to engage with his embassy. That changed on 10 January 1598.

On this Tuesday de Maisse was in the council chamber at Whitehall making small talk with Lord Burghley. They discussed the Gregorian calendar, used in most of mainland Europe for fifteen years but still stubbornly resisted by England. De Maisse said to Burghley that Italian and German mathematicians held differing opinions about it, to which the old lord treasurer replied that both were wrong. One might imagine the awkwardness of the conversation. But then other ministers began to join them. Burghley, Nottingham and Buckhurst took the bench on the right-hand side of the council table. Essex, Lord Hunsdon and Cecil sat on the opposite side. Burghley led the meeting.

He began by saying that the queen had commanded them to convey to de Maisse her decision. She would send commissioners to France. Peace, the ambassador was told, would bring its own challenges. Essex interjected to say that religion would be difficult – by this he meant any hope of reconciling the seemingly insoluble conflict between the Catholics and Protestants of France and Europe. Then Burghley told de Maisse plainly that the queen's ministers were divided over the peace proposal. Some (Nottingham, Buckhurst) wanted it, another (Essex) did not. According to de Maisse, Burghley said that Essex was a young man and wanted war, a comment to which Essex did not reply. This may have been a pre-arranged piece of theatre choreographed to emphasize just how delicately balanced views on the peace were – Henry IV could not take agreement and support for granted. Perhaps Burghley was simply trying to provoke Essex.

After the meeting de Maisse had an audience at which Elizabeth told the ambassador she hadn't yet chosen her commissioners. She would think about it. She assured him that no one was closer to King Henry than she.

Two days later de Maisse had a meeting in the afternoon with Burghley, who told him he wanted peace. Then the ambassador met Essex, who said that he himself was proposed as a commissioner but had refused, in part because he was cautious of being blamed for war if peace couldn't be achieved.

Monsieur de Maisse found out on Saturday 14 January that Elizabeth's chief negotiator in France was to be Robert Cecil. The gossip he picked up at court suggested Cecil's nomination meant the talks were serious. Some said it was a sign that peace was on the way.[7]

All this time of Monsieur de Maisse's embassy Burghley had been working busily behind the scenes to make sense of the peace proposal. In early January the ambassador had pushed both Essex and Cecil for a meeting of the Privy Council, hearing nothing. On one of those days, the 2nd, Burghley wrote a paper weighing up the negatives and positives for Elizabeth and her kingdom of peace with Spain. Struggling with his pen, his writing made jagged by the stiffness in his hand, he recognized the many benefits of ending the destructive conflict on mainland Europe. But he had too an old man's caution. 'It may not be denied but a peace assuredly obtained is better than any war.' 'Assuredly obtained' were the two key words here: the question was how to achieve peace, and what costs and consequences it would have for Elizabeth. It would mean the end of fighting in the Low Countries. Ireland could then be dealt with properly. Merchants would be free to trade openly and safely with Spain, North Africa, the eastern Mediterranean, the Baltic and northern Germany. Yet there were 'discommodities' also, especially if the English

garrisons and troops stationed in the fragile northern Dutch States were
withdrawn, so leaving the new republic potentially exposed to Spanish
aggression. Burghley saw a situation in which Dutch Catholics might
provoke a new civil war and religious upheaval in the Low Countries.[8]

His lordship came to no conclusion, at least for the time being.
Peace was better than war, but so often they were difficult to tell apart
from each other.

Robert Cecil was appointed ambassador to the French king a week
before Monsieur de Maisse knew it. Cecil hoped to be away from
court no longer than a month. It was to be ten weeks.

The secretary's embassy in fact wasn't a very closely guarded secret.
Within days there was a queue of volunteers asking to accompany
him. Young gentlemen, like Francis Norris, a twenty-year-old heir to
a barony, could use a special embassy to enrich their 'further experience' and education – a kind of court internship. There were also
willing experts: John Phelippes was asking to go with Cecil to France
at this time. Phelippes, a younger brother of Thomas, had been secretary to a recent resident ambassador in Paris, Sir Anthony Mildmay,
and for a short time chargé d'affaires at the French court.[9]

Mildmay wrote for Cecil an unvarnished analysis of those in France
in favour of peace (the king, Catholics) and those opposed to it (soldiers, Protestants). Sir Anthony included too a short essay on the
nuts-and-bolts practicalities of getting an embassy to France. The truth
was that Cecil had no direct ambassadorial experience. This was his
first visit across the English Channel since before the Spanish Armada.
Yet he was leading an embassy which might lay the foundation work
for the most important European treaties in nearly half a century.[10]

In the early weeks of 1598 Cecil instructed the drawing up of a document that laid out in extraordinary detail his intelligence-gathering
system across Europe. Where 'The names of the intelligencers' was a
well-thumbed working office file, this latest paper was a descriptive
snapshot of the whole setup. Just four pages long, it was drafted by
Levinus Munck (a native of Ghent, about thirty years old and another
of Cecil's growing team of private secretaries), who called it the
'Memorial of intelligencers employed by my master', which Cecil then

annotated. The purpose of the document was to brief those who stepped in to cover Cecil's work while he was away from home: his father (naturally) and, perhaps more surprisingly, the earl of Essex – a minister who (as he said pointedly a few months later) had never before lowered himself to the mundane offices of a clerk. Being away from court meant that Cecil had to open up to other ministers what instinctively he would otherwise have kept to himself and his circle.[11]

The 'Memorial' gave the details of every one of his intelligencers. It began with the Biscay coast of France and Spain, strategically the most important region in western Europe for England. Here there were, of course, Paolo Teobast (described as an experienced factor in Spain, wife and children in England, recommended by Sir Horatio Palavicino), Thomas Honiman and Edmund Palmer. Teobast, it turns out, supervised the operation of Honiman's secret reconnaissance ship, which operated under the cover of carrying contraband goods (iron, pitch, some wheat) in and out of the port of Ferrol. Also on the Biscay coast was an Englishman who called himself Hans Owter. He earned a big salary: where Honiman's ship cost Cecil five hundred ducats, he gave Owter four hundred ducats a year, which Owter was paid through merchants' bills of exchange in Rouen.

In Lisbon Secretary Cecil had three informants. Two communicated through and were paid by two separate London merchants. The third was serviced by George Gilpin, the queen's ambassador to the Dutch council of state in The Hague.

Bayonne was covered by one of Thomas Honiman's factors as well as by Honiman's brother. Two intelligencers operated out of Seville. First was Massentio Verdiani, who sent his letters to England through Rouen – while on his embassy Cecil wanted to communicate with him directly. The second was one Andover, whose letters went first to a merchant in Waterford before being sent on in Cecil's official post from Ireland.

In Brussels there was a 'discreet man' with no name, or at least not one that in January 1598 Cecil wanted to put on paper. This mysterious character was managed at long distance by George Gilpin. In Rome, intelligence came from a merchant's factor called Tucker. In Zeeland Cecil used a Scottish preacher, and from Amsterdam reports came from one Joseph Jackson, factor to a merchant in Harwich. In

Sweden Cecil had two sources, Castelvetro, and a fresh new recruit, one Smith of Yarmouth.

All of these intelligencers were settled and established. But Secretary Cecil, through Wade and others in his circle of trust, presided over a band of irregulars, 'spies and false brethren' at home. Of these the most notable was Lawrence Bright, a Catholic priest living on the Sussex coast who travelled regularly over to Normandy and was part of the deep network of Catholic dissidents abroad. One of these dissidents was the spider at the centre of the web of English Catholic secret communication across Europe: Hugh Owen, sixty years old, a Welshman by birth, a professional émigré, spy and co-ordinator of spies for thirty-odd years, a busy and intelligent man close to the heart of Spanish government in the Netherlands. (Owen will appear again in the Gunpowder Plot of 1605.)

Robert Cecil's intelligence network cost Elizabeth's government 4,500 ducats (about £13,000) in intelligencers' annual salaries. This was a fraction of that expended on garrisoning the Low Countries, sending field armies to France, or deploying fleets on grand adventures; in many ways it was a sum of money much better spent.

Scotland was left out of the 'Memorial' but Cecil's intelligencers there, both of them in plain sight at the court of King James, were Roger Aston – a confidant of the king described by James as his 'trusty servitor' – and George Nicolson. Each man occupied a few folios in 'The names of the intelligencers'. Cecil had for years now managed the in- and out-tray of diplomatic correspondence with Scotland. The kingdom was never far from his mind.[12]

Times changed. European war might give way to peace. Elizabeth would one day die. Wherever he was – in Westminster, at court, or on his way to France – Cecil had to consider both present and future. The present was Spain and the Low Countries. The future meant looking north of the River Tweed and to James VI, Scotland's mercurially unpredictable king.

It was a grand send-off to France. Cecil left for Dover from the Thames-side landing stairs of Duchy House on Friday 10 February, accompanied by a glamourous entourage: Lord Thomas Howard, Lord Cobham, Sir Walter Raleigh and – the most striking of all – twenty-four-year-old Henry Wriothesley, the earl of Southampton. At the coast Howard, Cobham and Raleigh returned to court. The earl was travelling with the embassy.

Southampton had been a friend of Robert's for a long time. As a royal ward in the 1580s he was a graduate of the elite finishing school at Burghley House on the Strand. Blue eyes, long brown curly hair, a flamboyant dresser, it was Southampton to whom Shakespeare had offered his *Rape of Lucrece* in 1594: 'The love I dedicate to your lordship is without end ... What I have done is yours; what I have to do is yours.'[13]

They must have looked like a small army on the move. Gentlemen, secretaries, chaplains, servants, trunks and baggage, all travelling down the post road from Gravesend to Sittingbourne. On Saturday, in the kind of stormy weather that had given such atmosphere to his first trip across the Channel ten years earlier, Cecil ate at the Saracen's Head in Canterbury before getting to Dover late in the afternoon. He lodged near the castle up whose tower he had marched in 1588 to take in the fresh cold air.

For the next few days couriers galloped up and down the post road between Westminster and Kent. The activity was constant. Letters from Burghley and Essex, which had Cecil busy writing replies. Notes to his friends. A jewel received from the queen. Servants dispatched to and fro. Planning the disposition of ships and their passengers: Cecil and Southampton on the *Vanguard*, the bulk of the embassy's senior team on the *Answer* and the *Quittance*, with the *Tremontane* taking most of Sir Robert's servants. There were long meetings with visitors, including a gentleman sent by King Henry. More letters, more dispatches, more interviews. Admiral Nottingham's worries about the seaworthiness of *Vanguard* after nine months' duty in the English Channel: he was preparing in its place the *Rainbow*. The king of France impatient to get started. Time ticked by; they waited for the weather.

'With God's blessing, you shall understand, that I know of no alteration by her Majesty to change the course of your journey, and negotiation', Burghley wrote to Robert from Whitehall on 14 February. The old lord treasurer had for so long relied on Robert for court news, but now their roles were reversed. 'Other things I have not, but for your comfort, to assure you of the Queen's continuance of her favour to you, which specially this day I found very abundant upon my thanks given her for her noble reward sent unto you': he meant the jewel. Robert wrote in reply that 'My Lord Cobham tells me by his letter how much I am bound to you, as he perceives, by the Queen.' No courtier, however important, wanted to be forgotten by Elizabeth – to be away from her was to feel a kind of grief.[14]

Three days later Essex wrote to Cecil with strict orders from Elizabeth. There was a report of a new Spanish fleet: the earl of Cumberland had been sent into the English Channel, and other commanders, including Lord Admiral Nottingham, had mobilized. Cecil must stay in Dover. Burghley was coming to court: Essex guessed that Cecil too would be sent for. On no account should Cecil put to sea: 'her Majesty's commandment [was] given me very directly and peremptory'.[15]

In a few days the panic was over, thanks mainly to the efficiency of Cecil's own espionage system. 'By all intelligences coming hither from such as you have used', Burghley wrote to Robert, 'there appeareth small ability in Spain for the arming out of any new fleet a long time.' William Wade was monitoring all reports. One senses the importance of Paolo Teobast, sent off on his latest mission – discreetly referred to as 'the service' – in the first week of January.[16]

As it turned out, both Essex (writing with those peremptory orders on 17 February) and Burghley (on 23 February) were too late. Cecil had already sailed for France. At 5 p.m. on Friday 17 February he went aboard his ship. Essex's letter he received in Angers on 21 March, the same day he met King Henry IV for the first time, along with his pregnant mistress Gabrielle d'Estrées, and their son. At Cecil's lodgings Henry took him out into the garden, where they talked informally for two hours.[17]

The real business of the embassy began next day.

Cecil was like any other ambassador thrown back on his own resources. Naturally he had mastered what his father called the course of his negotiation. Burghley had done some heavy background briefing: few ministers, after all, had so comprehensive a grasp of half a century of

international politics and diplomacy. Where Burghley's body was failing, his mind was not; his memory for facts was as capacious as ever.
Cecil's instructions were clear, amplified by a private letter from the
queen.

All of this was fine, up to a point. With the exception of his few
weeks in Ostend in 1588, Cecil had seen diplomacy only from one
side, safe at court. So many factors would surely come into play: distance, time, the fluctuations of Elizabeth's mind and moods, the sheer
complexity in this negotiation of balancing her orders against the
demands of the Dutch and French and the manoeuvres of the enemy.
Cecil had known in very early January that also going to meet King
Henry was Johan van Oldenbarnevelt, the most formidable politician
in the free Netherlands. The Dutch had dispatched a separate negotiating team to Elizabeth.

Though Cecil was pre-eminent, two other ambassadors travelled
with him to meet Henry IV: Sir Thomas Wilkes and Doctor John Herbert. Both had the kind of diplomatic experience that Sir Robert
himself lacked. Wilkes was a veteran of Anglo-Dutch diplomacy and
a key English link with Oldenbarnevelt, as well as a named candidate
for the secretaryship – back in 1591 he had been a wry commentator
on Robert Cecil's wait to get it. Falling ill in Dover, Wilkes died almost
as soon as he reached France. It was an unexpected and serious blow
to the mission.[18]

Yet Elizabeth's ambassadors were anyway late to the game. Cecil
had sensed this in Dover, five days before sailing. French diplomats
were already deep in discussion with the Spanish commissioners from
Brussels. As he put it to his father, 'I do confess the chiefest end of our
journey is inquisition [inquiry, search].' He fully expected to be an
observer of negotiations already in motion, not someone who would
shape the destinies of kingdoms.[19]

18

No Ordinary Ambassador

The negotiations in France were, as he expected, slow and complex. Cecil was tested and tempered by some of the most influential brokers of power and policy in Europe. They knew whose son he was. He knew he had a reputation to live up to.[1]

At Cecil's and John Herbert's first proper meeting with the king of France Henry was bracingly direct; in response Cecil was as plain as he could be. Their two hours in the garden on 21 March had been social. He and Cecil were getting the measure of each other. The following morning, Henry received his ally Elizabeth's ambassadors in the privileged intimacy of his own bedchamber.[2]

Stating their mission, Cecil explained to the king that Elizabeth had not sent them to dissuade him from making a peace without his allies. The queen was his friend, and she was not opposed to a general peace for Europe. She wanted to know what Spain's offers to France were, whether the king believed them, how he proposed to make peace, and what he would do if the Dutch, who deserved protection, refused to be partners in the treaty. To this preamble Henry listened very carefully.

His reply was disarming. He said he was glad that Cecil was not a Venetian – by this he meant a clever Italian full of only words. Cecil served a wise prince, and rhetoric was for pedants: he could truly and freely speak to Cecil in a way that he could not with ordinary ambassadors, knowing that Cecil spoke personally for the queen. He valued Elizabeth as his sister; he shared her suspicions of Spain; it was necessity that pushed him to peace. Spain had offered him everything except Calais, captured so recently. He knew that Elizabeth, not France, had damaged Spain, but Spain had damaged France. He accepted that Cecil's and Herbert's mission was to keep him in the war against Philip, but said he would be mad to refuse a peace with good conditions.

> Now is the time to consider. I have dealt faithfully with my sister, and the more because I see she doth in this sending [of the embassy] respect me, for if I believe what hath been beaten into my mine ears, I am told that your drift is to amaze me to leave me in the war for ever, and to account that your safety. But I am not of that faith.[3]

A peace between England and Spain, Henry said, was easily agreed. The problem was the Dutch States, on whose behalf England and France would be locked in war for perpetuity. It was a knotty question, Cecil replied, which he left to wiser men than himself. But Henry was quick to jump on the ambassador's evasion. He pressed Cecil: 'But what think you?'[4]

And so Cecil answered him. 'I heard many wise men hold it for infallible that it were a strange apprehension to all his neighbours to behold a king of Spain by conquest or contract owner absolutely of all seventeen provinces.' If Cecil was for peace – as, contrary to what King Henry believed, general reports of his embassy suggested – this was a bold thing to say: he feared Spanish rule of all the Low Countries, north and south. Henry replied – his words are as Cecil reported them: 'He rose up to me and said I was an honest man; he loved me for mine opinion. But, saith he, use no such speech to my council that I say so.'

This exchange was frank but friendly. But there was a sudden change of atmosphere – Cecil noticed it. Henry became defensive. He said he saw few alternatives ahead of him. 'There is but two ways', he said to Cecil: 'either I shall be driven to all necessity and fury of my people, who are ready to rebel for peace; or my friends must help me, which I see you mean not, by maintaining the war.' If England wanted war, Cecil should speak to his councillors; he should hear what they had to say.

Cecil replied that he feared he had already said too much openly; Henry's favour and command had made him bold and forgetful. He and Herbert would of course meet with the king's council. But their mission was to understand Henry's negotiations with Brussels, not to explain the queen's own justifications for continuing war against Spain. Cecil reminded the king of the cost of England's war, speaking some uncomfortable truths about how far Henry had been propped up over the years by Elizabeth – she, as Robert Cecil well knew, had privately raged at the king's failures to get on with the job of fighting both Spain and the Catholic League in France, especially when she had sent English armies to support him. This rankled with Henry, who disagreed over many of the details of Cecil's exposition. The king's response was to say that Cecil was the son of the lord treasurer. The way Cecil recorded the comment makes it sound like a barb.[5]

So far, Henry had talked about the painful impossibility of his own position – he had no choice but to make peace. Cecil countered by laying out Elizabeth's own difficult situation. This, Cecil told the king, was worse than Henry's or that of the Dutch States. France was supported by England; the Dutch grew rich (how rich, with their recent breakthrough voyages to the East Indies Cecil knew very well). 'She [Elizabeth] had new fires kindled still, and yet new importunities, so as her trouble was *infinitum*.' Rebellion in Ireland, the menace of Spanish fleets, food shortages, domestic rumblings of discontent: Cecil didn't need to give specifics. But Henry was unsympathetic. It was a strange message, he said, that when a man was in need all he heard in response was another's problems and an account of aid formerly given.

They had got to the heart of the problem. France needed a peace that Elizabeth may too have wanted. But the future of the Dutch States mattered and there had to be guarantees of their safety from Spanish aggression. King and ambassador agreed for the moment to disagree. But at least they had been plain with each other; at least there was hope. Near the end of their bedside meeting Henry told Cecil that 'you see I deal with you not like an Italian upon punctilios nor with devices. And the Queen shall see I will trust you and negotiate freely with you for her sake.'[6]

From his place of contemplation at Gray's Inn Francis Bacon wrote, probably in the March of 1598, to his cousin Cecil. Bacon was sorry that the mission to France was turning out to be longer than expected. His sense from Cecil was that the negotiations were difficult. But Robert was built for hard labour, was born for adversity. 'Because I know the gravity of your nature to be not to hope lightly, it maketh me despair the less. For you are *natus ad ardua*: and the indisposition of the subject may honour the skill of the workman.'

Bacon reported that he had visited his uncle Burghley. 'I had the contentment to see your father upon occasion: and methought his lordship's countenance was not decayed, nor his cough vehement; but his voice was as faint all the while as at first.'[7]

Fifty-year-old Johan van Oldenbarnevelt was one of the architects of the Dutch States that so far had resisted Spain's war machine. He was its advocate, next in authority to the stadtholder, Maurice of Nassau, son of the assassinated William of Orange. Elizabeth's government knew in late December 1597 from George Gilpin in The Hague that Oldenbarnevelt himself was going to meet King Henry, though the advocate had hoped to avoid the mission. Oldenbarnevelt found himself hoist by his own petard though; in the complex negotiations ahead only he knew his own mind on what had to be done – he could hardly leave the negotiations to anyone else.

For all his experience and political talents, Oldenbarnevelt found it difficult to think his way into someone else's mind. He left for France believing that Henry IV would embrace as his priority the protection of the northern Netherlands from Spanish power. It hadn't occurred to him that to make peace with Philip II, France would consider breaking the triple alliance with England and the Dutch States. So Oldenbarnevelt took with him to King Henry no other plan than for the continuation of the war; no contingencies; no room for compromise.[8]

The Dutch embassy spent a couple of weeks trying to catch up with Cecil. Oldenbarnevelt believed that Cecil supported a peace, but the fact was that his stance was as fluid as Oldenbarnevelt's was rigid. In late March (early April according to the Gregorian calendar), after some initial negotiations with Doctor Herbert, the Dutch embassy met Cecil, who tried from the beginning to reassure them. Elizabeth had instructed her ambassadors to make public her support for the

Dutch States. She did not – Cecil and Herbert were clear on this – want to 'seek her own quiet without respect of them'. They had tried to dissuade Henry IV's council from making a treaty with Spain.

Oldenbarnevelt thanked the Englishmen. The Dutch States could not accept any peace treaty, yet they had found all the king's councillors with whom they had spoken 'passionate for it'. Henry had told them that he did not desire peace with Spain but necessity forced his hand. Cecil and Herbert explained to the Dutch that they had emphasized to the king 'the strictness of the tripartite league, and the danger for him to trust to Spain'. Oldenbarnevelt replied that they would prevent any treaty, fully expecting that the Dutch embassy then in Westminster had secured Elizabeth's support for this rejection of peace.

Principles and statements were one thing. Practicalities were something else, especially when it came to money. If England continued to stay in the war on behalf of the Dutch States, Cecil explained, then some way would have to be found to ease the burden on the queen's Exchequer. Oldenbarnevelt was quick to take the point: Cecil and Herbert were suggesting that Elizabeth would have to run down her establishment of garrisons in the Netherlands. Was it a threat or a bluff? 'Monsieur Oldenbarnevelt seemed a little awakened with this', the ambassadors reported to the Privy Council, 'and then fell into protestations of their necessities, and withal disliking diminution of her Majesty's forces that ought to be in the Low Countries.' Cecil and Herbert replied that the Dutch owed the queen a great sum of money. Oldenbarnevelt cited treaty contracts. Such contracts, the queen's ambassadors suggested, cut both ways.[9]

The differences of opinion and position between all three parties to the triple alliance against Spain were impossible to reconcile. Henry IV needed peace at any cost, it would seem, even to Protestant allies; Oldenbarnevelt and the Dutch refused to give an inch. Sir Robert Cecil was caught between the two.

In their penultimate audience with Henry, Cecil and Herbert reminded the king of their task. Elizabeth had sent them to communicate her position and to understand his Majesty's; they were messengers and observers. Her position was unchanged. Henry should not believe those who persuaded him that she wanted (as they put it) 'to amaze him . . . to make him lose his opportunities'. It was time to show by tangible actions that faith he had sworn to her. Cecil asked Henry to state clearly whether the king wanted war or peace.

Henry replied by pleading necessity, as he had done from the start. He said he was sorry to find himself in the situation where either he must ruin himself or offend the queen. But he had no choice, for 'he should get by the hazard of a war no more than he should have with assurance by peace'. Cecil responded: 'I told him that this was strange that his necessities were such as that he must be forced on a sudden to compound with the common enemy, and to do it to the prejudice of the confederates.'

Cecil knew that the embassy had achieved as much as it could (in reality, this had been very little). It was time to go home. Elizabeth would soon know where she stood. 'Sir,' Cecil said to King Henry, 'I beseech you, let us have our passport . . . for if her Majesty's benefits past and your honour tie you only to respect yourself, the Queen knows what to expect hereafter.'

The king absorbed Cecil's extraordinary directness. After all, he had said weeks before how Elizabeth's secretary was no ordinary ambassador: now he said so again. Cecil stuck to his position. 'I answered him that I took myself to be sent from a prince that ought to be extraordinarily respected. And, if without arrogancy I might speak of it, I might take myself, considering my place, for no common ordinary ambassador.'

Robert Cecil's report of Henry's response to this communicates something of his feelings towards Elizabeth's brother king. They were not wholly complimentary. 'He [Henry] said it was true, and so slubbered up [i.e., carelessly put together] some speeches of kindness again.'[10]

On Thursday, 27 April 1598, the ambassadors joined their ships at the port of Ouistreham, a few miles north-east of Caen. Sir Robert Cecil was taken back to England by the *Adventure*, a ship commanded by Sir Alexander Clifton. By a combination of navigational errors and poor weather in the Channel they ended up on the Isle of Wight. Cecil set out from Portsmouth for London on the morning of 30 April. At

Staines in Middlesex, he found the earl of Essex's coach ready to take him to Westminster. It was about an hour's journey: Cecil was at Whitehall sometime after 10 p.m. The queen, always late to bed, saw him straight away; it was a short audience. Then it was to Cecil House for the first time in two-and-a-half months and a few hours of sleep.[11]

Waiting for Cecil on his return to England was a letter from his household steward Roger Houghton. Houghton had written it from Lord Burghley's mansion on the Strand on Saturday 25 March, a month before Cecil had sailed from Ouistreham.

> May it please your honour to understand that my lord your father hath many sudden fits and qualms since his last extremity of sickness, and at this instant his lordship is sore vexed with the gout and taketh small rest, which doth weaken his lordship very much. I could wish your honour's speedy return, for I fear of the worst, which is doubted by divers of your honour's friends.[12]

Lord Burghley's fragile health earned a comment by a keen observer of court news, John Chamberlain, in a letter to his friend Dudley Carleton, a gentleman on the staff of the queen's ambassador in Paris. 'Master Secretary returned ... somewhat crazed with his posting journey; the report of his father's dangerous estate gave him wings, but for aught I can learn the old man's case is not so desperate but he may hold out another year well enough.' On this occasion Cecil's friends were correct. But Lord Burghley had four months left to live, not John Chamberlain's twelve.[13]

In late April the Treaty of Vervins concluded peace between France and Spain. England, shackled to the Dutch States, was still at war. Elizabeth was fuming.

Johan van Oldenbarnevelt experienced her anger for himself when he arrived at court in May. She raged at King Henry's perfidy in negotiating with Spain separately from her own ambassadors and those of the States. Oldenbarnevelt tried to calm her, pointing out that the Dutch had acted to defend their religion, liberty and rights. But she knew she was diplomatically and militarily stuck. Making her own peace with Spain could only mean giving up her control of the so-called 'cautionary towns' of Flushing and Brielle, governed and garrisoned by the English: thirteen years of wasted and wasteful struggle – this was what Cecil was getting at when he told Henry IV what a 'strange apprehension' it would be to see Spain once again in control of all seventeen provinces in the Low Countries. She recoiled, above all, at the cost of continued war. 'God alive! God alive! How am I to defend myself? How can the affairs of Ireland be provided for? What repayment shall I get? Who will pay the Flushing and Brielle garrisons?'[14]

Oldenbarnevelt's final meeting on his uncomfortable whistlestop mission was with Burghley. He found the ancient and ferocious-looking lord treasurer in his bedchamber armchair. Burghley spoke frankly. He praised Henry IV's actions: the king had seized the best opportunity for bringing peace to his kingdom and people. Contracts and treaties had to be interpreted reasonably. Oldenbarnevelt replied that in his opinion kings and princes were bound by their contracts, oaths and pledges before God and man – Henry had abandoned the tripartite alliance.[15]

After the interview Burghley scratched out a policy memorandum, the last he wrote of many hundreds over his nearly forty years as the queen's minister. He was pragmatic, as ever. He wanted the best of both worlds, peace with security: he encouraged England's military disengagement from the Netherlands while still supporting an independent Dutch state. The only thing that mattered was protecting Elizabeth's interests.[16]

God and queen, Lord Burghley's alpha and omega, his beginning and his end.

The servants of the seventy-seven-year-old lord treasurer were keeping a close eye on their master's health and reported to Robert Cecil with regular bulletins. In May and June Burghley was still working, was still balanced between recovery and eternity: 'And so I will prove all good means either to amend or to make an end', he wrote to Robert on 9 June. Sometimes he was at Theobalds, where the suitors who had pestered him for years had now melted away; sometimes he was in Westminster. His stomach was delicate, his appetite variable, though a few artichoke leaves seemed to help; his gout came and went. The queen fretted and sent him frequent messages: Sir John Harington, at court, wrote that 'she did entreat heaven daily for his longer life'. A cold June kept Burghley more indoors than out, but even so he took at least two hours' fresh air a day. Some days he could write, some days he couldn't; Henry Maynard was never far away. He planned his itinerary day by day, as his health allowed. 'It seemeth as though', wrote Harington, 'this good man had little else to do on earth than die.'[17]

By early July Burghley was reinstalled in his mansion on the Strand. On the 10th he wrote to Robert about Elizabeth's kindness: on a recent visit she had fed him, and he compared her to a mother nursing her baby. He thanked his son for a gift of partridges, concluding with a postscript. 'Serve God by serving of the Queen, for all other service is indeed bondage to the devil.' He wrote the letter in his own hand – unsteady, stiff – and signed it as Robert's 'languishing father'.[18]

It sounded like a valediction. Yet two days earlier Master Maynard had sent to Cecil Burghley's book on the personnel of Elizabeth's armies in Ireland: 'I beseech your honour that great care may be taken to the safe keeping of it, and when you have done with it, to return it to me, for it is a book my lord often calleth for.'[19]

Burghley's stomach continued unsettled; he wasn't eating or sleeping well. The latest embassy of Dutch diplomats said they wanted to meet him, but they knew they couldn't (as Robert wrote to his father on 23 July) 'until they might find you so well'. Instead, they paid tribute to him in his absence. The words are again Cecil's: 'her Majesty could have no greater opinion of your lordship's merit than the world had of your reputation, you being accounted in all foreign states and so registered to be, the ancientest councillor of Europe.' Robert sent with the letter three more partridges, killed by one of Lord Cobham's hawks. Burghley weakened; he rallied. He asked Robert to send him physicians.[20]

On Friday 28 July Burghley was fading. He was comfortable, in no pain, eating just a little: the previous evening he had taken some broth and blancmange, a fish or meat jelly. At about 7 a.m. on Friday morning he asked for a drink of asses milk.[21]

On that day, and for the following few, Burghley was attended by Roger Houghton and another long-standing gentleman family servant, George Coppin. On the morning of Monday 31 July, he instructed Coppin to write to Robert. He was confined to bed by great pain in his arms and hands. His throat was so sore that he was finding it difficult to speak or swallow. He was very weak. But Coppin was still hopeful that Burghley might rally.[22]

For 4 August 1598 Levinus Munck of Cecil's private office made the following note in his journal of outgoing letters: 'In the morning about seven of the clock died my Lord Treasurer Burghley at the Strand house, being Friday.'[23]

19

One Heart, One Way

Four days later, on Tuesday 8 August, Robert Cecil wrote to Thomas, earl of Ormond. The letter was unavoidable, but his heart wasn't much in it. Ormond, as well as being Elizabeth's lieutenant general in Ireland, was Burghley's old comrade: 'My good lord, although my affliction is so great by my father's death as I shall be excused to use long writing, yet to you that are participant of it I think not amiss to advertise it, assuring you . . . that you have lost a most noble and constant friend.'[1]

The sudden silence following Burghley's death was tangible, almost physical. Robert's entire political career so far had been under his father's tutelage. Their busyness was constant – for Burghley, it had been that way for the whole of Elizabeth's reign. By the 1590s briefings, books and papers were shared between Cecil's and Burghley's offices in adjoining apartments on the Strand. Their working partnership had grown closer as Burghley's health weakened. The old lord treasurer hated being dependent on others: he hated having to dictate letters, detested having to scrawl with his pen like an infant. But as a loving father and his obedient son the two men found an equilibrium, especially so when Robert acted as intermediary between the queen and a Burghley kept by sickness away from court. Their sitting together in council meetings, Burghley's advices and aphorisms, the feel he communicated for power: all of this has left at least some evidence. Yet real for Robert, if not so transparent now, was the deeper history – the life behind the historical record – of his whole making. In Robert's boyhood years, Sir William Cecil had been the queen's principal secretary who notched up all the superlatives: no one could match the first Secretary Cecil at the height of his powers. So many moments in Robert's early manhood were necessarily under his father's scrutiny: 1584, the stay in Paris; 1588, the mission to Ostend and the tour of the Netherlands; 1592, investigating the great carrack the *Madre de Deus*. Every one of Robert's moves had been scrupulously choreographed, every one of his letters checked: to everything a purpose. The duke of Parma had got somewhere close to all of this when he addressed twenty-four-year-old Master Cecil as 'son to him who served always his sovereign with unfeigned sincerity'.

Now at court and in council Secretary Cecil was on his own. He had to find his own way.

In the days following his death the former lord treasurer's senior household men sorted through their old master's books and working papers, moving them from Burghley's office to Robert's. Government had to carry on – it was one of his late lordship's oldest principles of service to the state.

The letters of condolence began to arrive: from Lord Keeper Egerton and Robert's friend Fulke Greville, both at court; from Sir Horatio Palavicino and Edward Lord Zouche. Greville was waiting to visit Robert when the time was right. Egerton knew that sorrow was only increased by the usual phrases and formalities, so he stuck to saying how much he loved Cecil's virtues and cherished his good opinion. On 6 August Henry Maynard, Burghley's faithful private secretary, requested three or four days' leave of absence. Having heard nothing from Sir Robert two days later, he asked again.[2]

It was the old dean of Westminster Abbey, Gabriel Goodman, now nearly seventy and one of the Cecil family's closest friends and spiritual advisers, who helped Robert to make sense of his father's death. On Thursday 10 August Goodman quoted as 'a fine defence against affliction' a verse from one of Mildred Burghley's favourite Psalms (55:22): *Iactam super Dominum curam tuam* – 'Cast thy care upon the Lord'. He saw Robert's continuation of Burghley's work as a divine providence, a succession granted by God. Goodman considered Lord Burghley's motto, *Cor unum, via una*, 'One heart, one way', taken from the Prophet Jeremiah. Concord was the strength of church, commonwealth and the Cecils. For Goodman it was another of God's blessings that the lord treasurer had 'two sons, noble branches of himself, being the root, the strength of his honourable house, and all depending thereupon'.[3]

There was an age gap of a generation between Burghley's sons Thomas (now the fifty-six-year-old 2nd baron of Burghley) and Robert (now thirty-five). Both were guarantors of their father's legacy; both knew this. Their differences were complementary. One was a soldier, an administrator and a baron; the other was a courtier and councillor. Thomas was the sole surviving link with the Cambridge of their father's teenage years and the inheritor of the Cecils' patrimonial house and estates at Burghley, just outside Stamford in the English midlands. Robert, equally, was the only surviving child of Mildred Cecil, whose death in 1589 was the profoundest loss in Burghley's life. Thomas and Robert together lived their father's motto. Though two individuals, in William Cecil, Lord Burghley, the brothers were indivisibly complete.

This was the principle by which Lord Burghley had divided his inheritance between them in his last will and testament. There would be no dispute, no contention: Thomas and Robert were two brothers by the grace of God living 'brotherly together', as their father put it. Houses, estates, moveable goods, even the badges and robes of the Order of the Garter – everything was to be portioned out. Where seamless separation was difficult, time must be allowed to copy and preserve: a mirror record to be kept by both brothers. The family genealogies of the Cecils and their forebears, which Burghley had so lovingly compiled over the years, belonged now to his heir Thomas, but were shared with Robert:

> I give all my books in my upper library over my great chamber in my said house in Westminster to my son Sir Thomas Cecil, and namely all evidences and rolls belonging to my pedigrees, giving to Sir Robert Cecil the use of them for two or three months to take copies thereof for his information of the same.

Robert received his own special inheritance of Burghley's enormous working archive. His father's papers were stuffed into every available room in the great mansion house on the Strand.

> As for all such books and writings as are . . . in any of my bedchambers, pallet chambers or chambers used for suitors to resort unto me or in

my study over the porch, I give unto my said son Sir Robert Cecil, with all my writings concerning the Queen's causes, either her revenue or for affairs of council or state to be advisedly perused by him.

It was through this extraordinary accumulation of papers and files that Burghley's staff now navigated.[4]

And so perhaps the silence for Robert wasn't going to be absolute. He knew his father's methods, had internalized his philosophy of counsel, had absorbed the energy of his service to God, queen and kingdom. He had a legacy to fulfil. Burghley still spoke to him power-fully through old letters and memoranda. A voice survived: as the poet puts it, 'the communication / Of the dead is tongued with fire beyond the language of the living.'[5]

The late Lord Burghley's funeral on Tuesday 29 August was appropri-ately spectacular. Over five hundred mourners attended Westminster Abbey. The coffin had sat for six days in the abbey's choir, surrounded by heraldic escutcheons and pennons. In the great procession Thomas, Lord Burghley and Sir Robert Cecil walked behind their father's ser-vants. The abbey echoed to the music of the Chapel Royal. Dinner was kept at Burghley House on the Strand.[6]

All of this was for public show. In September Burghley's body was taken from Westminster and buried in a tomb in St Martin's Church in Stamford. This was just as he had intended, having instructed his executors to take his carcase up the Great North Road with as little expenditure and ceremony as possible, to lie with his forebears.

In August 1598 the earl of Essex was smarting from a spectacular fall-ing out with the queen. The episode is as elusive as it was dramatic: a moment, either in very late June or very early July, where Essex is supposed to have turned his back on Elizabeth and received a slap across the face for his offence. His response, allegedly, was a reflex movement of his sword hand to his rapier. Three others are said to have witnessed the encounter – Lord Admiral Nottingham, Cecil and Thomas Windebank. It was Nottingham, Essex's former comrade-in-arms, who had restrained the earl.

Weeks later Elizabeth was refusing to see or hear Essex, and three days before Burghley's funeral he did what the old lord treasurer, finding himself excluded from the queen's presence in early 1587 over the execution of Mary Stuart, had also done – though Essex did it with considerably less tact and utterly without contrition. To Elizabeth, Essex wrote a letter of which the earl's private secretary, Edward Reynolds, made an office copy.

In his elegant scrawl the earl marshalled his words for maximum effect. He had been sent away but was not, as he had expected to be, called back to court. He was clear that the fault was the queen's:

> As I had not gone into exile of myself if your Majesty had not chased me from you as you did, so was I ever ready to have taken hold of any warrant that your Majesty could have given me for my return. But ... your Majesty would neither endure that my friends should plead for me to you, nor by their visitations give comfort to me and ... your indignation did take hold of all things that might feed it.

On the grim news of recent military defeats in Ireland, which the earl and his fellow ministers heard by report, Essex wrote to the queen that he had offered his advice: she had rejected it. He appealed to the example of the late Lord Burghley. 'I did nothing but that which the greatest, gravest and most esteemed councillor that ever your Majesty had did when himself bare less discomfort and the cause was less dangerous.' Essex concluded by emphasizing that he was her servant 'in whom you would fain [force, compel] discourage better endeavours than ever you shall find elsewhere'. She was shutting out her own best minister, acting against her own best interests.[7]

An observer of Lord Burghley's funeral three days later noted that the earl of Essex had the 'heaviest countenance' of all the mourners. After dinner that Tuesday the wronged exile retreated to his house at Wanstead.[8]

A few months earlier Edward Gray, a deputy warden of the marches up in the wild border country of Northumberland, had written to Lord Burghley about a man he had taken into custody.

The man called himself Valentine Thomas; everyone else did too, though it wasn't his real name (this was either Thomas Alderson or Thomas Anderson). He had recently travelled out of Scotland into England, and in the post town of Morpeth, a few miles north of Newcastle upon Tyne, his presence had been noted. People talked about him; they said that he was an intelligencer who knew the king of Scots. Gray had him arrested.[9]

Valentine Thomas had a reputation as a horse thief and a Catholic agitator. But the story he went on to tell over the following weeks would seriously spook James VI. He said that he had encouraged James to ensure his succession to Elizabeth's throne by favouring English Catholics and – more stunning still – claimed that he and the king had discussed the queen's assassination. The jolt this accusation gave to Anglo-Scottish diplomacy was out of all proportion to the man himself. One rogue caused a storm.

By autumn 1598 King James was worried; even the consistently strong message from Westminster that the allegations were not being taken seriously by Elizabeth's government couldn't calm his nerves. George Nicolson, Cecil's agent and intelligencer in Scotland, spoke to James in Edinburgh in June, reporting that 'The King is very well resolved to please her Majesty in all things: yet this matter of Valentine's is now the only doubt ... for he accounts it slanderous and shameful to be suspected of such villainy.' This letter Nicolson marked for Cecil's eyes only: 'I beseech your honour read and keep close to yourself.'

On Saturday 1 July James and Nicolson spoke again. Nicolson wrote: 'He spake of Valentine Thomas's matter as an untruth also used to his slander. I replied that I thought her Majesty nor none in England gave credit to that report, nor preferred the same before his Majesty's good mind.'

James was not persuaded. 'Aye', Nicolson recorded him as saying, 'but what is that enough? I am publicly slandered.'[10]

At the end of July James sent Elizabeth a letter, his neat royal autograph the badge of his sincerity. He wrote that he was a king wronged, even though he pretended to brush off easily Valentine Thomas's allegations. 'In truth, I bear so little regard to so vile and treacherous lies ... as I, through mine only innocence, should have force enough to bear me through the foggy mist of such groundless calumnies.' But still Valentine Thomas troubled him. James wrote again, a letter delivered to Elizabeth by the king's emissary David Foulis. 'I doubt not but your honour and love towards me will move you not to see me innocently wronged.' Anxiety, however, was deep in James's bones.[11]

The king desperately wanted an assurance on Valentine Thomas that neither Elizabeth nor her ministers would give him. Quickly both sides were stuck. In early September James's representatives in London met Elizabeth's Privy Council, the Scots declaring that Valentine had 'confessed matter enough both prejudicial to his Majesty's honour and future hopes. To his honour, in respect of the objections that have been made, and may yet be made his honour ... To his future hopes, in respect of the statute of association.' By 'future hopes' was meant James's hardly secret ambition to be Elizabeth's successor, while the 'statute of association' was the Act for the Queen's Surety of 1585, which would squash the claim that any conspirator against Elizabeth's person might pretend to have to her throne – indeed, it would expose that pretender, whoever he or she was, to the full force of what was in effect treason law.

On James's future hopes and the Act for the Queen's Surety her Majesty's ministers were silent. They dodged the issues presented to them by the Scots. Their responses to the king were in Elizabeth's best style – answers answerless.[12]

During his summer weeks of unhappy domestic exile the earl of Essex wrote a long essay which came to be known as his 'Apology'. Written as a private letter to Anthony Bacon, his most loyal of followers, it was a manifesto as much as a defence; a vision for the survival of England and Christendom against the continuing menace of Spanish power. In the 'Apology' Essex was bullish; he was in no mood to give or compromise. This Christian soldier was no warmonger, yet he knew what had to be done.

I am charged that either in affection or opinion or both I prefer war before peace, and so consequently that all my counsels, actions and endeavours do tend [to] keep the state of England in continual war . . . But both my heart disclaims so barbarous an affection, and my judgement so absurd an opinion.

Any peace in Europe had to be of the right kind. 'Let any man show me, how we shall have an honourable, safe, and stable peace, and I will embrace both it and him with both mine arms.'[13]

For a time, Essex stayed away from Privy Council, refusing to return until the queen gave him a private audience. This she resisted. But in early September he developed a fever. Elizabeth sent him her own physicians. The bubble was burst. Essex had a way back to favour.

Two months after Burghley's death the office of master of the Court of Wards and Liveries was still vacant – not a surprise given that it was Elizabeth's appointment. Was it now Essex's turn to preside over that great patronage machine? So the gossip at court went: 'All men give him their voices to be master of the Wards', wrote John Chamberlain on 3 October.[14]

The early autumn weeks of 1598 were for Essex the flash of sunshine and blue skies between the storm clouds; a time of reconciliation, perhaps even favour. The Court of Wards might make his fortune. Burghley's holding of the office had paid for Theobalds and much more besides; in his thirty-seven years in the office, his lordship had creamed off huge sums of money from the trade in wardships, negotiating the futures of those minors left as future inheritors to lands in the tenancy of the Crown. Lord Burghley – along with Lady Burghley and senior members of the Burghleys' household staff – had over many years taken substantial fees for settling wards on guardians. Robert and Bess Cecil were also involved in this institutionalized corruption.[15]

The most flagrant abuse of the system was selling off a young ward to a new guardian before the minor's father was dead. One especially egregious example stands out, but there were most certainly others like it. Back in September 1596 George Goringe, a gentleman from Sussex, had proposed to Cecil a deal that would benefit them both. Goringe's neighbour and kinsman, one Master Pellate, was close to death. He held his lands from the Crown, his income was two hundred pounds a year, and he had a son. Goringe's proposal bypassed the court's process of first conducting an inquisition post-mortem on the deceased's estate – naturally so, given that Pellate wasn't yet dead. Goringe made his pitch to Cecil: there was no delicacy here, no embarrassment.

> I desire your honour would buy the wardship of his [Pellate's] son for yourself and if your honour please I shall like that your honour do use my name and yet your honour to take the benefit. If my Lord Treasurer have promised it already, then if your honour so please my Lady Cecil may get him of the Queen's Majesty. If the ward prove well, I would be glad to buy him at the full value off your honour for one of my daughters.

A disguised transaction, blatant use of insider influence with the queen through Bess Cecil, a nod and a wink.[16]

Essex wanted to know whether the mastership of the Wards was still going to be as lucrative as it had been for the Cecils. In October he wrote to the court's most senior official, who sent the letter on to his personal clerk with a warning: 'I would not have any man but yourself privy hereunto for a thousand pounds.' Essex got to the heart of the issue: 'How may the revenues of the court increase without offence to the subject, and the master of the Wards have the same authority as the last had?' How, in other words, could the court generate for the queen the money she needed, stifle grumbling about corruption and malpractice, and still make the master of the Wards rich? The receiver general's clerk, Edward Latymer, replied with a practised official's skill. He recommended serious reform of the court but left Essex to come to his own conclusion about the likely freedoms of the next master. The answer was clear in the silence. The good old days of massive profits for the master were apparently over.[17]

It was perhaps this response which caused gloom to set in. In late October John Chamberlain reported two rumours current at court. The first was that Elizabeth wanted to abolish the Court of Wards altogether and to find a better way of raising an annual tax. The second, that Essex was reluctant to take on the mastership under the court's current constitution. Both rumours fit the letter Essex wrote to Elizabeth when it looked unlikely that she would appoint him, or anyone else, master. It was the familiar cry from the heart, the usual note of resentment at an offence undeserved, the unforgiving sharpness.

'Since I cannot go up to solicit your Majesty by speech,' he wrote,

> I must in this paper put your Majesty in mind that you have denied me an office which one of my fellows [i.e., Lord Burghley] so lately and so long enjoyed, besides many things else ... If therefore your Majesty give it not at all, the world may judge, and I must believe, that you overthrow the office, because I should not be the officer ... Therefore if your Majesty value me as you would do any man that had done you half that service, think again of the suit of your Majesty's humblest servant.[18]

As usual, Essex would have to settle for disappointment.

In August 1598 Hugh O'Neill (or Aodh Ó Néill), one of the great landowners in the northern province of Ulster and known by his English title of earl of Tyrone, had routed the queen's army at the battle of the Yellow Ford in County Armagh.

Tyrone was, earlier in his life and career, a bridge between Gaelic Ireland and its English rulers. His power base in Ulster had been set up by one of Elizabeth's chief governors in Ireland, Sir Henry Sidney, in the 1560s. For many years the earl had enjoyed productive relations with English officials and he visited Elizabeth's court as late as 1587. But the colonizing ambitions for Ireland of the queen's administrators and commanders, which by the 1590s were aggressive and punitive, squeezed Tyrone and other Gaelic Irish leaders, challenging their power and the offices and lands they held. Attitudes hardened on both sides. Tyrone fought back: by 1595 he was the leader of Gaelic resistance and the English government in Ireland declared him a traitor. As a defender of Ireland and the Catholic faith, he looked to Spain for military aid – and Spanish armies landing in Ireland and using the kingdom as a back door for the conquest of England was one of the nightmares of Elizabeth's ministers. Yet Tyrone was also a deft operator: he kept open channels of communication with Elizabeth's government and there were temporary truces, even pardons. But the slaughter at Yellow Ford ended all ambivalence. Without decisive English action – without a victory – Ireland could be lost for ever.

Essex in his 'Apology' characterized the grim fight for Elizabeth's second kingdom as 'a miserable beggarly Irish war'. He was now the great hope as Elizabeth and her ministers gathered themselves to appoint him lord lieutenant of Ireland and dispatch him across the Irish Sea with an army. As usual, this was not a straightforward process. Essex's appointment was still ten days in the future when, on Wednesday 20 December, John Chamberlain described life at court.

> The world is little or nothing changed here since I wrote last, only the Queen is resolved to keep Christmas at Whitehall; and the matters of Ireland stand at a stay or rather go backward, for the Earl of Essex's journey thither that was in suspense is now, they say, quite dashed . . . From Tuesday till last Sunday it held fast and firm that the Earl of Essex was to go and all things were accordingly settled and set down, but a sudden alteration came on Sunday night, the reason whereof is yet kept secret.

Relations between Essex and Cecil seemed convivial enough, however. Together they played cards in the queen's presence chamber. On 31 December Cecil was optimistic about Essex's new command. He wrote to George Nicolson: 'I think my Lord of Essex shall go presently into Ireland . . . [where] I doubt not he will give her Majesty better account in one year than hath been in seven.'[19]

On 20 December 1598 Valentine Thomas made a short but arresting confession of what he said the king of Scots had recruited him to do, and the queen, at Whitehall Palace, put her sign manual to what for her was a final statement on the ruffian's activities.

Valentine claimed that James had asked him to kill Lord Treasurer Burghley. Countenancing this, the king of Scots had instructed Valentine to go further. Contriving an audience with the queen, Valentine would stab Elizabeth to death. As Valentine described it, the proposal was almost a casual afterthought. The words he said the king had used were chilling: 'I must have you do another thing for me, and all

is one, for it is all but blood.' Two of the witnesses to Valentine's confession were well used to the interrogations of other prisoners held in
the Tower of London and the dramatic statements to which they put
their names – they were Francis Bacon and William Wade.[20]

So Valentine Thomas said, although he continued to languish in the
Tower indefinitely (he would not be executed till 1603). Certainly,
Elizabeth seems not to have taken the supposed conspiracy at all seriously, though she was content enough to use it to keep James dangling
uncomfortably. Her statement for the Scottish king, which was meant
to put an end to the affair, was this: she recognized that, notwithstanding her clear messages previously communicated to James about
Valentine Thomas, the king of Scots, her dear brother, 'remaineth still
much grieved with the scandal of such an imputation'. James had
asked her to make a public declaration of his innocence. She sidestepped his request; this present document was as much as she was
prepared to do. The queen acknowledged James's detestation of Valentine Thomas's claims and accepted her brother king's professed
friendship and amity. She, for her part, had supported James since he
had been in his cradle. There was to be no trial for Valentine, and no
promise as to James's future. That was it, with neither explanation
nor justification: 'we are no way bound to yield account to any person
on earth of any our actions more than in love and kindness.'[21]

Elizabeth's haughty declaration of her untouchability annoyed James
as much as his quotation from Virgil's *Aeneid* over four years earlier ('If
I cannot prevail upon the gods, I will stir up hell') had maddened her.
Now he grumbled in response that they were equals; he deserved to be
treated as such. Delivered to James by David Foulis – who, when he
returned to Scotland, was lambasted by the king for accepting it –
Elizabeth's statement under sign manual and seal was all the assurance
he was ever going to get on Valentine Thomas and, by implication and
insinuation, his ambition for her crown.[22]

For James, it was not good enough.

A few days into the new year of 1599 Essex wrote to one of his old
noble soldiering friends, Peregrine, Lord Willoughby. He set his face
resolutely to a future which had been determined for him. He was

being asked to save Ireland and had heard the call of duty. And anyway, military service was preferable to the intrigues of court. Though fighting the earl of Tyrone would be hard, Essex hinted that his most dangerous enemies were at home:

> Into Ireland I will go. The Queen hath irrevocably decreed it; the Council do passionately urge it; and I am tied in mine own reputation to use no tergiversation [equivocation]. And as it were *indecorum* [for the moment] to slip collar now, so were it *minime tutum* [not at all safe], for Ireland would be lost, and though it perished by destiny, yet I should only be accused for it, because I saw the fire burn, was called to quench it, and yet gave no help. I am not ignorant what are the disadvantages of absence; the opportunities of practising enemies when they are neither encountered nor overlooked ... The court is the centre: but methinks it is the fairer choice to command armies, than humours.[23]

20

Armed on the Breast

In early spring 1599 – most likely it was mid-March – Sir Robert Cecil sketched out on two sides of a folio sheet his assessment of what was going on in the government of Scotland. This was no essay or policy paper, but a summary. He didn't waste words; he wrote quickly. He was interested in people.

To Cecil, it seemed that the whole governing establishment of Scotland leaned dangerously to Catholicism. Of the chief officeholders, the lord chancellor, the earl of Montrose, was a Protestant by profession but was allied to the papists. The treasurer, the earl of Cassillis, was in Cecil's judgement 'simple, young, governed by the King's Chamber'; Cecil had met him in England and clearly wasn't impressed. The king's secretary was 'Elphinstone of Elphinstone, a papist'. The list of bullet-point sentences he squeezed in at the end of the paper suggested that Cecil's impression of James himself was not a positive one. The embassies he had sent to England. His interview with a messenger from the earl of Tyrone. His toleration of aid from Scotland to the rebels in Ireland. His speeches to the conventions of estates (Cecil's shorthand for James's public pronouncements on his plans for the English succession). Every tale communicated to Cecil by his intelligencers was – these were his three final words on the page, squeezed in at the bottom – 'a sufficient condemnation'.[1]

If this was not a cheering assessment of the king of Scots, his court and government, it was also most certainly not the full story. James was necessarily a factor in any calculation of England's future.

Cecil's 'Elphinstone of Elphinstone' was forty-one-year-old Sir James Elphinstone, one of the high-flyers of James VI's government. A younger son of the third Lord Elphinstone and a graduate in law of the universities of Angers and Poitiers, he was twenty-eight when the king appointed him judge in the Court of Session, the highest civil court in Scotland. From the law he moved to finance and government. When in 1589 James sailed across the North Sea to marry Anne, the daughter of King Frederick II of Norway and Denmark, Elphinstone in Scotland handled the king's diplomatic correspondence. After that, first in the new queen's household, he served for a few years as a senior official in crown finance – one of the so-called 'Octavians' – before his appointment in 1598 as James's secretary. Smooth, urbane, skilful, commanding, Sir James Elphinstone had much in common with Sir Robert Cecil, although whereas the former served a thirty-two-year-old king who was sharp, mercurial and ambitious, the latter was secretary to a sixty-five-year-old queen long set in her ways. Elizabeth's and James's complex histories shackled together their past, present and future. Their secretaries knew that they had deep ties of mutual self-interest. Delicately, tentatively, the line of communication needed to stay open.

That was tricky when James prickled at Elizabeth's (as he saw it) ambiguous response on Valentine Thomas. In late February 1599 James instructed Elphinstone to send Elizabeth's statement on Valentine back to Cecil, something which Elphinstone tried to brush off as procedural: this was simply an expression of his Majesty's 'discontentment' at David Foulis, who shouldn't have accepted it in the first place. We can be sure Cecil got the point. After all, Elizabeth's sign manual and seal were being returned to her secretary like undeliverable mail. It was – and was surely meant to be – a snub.

On Valentine Thomas King James needed justice; through Elphinstone he wanted Cecil's help, for the latter to 'travail by all good means' to wrestle out of Elizabeth a clear and definitive statement on James's innocence. Elphinstone went further than this. He emphasized how they, the two secretaries, needed to work together in common interest: 'I look for an honest correspondence'. Elphinstone offered to Cecil his friendship.[2]

George Nicolson, Cecil's key intelligencer in Scotland, was a member of the small and secret group that, through friendly communication, promised a constructive way forward for Elizabeth and James on the problem of Valentine Thomas. Nicolson, who spoke regularly with Elphinstone, emphasized to Cecil how important it was to keep the two secretaries' letters to each other highly secret. The only others who knew about their delicate but necessary correspondence were the queen and the Scottish king.[3]

But Cecil didn't rush to reply to Sir James Elphinstone's February letter. He and Elizabeth took their time: it was mid-April when Cecil drafted his response. He was positive; he was reserved. He appreciated Elphinstone's professions of affection and honesty in the relations between James and Elizabeth. He expressed grief at the king's response to Elizabeth's statement, but on this Cecil had nothing to say: the queen would send an ambassador to the king. Cecil measured everything according to his service to Elizabeth. He made his statement, professed his loyalty:

> I shall stand free from any conceit of coldness to give furtherance to any of his Majesty's recommendations which shall not vary from my duty to my sovereign. And for yourself, sir, I pray you believe that, as I think, we are both born for nothing more than to study the conservation of royal amity between the two princes.[4]

Brisk and concise, Cecil was giving little away.

At about 2 p.m. on Tuesday 27 March General Essex began his farewell ride through the streets of London. Plainly dressed, accompanied by a large entourage of nobles and gentlemen, he set out from Seething Lane near the Tower and travelled the usual ceremonial route through the city, along Gracechurch Street, Cornhill and Cheapside. There was a great press of Londoners, shouts of 'God bless your lordship', 'God preserve your honour'. Essex was going at last to Ireland.[5]

The soldier poet Thomas Churchyard celebrated Essex's expedition in verse, comparing the earl to Scipio Africanus, the great Roman general who had defeated Hannibal. Churchyard foresaw with grim clarity the defeat of the traitorous rebel earl of Tyrone, felt the inevitable victory of the righteous:

Right makes wrong blush, and truth bids falsehood fly,
The sword is drawn, Tyrone's dispatch draws nigh.
A traitor must be taught to know his king,
When Mars shall march, with shining sword in hand,
A craven cock cries creak and hangs down wing,
Will run about the shrape and dare not stand.

Churchyard was likening the ensuing combat to a cockfight: the
shrape was the birds' fighting enclosure.[6]

Celebration, acclamation, expectation: hopes were high for a long-
awaited success in Ireland, after so many failures. But on the evening of
the earl's departure from London a contemporary chronicler observed
a natural event that was perhaps significant. When Essex and his entourage left the city, the sky was clear and the weather calm. But that
evening brought a storm: a great black cloud, sitting north of the city
over the outlying village of Islington broke, with lightning, thunder, hail
and heavy rain. The chronicler wondered – did others too? – whether it
was an ominous portent.[7]

With over 17,000 men in his command, the earl of Essex took to
Ireland the largest Elizabethan army ever to leave England. Expectations of Tyrone's defeat were almost as huge.

Sir William Bowes was the ambassador Elizabeth sent to King James.
Where Robert Cecil's mid-April letter to Sir James Elphinstone was
brief and ambiguous (an uncharitable reader of it might even say
terse), Bowes's instructions were quite the opposite. Many pages in
length, they covered every aspect of the Anglo-Scottish relationship,
from big diplomacy to the minutiae of fraught cross-border blood
feuds amongst the lawless reaver families. Embedded in Sir William's brief were some patches of very plain speaking. On dealing
with Valentine Thomas, the queen had been transparent and discreet: she wanted to protect the Scottish king. And she knew – and
had known for some time – that James was trying to recruit supporters, in Scotland and abroad, for his claim to her crown. She warned
him, for his own good, to stop it. 'And therefore', Bowes's instructions read,

we require you to make the King understand that in a time when he has used so strange intimations to prepare the minds of other princes in future time to further his pretensions, and when he shows himself so little to value our good will . . . therefore nothing must be thought acceptable.

His pretensions: just those two words, cool and dismissive, code for the future rule of her kingdom. Through her ambassador Bowes, Elizabeth hinted at some disagreeable consequences for the king if he continued to press on the succession. 'All this we will you plainly tell as a thing for which we are sorry, even for his own sake that he gives himself so great disadvantage.'[8]

At the top of one of the stone staircases in the old palace of Westminster, close to Westminster Hall and the Court of Requests, was the Court of Wards and Liveries. For such an important cog in the great machine of Elizabethan court patronage its physical proportions were modest. The building it occupied was much the same size as a modern doubles tennis court – about seventy feet long and between thirty and forty feet broad. The space inside was subdivided into an outer court for public business, at the heart of which was a large table, and then, behind a screen, a cluster of private rooms including a council chamber. The setting overall was not lavish: there were some cushions on the benches, and in pots the usual medicinal herbs to cleanse the air. The court's officers and staff had the treat of a mid-morning drink of white wine and sugar. This was no-frills bureaucracy.[9]

Robert Cecil's appointment as master of the Court of Wards was the last of three major appointments in May – a positive avalanche for the very late 1590s. Lord Buckhurst, for years one of the handful of core privy councillors, was, nine months after Lord Burghley's death, made lord treasurer on the same day – Sunday 13 May – that the lord chief justice, Sir John Popham, swore the Privy Council oath. Exactly a week later Levinus Munck made a note in his journal of outgoing business letters: 'My master Sir Robert Cecil is made master of the Wards and Liveries.'[10]

On the surface he was his father's successor to a role that had helped to make the Cecils rich and powerful. The appointment to the mastership suggested a happy continuity, for those at least who chose to forget that months earlier the earl of Essex had looked likely to be the queen's appointee. Bishop Richard Bancroft of London wrote to Cecil that he was one 'amongst many of your friends who rejoice for the attainment of your late office . . . heartily entreating your honour to begin . . . where your right honourable father left'. Bancroft, a sharp-eyed suitor, was certainly quick off the mark – Cecil's 'late office' was only three days old. But Cecil was not full of joy at taking on the Wards. He didn't much want to give up the Duchy of Lancaster. On the same day Bancroft wrote to him, Cecil commented glumly to the queen's ambassador in Paris, Sir Henry Neville:

> The domestical news we have these: that the Lord Buckhurst is Lord Treasurer, [the] Lord Chief Justice a councillor, and myself Master of the Wards, but so restrained by new orders, as in the office I am a ward myself. But seeing it was my father's place, and that her Majesty hath bestowed it on me, I will undergo it with as much integrity as I can; and yet I vow to you, I have resigned a better place of the Duchy for it.[11]

Such was the heavy and necessary burden of service, the steady accumulation of influence and power. And how some hated Cecil for it – certainly the earl of Essex's followers and, though they are harder to identify, ordinary Elizabethans who grumbled at the Cecils' riches and dominance. Poems and libels were common, the former hidden away in courtiers' private writings, the latter scattered in public places in London like Paul's Cross or the Royal Exchange. They were venomous: here Robert Cecil the suave technocrat and expert minister – the way he saw himself – was a monster of nature, Machiavellian, dissimulating, corrupt. As one libel ran:

> Proud and ambitious wretch that feedest on naught but faction
> Prevail and fill thyself, and burst with vile detraction,
> Detraction is thy game, and hath been since thy youth
> And will be to thy dying day; he lies that speaks the truth
> But well I know thy bosom is fraught with naught but scorn
> Dissembling smoothfac'd dwarf, would God thad'st ne'r been born
> First did thy sire and now thyself by Machiavellian skill

Prevail, and curb the peers as well befits your will
Secret-ary I know your crookback spider shapen
Poison to state and commons, foe to virtue, friend to rapine.[12]

'Detraction' was to present the qualities of the virtuous to seem like vices: this for the libellers was Cecil's lifelong skill.

Secretary, keeper of secrets, Machiavel, minister; the spider at the centre of the web. How easy it was for some to despise Robert Cecil.

Sir William Bowes's report on his audience with King James arrived in Secretary Cecil's private office on Tuesday 29 May. His secretary Simon Willis read and summarized it, neat and efficient as ever.

It had been quite a meeting. Bowes had made clear to James its seriousness – the time had come for a fundamental recalibration of the relationship between the two monarchs. 'I have let him [James] see the weighty importance of the substance therein contained,' Bowes wrote to Cecil, referring to his instructions, 'and that it is high time to put an effectual end [to] these jealousies depending between their majesties, of so dangerous consequences for him.' The king had more to lose than Elizabeth in continued frosty relations between England and Scotland.

The audience did seem to have cleared the air; James was now on something of a charm offensive, perhaps sensing that he wasn't in so grim a situation after all. Bowes told Cecil that the king would write to Elizabeth 'effectually signifying his resolution to deserve and retain ... her Majesty's kindness, which he acknowledgeth himself to have abundantly received heretofore, and which he esteemeth above all other on the earth'.[13]

On 31 May James corrected in his own hand Bowes's account of their meeting, adding long paragraphs of his own. James – on paper, in speech – couldn't resist an opportunity to discourse at length but, like Elizabeth, he wanted to get his words absolutely right.

He didn't refer explicitly to the English royal succession, but he did respond, disarmingly, to Elizabeth's challenge that he had been recruiting in Europe supporters for his claim to her throne. The cause of the misunderstanding was an embassy James had sent to

Germany. 'Touching that which your Majesty [Elizabeth] taketh for bespeaking assistance', it was David Foulis who once again took the blame for having misspoken in his explanation to the queen of the ambassadors' mission. The purpose of the embassy had been simply to bring about peaceful relations between Christian princes. 'He [James] trusteth your Majesty will not in so good and just a purpose remember the offence of one mistaken word, himself with earnest protestation wishing the continuance of your happiness by the good will of God.'

The issue unspoken – succession – was unspoken still, smoothed over, pushed ever so delicately to one side. For the time being.

While in May and June 1599 Sir William Bowes was occupied in delicate diplomacy at the court of King James and Cecil was pinned down by paperwork at Greenwich Palace, the earl of Essex was getting the measure of his lord lieutenancy in Ireland. His expedition against the Irish rebels was not running smoothly.

Most of the campaigning so far had been in the south of the kingdom, in a loop from Dublin that took Essex and his army into Munster and Leinster, completely avoiding the earl of Tyrone's own territory in the north. The English forces achieved some victories and breakthroughs, but the fighting was hard – much closer to Essex's predictions in his letter to Lord Willoughby than to Thomas Churchyard's heroic verse. By the time his army was back in the safety of Dublin – the base of English government in Ireland – in early July, both it and its general were exhausted. To Sir Henry Neville in Paris, Cecil offered a balanced assessment of Essex's progress, though recognizing that the main fight should be in Ulster:

> The lord lieutenant hath ranged the best part of Munster with his army and is come back to Dublin ... and so I fear this will be till my lord hath been in the north of Ireland and given a main blow, of which I doubt not, for he is preparing with all speed thither.[14]

Essex himself was not so optimistic. Twenty-four hours earlier he had written to the Privy Council with his latest news. 'I am armed on the breast but not on the back. I armed myself with confidence that rebels in so unjust a quarrel could not fight so well.'

He was more vulnerable from behind. But whom did he have in mind? The enemy in Ireland, or colleagues at court?

It might have been Rouen in 1591 again, or Cadiz in 1596. The pattern was so familiar. The general given clear instructions on what to do; the queen convinced day by day that he was deliberately ignoring her orders. Justifications, reproofs, temporary reconciliations, more reproofs. But in Ireland Essex was at last reaching the end of the line.

Cecil corrected the draft of Elizabeth's letter to the earl, which Thomas Windebank, on duty in the privy chamber that summer's day, dated 19 July. The voice, however, was wholly that of the queen. It seemed to her that in two months Essex had achieved only expense and waste. His few military successes had brought little benefit for her. Tyrone seemed now apparently unstoppable without a bigger army to oppose him. The world might perceive a suspicion that her commandments were being neglected – in other words, she knew full well that he was not obeying her orders. She had expected him to fight in the north. That was where he needed to go.

Put simply, Essex needed to isolate and defeat the earl of Tyrone:

> We must now plainly charge you, according to the duty you owe us, so to unite soundness of judgement to the zeal you have to do us service, and with all speed to pass thither in such order, as the axe may be put to the root of that tree, which hath been the treasonable stock from whence so many poisoned plants and grafts have been derived.[15]

Essex made slow progress from Dublin to the north. His plans for the next phase of his lacklustre campaign provoked from Elizabeth in early August a withering response. What he had achieved or supposed he would achieve amounted practically to nothing. Sitting under a huge 'Elizabeth R', the queen's instructions for Essex on 10 August read:

> The letter which we read this day from you ... concerning your opinions for the northern action doth rather deserve reproof than much answer. And therefore you shall hereby understand that when we

examine all parts of your writings and lay them together, we see nothing but insinuations to dissuade that which should be done in that point of great consequence.

Here, surely, was a deliberate poke at Essex the martial hero – he was trying to avoid doing the job that needed to be done.[16]

Essex's response was self-immolation. He wrote to Elizabeth that he had nothing left to give; he was exiled to cursed Ireland; death was his only release. 'From a mind delighting in sorrow; from spirits wasted with travail, care and grief; from a heart torn in pieces with passion; from a man that hates himself and all things that keep him alive, what service can your Majesty reap?'[17]

On Friday 7 September Essex met the earl of Tyrone, not in battle, but in parley. Facing the rebel army, Essex found his forces outnumbered. The two earls spoke, Tyrone's horse standing up to its belly in the Bellaclynthe ford over the River Lagan, Essex's standing on the river-bank. Essex reported after the meeting that they had agreed Tyrone's submission to the queen.

It was Henry Cuffe, one of Essex's senior household officials, who carried the message to Elizabeth at Nonsuch Palace. On Friday 14 September she dictated her reply, describing Essex's unauthorized parley with Tyrone 'a course more strange, if strange may be'. Two days later she responded again. Her warning to Essex was blunt. 'To trust this traitor upon oath is to trust a devil upon his religion. To trust him upon pledges is a mere illusory.' Essex was to do or agree nothing more with Tyrone without her permission.[18]

Robert Cecil sensed that events had come almost to a reckoning. 'At his return [to Dublin] my lord will fall to capitulations [bargains or treaties] more particularly, which will be the way to draw things to conclusion, so as I conceive my lord will not be long in Ireland.'[19]

This was true enough. But it was the earl of Essex, not Elizabeth, who made the decision for her lord lieutenant to leave Ireland on his own authority.

21

Sprigs of Gold

On the morning of Friday, 28 September 1599, Essex made a peaceable assault on Nonsuch Palace. It was perhaps his most accomplished tactical manoeuvre of that year. Arriving at court without any forewarning, he moved at speed through the queen's private rooms, appearing in her bedchamber soon after ten o'clock. Elizabeth was not long out of bed and not yet fully prepared for the day ahead. He knelt and kissed her hand. She 'gave him good words, and said he was welcome: and willed him to go to his lodging, and rest him after so weary a journey'.

He returned for a second audience an hour later; they talked for about ninety minutes. The atmosphere seemed cheerful, or at least Essex was. As the earl ate dinner, he received friends and followers and spoke positively about Ireland. But between Essex and one of those visitors – Sir Robert Cecil – there was a noticeable 'strangeness', a crackle of tension.[1]

By mid-afternoon the mood had changed. At a third audience the queen communicated to Essex her displeasure at his return to court, having left Ireland in so vulnerable a situation. She instructed a small group of privy councillors – Lord Chamberlain Hunsdon, Lord North, Cecil, Sir William Knollys – to meet the earl. They interviewed him for an hour. Between ten and eleven o'clock at night Essex received Elizabeth's command to stay in his chamber.

The Privy Council met for the whole morning the following day, 29 September, Michaelmas. At 2 p.m. they sent for Essex. When he entered the chamber, the councillors rose to salute him and then sat back down. He did not sit but stood bareheaded at the head of the table. No clerks of the council were present – this was a closed, secret examination. After three hours Essex returned to his chamber. The council met the queen.[2]

Two days later Elizabeth called for Lord Keeper Egerton, Lord Treasurer Buckhurst, Lord Admiral Nottingham and Cecil. They were in conference for most of the morning. The four councillors left, met together, and returned later to speak again to the queen. Afterwards they convened in Buckhurst's rooms. Then they sent for Essex. On this first day of October, a decision was made.

It took the courtier and keen political observer Rowland Whyte three days to piece together what happened at that meeting. 'When he [Essex] came to their presence, [he] made a low reverence, and stood still. They desired him to come nearer: then he went towards them, doing the like duty. A while afterwards, he went to his chamber again.' In the afternoon the earl of Worcester's coach arrived in the palace's stable yard and Lord Essex, who had been put into the custody of Lord Keeper Egerton, was taken in it to York House on the Strand, Egerton's official residence.

Whyte could reconstruct what had happened but he, like everyone else at court, could only guess at why, and at what had been said. He feared that Essex had greatly offended the queen. What Whyte also knew was that Robert Cecil was a man any courtier should want to have on his side: 'his love is very worth the seeking. He is one that her Majesty exceedingly values, and [is] most trusted by her in all great affairs, and business of kingdom.' This is perhaps what Essex himself was discovering.[3]

Palace and London buzzed with the Essex affair; to this Elizabeth's remove from Nonsuch Palace to Richmond Palace the day following the earl's departure from court made not one jot of difference. 'In this place,' wrote Rowland Whyte, 'all men's eyes and ears are open to what it will please her Majesty to determine with the Earl of Essex, who remains close prisoner at my Lord Keeper's. Her displeasure and indignation towards him is very great.'[4]

For the vigilant courtier there were indications and hints, signs to be read and interpreted. On 4 October Whyte saw Attorney General Coke at the queen's court. The following morning Egerton, Buckhurst and Cecil had a conference with the earl that began at eight o'clock and ended close to eleven. What the charges were against Essex was not public information, but Whyte made an informed guess. Essex's contempt of his command by returning to England. That in Ireland he had failed to follow his instructions. That his parley with the earl of Tyrone was dishonourable to the queen. That, contrary to Elizabeth's command, he had promoted his own men and made many knights – this was Essex's habit since at least Rouen in 1591 and had long been a sore spot for Elizabeth. 'These, and such like, are the fancies we dream of.'[5]

Whyte, as it happened, was close to the mark. Cecil wrote his own account of Essex's surprise appearance at court. He had disobeyed the queen's absolute command not to come home. The explanation for his return, according to Cecil, was that Essex, realizing the agreement he had made with Tyrone was not as substantial as he had claimed it was in his letters, was hoping to persuade Elizabeth in person. Cecil knew that her patience had run out. 'This . . . added to the breach of her commandments, did so much exasperate her mind, as she resolved to command him from her presence, and to commit him to the house of the Lord Keeper, where he is.' But this was temporary; its purpose was to make a point. 'A matter which must have an end,' as Cecil put it to Henry Neville in Paris, 'and will have shortly; though for ex-ample's sake her Majesty hath kept this form with him.'[6]

Thus, that was how Essex's situation looked a week later. He was con-trite and well-behaved (so at least Rowland Whyte reported), even if his followers were sometimes too vocal in toasting their patron and drinking to the confusion of his enemies. The situation had settled itself down; the earl's release was perhaps two or three days away. Whyte heard that Cecil had told Essex 'that he was glad to see her Majesty well pleased with his courses [and] that he would do any-thing to further his good and contentment'.[7]

'The Queen will not bear the blame of his imprisonment, and where it shall lie is not yet known.' So ran Whyte's analysis on 16 October, and it was entirely consistent with Elizabeth's long practice of deny-ing the consequences of her own commands and shifting responsibility elsewhere. A week later, Essex looked unlikely to be released from his house arrest. According to Whyte – the official record is tight-lipped – the Privy Council attempted to persuade Elizabeth to free him. She resisted; she was sharp and combative; she still felt Essex's offence keenly. 'She very angrily told them that such a contempt ought to be publicly punished; answer was made by them, that her Majesty by sovereign power . . . might do it, but it stood not with her honour and clemency to do it.' Elizabeth's response was to command that a list of the earl's offences be collected out of his letters and papers.[8]

But if the council was playing devil's advocate on Essex, relations between the earl and Cecil seemed to have collapsed. Whyte reported on 25 October that the two men were at war and that a mediation between them had been proposed but was not likely to happen: Cecil was 'unwilling unto it, because there is no constancy in his love, and says he is too violent in his passions' – the pronouns here belong to Essex. Perhaps he was beyond even Cecil's help – or maybe, with his finances and career all but ruined, Essex wasn't quite worth the effort.[9]

In late November Essex's fellow privy councillors conducted in Star Chamber a formal examination of his failures. All the charges were serious. Misuse of the queen's treasure. Lingering in England for two months after his appointment as lord lieutenant. Not engaging straight away with the earl of Tyrone and his forces. Talking to Tyrone without the permission of the queen and her council. Handing the command of his army to others. Leaving his lieutenancy and returning to England against commandment. The councillors queued up to offer their judgements. Essex had appealed to them by letter from York House as their humbled-hearted 'poor friend', but in Star Chamber their lordships of the council made a ruthless critique of his conduct in Ireland.[10]

Back in Ireland in very late November, officials and commanders were picking up the pieces of Essex's failures. On the last day of the month the earl of Ormond and Sir Geoffrey Fenton had a meeting with the earl of Tyrone across a river near Ferney in County Fermanagh. Fenton told Tyrone that Elizabeth 'had been informed by the earl of Essex that he found in him an internal desire to become a subject'. Here was her response, communicated, one senses, through her and perhaps Fenton's gritted teeth: she had a 'gracious inclination' not to reject Tyrone 'but to reserve her favour for him, so as she might find that his desire to be a subject proceeded from a sound heart, and that the world might know that he were truly penitent for faults past'.

Tyrone replied politely but coldly: 'her Majesty's favour was the thing he desired, and did never refuse it.'[11]

They discussed the demands Tyrone had made of Essex at their conference. Fenton told Tyrone that the queen wanted more time to give her answer. Fenton sent all twenty-two demands to Robert Cecil: in summary, the restoration of a Roman Catholic Church in Ireland, all offices in church or state to be held either exclusively or in majority by Irishmen, protections for Irish land, inheritance and trade, and the appointment of an English governor, to be called a viceroy, who had to be at least an earl and a member of Elizabeth's Privy Council.

Cecil wrote on the back of the paper 'Ewtopia' – 'Utopia': 'no place'.[12]

By December Essex was ill. Lord Keeper Egerton was worried enough to send urgent reports to Cecil. Tired with physic, Essex felt it was (as he put it) the patching up of an overworn body. The countess of Essex visited her husband, thanks to Cecil's influence with the queen; she wrote effusively, and significantly, to say that Cecil's 'honourable mediation' was proof for her and her husband that he would never be Essex's 'malicious enemy'. Popular opinion in London begged to differ. Rowland Whyte reported libels daubed in public places which suggested that Cecil was withholding from Essex medical treatment. There was a rumour that the earl was suffering with dropsy and that his life was in danger. His followers were saying that it would be a long time before he recovered his freedom and Elizabeth's favour.[13]

Writing to Sir Henry Neville in Paris, Cecil's view in late December was this:

For himself [Essex], his case and his punishment is at a stand. He hath been very sick, but is now well amended; and though I cannot certify you any other hard or severe course intended against him, yet I assure you the Queen holds a very strict hand over him, and doth exceedingly sharply throw all her misfortunes upon him in Ireland.[14]

Elizabeth was at Richmond for a convivial Christmas. She danced and saw plays and with Lord Buckhurst, Lord North and Robert Cecil played primero in her presence chamber.[15]

But much was unspoken, as Thomas Smith, a new clerk of the Privy Council, finding on 23 December some peace and quiet in the palace's council chamber, suggested in a letter to a friend:

> The court is the only school of wisdom in the world: it taketh not thought for anything or any person ... I shall tell you who hath the best grace, or showeth the best tricks in dancing ... otherwise I have nothing to say. For of other tricks in the court a man may not write ... Those that are in prison and in extremity of sickness find little comfort, notwithstanding all Christmas mirth.[16]

This holiday the usual courtiers' exchange of gifts felt especially charged with meaning. Elizabeth ignored the present Essex sent to her. It, like its giver, remained in a kind of no man's land.

Not so the gifts offered by Sir Robert Cecil. 'Master Secretary hath bestowed great and many New Year's gifts this year in court', wrote Rowland Whyte on Twelfth Night. What Cecil presented to his queen gleamed: 'Seven sprigs of gold garnished with sparks of rubies, diamonds and pearls pendant, and a jewel of gold like a hunter's horn, with a stone ... garnished with small rubies and a small pearl pendant.'[17]

Whyte continued: 'Her Majesty's favour increases towards him, so careful he is of her business and service: and, indeed, the whole weight of the state lies upon him.'[18]

By January 1600 Essex appeared to be well enough recovered for a trial in Star Chamber. His sisters and wife energetically petitioned the queen for clemency; they got nowhere. At York House, where Essex was still being held, the mood was sombre. Grieving over the death of his wife and feeling himself as much of a prisoner as his enforced houseguest, Egerton cut himself off from his official duties as lord keeper. Some courtiers (Rowland Whyte was one) wondered whether Egerton would retreat from public life entirely. Elizabeth was having none of that. 'Her Majesty sent to comfort him; and, as I hear, to tell him that the public service must be preferred before private passions.'[19]

After the hiccup of an early postponement, a date was set for Essex's trial: Wednesday 13 February. On that day the staff of Star Chamber prepared the court for a hearing and were ready to serve the judges and privy councillors their customary feast – proceedings in Star Chamber were always marked by a sumptuous meal at the queen's expense. Outside Westminster Palace large crowds gathered, anticipating one of the biggest political events for years. Amongst the public Essex the hero was lauded, while Cecil, the crook-backed politician, was libelled. But at Westminster nothing happened. Instead of a humiliating trial there was a pause, an intimation to Essex of her Majesty's mercy. The person Essex had to thank for it was Cecil.

Naturally the key events happened behind the scenes. The crunch week was 8–14 February. Between 11 a.m. and noon on Monday 11 February, Buckhurst and Cecil visited Egerton at York House to give Essex notice of Wednesday's judicial hearing. They refused to have contact with the earl, so they used Egerton to pass messages. Through the lord keeper they encouraged Essex to write to the queen. He composed a letter the same day.[20]

Essex wrote that the sentence of death would have been more welcome to him than Star Chamber.

> But be pleased, I beseech your Majesty, to remember how humbly and unfainedly I have acknowledged mine offence; and how patiently I have undergone your Majesty's indignations; and how much more it will agree with your princely and angel-like nature to have your mercy blazed by the tongue of your Majesty's once happy but now most sorrowful creature than to have a sentence given to ruin and disable him who despiseth life, when he shall be made unfit for your service.[21]

Cecil delivered the letter to the queen on Tuesday morning. Late in the afternoon, after Cecil had left court, Elizabeth decided that Essex's trial might after all be postponed: this was the advice of Lord Treasurer Buckhurst, Lord Admiral Nottingham and Lord Chief Justice Popham. Conscious that the hearing was scheduled to take place the following day, Elizabeth asked Thomas Windebank to write to Cecil. Windebank finished the letter at the stroke of six o'clock. She read it through three or four times. Was she satisfied with it? Perhaps yes: she asked Windebank to give it to the post to deliver. Perhaps no: she countermanded the instruction. Decision, indecision. At last, she instructed Windebank not to send it. A letter wasn't needed, she told him: Nottingham and the others knew her pleasure and meaning.[22]

The message was both communicated and received. The following day, Wednesday, Essex had his answer. Mercy, a reprieve, a lifeline. To Elizabeth, by letter, the earl vowed to dedicate the rest of his life.[23]

Cecil's apparent magnanimity divided opinion at court. John Chamberlain, the practised court watcher, thought any reconciliation between the two Roberts was simply a mirage; Cecil hadn't spoken to Essex since his close confinement at York House – he had merely delivered the letter that kept the earl out of Star Chamber. Rowland Whyte's interpretation was quite different – Cecil was not the enemy of Essex that many imagined him to be. 'Master Secretary hath won much love and honour by it,' he wrote, 'who in my conscience hath not been so adverse to the earl as was supposed.' And two days later, on the 16th: 'the Earl of Essex, by Master Secretary's means, was stayed from Star Chamber'.[24]

Robert Cecil's brother Thomas, 2nd baron of Burghley, took his own view. He wrote to Robert from York, his base as lord president of the Council of the North, the most important civil and military official in northern England. He thought that Cecil had been the decisive actor in reconciling Elizabeth and Essex, and it was to Robert's credit:

This great cause that hath so long hung in balance and bred so many discontentments in divers minds ... is now calmed by an humble submission by letter made by the earl and presented by you unto her Majesty; which charitable deed of yours I doubt not but will for this present procure you great honour and stop the tongues of the adversary.[25]

It was a moral victory for Cecil, and perhaps a political one too.

At the end of February Sir Henry Neville wrote to Cecil about a young Scottish nobleman he had met in Paris. John Ruthven, earl of Gowrie, he said, was a friend to the true Protestant religion and a friend also to Queen Elizabeth. On his journey home to Scotland the young earl wished to kiss Elizabeth's hand. Neville recommended him warmly. He gave Gowrie a passport to cross the English Channel.[26]

Gowrie arrived in London at the beginning of April. James Hudson, the latest of King James's agents at Elizabeth's court, described him for Cecil in much the same terms that Neville had. Gowrie was about twenty-two, one of the best accomplished young Scottish noblemen, a traveller for six years, handsome and educated. He looked like the perfect Renaissance nobleman.[27]

But in his family's history there was a shadow. The young Lord Gowrie's father, William, had been one of a group of hard-line Presbyterian nobles who, fearing that the king was falling more and more under the influence of the Catholic nobility at court, had in 1582 taken James into protective custody. At just sixteen years old James was kept as a prisoner at Ruthven Castle near Perth. He escaped to freedom in 1583, and a year later William Ruthven was executed.

Did the earl's sons ever reconcile themselves to their father's treason or forgive the king who, as a teenager, had seen to Earl William's destruction? In the high summer of 1600, there would be a reckoning for the Ruthvens, and for King James.

22

Feeling the Pulse

Spring 1600 was a season for new starts, for the green shoots of hope. On Thursday 20 March Essex left, after six long months, confinement at York House. Three weeks later Thomas Phelippes, decipherer and intelligencer, applied for a new job.

Now on parole, and under the supervision of Sir Richard Berkeley, Essex went to his house a little way along the Strand, a 'remove . . . agreeable to that I have formerly written', Cecil wrote to Sir Henry Neville, 'and so will be the rest of the proceeding, suitable to the Queen's benign disposition'. It wasn't so much favour as a lifting of disfavour; there was a subtle difference, even if at times it didn't seem like it. Any request Essex made still had to go through Cecil: so it had been with Lord Keeper Egerton, so it now was with Berkeley. Even a consultation with a doctor had to have Cecil's say-so. Yet it was a small step forward.[1]

Spring is a changeable season – it can be warm, it can be cold. Would Essex continue to submit himself to the queen? Would his followers contain their frustrations at his treatment? Would Elizabeth's disposition change?

For Thomas Phelippes the 1590s had been a hard decade. Lacking stable court patronage after Sir Francis Walsingham's death in 1590, a year later he was recruited by Francis Bacon for a new master, the earl of Essex, who wanted to use Phelippes's acknowledged skills as a runner of agents to build up his own reputation with the queen. The few missions of Phelippes's spies to infiltrate English Catholic dissident groups in Spanish Flanders in 1591 and 1592 did not yield the kind of quick and easy results Essex had wanted. By 1594 Phelippes's relations with the earl had soured into recrimination. Also distrusted by Lord Burghley, who saw Phelippes as Essex's man, there followed a period of unemployment at court.

But the real disaster for Phelippes came at the end of 1594 with an audit of the accounts of the London customs house; his job there, as collector of revenue on exports, he inherited from his father in 1591. The audit revealed that Phelippes was unable to pay into the Exchequer fourteen months' worth of revenue – the staggering sum of ten thousand pounds. We can only guess what he had done with an amount of money large enough to put an army into France. Lending it out at interest is the most likely possibility, for other courtiers with strong political connections – like Robert Cecil's friend Michael Hickes – built up businesses as moneylenders. This would explain why Phelippes was sure that he could pay his debt quickly, on the assumption that his debtors in turn would repay their loans. It turned out to be a vain assumption. Phelippes spent the next five years in and out of prison, pursued by Lord Burghley and the Exchequer for his debt. What assets of land and money he possessed were seized and his house was stripped of furniture, while his wife, Mary, tried desperately to recruit financial guarantors. Phelippes became ever more isolated. As the years 1595–99 ticked by, the likelihood of rehabilitation seemed remote. But now, at last, there was a particle of hope.[2]

Phelippes's long travails explain why in mid-April 1600 he wasn't rushing his letter to Robert Cecil. A first draft sat on his writing desk for four days. He checked every word of it; he measured every nuance. It had to be just right. It might draw some sort of line under his five-and-a-half years' humiliation. It might even make his future. He understood what the ancient Greeks had called *kairos*, the skill of finding the right moment to act. Friday 18 April was the day he chose to sign the letter and seal the packet with his father's old signet ring.[3]

To Robert Cecil, Phelippes offered his skills and talents as a provider of valuable secrets. He pardoned his presumption and lauded Cecil. He was self-deprecating and self-praising; he was a courtier. Most important of all on this spring day, he had a proposal. He wanted to serve Secretary Cecil: he wanted to make reparation for his mistakes.

'The principal point in matter of intelligence is to procure confidence with those parties that one will work upon, or those parties a man would work by', he wrote. 'I have found the way to have both in such sort as your honour will say you cannot fail of that you will pretend unto ... wherein I will be glad, and vow unto you to employ that dexterity I may have to the utmost of my power.'[4]

At some point he got his reply, in Cecil's own hand (this was always a good sign), addressed 'To my loving friend Master Thomas Phelippes'. Sir Robert wrote with the insouciance of a man used to power and command. Knowing what skills Phelippes had, Cecil thanked him for his offer. He accepted the proposal with, as Phelippes could not fail to have noticed, a conditional *if*. 'Where you desire my favour, if you do make your services fruitful, assure yourself I will very gladly do you any pleasure I can.' Cecil invited Phelippes to confer with him about his 'projects'.[5]

The equality Cecil suggested between himself and his new employee was pure fantasy. But Thomas Phelippes had a patron and a job.

The earl of Essex maintained that it was his enemies who got a manuscript of his 'Apology' to a printing press. It may have been instead some of his own over-enthusiastic followers trying to play on the earl's popular celebrity to advertise their hero's predicament. The irony of this was not amusing. Coming so soon after his release from York House Essex knew that the leak of his 1598 manifesto – that bullish explanation of his aggressive stance against Spain in the interests of Protestant Christendom – was a disaster. Quickly, urgently, he wrote to his brother-in-law, Lord Rich, to whom he made clear that the person who needed to know the truth about how the *Apologie* came to be printed was Robert Cecil: only he could find out the truth and end Essex's 'tedious troubles'.[6]

By the following day, Saturday 10 May, Archbishop Whitgift of Canterbury had seized 210 copies of the pamphlet and arrested its printers. They had admitted to printing 292. The archbishop was still examining his prisoners. He promised Cecil that he would bring their confessions to court the following day.[7]

To have out in the open Essex's aggressive defence of his actions and reputation after the Cadiz raid – a most unapologetic of apologies – was bad enough. Most damaging were the pamphlet's final three pages, a letter to the queen on Essex's behalf by his sister Penelope, Lady Rich. This exposed like an open wound the hatred she saw at court. She wrote that her brother could never expect a fair trial: 'For those combined enemies, which lay open false grounds to build his ruin, urging his fault as criminal to your divine honour ... have practised only to glut themselves in their private revenge.' Essex – and many others – must have been appalled at seeing those words in print.[8]

Having first secured permission through Cecil, Essex wrote to the Privy Council that he was the victim of libellers and secret enemies. And, of course, he petitioned Elizabeth. 'Before all letters written in this hand be banished, or he that sends this enjoins himself to eternal silence,' he wrote, 'I humbly beseech your Majesty to read over these humble lines.' He said that in his eight months of close imprisonment she had rejected his letters and refused to hear him. He was now like a dead carcase thrown into a corner, gnawed on by the basest creatures on the earth. 'The prating tavern haunter speaks of me what he list: the frantic libeller writes of me what he list: already they print me and make [me] speak to the world: and shortly they will play me in what form they list upon the stage.' Gossip, infamy, the worst kind of publicity. He sensed that he was ruined.[9]

Thanks to the leak of the *Apologie*, the postponed judicial hearing on Essex's conduct as general and lord lieutenant in Ireland in 1599 was now inevitable. This took place on Thursday 5 June in Lord Keeper Egerton's great chamber at York House. Joining the privy councillors at their long table were four more earls, two other barons, four judges: it was a trial in Star Chamber in all but name and place. The most junior of the four learned counsel who presented the case against Essex had once been one of his closest and most intimate advisers. Francis Bacon – bencher of the honourable society of Gray's Inn, essayist, first cousin of Robert Cecil, disappointed client and suitor, now thirty-nine years old – helped to lay out with devastating forensic precision the details of Essex's 'misgovernment and malversation in his office' in Ireland, above all his shocking dereliction of duty in returning to England against the queen's orders.[10]

The hearing began at 8 a.m. The earl knelt at the end of the table, holding a bundle of papers, his hat set down on the floor next to him. Christopher Yelverton, the queen's serjeant, made the opening statement. Attorney General Coke followed, with a withering attack on Essex's disloyalty. Then Solicitor General Fleming. Then Francis Bacon.

Essex spoke in his own defence; observers of the trial praised his discretion, mildness and patience. It counted for very little. Summing up the evidence presented by counsel, Lord Keeper Egerton offered his opinion: Essex deserved to be imprisoned in the Tower, fined as heavily as any subject ever had been, and stripped of his offices of privy councillor, earl marshal and master of the ordnance. Lord Treasurer Buckhurst agreed, though he didn't mention the Tower. Cecil made what one witness described as a 'wise, grave speech of these contempts of his, towards her Majesty'.

The session lasted for eleven hours, during which time the earl barely moved a muscle. Late in the evening Egerton at last gave sentence. Sequestered from all offices of state – though he retained his mastership of the queen's horse – the earl would be kept prisoner at his own Essex House in Westminster.[11]

Six weeks later Francis Bacon wrote to Essex an apologia of his own. Bacon said that he aspired to be a true servant to the queen – he wanted to be an honest man. He acknowledged his relationship with Essex. But he had made a choice which was in reality no choice at all: 'I confess I love some things much better than I love your lordship, as the Queen's service, her quiet and contentment, her honour, her favour, the good of my country, and the like, yet I love few persons better than yourself, both for gratitude's sake, and for your own virtues.' Bacon was sorry that Essex 'should fly with waxen wings, doubting Icarus's fortune'.[12]

In his letter of reply the earl said that he had never flown 'with other wings than desire to merit, and confidence in my sovereign's favour'. When one of his wings had failed him, he expected to fall at the queen's feet; instead, he wrote, she had 'suffered me to be bruised with my fall'. As ever, Essex was blaming Elizabeth for the situation in which he now found himself.[13]

At key moments – as her general in France in 1591, at Cadiz in 1596, in Ireland in 1599 – Essex had either ignored or disobeyed the

queen's orders. One of the extraordinary – actually, unique – qualities
of the relationship between Elizabeth and Essex was her capacity for
forgiveness. There was a pattern, neatly expressed by the court watcher
Rowland Whyte: 'her Majesty's anger, by the earl's submission and
acknowledgement of his errors towards her, is appeased'. The truth
was that Robert, earl of Essex *was* gifted and able; he was able to
inspire others to follow him unquestioningly, to offer him their uncon-
ditional loyalty. But Essex always had to be superlative, always believed
that he could make circumstances kneel before him. They didn't. And
so, the bursts of bad temper, his sulking retreats from court, his letters
of rebuke where he seemed to forget that it was Elizabeth, not he, who
was God's anointed monarch. He almost couldn't help himself. And
always he presumed the queen's forgiveness. Francis Bacon, as Essex's
friend, had made the correct diagnosis in autumn 1596: the earl's
inflexible self-belief, the royal favour he always expected and received,
his shaky finances, his popularity with the common people, his reputation for military heroism – there was an alchemy to all these elements
of Essex that made him both great and vulnerable. In the end everything rested on Elizabeth's favour. That seemed now to have run out.[14]

Thomas Phelippes was getting used to Robert Cecil as his employer.
He was dutiful, assiduous, delicately secretive: he was on his very best
behaviour.

By mid-June their work had begun. Under Cecil's direction Phelippes was trying to infiltrate one of his agents into a group of émigré
English Catholics. It was his familiar technique, the careful testing
and probing, working his way into the dissidents' trust: 'It may please
your honour to receive herewith the answer of the letter [which] was
written by your direction to feel their pulse on that side.'[15]

Phelippes was also writing regular digests of information from
Liège, much of it originating in Brussels and the northern Netherlands. In Holland the news from England was that Essex's case had
been heard; that the earl had behaved himself discreetly and mod-
estly; and that Cecil had shown himself 'very wise and temperate in
the action and to be most free from gall, where it hath been conceived
in those parts that he had been most galled by the earl's dependents'.

Was this really Dutch news, or was it Phelippes's attempt to tell Cecil what he wanted to hear? It could have been either. It might have been both.

But one paragraph in the same digest touched the most sensitive topic of all. In it there is little sense that Phelippes was guarding his words. Making the calculation that Queen Elizabeth did not have long to live, the Dutch were preparing to support James VI's claim, 'having resolved as soon as it shall fall out she die to ship over competent number of men with other necessaries for aid of the King of Scots whether by his solicitation or no'.[16]

Elizabeth would not live for ever.

Summer news out of Scotland from Cecil's agent at the court of King James, George Nicolson, sat neatly alongside Phelippes's information from Liège. Nicolson suggested a kingdom in flux, showing signs of instability and faction. The king was struggling to get his subjects to support his ambitions for England, and he had made a passionate speech to the convention of estates 'for having men and money for his honourable entering to the crown after her Majesty', as Nicolson put it. James grumbled that he could raise more money out of England and the Low Countries than from his own subjects.

The one pillar of stability in government and at court, so Nicolson intimated, was John Erskine, earl of Mar, a few years older than the king (he was about thirty-eight). They had known each other from childhood, both boys taught by the terrifying George Buchanan, a brilliant classical scholar of European reputation – hence King James's own formidable range and depth of learning – but an unforgiving and brutal tutor who believed strongly in the old schoolmaster's discipline of the birch rod. To the earl the king had entrusted the care of his six-year-old son and heir, Prince Henry. 'Mar now being of all others the most in the king's kindness for the time.' *For the time*: Nicolson seemed to have no great faith in the consistency of his Majesty's royal favour.[17]

Within the year Robert Cecil would get to know the earl of Mar very well indeed.

It was a breathless Nicolson who from Edinburgh a few weeks later reported to Cecil an event that Mar was both a witness to and a participant in, one shocking even by the unpredictable standard of Scottish politics. On Wednesday 6 August Nicolson's pen skated across the page, giving his handwriting a vivid clarity so often missing from his longer, smoother reports to Master Secretary. One feels the urgency. More than this, George Nicolson was worried.

The earl of Gowrie – that same well-travelled, erudite and promising young man who had met Queen Elizabeth – and his younger brother Alexander Ruthven had conspired to murder King James.

Nicolson's story was this. Early the previous morning, Tuesday 5 August, when the king had been hunting in the park of Falkland Palace in Fife, Alexander Ruthven had come with a message from his brother to tell James that he had great treasures at Gowrie House, the family's townhouse in Perth, seventeen or so miles away. Such treasures would ease James's need for money, and Gowrie wanted him to see them. The king was sufficiently interested to leave his hunting companions, the duke of Lennox and the earl of Mar, take a fresh horse and a few men, and to ride to Perth. On the way he met the abbot of Inchaffray. When they arrived at the earl's house Gowrie gave them dinner. Lennox and Mar had followed the king to Perth and they, too, were fed, and afterwards walked in Gowrie's gardens with the earl, while James had been taken on a tour of the house by Alexander Ruthven; the king had no weapon and no servant nearby. As the pair went from chamber to chamber, Ruthven locked the doors behind them. At last they came to a turret room – supposedly the chamber in which Gowrie had housed the treasure – where the king encountered a man wearing armour. James assumed he was there to guard the valuables. This was thirty-eight-year-old Andrew Henderson, one of Gowrie's servants from nearby Scone. Suddenly, Ruthven seized the king and drew his dagger. James had killed his father, Ruthven said, and now he would kill the king.

There were two reports of what they said to each other: James's, which was assumed to be the true one, and Henderson's, later taken under oath in the investigation into the treason. Nicolson's version for London came from the dispatch that had arrived in Edinburgh at 9 a.m. the following morning. James had sought to reason with Ruthven: he, the king, was a minor when Ruthven's father had been executed and was innocent of his death; he had ever since tried to make amends to the family. James told Ruthven that he would never escape: James had heirs to follow him. If he stood down, the king would keep it as their secret, and take no further action.

Ruthven's response was to strike at James. They wrestled each other to the ground. Ruthven called on Henderson to kill the king, but Henderson refused. The two men fought all the way to the turret's window, which, in the struggle, was opened by Henderson. (This is one of the details that for four centuries has prompted scholars to question Henderson's role, and indeed the authenticity of the official narrative and the Ruthvens' guilt.) The upper part of James's body was pushed out of the window. He cried out treason to anyone who could hear.

Lennox and Mar had finished their tour of the garden and, on being told that his Majesty had already left the house by a back gate, were themselves getting ready to leave. They were on the street, and still with an apparently guileless Gowrie, when they saw and heard the king at the window, red-faced and struggling. Not in Nicolson's letter to Cecil, but in a later statement under oath given by the duke of Lennox, were James's words: 'I am murtherit! Treason! My Lord of Mar, help! Help!'[18]

The courtiers struggled to get to the king: it was an effort to break down the doors. But one of James's servants, John Ramsay, knew a back way to the turret. There he found the king and Ruthven, James crying out to Ramsay that he was slain. With his rapier Ramsay killed Ruthven. Elsewhere in the house there was a battle between Gowrie and his men and the king's servants, in which fight Gowrie was killed. Two noble brothers – Protestant, sophisticated, cosmopolitan, until now apparently loyal – were dead.

It was the strangest of assassination attempts, and much of it – from the various accounts and depositions – feels contrived, all the more so, perhaps, given the principal conspirators' deaths and the decidedly peculiar part played in the affair by Andrew Henderson, the man in armour. But whatever happened in Perth, James thanked God for his deliverance.

The news of the assassination attempt caused a stir both in the palace of Holyrood and on the streets of Edinburgh.

George Nicolson reported to Cecil that the king's council met for the whole of Wednesday morning. At 1 p.m. all the councillors went to the city's market square to declare to the people what had happened. James's subjects were exhorted to praise God and to build bonfires. Bells were rung, the cannons of Edinburgh Castle fired in celebration. The council sent a messenger urgently to Queen Elizabeth.

But for all the joy and relief, Nicolson was troubled. There was a rumour in Edinburgh that he had planned to leave the city from its port of Leith at three o'clock that morning – this was thought to be a suspicious departure. Nicolson knew he was being smeared, and he spoke to Secretary Elphinstone about it. He wrote to Cecil: 'Thus your honour sees how the malicious here spite me, in what danger I live, and how subject I am to all accusation here.' Some, he explained, wanted the treason against James to have been planned 'in other parts'. Nicolson squeezed in one further word to make his meaning clear beyond doubt: 'England'.[19]

A few weeks later Sir Robert Cecil summarized the events in Perth for his friend Sir George Carew, and the queen wrote to King James.

Cecil took at face value the Ruthven brothers' conspiracy against the king but indicated how strange a puzzle it was: 'This earl was of the religion [i.e., a sound Protestant], and a very gallant gentleman. The causes of his discontent are not known.' Some said it was to revenge their father's death, 'but whatsoever it was, God forbid but all such barbarous attempts should pay just ransom'.[20]

Elizabeth celebrated James's preservation. In her letter she was disarming; there was nothing here of the familiar diplomatic coolness. She was glad that he was safe, glad that God had stretched out with his potent hand to defend his Majesty.

They were monarchs both, yet mortal. She knew too what it was like to be conspired against: 'And though a king I be, yet hath my funeral been prepared.' Her pen, she wrote, 'hath run further than at first' she meant, and certainly she intimated more than she wrote. 'If you will needs know what I mean, I have been pleased to impart to this my faithful servant some part thereof, to whom I will refer me and will pray God to give you grace to know what best becomes you.'[21]

Had the queen at last given James some idea of his future as she foresaw it? If she did – and who knows with Elizabeth? – they were words her special messenger, Sir Henry Brouncker, kept in his head as he travelled up the Great North Road on a mission which (as he later said) gave him little pleasure and cost him far too much money.

Late summer, autumn and early winter had Thomas Phelippes reporting to Cecil every few weeks. Nothing was too much trouble for him. He drew up reports full of detail derived from delicate sources in Antwerp, Brussels, Liège and Prague. He wanted and needed to show his range, his mastery of knowledge. Everything he tested for himself; it was a mark of his digests' authenticity. 'That in secret I know to be written bona fide.'[22]

All this time he was trying as hard as ever to clear his crushing debt to the queen: on this in autumn 1600 he was busy writing and petitioning. He could only hope to serve, only aspire to deliver, to push himself as hard as he could for Cecil against the enemies of the state; this was the other way he repaid what he owed. The basic formula he gave to Cecil a few months later was one he had written so many times before, and would write again and again, right up to the next diabolical attempt on King James's life, one more infamous than the Gowrie conspiracy, in 1605: 'If your honour be desirous to understand any other thing within the compass of my search I am at all times ready to do you what poor service shall lie in my power.'[23]

23

Insurrection

Summer and autumn of the year 1600 saw a loosening of Essex's bonds. In July Cecil wrote that 'Her Majesty stayeth the going over of the earl in the Tower'. A month later Essex was allowed to go to Oxfordshire under the guard of duty and discretion (as Cecil phrased it), though forbidden from approaching the queen or her court. By October he was in seclusion between London and the old Walsingham estate, Barn Elms. His followers were confident that he would regain favour, but the court observer John Chamberlain was sceptical: 'I shall esteem words as wind.'[1]

Essex continued to write to Elizabeth. She did not reply to his letters. He seemed fragile. 'I must sometimes moan, look up, and speak, that you may know your servant lives', he wrote in July. In early September he cut his own name down to a phonetic cipher: he was 'shaming, languishing, despairing S. X.'. Excluded, abandoned, wraith more than substance; while in the late summer and autumn Elizabeth and her court hunted and entertained embassies from Russia and Barbary, Essex was forgotten. After Michaelmas his monopoly on sweet wines, the earl's only remaining financial lifeline, was not renewed.[2]

The queen's accession day, mid-November, was celebrated with all the usual vigour and drama. Elizabeth's champion, the earl of Cumberland, gave the speech, from which one line stands out as resonant with the moment: 'He that spins nothing but hopes shall weave up nothing but repentance ofttimes of labour of languishing.' Essex wrote to Elizabeth on that 17 November: though dead to the world, he said, he did more true honour to her than any courtier in her presence. Miserable, full of sickness, full of sorrow, he wished her great happiness and happy greatness. He would lose everything in order 'to have this happy 17th day many and many times renewed with glory to your Majesty and comfort to all your faithful subjects, of which none is accursed but your humblest vassal Essex'.[3]

Five weeks later Essex wrote to King James. It was Christmas Day 1600, and the earl was building on his 'fame' as the guarantor of Anglo-Scottish friendship and James's hope of becoming king of England and Ireland. 'In me your lordship shall find faithful delivery in all that I receive from you or send to you', Essex had written in reply to the lord chancellor of Scotland's suggestion back in 1595 of a discreet 'reciproque' correspondence between James VI and the earl. Where one source of royal favour was by late 1600 cut off, Essex now went to another, knowing full well that where in James's eyes Robert Cecil could never quite be trusted to be in sympathy with his Majesty's cause, he himself most certainly would be.[4]

The confidence of Essex's Christmas letter was very different indeed from his lamentations as Elizabeth's languishing vassal. It was high time, he wrote, that he, so much and so injuriously talked of by others, should now speak for himself. He wanted to be understood and to be believed, not for himself, but for his country.

Essex explained to James that Elizabeth was the prisoner of a group that now governed court. This new ruling faction had attacked him – they had corrupted his servants, stolen his papers (probably he meant here his leaked 'Apology') and suborned false witnesses against him. They were planning the succession after the queen's death of the infanta of Spain, and had plotted against James's life. He, Essex, had waited for the right time to act. Now the moment had come to save his country; now also was the time for James himself to act. The first step was for the king to send, by the beginning of February, a discreet and trustworthy ambassador to England. Essex suggested as the best ambassador the earl of Mar.[5]

At the end of the first week of February 1601 Mar and Edward Bruce, abbot of Kinloss, were preparing themselves for their journey south as King James's ambassadors to Elizabeth – James had taken notice of Essex. Going ahead of them to prepare the way at Elizabeth's court was David Foulis. The purpose of their mission, as George Nicolson explained it to Cecil, was to 'settle the two princes in kindness without jealousy hereafter'. Rumours about James's dealings with Rome, with Spain and with Catholics (the stuff of Thomas Phelippes's secret reports of the last few months), along with accumulated bad feeling between Elizabeth and the king, meant that his Majesty wanted to clear the air.

But Nicolson sensed that the ambassadors had some other agenda also, and that King James was up to something. 'The conjectures and conceits of this embassage are exceeding strange and many,' Nicolson wrote to Cecil, 'yea with councillors and wise men. And the wisest are at a gaze to see what may follow it.' James was playing the embassy very close to his chest – not even Secretary Elphinstone was admitted to its secrets.[6]

The theme of the letter James wrote to Elizabeth three days later, on 10 February, was friendship. Mar and Bruce could be trusted, and the king hoped that 'by the labours of such honest and well-affected ministers, all scruples or griefs may on either side be removed and our constant amity more and more be confirmed and made sound'.[7]

To his ambassadors James gave private written instructions. 'Ye shall temper and frame all your dealing with the Queen or Council by the advice of my friends there.' He gave them secret instructions 'by tongue', putting nothing down on paper. There was, of course, one principal friend: Essex.[8]

On Saturday 7 February the acting company of the Lord Chamberlain's Men staged at the Globe theatre William Shakespeare's play about the deposing of King Richard II in 1399. The request to revive a play from the company's repertoire that hadn't been performed for a few years – a text of *Richard II* was first printed in 1597 – came from a small group of the earl of Essex's gentlemen followers.[9]

Essex had something of an association with the history of Richard II and Richard's usurper, Henry Bolingbroke, his successor as Henry IV. In 1599 the earl was dedicatee of a history of *The Life and Reign of King Henry IV* by one John Hayward, a thirty-five-year-old gentleman scholar with two Cambridge degrees. The book was an unlikely bestseller: some of its readers (John Chamberlain was one of them) saw straight away its relevance to Essex, who was addressed in Hayward's Latin as 'great indeed, both in present judgement and in expectation of future time'.

Hayward and his printer found themselves in trouble with the Privy Council. The history seemed to point subversively to commonalities between the failures of Richard's rule and the political atmosphere at the turn of the seventeenth century: misgovernment, private gain by corrupt courtiers, war in Ireland, oppression of the people, a powerful nobleman with his eye on the crown. On sale for only a few weeks, in late May 1599 Hayward's book was banned and both it and its author found themselves under the discomfiting forensic scrutiny of Lord Chief Justice Popham and Attorney General Coke. Coke went through *The Life and Reign of King Henry IV* page by page, making extensive notes on the historical details which seemed to him suspiciously contemporary. One of Coke's observations got to the heart of the problem: 'The king is deposed, and by an earl, and in the end murdered.' Was the usurper Bolingbroke really Essex in disguise, the monarch to be deposed Elizabeth?[10]

At the trial at York House in June 1600 Francis Bacon pointed to the link between Essex's ambitions and John Hayward's *King Henry IV*: 'Who was thought fit to be patron of the book, but my Lord of Essex, who after the book had been out a week wrote a cold formal letter to my Lord of Canterbury to call it in again, knowing belike that forbidden things are most sought after?' The following month Hayward himself was remanded to the Tower of London. He was still there, under lock and key, when he was questioned again by Sir Edward Coke in late January 1601 over a new preface (an 'epistle apologetical') that Hayward had written for a hoped-for second edition of his book. (Hayward survived, devoting himself to writing other, less controversial histories whose characters' words and speeches he lifted wholesale from classical authors like Tacitus: Francis Bacon joked with Elizabeth over Doctor Hayward's talent for plagiarism.)[11]

It is ironic, perhaps, that Robert Cecil himself may have seen an early private performance of Shakespeare's *Richard II*; Sir Edward Hoby had invited Cecil to his house on Canon Row where the unfortunate king would (as Hoby put it to his cousin) 'present himself to your view'. That was back in December 1595, in marginally less fractious times. Now, just over five years later, the play which showed a king deposed and his usurper crowned was commercially stale, or so the Lord Chamberlain's players complained to Essex's followers when asked to put it back on stage. Augustine Phillips, one of Shakespeare's fellow actors, said that the history was unlikely to draw a decent audience, so Essex's men offered them forty shillings in compensation.[12]

Within twenty-four hours, the play was about to become politically electrifying.

Essex and a band of about three hundred followers, some carrying firearms, began to march through the streets of London and Westminster soon after ten o'clock on Sunday morning, 8 February 1601. Their objective was to take the court by force and liberate – or imprison – the queen. They would occupy the Tower and the city of London. One of Essex's closest advisers was Henry Wriothesley, earl of Southampton, now twenty-seven years old, whose illicit relationship with one of the queen's maids of honour, Elizabeth Vernon, a cousin of Essex, had led to their hasty marriage in 1598. Essex and Southampton, who challenged so many of the norms of behaviour at Elizabeth's court, were fast friends and allies. They had served together against the earl of Tyrone in 1599 – indeed, Essex's unauthorized promotion of Southampton to general of horse had been one of the (admittedly many) causes of Elizabeth's anger at his behaviour in those few months in Ireland.

For weeks, Essex had felt himself to be under siege. The atmosphere at Essex House on the Strand had been heavy with suspicion. By February there was a sense of emergency. Essex convinced himself that a court cabal, including Lord Cobham and Sir Walter Raleigh, were plotting to kill him – he was afraid and desperate and, by now, paranoid. And so Essex threw himself at London just as he had stormed the defences of Rouen nearly a decade earlier: it was the same reflex, the need for release and action.[13]

Cecil described the events of the day. Elizabeth ordered Whitehall Palace to be protected by barricades. This blocked the rebels who, thrown back by a force of pikemen at Ludgate, retreated to Essex House, which was stocked with weapons. They held out till late afternoon, Lord Admiral Nottingham ready to demolish the house with two cannons brought from the Tower (only the fact that Essex's wife and sister were in the house prevented him from using his artillery). Cecil's brother Thomas, Lord Burghley, an experienced soldier and commander, rode into London to proclaim Essex and his men traitors. Cecil did not mention – but other accounts did – that Burghley had been shot at with pistols and that his horse was killed as he sat on it. Cecil was impressed above all by Elizabeth's steadiness: 'she never was more amazed [surprised, stunned] than she would have been to have heard of a fray in Fleet Street.'[14]

To Cecil, it was an attempted *coup d'état* averted by heaven: 'no small blow . . . to be given at the centre . . . if God had not in his providence hindered their [the rebels'] designs'.[15]

On 13 February the Privy Council met in Star Chamber. Each councillor had his say about the rebellion.

Cecil catalogued Essex's many promotions and the favour the queen had shown to him over many years. The earl was ambitious, his treason a long time in the making. 'In all this flourishing time of these his ill-deserved preferments, his head was hatching confusion to her Majesty's royal person, and the whole state of his country, and that by such degrees as his own mind could invent, and ill advice whisper in his attentive ears.' Essex had courted popularity, encouraged religious divisions, secretly supported Catholics and Jesuits, for years plotting treason, 'strengthening himself with vulgar opinion and the hearts of such subjects as by his dissembled affability and fair liberal promises of gifts he was able to maintain'.[16]

George Nicolson in Edinburgh received Cecil's report of the insurrection on Sunday 15 February. He went straight to see King James. With the king in his private apartments were the duke of Lennox, Sir James Elphinstone, Sir George Home and Roger Aston, another of Cecil's intelligencers.

Nicolson read Cecil's letter aloud. James was stunned: the report barely registered. He asked Nicolson to check the date and wondered how the rebels had intended to ransom London once they had

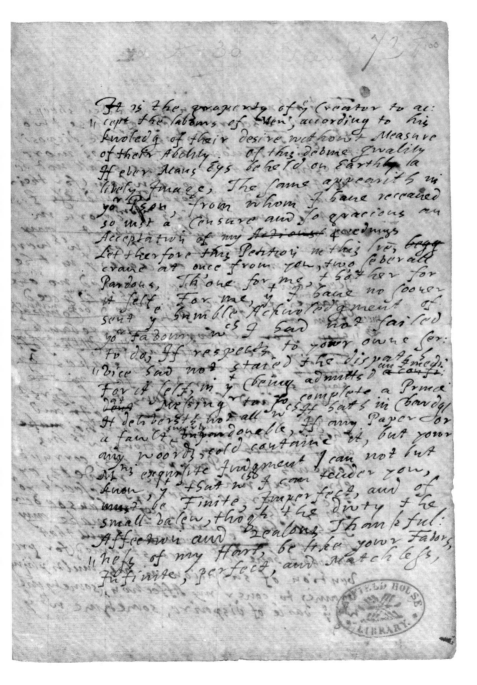

19. A draft by Robert Cecil of one of his many secret letters to King James VI, 1601: 'that which I can tender you, must be finite, imperfect, and of small value, though the duty, the affection and zealous thankfulness of my heart be like your favours, infinite, perfect, and matchless'.

20. From the same letter, showing Cecil's heavy alterations: in this delicate and dangerous correspondence every word had to be measured and correct.

The Masters of the *Agents for* Venice
Requests. *And the Estates*.
Julius Cæser & Roger
Wilbram.

The Lord Cheiffe Justice of
England Sr John Popham.
The Channceler of ye Exchequer.
Sr John Fortesoui.

The principall
Secretary.
Sr Robt Cicell.

Controller of ye Houshold.
Sr Edward Wotton.
Treasurer of ye Houshold.
Sr William Knowles.

Richard ye George Windsor
Herold of Armes.

The Banner of
borne by the E
Clanricard.

21. A group from the funeral procession for Queen Elizabeth I, April 1603, showing Secretary Cecil as the lone figure fifth from the right.

22. Ben Jonson, the poet who sought the patronage of Robert Cecil and wrote epigrams and masques for the newly created 1st earl of Salisbury.

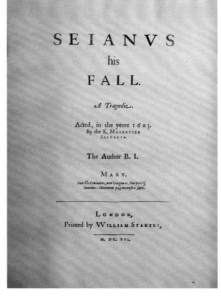

SEIANVS

his

FALL.

A Tragœdie.

Acted, in the yeere 1603.
By the K. MAIESTIES
SERVANTS.

The Author B. I.

MART.

*Non hic Centauros, non Gorgonas, Harpyásq;
Inuenies: Hominem pagina nostra sapit.*

LONDON,
Printed by WILLIAM STANSBY,

M. DC. XVI.

23. The title page of Jonson's *Sejanus, His Fall* from Jonson's folio *Workes* (1616): the play – a gritty critique of spies, informants and a surveillance state – was first performed in 1603 and printed, revised and expanded, in 1605.

24. The group portrait of the
commissioners who in summer
1604 signed the peace treaty between
England and Spain, bringing to an end
nearly twenty years of war. The setting
is Somerset House on the Strand in
Westminster. Shown on the left are
(nearest the window) Juan de Velasco
Frias, duke of Frias; Juan de Tassis,
count of Villa Mediana; Alessandro
Robida; Charles de Ligne, count of
Aremberg; Jean Richardot; and Louis
Vereyken. Shown on the right (again
from the window) are Thomas
Sackville, earl of Dorset, King James's
lord treasurer; Charles Howard, earl of
Nottingham, the lord admiral; Charles
Blount, earl of Devonshire; Henry
Howard, earl of Northampton; and
Robert Cecil, Viscount Cranborne.

Robert Winter · Christopher Wright · John Wright · Thomas Percy · Guido Fawkes · Robert Catesby · Thom Winte · Bates

25. The core group of Gunpowder plotters, 1605, shown in a contemporary Dutch print.

26. A late portrait of Francis Bacon, a supporter of the 2nd earl of Essex until Essex's disgrace with Queen Elizabeth, and an envious critic of his cousin Robert Cecil's power and privilege.

27. The Jesuit superior in England, Father Henry Garnet, tried and executed in London in 1606 for his involvement in the Gunpowder Plot: to Robert Cecil, Garnet's supposed crimes reached 'into the bowels of treason'.

Hatfield House in Hertfordshire, begun by Robert Cecil, 1st earl of Salisbury in the few years after
surrender of Theobalds to Queen Anne and King James in 1607.

The Marble Hall at Hatfield House, built in 1611, today the setting for the Rainbow Portrait
Queen Elizabeth I.

30. Robert Cecil's tomb in the Church of St Etheldreda in Hatfield, the work of Maximilian Colt, master sculptor to King James. The earl of Salisbury is dressed in the robes of the Order of the Garter and holds in his right hand the lord treasurer's wand.

captured the city. He said that he might delay his ambassadors' mission for a few days.

Then the king of Scots left the room.[17]

In the second week of February Cecil was compiling a list of which earls and barons would judge Essex and Southampton. Their trial was held in Westminster Hall on Thursday 19 February.[18]

Offering his own defence – traitors were allowed no learned counsel – Essex came, some way into the proceedings, to the matter of Elizabeth's succession. Cecil, he claimed, supported the title of the Infanta Isabella of Spain, the late Philip II's daughter. This damaging accusation had now become an article of faith for Essex and his loyalists.

Cecil knew, of course, that Essex would say this at his trial. He was ready and prepared, and quickly, ruthlessly on the offensive. 'The difference between you and me' – Cecil addressed Essex directly – 'is great; for I speak in the person of an honest man, and you, my lord, in the person of a traitor: so well I know, you have wit [intelligence, facility with words] at will.' He himself stood for loyalty, the earl for treachery. Cecil said it was true, as those privy councillors in the hall knew, that King James was a candidate for the succession (Cecil used the word 'competitor'): but so too was Essex, who had plotted to depose the queen, make himself king and call a parliament.

Essex responded with sarcasm: 'Master Secretary, I thank God for my humbling: that you, in the rust [corrosion, corruption] of your bravery, came to make your oration against me here this day.'

Cecil replied: 'My lord, I humbly thank God that you did not take me for a fit companion for you and your humours; for if you had, you would have drawn me to betray my sovereign, as you have done.'

Essex supported his claim about Cecil's Spanish sympathies by saying that a fellow privy councillor had told him about it. Cecil now asked the earl of Southampton who that councillor was. Southampton responded that he was Sir William Knollys, Essex's uncle. Again ready and prepared, Cecil announced with theatrical skill that Knollys was ready, with the queen's permission, to testify.

Knollys explained to the court that he had been present when Cecil had examined a book that 'had treated of such matters'. He meant *A*

Conference about the Next Succession to the Crown of England, the book by Father Robert Persons, printed under the pseudonym of R. Doleman, which had arrived at Elizabeth's court in 1595 – it was the book which Persons had so mischievously dedicated to Essex himself. *Conference* explained and justified the Habsburgs' Lancastrian claim to the English throne. So had Cecil acknowledged his own support of their title? Knollys said plainly: 'I never did hear Master Secretary use any such words, or to that effect.' Cecil said aloud to the court that he was glad to have found one honest man.

Really it was all over for Essex. In Westminster Hall Cecil told Essex that he forgave him from the bottom of his heart. Essex responded that he forgave Cecil. He meant to die in charity.

Essex and Southampton were found by their peers guilty of treason.[19]

After the verdict Southampton – now plain Henry Wriothesley, his treason having stripped him of his title – wrote to Cecil and the Privy Council with further evidence. To Cecil he excused his poor hand-writing. And in Cecil Wriothesley had a supporter. As Robert wrote to one of his correspondents in Scotland, Patrick, master of Gray, Southampton's life 'is in her Majesty's hands at an hour's warning', but Cecil felt compassion for the young man. He was a nobleman full of spirit and courage – there were precious few of those in the kingdom – and it was his marriage to Essex's cousin, not real affection, that in Cecil's judgement had made him so close to the earl. But there was an old obligation, too, and a sense of a deeper reciprocity of feeling between Cecil and Southampton, going all the way back to Henry Wriothesley's early upbringing and education at Lord Burghley's mansion on the Strand. This even survived the fracture between Cecil and Essex: 'he was bred in my father's house and ever (notwithstanding the separation between the earl and me) kept so good form with me as I protest I am persuaded he would have saved my blood if I had come within his power.'[20]

Other direct appeals for clemency and mercy arrived quickly, the earls' wives and mothers, stunned and distressed, hoping for compassion. Southampton's mother, the dowager countess, wrote that she could scarce hold her pen, let alone steady her heart. Essex's wife

Frances, holding on to the smallest particle of hope after receiving a letter from Cecil, appealed to him as a father:

Good Master Secretary, even as you desire of God that your own son never be made orphan by the untimely death of his dear father, vouch-safe a relenting to the not urging . . . of that fatal warrant for execution which, if it be . . . signed I shall never wish to breathe one hour after.'[21]

Young Southampton would live and, over time, be rehabilitated. For Essex it was a different story.

In Cecil's papers there is an eyewitness account of what took place in the Tower of London just after 8 a.m. on Ash Wednesday, 25 February 1601. He was not himself there to see it.

Dressed in a black velvet gown and black satin suit with a small ruff, thirty-five-year-old Essex was led to the scaffold by three chaplains and the lieutenant of the Tower with a guard of sixteen men. Essex removed his hat to the six noblemen who were there to witness the execution of justice. He made a short speech. He spoke about his loyalty to the queen. He prayed.

Removing his ruff and gown, he laid himself flat along a board, stretching out his arms, placing his neck on the block. His last words were 'Lord Jesus receive my soul'.

The executioner's first blow killed him. Two more severed his head from his body.[22]

Walter Devereux, earl of Essex, had been thirty-seven when he died, leaving his earldom to an eleven-year-old boy as delicate as he was promising. In spite of his fragile patrimony, Edward Waterhouse, Earl Walter's secretary, thought the young new earl, Robert, had before him a bright future. He could achieve even more than his ancestors. He would become 'a man well accomplished to serve her Majesty . . . as well in war as peace'.[23]

The corpse was buried in the Tower's chapel of St Peter ad Vincula.

24

Thirty, Ten

Libels were nothing new or surprising to Robert Cecil. Anonymous enemies had been libelling his family for years. The death of Robert Devereux, former earl of Essex, simply made more prominent an annoying fact of life.

The libellers left their handwritten papers in public places like the Royal Exchange. Sometimes the attacks were personal. Sometimes they were not. Certain codewords sufficed to make the point clear. They suggested a resolve to rid Elizabeth of meddling and criminal ministers who were eating the heart out of her kingdom. At court, in taverns, in conversation, on paper, Robert Cecil was hated and mocked: 'Little Cecil trips up and down, he rules both court and crown.' Occasionally, but not often enough, the libellers were caught. Two days after the earl of Essex's rising, one William Buttes of the county of Essex was picked up by a local magistrate: 'the said Buttes did vaunt and brag and publish rhymes and libels' against both Lord Admiral Nottingham and Master Secretary Cecil.[1]

One paper that Cecil read in the weeks following Essex's execution looked from the outside respectable enough. The packet was folded and sealed in the usual way. But the phrasing of the address suggested mystery: 'Into the hands of our most noble and gracious Queen of England deliver me.'

Its author wrote, not as an 'I', but a 'we' – as many, all loyal, loving and obedient subjects, all who saw the corruption in the commonwealth. The vineyard of the kingdom was being eaten by worms which 'have pierced the tender roots of the chiefest plants ... and now like caterpillars do climb'. Loyal subjects were poor sheep whose shepherds were preyed upon by wolves and foxes. They asked Elizabeth to consider their petition, and with speed – otherwise they would all perish together.

The paper got only as far as Cecil. He read it; he dismissed it. He wrote on the back of the packet, near the seal he had broken, one word: 'Libel'.[2]

In *Richard II* a gardener and his assistant discuss how to tame a garden which has grown out of control. The garden is the kingdom. Corruption has to be pruned away. Heads need to roll. Indeed, some have been lost already, those of Richard's favourites, Bushy, Bagot and Green.

The gardener says to his man:

> Go thou, and like an executioner
> Cut off the heads of too-fast-growing sprays,
> That look too lofty in our commonwealth,
> All must be even in our government.
> You thus employed, I will go root away
> The noisome weeds which without profit suck
> The soil's fertility from wholesome flowers.

His assistant replies:

> Why should we in the compass of a pale,
> Keep law and form, and due proportïon,
> Showing as in a model our firm estate,
> When our sea-wallèd garden the whole land
> Is full of weeds, her fairest flowers choked up,
> Her fruit trees all unpruned, her hedges ruined,
> Her knots disordered and her wholesome herbs
> Swarming with caterpillars.

This was the scene as it was printed in 1597 in *The Tragedy of King Richard the Second*, on sale in Paul's Churchyard at the bookshop of Andrew Wise at the sign of the Angel – the script as it had been performed by the Lord Chamberlain's Men.[3]

On 7 February 1601 the gardener and his man once again spoke on stage about pruning back the too-fast-growing sprays of the commonwealth. Within days their speeches had a new, stark significance. But it was Essex, not Cecil, who had been rooted out.

We might wonder whether Robert Cecil's libeller was somewhere in the audience listening attentively.

On Shrove Tuesday, 24 February, David Foulis, by now lodged in London, was co-ordinating with Cecil the arrival of King James's ambassadors. They would need accommodation for about forty: the earl of Mar and Edward Bruce were not travelling light. Cecil liaised with the Privy Council, and the council wrote to the lord mayor of London. Within three days the mayor had found what he thought was the perfect house in the city, large and seldom used: Sir John Spencer's Crosby Place on Bishopsgate Street, in the heart of London.

What did James want his ambassadors to achieve? When on 15 February he heard Cecil's account of the Essex rising read out loud by George Nicolson, every calculation the king had made about the embassy had to change. No Essex, no clear plan for the future. To James, Robert Cecil was an unfriendly spirit – the Cecils, father and son, always had been. Most probably the earl and the abbot would be operating in unfriendly territory. And then there was the most important, and most unpredictable, factor: the queen.

Robert Cecil had no illusions about his reputation in Scotland. His father had been held responsible for the execution of Queen Mary, and Mary's son James believed that Robert, like Lord Burghley, was dead set against him and his claim to the English throne. Cecil wrote to Nicolson a week before Essex's insurrection that he had given up caring about the slanders and gossip at James's court. It took just too much effort to confute the malicious untruths.[4]

It was from several sources that Cecil discerned the true purpose of the Scottish embassy. Henry Cuffe, Essex's servant and a chief conspirator in the February insurrection, confessed what Essex had known about Mar's secret instructions from James. The king had 'infallible proof' from Essex that Elizabeth had been captured by a clique 'of extraordinary ... power and malice': Buckhurst, Nottingham, Cobham, Cecil and Raleigh, all scheming to thwart James's claim. This clique controlled and ruled the whole kingdom. They conspired with Jesuits and Catholics. They favoured as Elizabeth's successor the Spanish infanta.[5]

Cecil called these allegations 'hyperbolical inventions'. But they mattered. Smearing him and the others as Spanish sympathizers had been a deliberate effort by Essex to gather support against Cecil. This is why the secretary had used the earl's trial in Westminster Hall to refute the slander once and for all. The real traitor had been Essex: 'He had no other design than to have possessed the Queen under colour of changing of the court, and for some small time to have governed in the Queen's name until he had seen how the world would have liked the first act of his comedy and then to have given the *coup de maître*' – the masterstroke, to take the throne for himself.[6]

Ambassadors Mar and Bruce were in London by the end of the first week of March. The earl had come to build bridges, to come to an understanding.[7]

Mar waited over a week before asking for an audience with the queen. This was not a happy beginning. His delay was noted, and it felt like a discourtesy. He met Elizabeth at last on Sunday 15 March in the presence chamber at Whitehall Palace. Cecil wasn't at the meeting, but the topic Mar brought to the queen – justice for James over the outrageous accusations of Valentine Thomas – left both Cecil and Elizabeth underwhelmed. The case of Valentine seemed to them now concluded and irrelevant.[8]

What James really wanted was impossible for Mar to discuss. There was no way he could talk about the succession openly, and without Essex he had no obvious supporter at Elizabeth's court. So, the days ticked by, audiences, meetings with the council, but nothing was achieved. By April both sides were feeling frustrated. Elizabeth wrote sharply to James: Mar and Bruce had presented her with issues which had already been settled. Sensing that their embassy would soon be over, the ambassadors wrote to Cecil in the hope that he could do something, appealing to the common interests of Scotland and England.[9]

At the turn of the month Mar and Bruce sent to James a justifiably pessimistic assessment of their lack of progress in Westminster. At

Linlithgow Palace on Wednesday 8 April the king replied. It was time, he realized, for a new plan.

> Ye must so deal with Master Secretary and her [Elizabeth's] principal
> guiders as ye may assure them that ... I will make account of their
> affections towards me accordingly, and ... that ye have power to give
> them full assurance of my favour, especially to Master Secretary, who is
> king there in effect.[10]

Master Secretary was on King James's mind, and he sought from anyone he met their opinion about Cecil. In late April one of Cecil's intelligencers, a Scot called Thomas Douglas, delivered the earl of Mar's letters to James. Douglas talked with the king about the embassy and about what was happening more generally in England. The king pressed him for more. What did the common people feel towards James? And the nobility, especially Secretary Cecil?

'For that, said I, my Lord of Mar can best answer, but for Sir Robert, said I, he is a man impechit [charged] with the most chief affairs of the land.' There was, Douglas told the king, no better man.[11]

It was the most important, certainly the most secret, meeting of Robert Cecil's life. For Cecil it changed everything. What it began risked his whole career.

He met Mar and Bruce at Duchy House, the headquarters of the Duchy of Lancaster, in early May. They discussed Cecil's support for James's title to the crowns of England and Ireland. 'I took no long deliberation at first to make an answer to your ambassadors' summons', Cecil later wrote to James. But he understood the seriousness of what he was about to do, for he was being invited to negotiate personally and secretly with a foreign prince, and one whom he had for many years viewed critically, even sceptically. Cecil had in front of him some serious reprogramming of old and deep assumptions, as well as the task of convincing James of his support and building a relationship with the king of Scots strong enough to stand the tests of the next few years. Cecil knew that even to mention the succession was taboo. In opening communications with James, he was risking his career and his freedom.[12]

He surely spoke to Mar and Bruce as plainly as he wrote to the Anglophile Patrick of Gray, on the Spanish smear against him. To Gray he reported what he had said in Privy Council: concerning 'the matter of the Infanta I spake as God . . . doth know it truly, that . . . I hated the nation, that I abhorred to be their subject'.[13]

He was James's man. He made his commitment, his Rubicon decision. He was loyal to Elizabeth – and to the future claim to her throne of the king of Scots.

Why did he agree to James's offer? His own answer to that question, a few years later, was that his actions kept both Elizabeth and the king of Scots safe and secure. We might add that he had his own future to think about. He was being pragmatic and realistic.

Why was it a secret? Cecil answered that question too, in 1608, with a few years' perspective on the late queen. For decades she had squashed succession plans and planners, those brave individuals who saw that something would have to be done about the future at some point. Now near the end of her life she was just as resolute, just as she was failing in her powers. She might misinterpret what was being done for own best interests, and wouldn't have recognized it as such. 'Her age and orbity,' Cecil wrote, 'joined to the jealousy of her sex, might have moved her to think ill of that which helped to preserve her.' Orbity, from the Latin root word *orbitas*, bereavement or childlessness, a woman not what she once was, a virgin queen near the end of her life.[14]

So the agreement was made. After the Duchy House meeting, James wrote to Cecil a letter which was fastened in two places with pink silk and sealed twice. It was almost certainly handed to Sir Robert by the earl of Mar. For reasons of security James signed it with a number, 30, and sealed it with a courtier's seal. Sir Robert Cecil was '10', and a third correspondent in this very secret circle, sixty-one-year-old Lord Henry Howard, '3'. It was hardly deep cover: 30 wrote to 10 in the distinctive handwriting of the king of Scots.

James said that he was glad that Cecil had 'made choice' of his ambassadors. Because Cecil and the king could not speak face to face, James suggested Howard as an intermediary, 'a sure and secret interpreter', the king called him 'long approved and trusty'. James now distanced himself from the earl of Essex, whose 'aspiring mind', he noted, Cecil had long mistrusted. James took this to be 'a sure sign that 10 would never allow that a subject should climb to so high a room'. Here was a neat dismissal of Essex's pretensions and a warning to Cecil not to overstep himself.

And then there was the promise, the kernel of the deal. For a safe and secure accession there would be a future reward: 'when it shall please God that 30 shall succeed to his right, he shall no surelier succeed to the place than he shall succeed in bestowing as great and greater favour upon 10 as his predecessor doth bestow upon him.'[15]

So it began. Five men, five numbers, and the oddest of groups. The king, the earl, the lord, the minister, the lawyer; three – Cecil, Mar and Bruce – steady and discreet, two – James and Howard – more quixotic, less predictable. The strangest character of all was Lord Henry Howard, the son of an earl executed by King Henry VIII, a crypto-Catholic and former ally of the earl of Essex, a scholar and intellectual, and a shameless flatterer. Cecil called Howard 'My friend 3'.[16]

Cecil's reply to King James is its own kind of masterpiece; frank as well as subtle, it had moments of rhetorical play that James would have savoured. How carefully he used his words. Robert Cecil fashioned himself into the servant of two sovereign masters. Where he served Elizabeth, he counselled and advised James. He reconciled present and future. He was rooted in both, elastic in whom and how he served, scrupulous in his duty.

Cecil began by writing that he needed to speak for himself. He expected the king's eventual succession, knowing that James would reward those who had supported him. He was careful to avoid any imputations of plots or secrecy or disloyalty to Elizabeth: 'I perceive when that natural day shall come wherein your feast may be lawfully proclaimed (which I do wish may be long deferred) . . . those shall not be rejected . . . who have not falsely or untimely wrought for future fortunes.' Cecil was not hoping for a hastening of what he knew would one day happen.

In now revealing the truth of himself to James he had waited for the right moment. He acknowledged the allegation made against him that he was 'one that was sold over to Spanish practice, and swollen to the chin with other dangerous plots' against the king. Here, in one of the most subtle passages of the letter, was Cecil's explanation for speaking and writing now: it was these claims which had made James believe that Elizabeth had towards the king 'an alienation of heart'. Cecil, in other words, was himself the barrier of clear communication between the queen and the king. And so to clear that blockage, he had committed himself to James, something Elizabeth did not need to know about. This was for her own good. 'Sir,' he wrote to James, 'I know it holdeth so just proportion, even with strictest loyalty and soundest reason, for faithful ministers to conceal sometime both thoughts and actions from princes, when they are persuaded it is for their own greater service.'

Cecil reflected on his relationship with the former earl of Essex, looking back to happier times:

> Such were the mutual affections in our tender years, and so many recip-
> rocal benefits interchanged in our growing fortunes, as besides the rules
> of my own poor discretion, which taught me how perilous it was for
> Secretary Cecil to have a bitter feud with an Earl Marshal of England,
> a favourite, a nobleman of eminent parts, and a councillor, all things
> else in the composition of my mind did still concur on my part to make
> me desirous of his favour.

Cecil had done and would still do his duty to Elizabeth. He looked now to James's future happiness. He offered practical advice to the king. James should keep silent on minor matters which seemed to question Elizabeth's judgement. Instead, he should secure her heart by 'clear and temperate courses'.

Close to the end of the letter was a last piece of advice, for the time being. There was no need for James to build in England a mass following. To secure a kingdom took only a select few.[17]

The stalking-horse for the secret correspondence was a travelling French nobleman, the duke of Rohan. Monsieur de Rohan had visited Elizabeth's court in autumn 1600 on his way to Scotland, when at the end of October he had an interview with Cecil. In mid-November Rohan was feasted at James's court. He was back in England by early

February, signing a letter to Cecil from Dover on the day, 7 February, that the Lord Chamberlain's Men performed *Richard II* at the Globe theatre. In April the French ambassador in London sent Rohan a letter about Essex's arraignment – it was intercepted and copied by a watchful Thomas Phelippes.[18]

By late spring 1601 Rohan was a perfect cover for letters moving between the courts of Elizabeth and James, which would raise few suspicions. Rohan himself, back in France, was unlikely to get in the way. Cecil instructed George Nicolson to hand any letters from Monsieur de Rohan, which travelled up from Westminster with Cecil's own, to the earl of Mar personally. Nicolson, of course, had no idea about the correspondence, and Cecil would have to work very hard to keep it that way. Mar's replies to Rohan should be handed only to Cecil.[19]

By August 1601 Nicolson had noticed something he thought might interest Cecil. He was beginning to see a pattern for which he had no good explanation. When he delivered Monsieur de Rohan's letters at court, the king went into private conference with Mar and Bruce. Nicolson wondered why.[20]

In June 30 replied to 10. After his ambassadors had spoken to Cecil, James had hoped that his favour 'was to be grounded upon a fixed star and not a mobile or wavering planet'. On receiving Cecil's letter, he was now sure; Master Secretary had broken his silence and James wholeheartedly welcomed it.

His Majesty recognized the role Cecil was proposing to play, promising that he would not press him beyond 'dutiful fidelity to the Queen'. A wise man always judged things 'by certain effects and not by outward and deceivable appearances'. James would treat Cecil as one of his councillors. He had listened to his advice to James to convert the few, not the many. The king quailed at *mobile vulgus* (the fickle mob) and at democracy, of which James had had his fill in Scotland. He was no Absalom, the Old Testament rebel against his father King David. 'I am no usurper; it is for them to play the Absalom.'[21]

James quoted for Cecil a Latin proverb: The drop hollows out the stone not by force but by repeated falling. They were in for a long and delicate game.

25

Factions and Fantasies

Sunday, 4 October 1601, the quick and fluid movement of Robert Cecil's pen on paper. This was the most secret of letters, composed alone, well away from secretaries and staff. There was the usual wrestling with words and meanings, heavy corrections and re-writings; a meeting of Latin maxims and deep political experience; the laying out of a plan; a calming draught for a nervous monarch.

It was a letter to James of reassurance. Cecil would resist writing unnecessarily, acting and reporting when he needed to, standing sentinel should the question of the royal succession be raised, ready to defend James's interest 'as tongue or power is able'. He reiterated what the king already knew: Elizabeth refused even to acknowledge her succession. 'The subject itself is so perilous to touch amongst us, as it setteth a mark upon his head for ever that hatcheth such a bird.' James should not worry about silence, listen to rumours, or fret that those acting on his behalf weren't busy working simply because they didn't give him hourly reports. Trust us to get on with the job, Cecil was saying: stay calm, resist the urge to overmanage. If James did all this, he wrote, then the king's supporters at Elizabeth's court had 'found in you a heart of adamant in a world of feathers'.[1]

Patience, trust and time.

Autumn 1601 was a turbulent season in Westminster. A bad-tempered parliament, Elizabeth's tenth, sat from 27 October, grumbling over the ever-increasing sums of taxation that were needed to pay for the garrisons in the Netherlands and the continuing fight against the earl of Tyrone in Ireland, where in September at Kinsale, not far from

Cork, a small Spanish army of 3,400 experienced troops had landed to support the rebel earl. Eventually, by January 1602, Elizabeth's forces under the command of Lord Mountjoy succeeded in breaking both the Spanish and Irish armies, negotiating the Spaniards' surrender. It was a small but important victory – and much too late.

Stung by the criticism of those she called 'malcontents', the queen gave two speeches to her parliament. She fell back on her familiar technique, imperious and self-justificatory. She spoke about her sense of justice and uprightness, about how much she had sacrificed for the security of the kingdom, 'content to be a taper of true virgin wax to waste myself and spend my life that I might give light and comfort to those that live under me' – her words are from Lord Henry Howard's copy of the speech. In the other, earlier address she reminded her Lords and Commons of a monarch's deepest responsibilities. 'You must not beguile yourselves, nor wrong us, to think that the glossing lustre of a glittering glory of a king's title may so extol us that we think all is lawful what we list, not caring what we do.'[2]

Elizabeth's short histories of her reign and her reflections on the burdens and costs of absolute power sounded like valedictions.

On one matter parliament and monarch were silent. Lord Howard, one of the initiates in the secret correspondence, wrote about it to the earl of Mar near the end of November. He believed that there was clear though unspoken unity and unanimity in parliament on James's future as king. 'Touching the succession, nothing propounded in figure, nothing conceived in prejudice; but all minds as thoroughly persuaded of one truth, one right, one claim as if all the estates [parliament] had concluded it.' This was too easy an assumption to make. In being certain about the future beyond Elizabeth there was a very long way yet to go.[3]

By early 1602 Howard was a busy writer of epically long letters to James, Mar and Bruce – even the king, who loved words, found their length overpowering. But without Howard, supporting Robert Cecil at Elizabeth's court, the deep preparations for James's future would not have been possible.

Thus the letters addressed to and from Monsieur de Rohan went north and south – 'great packets' as George Nicolson often called them, sealed for security with various courtiers' seals, carried by David Foulis and others, containing messages of common endeavour and resolution. Nicolson had no idea about what these packets actually contained. That was a problem for Cecil, for the smallest slip or miscommunication risked the whole correspondence and might have sent him to the Tower. Even Nicolson – we might say especially Nicolson, whose wits were sharp enough – was a danger. 'The world is now become so suspicious (as somewhat by George Nicolson's speeches to myself) I did gather', Mar wrote to Cecil in April. The king loved to talk and discourse. For him discretion was no native instinct. A leak was always possible.[4]

Robert Cecil had lived and worked for so long in a court of secrets and was himself trained up for secrecy. He was the consummate manager of information. When, for example, he advised Sir George Carew in Ireland to send him two versions of the same letter – one for the queen, another fuller, franker one for himself as secretary – Cecil was doing what his father had done. For Cecil's eyes only: 'that which is fit for me to know apart'. This was his job. As he wrote, 'all honest servants must strain a little when they will serve princes'. *Strain* was no accidental verb, and for Elizabethans it had several meanings: to bridle or control; to grip or grasp tightly; to seize; to constrict or pinch; to filter. Or – Shakespeare used it in this sense, as now did Robert Cecil – to transgress and go beyond.[5]

But the intensity of the secret correspondence was new territory even for Cecil. He and Howard saw from all sides the manoeuvres and counter-manoeuvres at court: 'What a world we live of factions and fantasies', Howard wrote to Edward Bruce. And Cecil was playing a familiar part, though with a new intensity – the master of dissimulation, the most formidable of all political operators, quick and persuasive. Reporting a sharp encounter with the queen about the poverty of her Exchequer and the burdens of war, Howard praised him to the skies, writing to James: 'No man could answer more judiciously and honestly than Cecil to every point, tempering her fears, improving causes of hope, excusing persons in employment, and abating passion.'[6]

Cecil knew, too, that he might be dissimulated against. When in January 1602 George Nicolson spotted that the intelligencer Thomas Douglas had been fabricating his whereabouts and was claiming ten pounds' worth of expenses for it, Cecil wasted no words. He knew how his spies, when they saw that their time and trust was up, had tried to mislead him. 'I have been so often bitten with the discontented humour of intelligencers when they have spent my money a good while and think I begin to find it, and so play me some slippery trick at farewell.'[7]

Douglas was quick to apologize and justify himself, careful over 1602 to send reports from Scotland every few weeks. Nicolson paid him a decent regular salary: ten pounds every quarter year. But Cecil trusted his spies just as he trusted others to keep his secrets – never as completely as he would have wished.[8]

From Falkland Palace the king of Scots communicated with his secret facilitators in England.

To his 10, Sir Robert Cecil, on 3 June: 'I cannot omit to display unto you the great contentment I receive by your so inward and united concurrence in all the paths that lead to my future happiness.'[9]

To his 3, Lord Henry Howard, on 29 July: 'The deep and restless care that both worthy 10 and ye have of my safety I shall never be able to recompense.'[10]

The queen went on progress in late July, while in August reports began of Spanish forces preparing to land in Ireland. There was no peace and quiet for Robert Cecil.

When it came to the greatest secret of all, James's characterization of Cecil's 'restless care' was right on the mark. What Cecil made, with the conscious knowledge of Lord Henry Howard and the unconscious aid of George Nicolson, was a closed information loop between himself and James and their circle that was secure only superficially – an easy mistake risked opening it up to outsiders. The biggest dangers here, in terms of the human factor, were two: Nicolson's loyal and legitimate suspicions of what he saw and heard at James's court, and the unwitting indiscretions of the Scottish king and those around him.

Here Cecil had to handle Nicolson gingerly, changing nothing in their routine, steering him away from raising questions it was better for Cecil not to have answered. Henry Howard was less circumscribed: King James, Mar and Bruce were part of the great secret. Howard had the additional advantage of being briefed at court by Cecil, who showed him Nicolson's reports, which Howard then shared with Mar and Bruce.

The benefit of all this – though it revealed the risks too – was that Cecil and Howard were able to alert their secret correspondents to any potential breaches of security. In August 1602, for example, James told Nicolson that 'the Secretary is very honest and faithful to the Queen his mistress, but yet honest and friendly towards him'. More worrying was Nicolson's report that the king 'hath of late very strange intelligence' which James wasn't doing a good job of keeping secret. In his reply to Nicolson, Cecil avoided any reference to these lines, but he made sure to let Howard know about them.[11]

What Cecil feared most was the mis-delivery of a confidential packet. This too had happened by August 1602, though Howard managed to keep the fact from Cecil – just. He had noticed that in one of Edward Bruce's letters a piece of paper, an important enclosure, was missing. That something had gone astray was obvious from the context of the letter. Howard managed to avoid sharing the letter with Cecil, but he told Bruce that it could have brought the whole secret correspondence crashing down. Cecil was alert for the smallest mistake and living on his nerves. 'For if . . . he must have seen that misadventure of the packet,' Howard wrote to Bruce, 'upon the multiplicity of doubts his mind would never have been at rest, nor he would have eaten or slept quietly; for nothing makes him confident but experience of secret trust and security of intelligence.' Cecil himself wrote to James of his 'doubt and fear lest the treasure of such a prince's secret trust' – those same two words: did Cecil say them to Howard? – 'coming to light, either by the levity of those that have offered traffic [i.e., those who carried the letters] or by their own election of loose instruments, might call in question . . . my sincerity in making use of such a confidence'.[12]

By October 1602 one of the mainstays of Secretary Cecil's private office, the longest serving of his secretaries, Simon Willis, had been dismissed from his service. The reason – which could not be acknowledged – was the secret correspondence.

A disagreement had been rumbling over a piece of patronage that Willis wanted. He and Cecil argued about it; Willis spoke sharply, though in July he had written to Cecil to apologize, asking forgiveness for his mistakes. It was not enough to save his career. He was dismissed some time before Michaelmas, 29 September. A few days later the court watcher John Chamberlain had heard from two senior officials close to Cecil that Willis had been sacked because of 'his insolent and harsh behaviour towards his master'. Cecil himself later noted Willis's 'pride', a word that Willis had used, though perhaps not acknowledged, back in July, answering accusations of 'the pride of my spirit'.[13]

But this was only half the story. Willis had unrivalled access to Cecil's papers. He also now had a grievance. On Cecil's mind were the highly secret packets purportedly from Monsieur de Rohan which could so easily have been handed by mistake to Willis. He could guess what Willis might have been tempted to do: 'he mought [Elizabethan past tense for may] have raised some such inferences thereof, as mought have bred some jealousy in the Queen's mind, if she had known it, or heard any such suspicion to move from him.' Cecil's careful words from 1608 suggest something of his mindset in October 1602. He was jumpy. And now Willis, a man who had known the innermost secrets of Cecil's office for over a decade, a man who knew the secretary better than most, found himself unemployed, and Cecil without an old and familiar retainer.[14]

Cecil was seriously ill in autumn 1602. He noted in the last week of October that he was struggling with sore eyes. In mid-November John Chamberlain wrote that after catching a sudden cold Master Secretary's throat had swollen so much that he could neither swallow nor breathe properly. At the end of the month Cecil himself described it to George Nicolson as an 'indisposition which held me from court in my own house longer than ever I was these thirty years'. It made him wonder for how long he could stand the physical strains of his job, to 'undergo burden of prince's service'. Office brought with it care and pain, inseparable from duty: these caused 'anxieties of mind and decay of health' even in the best constitutions – 'a contemplation fit for me of any other, whose infirmities promise not long health'.[15]

Cecil spent his weeks of sickness and introspection at his new house in Westminster. Robert's brother Thomas had inherited their father's great mansion on the Strand, where Robert had had an apartment since the mid-1580s. So, he built himself a new house practically across the street, just off the Strand on Ivy Bridge Lane, close to the old Savoy Palace: 'a large and stately house of brick and timber', as the London antiquary John Stow described it. In September 1602 it was just finished: only the wainscotting in Cecil's bedchamber had yet to dry out properly. A flushing privy was an early summer gift from Sir John Harington, its inventor, 'a homely present . . . worth gold and silver to your house'. Harington wrote that Cecil would find 'as well for your private lodgings, as for all the family, the use of it commodious and necessary, and above all in time of infection most wholesome'.[16]

The new Cecil House – as Sir Robert may have reflected as he found himself confined there ill for a few weeks – was a house fit for a courtier whose service was exacting a heavy personal price.

Sir John Harington was also a behind-the-scenes supporter of James VI as Elizabeth's successor. Harington was one of those precocious talents whose career never quite got purchase at court or in government. Eton; King's College, Cambridge; the academic star of the MA commencement eighteen-year-old Robert Cecil had attended in 1581; Elizabeth's godson, favoured and encouraged – her 'Boy Jack'. As a poet and linguist, his most accomplished work was the first published translation in 1591 of Ludovico Ariosto's epic romance *Orlando Furioso* ('in English heroical verse'), a source for Shakespeare's *Much Ado About Nothing*. Before Christmas 1602 he completed a long essay laying out the case for the claim to the English throne of the king of Scots – a magpie collection of observations and discussions on the laws of succession, on potential successors to Elizabeth, on British history and Anglo-Scottish unity. Harington examined how division and bitterness over faith might be ended, even – and here he challenged the deepest assumption of his times – separating religion from the secular arm of government. The essay was part exposition, part polemic – a meditation on a queen who was nearing her end as well as an affirmation of a king who was full of life and possibility. Affable, open, generous, wise, magnanimous: James had all these qualities. 'Oh that princes did know how sweet a thing it is to give with reason and due desert, not lingerly and against their wills, as it were, which takes away the thanks.'

Times were changing. 'God hath blessed our sovereign with a prosperous reign and a long life; she is now this September ... full sixty-nine.' 'Long may she live to His glory: but whensoever God shall call her, I perceive we are not like to be governed by a lady shut up in a chamber from all her subjects and most of her servants, and seen seldom but on holy days.' From the beginning Elizabeth had suppressed discussion of an heir apparent, 'saying she would not have her winding sheet set up afore her face'. But privately, Harington claimed, she recognized the Scottish claim, for which, so he maintained, there was widespread support at court and more widely in the kingdom. There were other, notional claimants – the Spanish infanta, and James VI's cousin under close watch in England, Arabella Stuart (through her great-grandmother Margaret Tudor, daughter of Henry VII) – but Harington dismissed them. Elizabeth's successor was and had to be the king of Scots.[17]

There were two Queen Elizabeths at Christmas 1602: the tired woman Harington met at court, and the imperial queen whose majesty was praised on her early December visit to Cecil House on Ivy Lane Bridge.

Perhaps Harington saw his godmother as she was. Perhaps, privately looking forward to the future, on some level he saw Elizabeth as he wanted to. He observed that the queen was visibly declining: she 'doth now bear show of human infirmity, too fast for that evil which we shall get by her death, and too slow for that good which she shall get by her releasement from pains and misery', as he wrote to his wife. Elizabeth was irritable and unhappy, and her memory seemed fragile: she called for officials but when they arrived angrily dismissed them. 'But who', Harington asked, 'shall say that "Your Highness hath forgotten"?'[18]

When she had visited Cecil House on Monday 6 December, Cecil had put on for her a show of presents and jewels. Elizabeth, apparently relaxed, took a special interest in the display of weapons in the hall – a surprisingly martial theme for a most civilian of ministers. Cecil had commissioned the usual entertainments. One of these was a dramatic dialogue between one of the queen's gentlemen ushers – an official who controlled admission to her private rooms – and a courier just arrived at court with an urgent packet for Master Secretary, a letter from the emperor of China. The dialogue's purpose was to celebrate Elizabeth's deep learning and erudition and her secretary's skilled and busy service.

The courier (or post) arrives breathless. He needs to see the secretary.

> *Post*: Is Master Secretary Cecil here? Did you see Master Secretary? Gentlemen, can you bring me to Master Secretary?

> *Usher*: Master Secretary is not here. What business have you with him?

> *Post*: Marry Sir, I have letters that import to her Majesty's service.

> *Usher*: Then you were best stay till he come; he was here even now and will be again by and by, if you can have the patience to stay a while.

> *Post*: Stay: the matter requires such post haste as I dare not for my life stay anywhere till I have delivered the letters. Therefore I pray direct me where I may find him, for without doubt it is business that especially concerns the Queen's service.

> *Usher*: What business is here with you? If the letters concern the Queen why should not you deliver them to the Queen? You see she is present, and you cannot have a better opportunity, if the intelligence be so important and concern herself, as you say.

> *Post*: I cannot tell what I should do: they concern the Queen's service indeed, but they tell me they ought to be delivered to one of them to whose place it is proper to receive them.

The entertainment suggested – only Cecil knew it – a deeper, secret truth. And surely it spoke to his anxieties: the urgent packet for the secretary's eyes misdelivered; the queen reading what she could not know; the letter which leads to the unravelling.[19]

But the reign was unravelling anyway, winding down to its end.

Nine days after the queen's visit to Cecil House, Simon Willis wrote to his former master. He felt that time was precious and his new idleness to be a burden. After serving 'a full double prenticeship spent in painful service' under a minister of state, he asked that minister for the patronage he felt he had earned. The private secretary who for over a decade was Robert Cecil's shadow – and the man who might one day have known too much – had to content himself with a small annuity and a lodging with his brother on Aldermanbury, not far from the London Guildhall.[20]

New Year meant the exchange of gifts. Some mattered more than others. George Nicolson in Edinburgh sent Cecil 'one fair standing bowl', a piece of tableware like so many others: Cecil sold it. More welcome for King James in Scotland was a manuscript Latin treatise by the poet and legal jurist Sir Thomas Craig of Riccarton. It was a behemoth of a work, a confutation of every argument made against James as Elizabeth's successor. Craig's main target was Robert Persons's *Conference on the Next Succession*, the same poisonous book that had been used to smear both Essex and Cecil. To the pseudonymous Doleman – Persons – there had been no answer. The English had covered themselves in silence, as Craig put it. No Scot had ever attempted it. And so, now, Craig took up the job.[21]

Near the end of his treatise, Craig examined whether it was necessary for princes before they die to name their successor. It was better if they did, he wrote, but he understood why often in history they hadn't: it was natural for men 'to worship rather the rising than the setting sun' – ambitious courtiers would always look to a successor.

Yet Craig believed that Elizabeth would, in the end, do something, as fragile and human as she was.

> She is a sovereign queen, and kings are often liable to jealousies and
> suspicions. She is a woman and that infirmity is common to that sex;
> and now she is become ancient, and that age is conscious to itself of
> infirmity, is credulous, fearful, and most full of suspicions; and when

people are of a great age they are always apt to fancy themselves neglected and forsaken.

They should not despair: she would act to prevent all approaching
evils and mischiefs.[22]

Elizabeth didn't. Fortunately, Secretary Cecil did.

On 4 February 1603 Thomas Douglas, Cecil's intelligencer in Scotland, reported that King James had spoken about Cecil. Douglas
didn't quite know what to make of his words. 'The King ... doth
highly commend your honour, speaking openly at his table that you
have performed the part of a friend and an honest man, with many
other (I think upon my soul) ironical speeches ... But time will try his
love.'[23]

Douglas could have had no idea of how true his words were, and
how soon for James and Cecil that trial would come.

26

Accession

One account of Elizabeth I's final days has Lord Admiral Nottingham, Lord Keeper Egerton and Secretary Cecil at Elizabeth's bedside and the queen, asked by them to name her successor, giving them an answer answerless: 'I will have no rascal to succeed me: and who should succeed me but a king.' The same narrative – and a second, much later one – says that when the next day she lost the power of speech she acknowledged James, when his name was put to her, by putting 'both her hands jointly together over her head in manner of a crown'.[1]

Was this fact or fiction or a little of both, manufactured in a new reign for the sake of dynastic continuity? Even with the substance of vapour, it was as close as the queen had ever come to deciding her succession.

She died at Richmond Palace on Thursday 24 March between two and three o'clock in the morning. Following a few months of melancholy detachment, it was a quiet end: *cum leve quadam febre, absque gemitu* – 'with a slight shiver, without a groan' – was how one of the royal chaplains, praying at her bedside, described it.[2]

The queen was dead, long live the king. Almost.

In the previous few weeks Secretary Cecil had closely controlled news of Elizabeth's health. He wrote and reported only what he needed to, choosing his words carefully. He didn't wholly trust the couriers.

His brother Lord Burghley, from his base in York, was able to read between the lines of Robert's letters. He knew the queen was near her end, and he was ready. He wrote to Robert: 'I pray you when that fatal matter cometh to pass let me [hear] from you by post and you shall always hear from me.' With George Nicolson Cecil was more circum-spect, writing on 9 March: 'I must confess unto you that she hath been so ill disposed these eight or nine days as I am fearful lest the continu-ance of such accidents should bring her Majesty to future weakness and so to be in danger of that which I hope mine eyes shall never see.'[3]

In mid-March the Privy Council ordered county sheriffs and mag-istrates to suppress gossip about the queen's sickness. Lord Burghley heard the rumours in York. By 19 March he was worried:

> Your letters I received last by my man, whereof I picked out your mean-ing, much satisfied me, but the uncertain estate of her Majesty's health much perplexed me, and therefore [I] cannot rest [from] sending or writing unto you, by a special messenger, that [by] him you may write more particularly than I know by posts you dare venture.[4]

On Tuesday 22 March Elizabeth was confined to bed, and the council began to prepare for her death. They wrote to the lieutenant of the Tower of London, Sir John Peyton, and Peyton received their lord-ships' letter just as the Tower's gates were being closed for the night. Peyton knew his duty: he was ready to resist 'an opposition against right intended'. Whose right Peyton didn't say.[5]

The same day Secretary Cecil wrote to King James VI a letter which has not survived, but whose theme we might make a plausible guess at: prepare yourself.[6]

But another of Cecil's letters to James has survived, one he began in Elizabeth's final hours and finished, a couple of hundred words later, in a new reign. The giveaway is the change in grammatical tense. He began by hoping that James would 'make my sincere and undivided service unto my present mistress, an argument of my future fidelity unto yourself' and ended by humbling himself before the authority of his new king, offering himself in service as 'a member of that house [i.e., the Cecil family] which hath yet never been unfaithful to their masters'.[7]

What he didn't explain to James, however, was his own role in cho-reographing the early hours of Thursday 24 March his Majesty's accession – the hours between the start and finish of his letter.

*

Soon after 3 a.m. that morning the dead queen's court was sealed. The porters were instructed to let no one in or out of the gates without the say-so of the Privy Council. Councillors and noblemen, gathered in the privy chamber, moved to Secretary Cecil's apartment to go into conclave. Of what was discussed and concluded no account was kept, no minutes taken. This was too important a gathering to record; this was the silence of absolute secrecy.

Was it simply a ratification of a decision already made to choose James? That is what Cecil himself suggested to the king of Scots: 'I do hold it my duty to testify thus much . . . but it was an universal assent of all that gave this speedy and dutiful passage unto your Majesty's rightful claim.' Of course we might think here that Cecil was bound, out of form and politeness, to write this. But he added a few other words which suggest something of the atmosphere in those intense pre-dawn hours: 'fear and necessity working the same effect in the ill-affected (if there were any such) that duty and allegiance did in all the rest'. Fear and necessity: the moment of decision had come at last.[8]

Of course, Robert Cecil would have had a plan. To the Scottish king he had made a commitment which was absolute and unyielding. And he had had time to organize, over months, weeks, days, hours. What helped was that in Master Secretary's chamber there was present an ally; both were conscious of each other and had indeed co-ordinated their efforts since June 1602. This was '40', recruited by Cecil, and a 'faithful colleague' (to use King James's phrase to Cecil) who had been powerful enough to influence Elizabeth's Anglo-Spanish policy and to have 'preserved the queen's mind from the poison of jealous prejudice' of the Scottish king and his rights (the words are again James's). Only circumstantial evidence gives us the most likely identity of '40': Lord Admiral Nottingham, the hero of 1588, and one of the inner quartet in Elizabeth's council.[9]

Cecil's task was to secure for James the crowns of England and Ireland; that point is fixed. This was agreed and settled within hours: the proclamation was made (written by Cecil); messengers were sent off to James. We can assume that Cecil guided the council and the other noblemen through all the arguments in favour of James's claim. If we take as a necessary politeness those few words in parenthesis in Cecil's letter ('if there were any such'), then some councillors may have dissented. But who would they have been dissenting for? The disparate remnants of the medieval Plantagenets, like the earls of Huntingdon? Or Arabella Stuart, King James's twenty-seven-year-old cousin? Or Infanta Isabella of Spain?

Arabella was born in England while James wasn't, which fact potentially resurrected the long legal debate, familiar from the years of Mary Queen of Scots, about whether a claimant of foreign birth could inherit the English Crown. Ironically, the principal argument that had been used by Mary's apologists to defend her claim to Elizabeth's throne – that the Crown was not really inheritable property and that a blood claim trumped everything – now stood in James's favour. With Isabella, what possible right might she have, for all the genealogical byways which took her ancestry back to John of Gaunt, duke of Lancaster, as a Spanish Catholic? And why either woman over a married king with two male heirs of his own? Sir Thomas Craig – and certainly Cecil – would have made short work of all this. But perhaps the claims and counterclaims were aired, doubts settled, the plain reality made clear. We can imagine that Cecil and the Privy Council worked through those justifications for James's title which would be deployed to persuade the new king's subjects of the soundness of his claim.

As privy councillors' servants prepared horses and coaches for the journey to London, a feature of this new regime was an unspoken confidence. The council did not go off to the security of the Tower of London – the fact is striking. This was the most delicate dynastic transition in fifty years; against the realities and uncertainties of 1603, Elizabeth's own accession in 1558 had been easy in comparison. At the beginning of this new century there were rumours, stirs, uprisings. Anything was possible: invasion scares, crop failures, trouble on the streets of London, the pain of war and economic collapse had had the council on a hair trigger for months. And yet they went to London, to visit the city's sheriffs on Milk Street, to square the lord mayor and aldermen and get their signatures on the proclamation of King James's accession, to set up their base of operations at Whitehall. There was no panic, rather, a sense of calm transition, at least outwardly. Here was an interregnal aristocracy preparing for a new monarchy.[10]

At 10 a.m. Master Secretary Cecil read the proclamation at the gates of Whitehall Palace. The king of Scots was the lineal and lawful descendant of the royal houses of Lancaster and York. On the queen's death her crown imperial passed to him absolutely and solely. His undoubted right was asserted by the temporalty and spiritualty of the realm, the Privy Council, other leading gentlemen, the lord mayor, aldermen and sheriffs of London, who would maintain present peace and James's future right, spending the last drop of their blood defending his claim against any challenger. Of the thirty-seven men who signed the document, Robert Cecil's name was third from the bottom: humble Master Secretary, author of the proclamation, the consummate manager of the whole process.[11]

After weeks of discreet behind-the-scenes preparation – and purpose and resolve in the hours before daybreak on a Thursday morning in early spring – the temporary rulers of England and Ireland settled themselves in the privy chamber at Whitehall, 'taking upon them the provisional government of the state'. The words belong to Levinus Munck, Cecil's private secretary. He most likely heard them from his master.[12]

Robert Cecil likened a king and his secretary to lovers whose secret counsels went undiscovered by their friends. His secret correspondence with James was a courtship. Through it they came to know each other, at least at a distance. There were protestations of love and duty, of mutual obligations. There was a sense of a future not quite yet fully mapped. They revealed to each other something – just something – of themselves.[13]

James in the autumn of 1602 had congratulated Cecil on his 'discreet fidelity' in handling Elizabeth. The Scottish king was effusive: nothing, he wrote, 'ever will breed the least suspicion in me of any crack in your integrity'. He said that he trusted Cecil as much as he trusted the earl of Mar 'that was brought up with me'.[14]

They corresponded over months about two matters which pressed so oppressively on the late Elizabethan age. First, after nearly two decades of uninterrupted and cripplingly expensive war, the most burdensome element of which was the English military commitment to the Low Countries, what hope was there of a peace with Spain? Secondly, the deep fractures in England of faith and religion, the long, painful consequences of the Reformation.

When it came to Anglo-Spanish peace, James thought only about himself and his right to the queen's crown. In late 1602 and early 1603 peace was out of the question, at least while Elizabeth was still alive: 'greatly prejudicial' to religion and 'most perilous for my just claim', was how James put it. In his mind succession and religion were connected. Peace would only underpin support in England for the Spanish infanta's title (at least in his view), and the king of Scots was having none of that. James also believed that a peace would encourage the missionary efforts of Jesuits and other Catholic priests, 'that rabble wherewith England is already too much affected', which he likened to the swarms of caterpillars and flies of biblical Egypt. The king wanted to see the strict enforcement of the recent proclamation that had banished them. Drafted by Cecil, the date of that proclamation – it has a significance when we look three years into the future to the Gunpowder Plot – was 5 November 1602.[15]

Cecil had replied to James's letter probably in January 1603. He had thought of Homer's *Iliad* and the creation myth of Oceanus, the stream from which originated all gods and living creatures: 'and so, once and for all,' he wrote to James, 'I acknowledge your own virtues to be the only springhead of all my confidence'. He felt the 'unspeakable favour' of the king sharing with him 'the inward temper' of his mind on religion. Then Cecil explained his own.[16]

The problem was decades old. It was difficult, divisive, poisonous. When the queen demanded from her subjects total obedience to the Church of England, could Catholics – with a different creed, with another spiritual authority, the pope, not the queen – ever be loyal or ever be trusted? Were Catholic priests secretly living in England holy men or traitors? Over the years treason and penal statutes had isolated those Catholics who stayed in England. Some of the dissidents who had gone abroad – Robert Persons, Richard Verstegan – had bitterly denounced what they called the English persecution. Cecil knew this. As a young man in parliament he had given his voice to the penal laws against priests and recusants, and he believed in them still. On his early travels he had met Catholic émigrés who wanted to be reconciled and forgiven. He had used priests to spy, men torn between queen and God, divided against themselves.

Now to King James, Cecil condemned Catholic priests, especially 'viperous' Jesuits, though he wrote that he shrank back from seeing them die on the gallows in their dozens. Some taught rebellion and treason: for them he had no compassion. But there was hope for others – or at least those who supported James's claim to the succession. This wasn't a call for enlightened toleration, or for any kind of separation of Church and State, just as it wasn't the suggestion of lenient treatment for rebels and traitors. It was instead a delicate request to the future king to exercise judgement in discerning his kingdoms' enemies – for James to use, as Cecil put it to him, 'the mystery of your own wisdom'.[17]

As Elizabeth in melancholy detachment was slipping away from human concerns, James had replied to his 'dearest 10'. He was receptive to Cecil's careful, subtle analysis. But Cecil had prodded a sore spot for a king who, as he said now, hated extremities and valued in his philosophy the middle way. He recommended to Cecil his long essay on monarchy and the art of ruling, *Basilikon Doron* ('Royal Gift'), written for his heir Prince Henry and printed in Edinburgh in 1599 (there would be many London editions of it from 1603 and even a translation into Welsh). If Cecil believed that the king was calling for a persecution, he had misunderstood James's meaning. No one should die for their faith: persecution was the mark of a false church. The punishment of rebellion, however, was a different matter.[18]

Saturday, 26 March 1603, was a day for the quick and the dead. The Privy Council escorted the corpse of Elizabeth Tudor from Richmond to Whitehall, where it arrived late in the evening. At about the same time, hundreds of miles away in Edinburgh, James heard the news that he was now king of England and Ireland as well as king of Scots. The following day he wrote to his right trusty counsellor Sir Robert Cecil and signed the letter James R. Numbers were no longer needed.[19]

James praised the good advice and grave judgement of those who had proclaimed him king: his new monarchy he owed to divine favour and human agency, to the wisdom, providence and policy of his dearest friends. David Foulis took the letter, with the king's thanks to Cecil for the 'earnest care you have begun and half accomplished of our good fortune and prosperity', and a 'ratification' that Cecil would continue in all his offices, honours and dignities.[20]

In early April Westminster, London and the Great North Road hummed with activity. Cecil was busy at his house on the Strand and a frequent visitor to Lord Treasurer Buckhurst, while his secretaries and servants might be found anywhere between Whitehall, Greenwich, Theobalds and London. Cecil, as he had written to James on 25 March, knew that his place was in London, especially in the hours after the proclamation of the accession: 'Though my longing be great to present my service to your Majesty in person . . . yet I shall be forced to stay a few days to perform those rights . . . in the behalf of your Majesty.'[21]

The new king got ready to travel south. From Holyrood Palace in Edinburgh on 2 April he drafted a letter for the nobility and 'late Council' of England, dating it in the first year of his reign. On the day he left Holyrood – 5 April – he put the provisional government in Westminster on an official footing. To Cecil he gave full authority to use the signet and privy seals in his possession.[22]

Cecil's role in securing James's accession was recognized. The earl of Montrose, remaining at Holyrood, wrote to him on 8 April. 'It hath pleased God . . . to bless our King and master with his due crown of England so happily without shed of blood or trouble to his Majesty . . . chiefly by the wisdom and assistance of your lordship.' All subjects would keep Cecil's services in perpetual memory.[23]

King James entered York, the second city of his new kingdom, eleven days after leaving Holyrood, on Saturday 16 April, the day before Palm Sunday.[24]

It was as late as Friday that Cecil had received his call to go to the king. He was on the road straight away. On Saturday he was in Huntingdon, managing communications between James and the Privy Council at Whitehall. That night he planned to sleep in either Grantham or Newark, pressing on to York on the Sunday. He arrived at James's court in York a little after midnight on Monday 18 April.

A few hours later Cecil had his first audience with the king he had served at a distance for two years. They had never before met, only exchanged letters. They knew about, but did not yet know, each other. Cecil kissed the king's hands.

Cecil had brought with him a briefing paper from the council. For an hour they went through the agenda items, discussing the date of Elizabeth's funeral, the arrangements for the coronation, and the naturalization of any Scottish courtiers in England (which needed an act of parliament but could be done, for the time being, under the great seal). In a sense James's accession was only the beginning of something wholly new: for England, a king from Scotland; for the Scots, the relocation of their monarch to Westminster. All of this was a challenge to protocol, convention and law. One thing at least was decided, the most important to James himself: he would be crowned with Queen Anne. He chose the second of the dates suggested by the council, 25 July.

The audience was short because the king had a dinner engagement ten miles outside the city. Cecil found himself trying to keep up – and trying to find lodgings at his Majesty's court.[25]

In York Cecil had tried to manage the tricky choreography of putting Elizabeth Tudor in her tomb and welcoming King James to London. The problem was timing. 'Their Lordships and the State' – his phrase for the provisional government at Whitehall – couldn't be in two places at once. With Elizabeth's funeral at Westminster Abbey fixed for the week following Easter (with James he discussed 29 April, though it took place on the 28th), Cecil had to slow the king's journey down the Great North Road. His Majesty didn't seem to mind as he moved from estate to estate. He hunted with Sir John Harington, who at Burghley House presented James with a verse of welcome. Cecil arranged for the king to stay at Theobalds, too.[26]

Monarchy, as Harington had put it, was no longer shut up in a chamber. England and Ireland now had a king two months away from turning thirty-seven, liberated at last from the oppressive horrors of Scottish politics. Made king of Scots a month after his first birthday on the forced abdication of his mother, over the years James had been plotted against, imprisoned, challenged and lectured, all by his own subjects. One senses that he couldn't wait to journey south. He loved to talk, to philosophize and to write. He believed in the divinity of kings, of being in charge. He liked to be generous, to spend money. He was a new master for a thirty-nine-year-old secretary to get used to.

In York Robert Cecil started to make sense of King James. To the master of Gray on 25 April Cecil was appropriately effusive. 'His virtues are so eminent, as by my six days' kneeling at his feet, I have made so sufficient a discovery of his royal perfections . . . Now that I am become his humble subject and servant, I am fully resolved (while breath lasteth) to depend upon himself only.'[27]

In June retributive justice caught up at last with Valentine Thomas, the rogue in the Tower of London who once upon a time had alleged James's knowledge of a plot to kill Elizabeth. The queen had refused to try him. For nearly half a decade James had fumed at her inaction.

Attorney General Coke was busy on Friday 3 June preparing for Valentine's trial next day in King's Bench in Westminster Hall. He expected a guilty verdict; the traitor would most likely die on Monday. 'In this case that so concern[s] his Majesty's honour,' Coke wrote to Cecil, 'I cannot in mine own opinion be too careful and vigilant.'[28]

That same June Thomas Phelippes was feeling an unseasonably cold wind of change. The enormous debt he still owed to the Exchequer was bad enough, though he had begun, indirectly through his secret service for Cecil, to work that off. But Phelippes's more distant past was now against him. He had been the primary instrument in sending the new king's mother to her execution. James remembered.

Phelippes's reports in 1602 had been as full as ever; his espionage was consistent; he dispatched spies; he gathered and synthesized intelligence. His targets were the usual ones, the dissident Catholic groups on the Continent, whose plots and schemes he sought to expose. Phelippes told Cecil that he owed him everything: 'I have chosen to myself no other saint but your honour.'[29]

Phelippes wrestled with his own private affairs; behind the scenes he had more problems over patronage and money. Since March information had been harder to come by than usual, though Phelippes wasn't admitting defeat: 'some things not vulgar have fallen within the compass of mine intelligence'. But he couldn't disguise the wobble, the uncertainty, the nagging feeling that his credit with Cecil was draining away. 'I have had since the Queen's death occasion ... to think myself not so charitably nor justly dealt withal.' Yet he so wanted to serve.[30]

King James was as giving and generous with titles and promotions as Queen Elizabeth had been conservatively parsimonious. On 13 May Sir Robert Cecil became Baron Cecil of Essendon: Lord Cecil, principal secretary to the king's Majesty. He was the first baron to hold the principal secretaryship since Lord Burghley thirty-two years earlier.

Robert Cecil inherited from his father a practice of duty which contained two necessary responses to the paradox of Elizabethan monarchy, one with no clear succession. The queen was everything: she might one day – God preserve us – be nothing. To the first, 'Serve God by serving of the Queen, for all other service is indeed bondage to the devil.' To the second, 'The government of the realm shall still continue in all respects.' The last declaration by Lord Burghley – a piece of position paper theorizing in 1585 – imagined what his son had had to face as a reality in March 1603: the death of the queen without a successor named in her last will and testament (she left none) or an act of parliament. No monarch, consequently no government, and probably a civil war or at least a fight between contenders for the crown – this was the fear. But it had been avoided by rigorous planning and Robert Cecil's skill.[31]

Cecil was pragmatic, never dogmatic. Flexible, sinuous, he shaped his actions to the play of circumstances. He maintained a politic secrecy: even a faithful minister might keep concealed from his prince – certainly Elizabeth, potentially James too – those things which he knew were for that prince's greater service. Yet monarch and minister should always share an intimacy, a deep understanding of each other. In about May 1603 the new Baron Cecil wrote that 'a prince must make choice of such a servant ... as the prince's assurance must be his confidence in the Secretary, and the Secretary's life his trust in the prince'. The secretary was hated by foreign monarchs and envied by other councillors for his free and easy access at court. He watched and listened. He discerned and weighed. He acted and judged.

And when it came to aspirers or conspirers he would, in his prince's interest, be ruthless. For in Cecil's view it was the job of the secretary 'either [to] kill those monsters in their cradles or else tract them out where no man else can discern the point of their footing'.[32]

In late June Baron Cecil, with the court at Windsor, dictated to his secretary Levinus Munck a letter for Lord Treasurer Buckhurst. It was routine enough: a request for the midsummer instalment of an annual subvention of money paid to the secretary quarterly. A polite reminder that an arrangement from another reign should continue.

Cecil asked Buckhurst to give the order for two hundred pounds to the letter's bearer. This may have been Richard Percival, or Roger Houghton (now twenty-eight years in his master's service), or Master Levinus himself. Whoever it was had to be discreet: Lord Cecil's funds were 'for matter of espial'.[33]

The king's loyal secretary tracked the prints left by his Majesty's enemies.

27

Little Beagle

At nearly sixty Richard Bancroft had a talent for sniffing out subverters of authority in Church and State. There was nothing of the ivory tower about him; he was a skilled politician, close to high officialdom. A former Cambridge scholar and administrator, he had been a chaplain to Lord Chancellor Hatton, had aided Archbishop Whitgift of Canterbury in isolating dangerous elements within Elizabeth's Church of England, and by 1603 had been bishop of London for six years. Many in both Church and government recognized Bancroft's effectiveness as preacher, enforcer and expert on the Catholic underground in London. By 1601 – and almost certainly before then – he was working closely with Cecil, to whom he wrote: 'By your means, and next to yourself, there are not many that are better acquainted with the current humour amongst [Catholic] recusants at this time than I am.'[1]

A new reign seemed to present a fresh possibility for religious peace and an opportunity for Catholics formerly denounced as dissidents and traitors to prove their loyalty to the king. But old habits were hard to break. Summer 1603 was busy with reports of the arrival of Jesuit and other priests into England, at ports on the English south coast, in London and in Westminster. They were still travelling secretly, and the authorities – Bancroft, Cecil, other ministers and magistrates – responded as they had done for decades, arresting suspicious individuals and seizing great chests of prohibited Catholic books. In July in Westminster, not far from Cecil's house, searchers discovered a hidden Catholic printing press with all the equipment needed to use it and a stash of paper.[2]

For those Catholics who were prepared unconditionally to profess their loyalty to the Crown, it was a time of homecoming. But not all

English Catholics trusted James and his government, or indeed their fellow Catholics. There emerged over 1603 a schism between those priests who would swear to be loyal subjects and those – including the Jesuit Robert Persons, author (amongst very many works) of the pro-Spanish book *A Conference about the Next Succession to the Crown of England* – who found the notion appalling. These two groups now directed at each other the kind of abuse that once upon a time they had directed at Queen Elizabeth's ministers. Much of it was in print, much of it viciously personal. It was Richard Bancroft who in November 1602 had secured from some priests support for an oath of allegiance. And those Catholics who distrusted the government's intentions were right to be sceptical. The oath was really a device to disengage moderate English Catholics from others who held a more inflexible recusant position. And indeed, to some Catholics it sounded like the prospect of religious toleration – the king's 'promise', as a later Gunpowder plotter, Robert Catesby, is reported to have said.[3]

Even for those who swore loyalty, hopes of a happier future of Catholic toleration quickly soured. A minority began to plot. One of these disappointed Catholic loyalists was a Father William Watson, who as early as summer 1603 had joined up with a disaffected former cavalry officer in Ireland, Sir Griffin Markham, to form a plan to seize the king and take over the government of Ireland. It was one of those madcap conspiracies that had kept Sir Francis Walsingham, Thomas Phelippes, Lord Burghley and Robert Cecil busy for so many decades – a *coup d'état* that could never work. It was more a release of the plotters' anger and frustration, their fantasies and grievances, than anything of substance.

That was not, of course, how it appeared to the authorities. It was Bishop Bancroft who first saw the shape forming around Watson of a conspiracy against King James.

In June Bancroft received from one William Clark – another priest, like Watson – two letters, one for himself, the second for the king. Bancroft's instincts were sharp. He held back from delivering the letter to James but instead opened and read it, noting, for Cecil, that it was 'a saucy part of Clark to make me his carrier'. Both letters contained a heartfelt statement of Clark's loyalty to James and the strongest possible denunciation of their common enemy, the Jesuits. The letter to

Bancroft suggested that loyal Catholic gentlemen in London were ready to act to protect the king, whatever that meant. But the bishop had heard reports from other sources that Clark had been nominated by some plotting with Watson to seize James. So, was Clark loyal or was he a traitor? Bancroft suggested to Cecil that he should be questioned, ideally by Cecil himself, on conditions of personal protection – the best and quickest way to get to the truth.[4]

A week later – Wednesday 13 July, twelve days before the king's coronation – Bishop Bancroft informed Cecil from the Tower of London of two things. The first, that William Watson had disappeared. The second, that he and the other investigators – one was William Wade – had identified Sir Griffin Markham as a principal in the plot. The bishop was sure that he would soon be able to brief Cecil on what he called a great and detestable treason.

And so began the search for Markham and Watson: for a tall, dark-haired gentleman with a large nose, a thin beard, and one of his hands maimed by a bullet wound; and for a short-sighted priest with light brown hair and a long beard of the same colour – though it was possible that the beard was now trimmed. James's Privy Council alerted the ports of the English south coast, and on 16 July Markham was proclaimed a traitor. Meanwhile, Clark too had disappeared. Bancroft described him for Cecil, just in case there was time for a description to be squeezed into the proclamation: of middle height and moderate build, about thirty-six years old, auburn to blond hair, a beard cut short.

As fate would have it, the conspiracy brushed Cecil's own extended family. A collateral plotter was his brother-in-law George Brooke, brother of Lord Cobham. Through Bancroft, Brooke asked for an interview with Cecil: the bishop suggested a meeting either in the episcopal palace at Fulham or, knowing how busy Cecil was, in a quiet room in one of the outer precincts at Hampton Court Palace. Brooke was already claiming that he had helped to break up the plot, a notion Bancroft, recognizing its thinness, called a conceit.

For days posts galloped up and down the roads between London and Dover. They rode all night: a letter posted from the coast at 7 p.m. was in London by 9 a.m. the following morning – this is what writing on the packet 'Haste, haste, post haste, haste, with diligence' could achieve. But the discovery of Sir Griffin Markham's whereabouts was not in the end very dramatic. On about 20 July a royal messenger and four magistrates, with a warrant signed by Bishop Bancroft, searched Markham's house. He was not at home, but after being told of the search Markham wrote to Bancroft, assuming – surely feigning – that the raid must have had something to do with a court case over debt. On 21 July he surrendered himself by letter to the bishop: 'upon notice from you at any time I will wait upon you, for I hope your lordship's sending me summons will serve me for a protection'.[5]

When prisoners were questioned in the Tower of London, no plot was ever found to be less serious or pernicious than first suspected. The routine of rounds of interrogatories and confessions, sometimes with the suggestion of torture, always seemed to produce evidence which condemned prisoners; rarely did the questioning exonerate them. In the sixteenth and seventeenth centuries, conspiracies ran like ink spilt on paper, deep into the fibres.

In August Watson, Markham and Clark – the latter eventually captured in Worcester – all confessed. Separately, George Brooke, another conspirator, wrote to Cecil that he had fallen into hell, appealing to his brother-in-law for help that never came.[6]

The conspirators were tried and condemned at Winchester Castle in November. At the end of the month Watson and Clark were hanged, drawn and quartered in the city's marketplace. The scaffold for George Brooke was being built in the castle in early December. On it he was beheaded. Sir Griffin Markham, still in the Tower, was spared the gallows. He had appealed to the king for mercy. He had written to Cecil.

George Brooke's brother Lord Cobham told Cecil that he knew the alliance between the Brooke and Cecil families was not enough to support any special pleading. But the old bonds were there nevertheless, and Cobham rehearsed them, remembering above all Bess Cecil. 'I hope not but that you will remember the ancient love that was betwixt our fathers, the happiness and comfort you had with my sister, the blessing that from her you have in your children.'[7]

In the summer Lord Chief Justice Popham had sent to Lord Cecil a report by one of his informants. For a man so frequently libelled and slandered as Robert Cecil, the theme of one paragraph was not surprising.

Catholic dissidents and émigrés had said that the plotting of William Watson and William Clark was engineered by Cecil. For what purpose wasn't quite clear to them – either it was 'to make Catholics more odious in the opinion of the world' or to help force their religious toleration. That these two things pointed in opposite directions hardly mattered: logic has no authority over rumour. What did matter was the popular belief, talked about on the streets of London and throughout the country, that Cecil was behind the scenes pulling the strings.[8]

Cecil felt that he did not need to defend himself against these malicious accusations; he rose above them; his conscience was clear. 'I have that knowledge which is the most necessary, which is to know God and myself', as he wrote to Sir John Harington, 'and have been taught patience by undergoing the sharp censures of busy brains.'

Working harder than anyone else in James's government and so easy a target for slander, libel, abuse and conspiracy theories, Cecil told his old friend Michael Hickes that he had no hope of ease but left all to God's providence.[9]

A new reign, a new life. For Robert Cecil and Queen Elizabeth's former ministers and courtiers it was like emerging from a dark cloister where people spoke in whispers into a busy, noisy marketplace in full sunlight.

In all of Cecil's formative years there had been nothing like the atmosphere, the tone, the activity, the jostle of James's kingship. The king expanded his Privy Council to treble its late Elizabethan size. He opened the doors of his private chambers to greater numbers of courtiers, many of them Scots who had served him for years. English ministers found themselves outranked by newcomers; some long overlooked were now noticed. Francis Bacon, for example, courted the philosopher king with essays and discourses, and with success – Bacon found himself favoured and promoted at long last, after so many years of frustrations and disappointments, blocked (so it was easy to assume) by his uncle Burghley and cousin Cecil. Royal officials now had to consult books of protocol on which had gathered decades of dust, for some aspects of the new life at court had not been practised in two generations. The last monarch to have a consort with her own household was Henry VIII – strange to think that Anne of Denmark's predecessor was Queen Katherine Parr. Change and fresh air had come to Gormenghast.

In his letters James liked to use to his intimates the old numbers of their secret correspondence – a kind of cipher of familiarity and trust. Like Elizabeth, he sometimes gave courtiers pet names. By 1604 Robert Cecil was his 'little beagle'. Without the sly malice of the late queen's Pygmy, it was in its own way perfect. Used to catch hares, the beagle was the smallest English hunting hound. Was it wholly coincidental that Elizabethans also used the word to mean a spy?

James himself loved to hunt. His English ministers soon learned that business often had to be done at a distance. The king knew and recognized this. He did not apologize for it; it was the way of monarchs and servants. The letter he wrote in spring 1604 to his little beagle – a letter wry, engaging and personal – is a sidelight on their relationship:

> Although I be now in the midst of my paradise of pleasure yet will I not be forgetful of you and your fellows that are frying in the pains of purgatory for my service . . . Only your care must be to preserve things from extremities in case crosses do fall out, and to keep things from such conclusions as may be justly displeasing to me . . . and I do strengthen myself by the trust I have in so good servants whom to I hope no virtuous things, how difficult soever, being undertaken *meis auspiciis* [under my auspices] shall be impossible . . . And so I make an end with my hearty commendations to all your honest society and hoping that 3 [Lord Henry Howard] and 10 [Cecil] will pardon me for my overwatching them the last night and morning that I was amongst you.[10]

King James was puckish and charming and a frequently absent micromanager. He had some fun at the expense of his earnest secretary, joking that Cecil preferred restful home life to outdoor exercise: he addressed one letter 'To the little beagle that lies at home by the fire when all the good hounds are daily running on the fields'. Really James meant that Cecil was stuck, as ever, at his desk.[11]

*

On 20 August 1604 Baron Cecil of Essendon was elevated once again. He became Viscount Cranborne, a title he took from an estate in Dorset he had owned since Elizabeth's reign. A week later English commissioners, of whom Lord Cranborne was one, signed a peace with the kingdom of Spain, the old enemy. This was safe to do now that James had his throne; the king was no longer looking over his shoulder at the Spanish Infanta Isabella and her notional claim to England and Ireland. This peace was what Queen Elizabeth had wanted for so many years of her later reign but could not afford to do strategically, even though the sea war with Spain and the English garrisons and armies stationed in the Netherlands to protect the Dutch had drained her Exchequer dry. That war had seemed endless, stretching for the whole of Robert Cecil's life at court. As a young man, in 1586, he had wanted to travel with the earl of Leicester and the first army deployed to the Netherlands against Philip II's crack troops. In 1588 he had seen the charade of the duke of Parma's peace negotiations with England; the Armada followed a few months later. At every point in his career he, like his father, had been alert to Spanish aggression – at sea, in the Low Countries, in Ireland, the supporter of plots and conspiracies against the queen herself. Peace was another fresh start.

Treaty commissioners from the Spanish Low Countries had arrived in London in May. The English delegates were Lord Buckhurst (now the earl of Dorset), Admiral Nottingham, the earl of Devonshire, Lord Henry Howard (now the earl of Northampton) and, naturally, Robert Cecil – a meeting of the old establishment and the new. Given the usual contortions of peace diplomacy, progress was rapid. The two teams of commissioners agreed terms in July.

The peace agreed and ratified at Somerset House was celebrated in a great painting, probably by a Flemish artist, which shows both groups of delegates sat facing one another. The table is covered by a richly patterned carpet. A window of small, delicate leaded panes opens out into a sun-lit courtyard. There are shrubs and flowers, and the walls are hung with tapestries. Four of the English commissioners incline their heads towards the viewer. Devonshire sits in profile. Northampton looks like he is about to pass a paper to the minister on his left, Robert, Viscount Cranborne.

With his right arm drawn up across his chest, Cranborne's hand rests gently on his heart. In his features there is a little of his father, a little of his mother. A pointed reddish beard. Full dark hair combed back high on his head. Steady eyes, pale skin; his face looks drawn but relaxed; there is even the beginning of a smile. In front of him on the table sit the tools of his vocation: a pewter ink pot, a quill, a long sheet of paper folded longways down the centre.[12]

Sometimes all that is needed is the smallest opportunity – it might be an accidental encounter, or a letter intercepted – to build a covert operation against the enemy that takes on a whole life of its own. So it occurred to Thomas Phelippes as he sat in a cell in January 1605, trying to set out for his master Lord Cranborne as clear a narrative as he was able of the eight-year-long intelligence operation that had put him in prison.

He traced it back to an old spy of his, William Sterrell, whom Phelippes had employed, at the earl of Essex's expense, on a mission into the Low Countries back in 1591. In about 1597 Sterrell had shown to Phelippes a letter that he had received from the oldest, most experienced, most devious dissident Catholic intelligencer in Europe, Hugh Owen, who for years had organized his operations from Brussels. Phelippes had been careful (so he said now in 1605) to brief the late Queen Elizabeth about this contact with Owen.

Phelippes had established a false correspondence with Owen and other dissidents. Usually one of his agents (someone like Sterrell) would pretend to be a renegade English Catholic. Phelippes would then read the dissidents' papers his agent passed to him and draft the letters back to them. Once – and this was the problem he now faced in 1605 – he invented a character from whom he pretended to receive information, then fed this to the enemy. This character was supposed to be close to Cecil. Phelippes called him 'an imaginary intelligencer' and called him Vincent. It was the art of the double cross.

He claimed in 1605 that he had been running the operation since Elizabeth's reign, pausing it at the queen's death, and then restarting it. Since James's accession he had used this false correspondence to gather intelligence on what was happening politically and diplomatically in

France. It had also allowed Phelippes (again so he said) to stay a step ahead of Jesuit plots. He had thought – it turns out incorrectly – that the new king would thank him for his secret service. Unfortunately, James remembered very clearly Phelippes's role in the downfall of his mother Mary Queen of Scots.[13]

By January 1605 the communications between Phelippes, Sterrell and Owen were revealed to Cranborne. It is not clear by whom. But the significant point is that Cranborne knew nothing about them, a fact that is clear from the written interrogatories he put to Sterrell, now a prisoner like Phelippes, on 26 January. In what circumstances, Cranborne wanted to know, had Sterrell and Phelippes first made contact with Hugh Owen? What payments or gifts had been exchanged between them? Why had they corresponded when they had no authority to do so? What money had they received from the enemy abroad since the king's accession?[14]

Sterrell wrote that he had first been in touch with Owen indirectly, through an English priest in Antwerp. He had met Owen in person in the town of Spa, close to Liège. In return for secret information, Owen had promised Sterrell a salary of thirty crowns a month. Sterrell confessed to Cranborne that he was lucky to receive thirty crowns a quarter, but what money he received was delivered by one of the professional couriers travelling between England and Antwerp. The late earl of Essex had known about Sterrell's meeting with Owen, as had Francis Bacon, William Wade (who had clearly never mentioned it to Robert Cecil), and of course Thomas Phelippes himself, 'whom the earl then used [i.e., employed]'. Essex had informed the queen herself, the earl personally and explicitly sanctioning Sterrell's exchange of letters with Owen. 'I was told by Master Phelippes that your honour [Cranborne] was privy to it also, but I never spoke with your lordship about it' – so Sterrell now claimed.

Sterrell's defence, in essence, was to play down the operation. He had received very little money from Owen, who had promised more for better and more frequent reports; he couldn't speak for what Phelippes had got. He did think that the dissidents had not known that Phelippes was involved in writing the letters 'but took him for some other'; Sterrell did not mention the fictional Vincent. Few letters had been exchanged with Owen after 1601, and Sterrell undersold their importance. But he couldn't resist writing, perhaps out of professional pride, that 'her Majesty, with the earl of Essex, did often acknowledge that by my means there was good intelligence came to them'.[15]

Phelippes was caught fast. Cranborne knew nothing about his contact with Owen. What Phelippes had said was an old operation against the Catholic enemy looked like a highly suspicious piece of private enterprise for Phelippes's own enrichment. Most serious for Phelippes, King James himself knew about the allegations.

In January 1605 Phelippes wrote every few days to Lord Cranborne: Cecil was his hope, his intercessor, the man who knew the value of his service to the king. For a prisoner denounced by others and unable to speak for himself, Cranborne was the only courtier who could remove what Phelippes was desperate enough to call James's 'vain imaginations' of his disloyalty.

> [I] do confidently affirm that there was not a more truly and substantially carried intelligence set afoot for the service of a state . . . I humbly beseech your lordship therefore to prevent his Majesty's further displeasure . . . not knowing what to think or say seeing myself condemned as it were aforehand . . . And therefore there being nobody so able I beseech your lordship to stand my friend.[16]

28

The Variable Motions of Men

Ben Jonson detested agents and informants. After a spell in prison in the late 1590s, where he was surrounded by them, he wrote a pungent epigram. Such men got what they deserved:

> Spies, you are lights in state, but of base stuff,
> Who, when you've burnt yourselves down to the snuff,
> Stink, and are thrown away. End fair enough.[1]

The playwright was a formidable character. He was thirty-two years old in the spring of 1605; one literary collaborator and rival, Thomas Dekker, described him as 'a staring Leviathan' with 'a terrible mouth' and 'a parboiled face ... punched full of oilet holes like the cover of a warming pan'. The talent was as uncompromising as the visage. A play by Jonson might be a runaway success or a commercial flop, a comedy or a political drama; he gave audiences what he wanted to, whether they liked it or not. He was used to being hauled before the authorities and to spending time in a cell. He made enemies of privy councillors – the earl of Northampton was one. Jonson was pugnacious and combative; a felon who had avoided the gallows but was branded for his felony – a conviction for manslaughter – on his thumb; a secret Roman Catholic convert who wrote masques and entertainments for Protestant courtiers; a prisoner for his art who knew how to plead with powerful men when he needed to. 'God himself is not averted at just men's cries; and you, that approach that divine goodness, and supply it here on earth in your place and honours, cannot employ your aids more worthily than to the common succour of honesty and virtue, how humbly soever it be placed.' This was a letter to Robert Cecil, one of his patrons, in the spring or summer of 1605.[2]

Yet on the state surveillance of his time – Cecil's system – Ben Jonson was damning, even if on stage and in print he had to disguise his critique of it. The present day was out of bounds, and the history of England too dangerous to write about – as John Hayward knew after publishing his book on the reign of King Henry IV and associating it with the earl of Essex. In *Sejanus, His Fall* Jonson used the court of Emperor Tiberius in early imperial Rome, which was just about safe enough as a vehicle for his unsparing analysis of power and government corrupted beyond hope. Or nearly safe. On stage in 1603 or 1604, with William Shakespeare in a leading role, a first version of his Roman play got Jonson into trouble at court, principally with Lord Northampton, whose sharp brain missed very little – this encounter and its consequences for Jonson may explain his appeal from prison to Robert Cecil. But the poet was not put off: he had something urgent to say. By 1605 Jonson had adapted and expanded *Sejanus* into a printed play text unsuited for performance (about four hours on the stage), perhaps deliberately so. Dense, austere, full of notes and references to the heavy works of classical literature and history he had used – a neat way of disowning any political motive which would have fooled no one at James's court – Jonson's book was printed in summer 1605.[3]

In *Sejanus* spies and informants are the instruments of a pervasive tyranny. There is no tolerance in Tiberius' Rome, no free speech or action. Men and women who love freedom are watched and reported on by the creatures of politicians who are sick with power. There is no privacy: the watchers watch even during meals, even in private apartments. They hold in their reports the lives of those they watch. There is no trust, no hope, but a system which feeds itself:

> your state
> Is waited on by envies, as by eyes;
> And every second guest your table take
> Is a feed'd spy, t'observe who goes, who comes,
> What conference you have, with whom, where, when
> What the discourse is, what the looks, the thoughts
> Of every person there, they do extract
> And make into a substance.

Every minist'ring spy
That will accuse and swear is lord of you,
Of me, of all, our fortunes, and our lives.
Our looks are called to question, and our words,
How innocent soever, are made crimes;
We shall not shortly dare to tell our dreams,
Or think, but 'twill be treason.

In Jonson's world there were no happy endings, no redemption, no eventual victory for the good and just. A single consolation – a bleak one in reality – is that tyrants and their henchmen were consumed and destroyed by their own corruption and criminality.[4]

Sitting beneath the crust of Jacobean optimism and fresh kingly style was a deeper, heavier reality – one Jonson saw and which in this year of gunpowder treason would before too long break shockingly through the surface.

Ben Jonson in his letter of supplication addressed Robert Cecil as 'thrice-honoured Earl of Salisbury'. First Essendon, then Cranborne, now Salisbury, a title which, going back to the fifteenth century, had a distinguished Plantagenet lineage. James of Great Britain was a king whose generosity with preferments and promotions now gave him Lord Salisbury as his principal secretary.

Levinus Munck, occupied with the usual correspondence in his master's private office, was commendably businesslike in recording the event: 'The creation at Greenwich of noblemen, where my lord was created Earl of Salisbury.' One of the other creations that Saturday was Thomas, Lord Burghley, already from Elizabeth's reign a Garter knight, as earl of Exeter, the day before his sixty-third birthday. Two brothers so different yet bound together in temperament and affection; their father's motto 'One heart, one way' was reformed in a new reign, a happy meeting of past, present and (providence willing) future.[5]

So different from Master Levinus's short note is the patent of Robert Salisbury's title to his earldom, a great illuminated charter, attached to which with twisted cord was James's great seal. At the ceremony where it was handed to Viscount Cranborne were, amongst others, the king's heir and successor, eleven-year-old Prince Henry, the prince's uncle (Queen Anne's brother) Ulric, duke of Holstein, the steely Richard Bancroft (five months' archbishop of Canterbury after the death of John Whitgift), and Lord Chancellor Egerton.[6]

The king himself dined with Lord Salisbury at his house on the Strand – now Salisbury House – three weeks after the ceremony at Greenwich. It was a Monday, 27 May, and they ate pork, fish, potatoes and pies, with a dessert of strawberries and pomegranates. Secretary Salisbury always ate well, whether on the Strand or at Theobalds, at least on the rare occasions he could get out to Hertfordshire. The visit was a mark of favour by James, a show of status for Salisbury, and worth every penny of the nineteen pounds it cost him in additional labour and supplies, all scrupulously accounted for.[7]

The king knew how much he owed to his secretary who, while James was out and about on his hunting expeditions, kept the machinery of government moving. 'My little beagle, That I have been so long unwriting unto you, ye may only impute it to lack of matter, for I daily hear . . . of your so continual consultations upon all my affairs, as I protest I was never so void of care for all my great turns.'

James was finding political life as Elizabeth's successor – that longed-for inheritance he had felt for years was rightfully his – more difficult than he had perhaps expected. His early hopes for a full union of his two crowns into one Great Britain made little progress. How to make one unit out of three kingdoms kept the writers of essays and position papers occupied for months, working through the practicalities and difficulties of integrating the kingdoms' quite different legal systems and government institutions, and even what a new union flag might look like (there were a number of designs for it). It was the Scots who were the enthusiastic unionists, but in the English parliament they met firm resistance: there could be no encroachment by Scots on England's institutions and privileges. Eventually, in 1606 and 1607, the whole issue would get stuck fast in a parliamentary mire of bad temper and apparently insuperable technicalities.

More worrying was that his English revenue as king was stretched beyond what James wanted and needed: Elizabeth had left her Exchequer bare. So he looked to his advisers: 'when I consider the extremity of my state at this time, my only hap and hope that upholds me is in my good servants that will sweat and labour for my relief'.[8]

But there was hope for the future. Fortunately, a new session of James's first parliament was imminent, scheduled to gather on Tuesday, 5 November 1605.

Not to be forgotten – he was too skilled a suitor for that – Ben Jonson wrote an epigram to celebrate the earl of Salisbury's glory. Knowing that his lordship's achievements spoke quite well enough without the need for poets ('What need hast thou of me, or of my muse, / Whose actions so themselves do celebrate?'), Jonson hoped he might be able to assume by association just a little of Salisbury's fame:

> Yet dare not to my thought least hope allow
> Of adding to thy fame; thine may to me,
> When in my book men read but Cecil's name,
> And what I write thereof find far and free
> From servile flattery (common poets' shame)
> As thou stand'st clear of the necessity.

Thus the poet supplicant courted the most powerful politician in the kingdom.[9]

Two October suppers, both connected to a treason.

The first, on or about the 9th, was a dinner at the lodgings of a Catholic gentleman called Robert Catesby at a hostelry on the Strand owned by William Patrick, not so far, as it happened, from the considerably more distinguished Salisbury House on Ivy Bridge Lane. Catesby was the organizer of a group of dissidents whose patience with the new government, if they had had any in the first place, was exhausted by 1604. Catesby, his cousin Thomas Wintour, John Wright and Wright's brother-in-law Thomas Percy formed the core of the group, with others joining later, most infamously Guy Fawkes.

Their plot to kill the king, the queen, Prince Henry and all the members of the Lords and Commons by blowing up the parliament with gunpowder is the most infamous and contentious in British history. The summary Guy Fawkes later gave of it under interrogation gives us its basic shape and timeline. Fawkes was first approached by Wintour at Easter 1604 in the Spanish Low Countries. Catesby, Percy and John Wright were by then already involved. It was Catesby who 'propounded' to this group of five the notion of using gunpowder to blow up the chamber of the House of Lords. To destroy parliament, where the penal laws against Catholics had been made, was a deliberate choice, 'because religion having been unjustly suppressed there, it was fittest that justice and punishment should be executed there'. So they had set to work, with Percy renting a house in Westminster, from which in December 1604 the conspirators began to dig a tunnel through to the cellars below the House of Lords' chamber close by. Barrels of gunpowder and stacks of wood were procured. The plot developed. On the day of parliament's destruction, some of the growing group of conspirators would seize James's daughter, nine-year-old Princess Elizabeth, and proclaim her queen, presumably with the intention of using her as a puppet monarch. They couldn't come to a decision over what to do with the king's second son, Charles.[10]

At the dinner on the Strand on or about 9 October were Catesby and Wintour and a few others. One was Francis Tresham, who had taken part in the Essex rising of February 1601, though he had been later pardoned. Another guest was Ben Jonson. Most likely, in the absence of contrary evidence, Jonson was himself no plotter, but simply a poet having a discreet supper with likeminded Catholic gentlemen – he was one of their wider social circle. Yet we might wonder what was said at the supper, or hinted at, or suggested? What did the author of *Sejanus*, that play of the watchers and the watched, hear or sense?[11]

Jonson's presence at the meal was either coincidence, accident or happenstance, or perhaps something of all three. He belonged to the conspirators' world.

About five days later, on 14 October, Francis Tresham became the last sworn conspirator of Catesby's group, the thirteenth member, bound, like the others, by an oath of secrecy. The destruction of king and parliament was days away.[12]

The other supper, near the end of the month on Saturday 26th, was at the lodging of Lord Monteagle at Hoxton, a little way out of London north of Moorfields, on a dark autumn evening. At 7 p.m. Monteagle, thirty years old, a veteran of the late earl of Essex's expedition to Ireland and a brother-in-law of Francis Tresham, was about to have supper when he was interrupted by one of his footmen. Running an errand, the servant had met in the street outside a man he did not know. The man had given him a letter and asked him to put it straight into his master's hands.

He opened and read the letter addressed to 'the right honourable the Lord Monteagle'. Fifteen lines packed densely together. A more-or-less educated hand, though heavy, clotted and awkward – one might think a hand disguised. It was a warning from a well-wisher, a piece of timely advice, as clear as it was obscure. For his own preservation, Monteagle should stay away from the parliament and retire himself into the country. God and man had concurred to punish the wickedness of this time. 'Though there be no appearance of any stir, yet I say they shall receive a terrible blow this parliament and yet they shall not see who hurts them.' This knowledge could do his lordship no harm so long as he burned the letter. Though it was late and dark, Monteagle took it straight away to Whitehall Palace.[13]

What Monteagle did with the letter is described in the official public narrative of the gunpowder treason, the so-called 'King's Book'. This was the printed account dictated by the earl of Salisbury to Levinus Munck, which in its manuscript form Salisbury checked and corrected with great care. The 'King's Book' published by the king's printer slightly compresses some of the details from the manuscript, but their accounts of Monteagle's reception at Whitehall are close to identical. There he found the earls of Suffolk, Worcester, Northampton and Salisbury ready to go to supper. Monteagle took Salisbury only into a nearby chamber and showed him the letter. Salisbury praised Monteagle for his discretion and told him that, 'whatsoever the purpose of the letter might prove hereafter', he had been receiving 'divers advertisements . . . from beyond the sea' that Catholics were 'making preparations for some combination amongst them against this parliament time'. He had already briefed James and the Privy Council – 'acquainted the King and some of his Majesty's inward councillors that the priests and laymen abroad and at home were full of practice and conspiracy', as Salisbury dictated it to Munck.[14]

But Salisbury may not have treated the mysterious letter as seriously as his own narrative, both in manuscript and print, suggested. His smooth words to Monteagle were probably a neat and necessary later backfilling, or a bit of ministerial vanity: he had a reputation to maintain. His knowledge was probably patchier than he would have admitted. For all the suspicions over his secret communications with Hugh Owen, Thomas Phelippes operated only on the outer edges of the dissident groups in France and the Low Countries. There were priests and recusants who reported to Salisbury, the 'false brethren' whose reports were as occasional and self-promoting as they were helpful. The many letters written by one of them, William Udall, an informant who had reported to Salisbury for a decade, he most likely took with large pinches of salt: Udall years later claimed that he had given information about the gunpowder treason nearly a year before its discovery, but that Salisbury had treated it as a joke. A thicket of putative treasons, and a mindset of conspiracy, made plots of genuine substance more difficult to identify.[15]

Having consulted fellow ministers, with Monteagle present, Secretary Salisbury did nothing about the letter. This, according to the 'King's Book', was for two reasons. First, he wanted to show it to James, who was away in Hertfordshire hunting, waiting for the king's 'fortunate judgement in clearing and solving of obscure riddles and doubtful mysteries'. The second reason is more convincing: Salisbury wanted to wait 'for the practice to ripen', to see what, if anything, might happen, to find out whether there was any reality to it. The truth was that the letter to Lord Monteagle said almost nothing of substance.[16]

Enjoying his time at Royston in Hertfordshire, James wrote to his little beagle: 'And thus hunt ye well there, for I am going to hunt here.' What Secretary Salisbury was hunting the king didn't yet know. Nor probably did Salisbury.[17]

He went to the king in his privy gallery at Whitehall on the afternoon of the feast of All Hallows, Friday 1 November; James had returned to Westminster the previous day. The account of the audience in the published 'King's Book' has the two of them alone together, but Salisbury's dictation to Munck suggests that the meeting may have happened on

31 October and that Lord Chamberlain Suffolk was 'hard [close] by' in the gallery. Either way, the story is, again, Salisbury's.[18]

He gave James Monteagle's letter with no judgement, no analysis, just the circumstances of its mysterious delivery. The king read it, paused and read it again. He didn't dismiss it; the writer's style seemed to him 'more quick [alive] and pithy' than other pasquils and libels. Salisbury sensed the king had discerned a deeper meaning, so, in counterpoint, he pointed to one sentence: 'For the danger is past as soon as you have burnt the letter.' Only a fool would write that, he said; it was a warning of nothing. James responded by pointing to the previous sentence, on the 'terrible blow this parliament'; already, according to the 'King's Book', James was thinking of gunpowder, even suggesting a search of the cellars of Westminster Palace. Salisbury was still unconvinced, but humoured the king, and – a deft secretary's old trick – left James with a parting witticism.

But the letter nagged at Salisbury, and the following day he went, with Lord Chamberlain Suffolk, to the king. They agreed that Suffolk would search Westminster Palace, a great jumble and tangle of ancient dwellings and easily penetrated by outsiders, both above and below ground. Taking with him Lord Monteagle, Suffolk made his inspection late on Monday 4 November. In the cellars they discovered thirty-six barrels of gunpowder and watching over them a man who called himself John Johnson.[19]

From Tuesday 5 November the plot which lay behind Lord Monteagle's letter came vividly into focus. Johnson – eventually he was identified as Fawkes – was interrogated closely over the following few days, the king himself drawing up the interrogatories, giving clear instructions for Fawkes's examiners in the Tower: 'If he will not otherwise confess, the gentler tortures are to be first used unto him, *et sic per gradus ad ima tenditur* [and so by degrees proceeding to the worst]. And so God speed your good work.'[20]

Salisbury presided over the commission of ministers and law officers that examined the gunpowder treason. He drew together the evidence, reading and annotating it. He was interested in every possible document. On the signed and witnessed agreement between Thomas Percy and Henry Ferrers for the sub-lease in 1604 of the 'house in

Westminster belonging to the parliament house', Salisbury wrote: 'The bargain between Ferrers and Percy for the bloody cellar, found in [Thomas] Wintour's lodging.' With Munck, Salisbury did some investigative work, reconstructing the secret negotiations of Guy Fawkes and Wintour with the king of Spain. As ever more letters about the plot and its consequences – including the shoot-out at Holbeach House in Staffordshire in which Catesby, Percy and the Wright brothers were killed on 8 November – arrived in Salisbury's office, Munck kept a detailed calendar of them.[21]

Most certainly Salisbury fashioned the official narrative, just as his father had done for Elizabethan plots. The story had to be told, the evidence published, all with the appropriate omissions – for where the king's subjects had to understand the facts of a monstrous treason against a monarch ordained by God, they shouldn't know everything. From this we should not assume that Salisbury was involved in some kind of deep state conspiracy, manufacturing the plot for his own ends; as we will see, Jacobean Catholics claimed this at the time, and some scholars have agreed with them (the debate became especially heated in the late nineteenth and twentieth centuries). When working with this kind of evidence it is too easy to multiply causes and explanations to engineer elaborate conjectures that satisfy our own prejudices.

Yet so much did happen in shadows, in 1605, and in other years. We know this. We feel it in the gaps, the records not kept, the conversations and discussions unrecorded.

On 7 November, with Fawkes under heavy interrogation in the Tower, the Privy Council instructed Ben Jonson to locate a priest, unnamed, who had testimony to give about the powder treason. Jonson's connections and affiliations were known and used, making it all the more important for him to emphasize with all the persuasive words he possessed his loyalty to king and God. Not able to find the man – he observed it wasn't surprising that Catholic priests 'have put on wings' – he wrote straight away to Salisbury, offering himself 'with as much integrity as your particular favour ... can exact'.[22]

Reporting on the gunpowder treason, Salisbury wrote on 1 December to the earl of Dunfermline, lord chancellor of Scotland, that he would rather die than 'be found slack in searching to the bottom the dregs of this foul poison'. His energy and passion were well known. His enemies hated him for it.[23]

He was well used to scurrilous libels. Death threats were rarer, and a paper left in the court of Salisbury House on Wednesday 4 December, which explained how five Catholic men had each sworn to kill him, touched a nerve. Salisbury on the whole preferred silence to apologia. This paper was different and needed another kind of response. Employing the king's printer, Robert Barker, Cecil went public: he wrote an essay which became a short pamphlet, *An Answer to Certain Scandalous Papers*.

The libel stated that the gunpowder treason, which was both wicked and indefensible, had made the Catholic cause in England more scandalous than ever. Behind it was Salisbury, the plot's prime mover, and his purpose was to use it as a justification to destroy the Catholic religion by banishment, massacre, imprisonment and the introduction of further cruel penal laws. So it was that 'some good men', wanting to defend their faith and to save souls, had, having taken the sacrament, vowed to kill Salisbury if he continued his persecution of Catholics. Each assassin did not know the identities of the four others, but it had been decided which of them would fire the first shot. Each was either sick or in distressed circumstances; each expected and embraced death, understanding Salisbury's 'transcendent authority' in the kingdom and his closeness to the king. The paper was not a hoax but a deadly serious warning – 'a charitable admonition' that the rage against Catholics had to stop.[24]

The truth was that the penal response to the gunpowder plot was sharp, as the official reaction always was after revelations of treasons and conspiracies. Counterweighing this, in words, was the king's recognition, in a speech to parliament following the plot, that not all Catholics were traitors, as well as the measured moderation (so Salisbury hoped) of his *Answer*. What Salisbury sought to achieve was a response to the assassins that was considered, scholarly, full of Church history and classical literature, seasoned with Latin tags and quotations – a masterclass in coolly academic hauteur.

He was serene, he was pious. 'Proscribed for a man of blood', he examined what he called 'the variable motions of men', putting to one side his business as a minister and assuming for a time a state of contemplation. He went to scripture, to the Church Fathers like St Augustine ('of whose books . . . I have turned over some few leaves'), to canon law, to Seneca. He challenged the Catholic Church's old justifications for the papal deposing of disliked kings – a familiar bugbear for Protestant writers since Henry VIII's break with Rome in the 1530s, and relevant because of Elizabeth's own excommunication by Pope Pius V in 1570. He condemned what he called 'the most strange and gross doctrine' of equivocation, the word and idea incendiary and electrifying in 1606, used by Shakespeare to brilliant dramatic effect in *Macbeth*. To equivocate was to hide wickedness with ambiguous words, to dissemble with double meanings, to reconcile consciences to evil acts. For Salisbury, this was the technique employed so effectively by the smoothly malevolent Jesuit priests who pulled the strings behind the scenes, encouraging English Catholics to treason. (Shakespeare's Porter captures all this in a sentence: 'Faith, here's an equivocator that could swear in both the scales against either scale, who committed treason enough for God's sake, yet could not equivocate to heaven.')[25]

So it was that Salisbury turned on its head the allegation that he had planned and instigated the gunpowder treason. Really to blame were the manipulators of credulous Catholics. 'These men that rule your consciences have first dazzled your eyes with fearful, but false, objects, thereby hoping to engage you more deeply in their pernicious attempts.' They had, as he put it, sought with Nero to set Rome on fire and to lay the blame on the Christians.[26]

He was resolute, fundamentally unmoved by the calumnies and lies used against him. A secretary's vigilance, he wrote, was 'to stand sentinel over the life of kings and safety of states'. He served and did his duty to God, king and country. He knew he was mortal. He was satisfied with his *Answer*: 'Thus have I given my pen her liberty to run her stage, thereby to free my mind travailing (as a woman with child) with more weighty cogitations than I could contain in silence.' For a man who had lost his wife in childbirth this was a statement with power and meaning. The *Answer* had been a labour, a hard yet necessary effort to explain himself in a way that he had never done before.[27]

Moreover, he had said enough to answer his anonymous enemies.

Further replies expect not ... at my hands: I will henceforth rest in peace in the house of mine own conscience ... If this may not suffice, but that you will still threaten and exclaim, I must hear with patience, and say with Tacitus, you have learned to curse, and I to condemn.[28]

Salisbury's *Answer* would have been on sale in London as the surviving gunpowder plotters, tried and sentenced, were executed in two groups, the first in London in Paul's Churchyard on 30 January 1606, the second a day later in Westminster in Old Palace Yard near the parliament house.

In mid-February the boys of the company of the Queen's Revels performed at the Blackfriars playhouse *The Isle of Gulls* by John Day. A busy London dramatist, Day's play was a piece of daring satire on the new British court of King James: the boys spoke in both English and Scottish accents. Even the title was provocative. A 'gull' was a dupe or a fool.

The play's crooked politician, Dametas, Day took from Sir Philip Sidney, who in turn had borrowed him from the Roman poet Virgil. Dametas in Sidney's *Arcadia* was a low-born herdsman who rose to an authority for which, as a graceless flatterer and fool, he was unsuited. Day turned him into a sinister, Machiavellian figure, a 'monstrous and deformed shape of vice'. It was a vicious swipe at the earl of Salisbury. Dametas's villainy gave 'the greater lustre to the virtuous dispositions of the true-born gentility'. He was 'the most misshapen suit of gentility that ever the court wore'. He sees himself as invaluable to the ruler of his master, the Duke.[29]

A villain to his fingertips – a gift for the stage – Dametas preens himself with self-justifying gravitas. Grand, condescending, self-serving, boastful, he feels himself to be more important than monarchs:

inferior persons, aye and princes themselves, fly from my presence, like the chirping birds from the sight of the falcon: my very breath like a mighty wind blows away inferior officers (the court rubbish) out of my way, and gives me a smooth passage: I am the morning star, I am seldom seen but about the rising of the sun: indeed I am never out of the Duke's eye ...[30]

It was a daring play with a punch worthy of Ben Jonson. And it was a step too far. Remarkably, John Day himself appears to have escaped punishment, but the trouble caused by *The Isle of Gulls* meant that the company was put under new management and lost the patronage of Queen Anne, and its leading boys had a bitter taste of Bridewell prison.[31]

29

Equivocations

Two dangerous old men brought to the new Jacobean age unfinished business from Elizabeth's reign. The first was Hugh Owen, the veteran Catholic intelligencer; the second Father Henry Garnet, the Jesuit superior in England. Owen finished off the career of Thomas Phelippes once and for all. Garnet – in 1606 captured, questioned, tried and executed – gave Salisbury one of the most significant public moments in his political career.

In the weeks after the discovery of the gunpowder treason Hugh Owen, hidden away in Brussels, worried Salisbury. The confessions of the conspirators suggested his importance to the plot. By Christmas 1605 King James's government wanted justice. They wanted Owen himself.

It was a test of the new Anglo-Spanish peace. The Spanish authorities did James the courtesy of arresting Owen, but Archduke Albert in Brussels sidestepped the request to have him extradited to England. James's ambassador to the archduke, Sir Thomas Edmondes, believed that a cache of Owen's papers held the key to his deep conspiracies: they promised important revelations. Owen denied that even a single word in them was relevant to the gunpowder plot. The archduke promised Edmondes that the papers would be read and that any information relevant to the November treason would be passed to his Majesty's government. In reality, Albert did nothing at all.[1]

Earlier in 1605, his unauthorized communications with Hugh Owen had put Thomas Phelippes in prison, desperately trying to petition his way out of the charge, implied by Salisbury, that Phelippes had gone over to the Catholic enemy. In those weeks Salisbury had read through Phelippes's digests of intelligence from Brussels – he had read the poison they contained: 'wicked letters directed from Owen to Phelippes' he wrote on one of them, dating from May 1601.[2]

In December 1605 Phelippes made another miscalculation. Rather than leave Owen well alone, he tried to re-establish contact with him, ostensibly to coax out of Owen secret information about the gunpowder treason. Phelippes would frame his letter as a report on the latest investigations into the plot. It was meant – so he claimed – as bait.

Given Salisbury's suspicions over Phelippes and Owen, the effort failed spectacularly. Told at Whitehall that Phelippes was up to something suspicious, Salisbury ordered a search of the ports. The physical features of Thomas Barnes, the courier Phelippes was using and his oldest spy, happened to match the description of a gentleman on the watch list of individuals still wanted on suspicion of their involvement in the gunpowder conspiracy. Barnes's bag was searched by officials. In it was the letter by Phelippes for Owen. This was taken to Salisbury.

The report never reached Owen, but Salisbury read it at Whitehall Palace. Phelippes found himself once again in the Gatehouse prison.[3]

Thursday 6 February 1606 had been for Salisbury a busy day in parliament, but he returned home late to the Strand in a playful and reflective mood. He warmed himself by the fire, writing up the events of the day to be passed on to the king, 'being close by my chimney end,' he wrote, 'a proper place for beagles'.

Lords and Commons had met in conference to discuss the framing of further penal statutes against priests and papists. There was unanimity: the more stringent the laws the better. Salisbury had spoken, and that evening he remembered what he had said. He had begun by saying that subjects were happy when they lived under the rule of philosophers or kings that were also philosophers: and their own sovereign was rich in wisdom and zeal.

That winter's night he renewed his own service to James, secretary and monarch, never to be parted. 'Whilst my worn body hold my mind, it shall serve him till by serving him I shall trouble him; for my love to his person hath no dimension.'

There was a final piece of news to communicate to the king. Salisbury and other privy councillors had that night committed two priests to the Gatehouse prison. One of them called himself Whalley.[4]

The beagle was alert as ever.

A week later Secretary Salisbury was watching Thomas Barnes carefully. Barnes was now working as Salisbury's courier into Flanders, having promised to behave himself. On Phelippes, whose house had been searched, Salisbury hadn't yet made up his mind.

This was the month that the heads of two of the gunpowder conspirators, Thomas Percy and Robert Catesby, were put on display over the parliament house; the job was done at the cost of twenty-three shillings and ninepence, the invoice sent to the Lord Secretary. Interviewed by Salisbury about his connections to Catesby and Francis Tresham, Phelippes acknowledged he knew one of them, but denied any association with their treason. From the Gatehouse he wrote a long letter of justification: 'God and his ministers confound me body and soul if I be ... touched with the least ... drop of guilt in that foul project.' He professed his loyalty and his religion, explaining how he had seen in Thomas Barnes's travels and dissidents' ciphered letters rich possibilities for discovering secrets. Hoping for banishment to a remote house rather than more time in prison, Phelippes played upon an old association between his family and Salisbury's that the late Lord Burghley had valued. Over a century earlier, Salisbury's paternal great-grandfather had left Wales for Stamford in the service of one of Phelippes's own ancestors, Sir David Philip. And so, he wrote to Salisbury, 'One of my name and house first brought that scion ... that is grown to a tree of such honourable greatness as your lordship's family is.'

It was an appeal to the heart, to old instincts of service and loyalty. It didn't work. Questioned at the end of the month, a younger brother, Stephen Phelippes, offered information about clandestine meetings at the Exchequer with suspicious individuals, opening his written statement with ominous words: 'My brother did write in several notes sundry things concerning himself and his own private business ...'[5]

From the Gatehouse Master Phelippes went to the Tower.

*

The priest named Whalley in the Gatehouse was really Henry Garnet, twenty years secretly in England. As the Jesuit superior in England, he had long been sought and very occasionally the authorities got close to him; for a decade at least, both Thomas Phelippes and William Wade had promised his capture, but neither had succeeded. In early 1606 he was discovered at last hiding in a cramped priest hole in a Catholic manor house near the city of Worcester.

Accusing them of being 'practisers' in 'bloody and cruel crimes' – their association with the gunpowder treason – a proclamation had been issued on 15 January for the apprehension of Garnet and two other Jesuit priests: 'Henry Garnet, alias Whalley, alias Darcy, alias Farmer, of a middling stature, full faced, fat of body, of complexion fair ... of age between fifty and threescore ... his gait upright and comely for a fat man.' Twelve days later he was in custody.[6]

It would be hard to overstate the significance of Garnet's capture. So many plots, such poison: here, in the view of the authorities, was the sinister Jesuit behind it all, the master of dissimulation and equivocation, for whom men's consciences were raw disposable material; the priest who (as Salisbury put it in his *Answer to Certain Scandalous Papers*) set Rome on fire and laid the blame on the Christians.

The council examined him in Star Chamber on 13 February: Salisbury, the earls of Northampton and Worcester, Lord Chief Justice Popham and Attorney General Coke, with Sir William Wade, now lieutenant of the Tower of London, in attendance. Garnet's manuscript on equivocation – which he called a 'treatise against lying and fraudulent dissimulation' – lay on the table. This examined the problem painfully relevant to a faith practised in secret: 'Whether a Catholic ... before a magistrate, being demanded upon his oath whether a priest were in such a place, may ... without perjury, and securely in conscience, answer "No".' But this was only one strand of the issue. Most significant to the king's ministers and law officers was Garnet's complicity in the gunpowder treason.[7]

This first session was not aggressive; it was delicate, exploratory and probing. Salisbury and his colleagues wanted to find out who Whalley was for certain; they had to be sure they were dealing with Henry Garnet. Early questions had the style of a university disputation. Salisbury began. Were the king and his council heretics? Their religion was heretical, Garnet responded, feeling his way round the trap: 'of their persons I would not judge'. To be a formal heretic one had to have sufficient knowledge of the true faith – a point of theology that Northampton, the outstanding Catholic conformist of his generation, would have known very well. Pressed on James being a heretic, Garnet refused to pronounce a judgement on the king 'out of reverence for him'.

The interview, with other questions, lasted for over three hours. Attorney General Coke took notes. And next day, following in the footsteps of Thomas Phelippes, Garnet was moved from the Gatehouse to the Tower of London and Wade's very close supervision.[8]

There were watchers and eavesdroppers in the Tower. Father Garnet's interrogations became heavier and more intense, some perhaps either under torture or at least the threat of it. Popham and Coke led, and over the weeks between mid-February and mid-March believed they had come to understand the details of a story that in broad terms was this: Garnet had known the gunpowder plotters, had understood the horror of what they were proposing to do, and lifted not a finger to stop them. He maintained that the seal of confession could not be broken and admitted to his own perplexity at what to do with the knowledge he possessed: 'Every day I did offer up all my devotions and masses that God of his mercy and infinite providence would dispose all for the best, and find the best means which were pleasing unto him to prevent so great a mischief.' And really he hadn't wanted to know: 'For in respect of their [Robert Catesby's and Thomas Wintour's] often conversation with us [Garnet and other Jesuits], we should be thought accessory.'[9]

Lord Chief Justice Popham had no time for what he believed were Father Garnet's evasions. He composed fourteen articles which demonstrated that Garnet had been a principal conspirator. Salisbury read his paper.[10]

Salisbury wanted Henry Garnet's trial to make clear the difference between religious truth and treason disguised as faith. He expected the Jesuit to be 'condemned by clear justice to have been privy to the foulest treason'. Whether Garnet lived or died was not, for Salisbury, significant: 'For his life, it is not it which is of value.' Kings rightly used the law to prevent the destruction of their kingdoms 'practised under the mantle of religion'. The supposed faith of Garnet and priests like him reached 'into the bowels of treason'.[11]

The choice of London's Guildhall, the most public venue possible for Garnet's arraignment, was deliberate. On 28 March, a Friday, the court sat from 9 a.m. The hearing lasted for eleven hours. King James was there for the whole day, observing the session privately. Father Garnet, set apart in a box which looked to observers like a pulpit, faced James's judges, law officers and five earls: Nottingham, Suffolk, Worcester, Northampton and, of course, Salisbury. Here was a trial that was also an intellectual contest, a search for theological truth – the evidence gathered by the Crown of Father Garnet's complicity in the gunpowder treason, heresy, equivocation, the pope's supposed authority to depose and execute heretic monarchs. Salisbury had prepared meticulously; he was focused; this was his moment. Northampton was ready to apply his formidable intellect, and his easy mastery of words, to pounce on principles of law and theology. Much of the surviving account of the trial is the record (in a bare summary) of the sustained and complex exchanges between Garnet, Northampton and Salisbury. King James, the philosopher prince, would have been gripped: before the trial his Majesty, as fascinated as he was appalled by the Jesuit superior, put to the prisoner his own set of theological questions. But it was academic only up to a point. No one doubted what the jury's verdict against Garnet would be.[12]

Salisbury wanted to know why Garnet had refused to hear from Robert Catesby the details of the gunpowder conspiracy. Catesby had offered to communicate them: Garnet would then have been able to act to prevent the plot. Garnet responded that his soul had been 'so troubled with mislike of that particular, as he was loath to hear any more of it'. Salisbury had made his point. 'Well then,' he said to the Guildhall, 'you see his heart.'[13]

Salisbury explained that it wasn't his part to speak to the jury or to debate with Father Garnet about the doctrine of equivocation – in other words, he was neither a lawyer nor a theologian. But it was his responsibility to defend King James and God's Church, and so again he addressed Garnet directly 'as the man in whom it appeareth best what horrible treasons have been covered under the mantle of religion'.[14]

The subjects of equivocation and evasion were unavoidable. Garnet had, according to Salisbury, simply manoeuvred his way around the plot, pretending either not to hear what he had been told by the conspirators, or arguing that it was impossible for him as a priest to make public what they had said to him in confession. Garnet knew about the plot; there was proof that he had written about it to the pope. To Garnet's argument that he 'was not consenting to the powder treason', Salisbury asked: 'Master Garnet, give me but one argument that you were not consenting to it that can hold any indifferent man's ear or sense, besides your bare negative.' To which the official account of the trial has four words: 'But Garnet replied not.'[15]

For Salisbury, this (admittedly highly one-sided) exchange got to the heart of how he believed religion was used by the Jesuits and their allies as a cover for plain treason. Garnet himself said 'he was bound to keep the secrets of confession, and to disclose nothing that he heard in sacramental confession', in response to which Admiral Nottingham posed a scenario: if someone confessed to Garnet that tomorrow morning, he meant to kill the king with a dagger, must Garnet conceal his knowledge? Father Garnet answered that, yes, he had to conceal it.

Salisbury took up the issue. On this he was prepared: his own briefing notes on the subject began with precisely this scenario and a clear principle – 'No future action can fall under confession'.[16]

Salisbury asked: Must there be confession and contrition before absolution? Garnet: Yes. Salisbury: Was Greenwell (or Greenway, alias of Father Oswald Tesimond, a Jesuit who was also involved with the gunpowder conspirators' planning) absolved by Garnet or not? Garnet: He was. Salisbury: What did he do to show that he was sorry for it, and had he promised to desist in what he was doing? Garnet: He had said he would do his best. And then Salisbury brought this theorizing to the chronology of the conspirators' secret movements, a reconstruction of which showed that either Father Garnet had heard from Tesimond about the plot outside confession, or that in confession Tesimond had offered no penitence and was thus in no condition for the absolution Garnet gave him.[17]

Before the law officers concluded the trial – and before the earl of Northampton began a characteristically long oration, which he began with observations from Plato – Salisbury said to Henry Garnet: 'Alas, Master Garnet, why should we be troubled all this day with you, poor man, were it not to make the cause appear as it deserveth? Wherein, God send you may be such an example, as you may be the last actor in this kind.' Salisbury spoke every one of these words with care and meaning. For him it was a declaration of final victory for God over the Antichrist – a victory for the king, a statement of his own implacable service as James's guardian minister, and a settling of accounts too for his father, for Lord Burghley had been an old foot soldier in the war for true religion, who saw the Jesuits for the traitors they were.[18]

But it was a comment by Lord Admiral Nottingham which quickly found its way around London. He said that Garnet had done more good that day standing up in his Guildhall pulpit than he had done in any other pulpit over the whole course of his life.[19]

To the jury, of course, Henry Garnet's guilt was clear. It was a catharsis – and a moment to pause. 'It is thought he shall not die yet, if at all,' wrote John Chamberlain, 'for they hope to win much out of him: and used him with all respect and good words, and he carried himself very gravely and temperately.'[20]

Also immured at this time in the Tower of London, Thomas Phelippes wrote out for the king a long essay on his letters to Hugh Owen and on his imaginary agent close to Salisbury. 'The truth is that there was never any real or direct correspondence held with Owen'; it was 'a mere stratagem and sleight'. Salisbury knew about his secret work, he said – a statement which rather stretched the truth, given that Salisbury had only discovered months before Phelippes's communications with Owen. Phelippes had now satisfied his master with what he called 'an ample declaration of his proceedings from the beginning'. Or so he hoped: he was circumspect enough to leave that for Salisbury to explain to James.

He said he was loyal, that he had only ever served; he gave all the facts and told the truth. And so he asked that 'the King's Majesty may be moved to descend into a gracious consideration of his case and he doubteth not but his Majesty shall find cause to conceive much better of his proceedings than it seemeth he doth'.[21]

There was no response. No such consideration was forthcoming, no cause found for a re-evaluation.

The pause in executing Henry Garnet lasted for five weeks and a day. Scheduled for the May holiday, the prospect of a large and possibly riotous crowd led to a postponement of two days. After the trials of the gunpowder conspirators one official had had doubts about Paul's Churchyard as a place of execution, so close to the cathedral. Should so sacred a place be defiled by the blood of traitors? Secretary Salisbury had then been unmoved by the objection. This was where Henry Garnet too would die.

On Saturday 3 May he was taken from the Tower to the Churchyard, hanged, drawn and quartered, and his remains dispersed across the city.[22]

30

Yielding the Keys

In June 1605 Viscount Cranborne, Salisbury's son and heir, went off to university. 'I came (God be thanked) safely to Cambridge . . . and am entered into my wonted course of study', he wrote to his father from St John's College a few days after his arrival. He marked out the lines of his letter with ruler and pencil, practising his best hand-writing, for Salisbury, whose own hand was no writing-master's model, was a stickler for perfection in that of his son. The words were formal and conventional, a little flat, but then Cranborne was only fourteen years old. It was the age of the viscount's grandfather, the original William Cecil, when, in the reign of Henry VIII, he had walked through the same college gateway, decorated with the wild heraldic beasts of the Lady Margaret Beaufort, King James of Great Britain's great-great-grandmother. May 1535, June 1605: seventy years, almost to the month.

The College of St John the Evangelist had long and deep connections to the Cecils, who had endowed it with studentships, donated valuable books and given money for winter fires in the hall. Each year Cecil scholars from St John's journeyed from Cambridge to Burghley House and to Theobalds to read their verse compositions on passages of scripture chosen by the 1st baron of Burghley; the writer Thomas Nashe, a contemporary of Ben Jonson, was one of them. Over the college – in fact over the whole university, as its chancellor – Salisbury was a powerful influence. Going off to Cambridge in 1605 wasn't simply a personal adventure for Lord Cranborne: it was piece of family business.[1]

The expectations were clear. Young Cranborne went to Cambridge with a purpose. His college tutor, Roger Morrell, knew exactly what

Salisbury expected, and his reports on his pupil's progress have the suppressed anxiety of one who knew very well that he would be held to account for his teaching. First indications were positive: after a month the new student was applying himself diligently to academic work. Master Morrell felt that William needed sport and recreation; he asked for Salisbury's instructions as to what was appropriate. Morrell tiptoed delicately around the issue of whether vacation-time Cambridge, where 'gentlemen of note' were few and there were no lectures, was quite the best place for his pupil to be, especially in an unseasonably hot summer; he worried (as all tutors did) about sickness. But one thing he emphasized, as of course he really had to: Cranborne went to his books with alacrity and cheerfulness.[2]

Where St John's was a fixed point of reference for the Cecils, Theobalds ran even deeper. Cranborne was at home for a couple of weeks in autumn 1605, at the time when his father was in Westminster dealing with the gunpowder treason. In mid-November he was at Theobalds on his own, but in October a friend had visited, another boy of fourteen, and an earl – though Robert Devereux, 3rd earl of Essex, had had to be restored in blood and honours by an act of parliament before he could succeed to an earldom that had temporarily ended with the execution of his father in 1601. Only the steward's dining accounts offer us the image of two teenaged friends being served dinner and supper at Theobalds in late October 1605, at the same table where their fathers had met a generation earlier, in the weeks before Cranborne's grandfather Burghley had the 2nd earl of Essex shipped off to Cambridge. Cecil and Devereux: two Roberts in 1577, William and Robert in 1605. Two families still connected: out of a tangled history and rivalry, friendship.

Salisbury, like his father Burghley, felt the linkages between past, present and future. To be a Jacobean dynast was to be able to see all three aspects of time co-existing in a single reality. What has been, what is, what will be, celebrated and marked, consolidated in the moment, planned for in the interests of later generations. This was a trust, a continuation of work already started, pointing ever forward. This was what the hermit of Theobalds had said to Queen Elizabeth and her court all those years before in the great entertainment of 1591: after Burghley, Master Robert Cecil would continue to serve his monarch, and beyond him William Cecil, then a baby two months old. Now – deliberately, consciously – Salisbury sought to raise and shape William Cranborne, just as Lord Burghley had shaped him, fitting him for his future. It was the old pattern, tried, tested and trusted: where a wise father directed, a diligent son obeyed.

By spring 1606 Master Morrell was applying himself to Salisbury's instructions as assiduously as his pupil was studying his Latin and logic. Salisbury knew what he wanted, and Morrell thanked his lordship for the 'most pithy and judicious letters full fraught with many excellent rules, both for order in study and direction in life' – the guidance was for both Master Morrell and Lord Cranborne. The words might have been those of a twenty-something Robert Cecil writing with thanks to his noble father the lord treasurer of England. In Cranborne's education, 'True congruity in speech and orderly reasoning in disputation' were particular emphases, for these were the foundations for public life and service. But the student also needed a short break from his studies. 'I perceive in him a longing desire to see your lordship,' Morrell wrote, 'as also for that I am persuaded that a little intermission for a few days would very much refresh his wit and revive his spirits.' To the hardest working of King James's ministers, the fellow of St John's suggested that Cranborne might spend holy days at Theobalds.[3]

With high influence came great expense. Lord Burghley had known this; Robert, earl of Salisbury felt it too. Royal favour weighed heavy on the purse. At Theobalds in July 1606 Salisbury entertained King James and his brother-in-law, Christian IV of Denmark, something of a bon viveur: five days' entertainment, the final sum of money in the household accounts one thousand one hundred and eighty pounds, just over fifty-five of which were spent on a dramatic tableau.

Sir Walter Cope supervised the preparations for the entertainment, buying the silks and other essentials for the show. Cope was both kinsman and servant of the Cecils, one of the most trusted men of Salisbury's inner circle. A second cousin to Robert's mother, a gentleman in the 1st Lord Burghley's service from the mid-1570s with a long career in the Court of Wards and Liveries, Cope was now aged about sixty. He co-ordinated the work of three other, younger men: a scrivener, a painter and a writer of verses. The painter was a thirty-three-year-old Londoner, Inigo Jones, whose first experience as a designer of sets and costumes at court had been in the previous year. The poet was Ben Jonson.

It was an entertainment at the very opposite end of the scale from Jonson's *Sejanus*, his brooding study of Roman tyranny. On Thursday 24 July King James and King Christian entered the inner court at Theobalds to see set over the porch the characters of Three Hours, sitting on clouds, whose names were Law, Justice and Peace. The two monarchs were addressed in Latin verse: 'often has Theobalds, blessed with good fortune, received its gods under its dutiful eaves; but hardly a pair at once ... But now the house, fortunate already, is blessed in every way, yet how much more so the master, if that much is possible.'[4]

Salisbury was the master of Theobalds; the house was in his bones, in his heart; it was his past and present; it would surely be his son's inheritance. But the king too liked the house and its parks, and soon enough the most dutiful of his ministers would find it impossible to refuse James.

At Theobalds in July 1606 Law, Justice and Peace addressed two kings in Ben Jonson's Latin. A few weeks later Thomas Phelippes wrote once again to Secretary Salisbury – eternal hope over hard reality.

Phelippes's conscience was clear in his devotion to James. He asked for compassion and consideration. He had written to the Privy Council but knew that only Salisbury could free him from prison, indeed that only Salisbury knew the truth of a case which – he expressed this delicately – 'may be to others not so excusable in appearance'. He was relying on his lordship's wisdom and equity. He would do anything to serve or satisfy, to make a living for his poor family. He asked God to preserve Salisbury with the increase of all happiness.[5]

In late summer Salisbury fell dangerously ill. A 'distemper' was how Sir Fulke Greville described it, brought on (supposedly) by a

ferocious encounter with the Spanish ambassador over the gunpowder plot. By mid-September he was recovered, or at least recovering,
but the rumours that had had both court and London buzzing had
suggested that Salisbury would soon die.[6]

On Lord Secretary Salisbury there rested so much: 'your little finger
cannot ache, but the whole state hath cause to be sensible', said Sir
Edward Wotton. Without Salisbury, Lord Zouche, himself sick and
lame and taking the waters at Bath, told him that the king's enemies –
the 'enchanting papists' – threatened the state.[7]

How fragile it all was. As a minister of King James, God's vice-
gerent on earth, Salisbury was gifted and powerful: he was an earl, a
knight of the Garter, one of the elite, born and trained to serve. And a
man possessed of a penetrating mind who knew – who had known
from at least early manhood – how weak his body was. 'My own not
strongest constitution' was how he had described it to his mother in
Armada year, 1588. Energy and sheer willpower overcame the physical weaknesses: in the end, the bear's whelp licked himself into shape.
But the pressures of office only increased, that 'burden of prince's service' as he had put it in 1601. His mind and his body were always
under assault: 'a contemplation fit for me of any other, whose infirmities promise not long health'.

In May 1607 Salisbury cut one of the most significant links with his
past. Theobalds – the house built for him, where he had been raised
and taught, the place which celebrated in solid dimensions the Cecils'
lineage and service to monarchs – he exchanged with Queen Anne
and King James for other Hertfordshire lands and estates about nine
miles away, at Hatfield. The act of parliament which authorized this
complex transaction explained in its preamble why it was done: James
had 'taken great liking to Theobalds house and two parks of the Earl
of Salisbury's . . . the one replenished with red deer, the other with
fallow deer, most convenient for his princely sports and recreation.'
What the king wanted the king got. At Theobalds Salisbury would
now be a visitor.[8]

Hatfield gave him the opportunity to build a statement house of his
own, and a month before the exchange he went with the earls of

Suffolk, Worcester and Southampton (Henry Wriothesley, condemned with Essex in 1601 but rehabilitated to favour after 1603) to reconnoitre his new estates and find the best site for building. From the beginning Salisbury threw all his resources at the project – tens of thousands of pounds, the skills of a formidable team (Thomas Wilson as financial controller, Robert Lyminge as architect, Simon Basil the royal surveyor), as much energy as he himself could spare, and aspirations for a new Theobalds or Holdenby, Sir Christopher Hatton's own remarkable house. Hatfield was Robert Cecil's motto in stone and brick: *Sero, sed serio* – 'Late, but in earnest'.[9]

Ben Jonson wrote the entertainment performed at the formal delivery of Theobalds to Queen Anne on Friday, 22 May 1607. Was there an ambivalence about the exchange? Jonson's character of Genius says:

> To yield these keys, and wish that you could see
> My heart as open to you as my hands.
> There might you read my faith, my thoughts – but, oh,
> My joys like waves each other overcome,
> And gladness drowns where it begins to flow!
> Some greater powers speak out, for mine are dumb!

And then a song, which began with a solo:

> O blessèd change!
> And no less glad than strange!
> Where we that lose have won,
> And, for a beam, enjoy a sun.[10]

How hard Salisbury had to work for his king; how much he had to give. His service was sacrifice.

Hatfield House would one day be Viscount Cranborne's, his inheritance just as Theobalds had been Salisbury's. In 1607 that was some way off. Cranborne, still studying at the College of St John the Evangelist, was preoccupied by other matters. Salisbury was frustrated by his son's lack of progress in Cambridge. He was not pleased.

Cranborne's handwriting was undistinguished. He still ruled lines like a child, folding his letters like a grammar schoolboy. This was not a compliment: Salisbury sent him a packet folded as a gentleman should do it. The fatherly admonitions were direct without being crushing; he spoke to what he knew his son was capable of. And Salisbury didn't believe that William's faults were entirely his own, sensing in Cambridge more generally a sloppy inattention to learning – a telling judgement from the university's chancellor. To his credit, Cranborne responded; he worked harder. 'Will, such is the change I find in your hand from worse to better, as I am very much pleased with it', his father wrote at about the time he handed the keys of Theobalds to Queen Anne. 'I perceive you do respect your own good, the rather because I tell you wherein it will consist, which is next the service of God, in enriching yourself with learning.' It had been Lord Burghley's philosophy too: he had read and judged Robert's exercises in just the same way, his eyes sharp, his pen ready to correct. For the Cecils, standards – the very highest – could not slip.[11]

Salisbury's letter to Master Morrell was withering. 'I may not conceal it from you that my expectation is deceived', he wrote. Salisbury took upon himself some responsibility for Cranborne's faults – but only some. Morrell's curriculum for his pupil was so dry and uninspiring that Lord Cranborne could speak barely six words in Latin and could not recite from memory more than five lines of his history books. But Morrell had not failed completely. He had saved Cranborne from the most damaging effects of bad company: 'if your eye had not been a watch over him it would have been much worse with him'. Morrell was not dismissed, though Salisbury demoted him, handing to others oversight of his son in chapel and at lectures, and more generally around Cambridge.[12]

Under his father's scrutiny, William Cranborne was a young man to be fashioned for his own, and his dynasty's, good.

On Tuesday, 19 April 1608, Lord Treasurer Dorset – Thomas Sackville, the old Lord Buckhurst – died in the council chamber in Whitehall Palace; it was as if he had fallen asleep at the table. By then in his early seventies, Dorset had been at the apex of power for twenty years, lord treasurer since 1599, reappointed to the office for life on James's accession in 1603. He and Salisbury were close:

I thank you a thousand times for your letter, which hath given me satisfaction and comfort. I beseech God to preserve you and your health not only for yourself and your friends, but for the King and the state. For when your hand is from the helm God doth know what I am resolved to do.

This was in 1606 on Salisbury's recovery from his distemper.[13]

King James's appointment of Dorset's successor was made at a speed which would have left Queen Elizabeth dizzily disorientated. A fortnight and a day after Thomas Sackville's most definitive of resignations, Salisbury took the helm of the king's Exchequer.

The treasurership was the impossible job in James's government. Words and deft negotiations might keep diplomacy working. The little beagle hunted the king's enemies. Talented administrators could deal with mountains of complex paperwork, keeping it ever moving – in both the Privy Council office and Salisbury's private secretariat were individuals of sometimes polymathic brilliance. The Exchequer was different: what Salisbury inherited there, at least according to Sir Walter Cope, was 'a chaos of confusion'. To keep the Crown's finances from total collapse and James from penury, and to confront a system of parliamentary taxation broken beyond repair (if it had ever really worked) where the king's resources were eroded year on year as he himself, the most generous royal benefactor, spent ever more money – these were labours beyond those of Hercules. Even if they should succeed, ministers were rarely thanked for their efforts. If they didn't, their travails were even greater.[14]

Wrestling with his declining health, fashioning his legacy, Salisbury took on more work. He experienced after 1608 the deepest frustrations and humiliations of his career. It was, in his own mind at least, the end of his meaningful service to the king. And it was the last painful chapter of his life.

31

The Plagues of Job

Two aspects of Robert Cecil existed in creative tension. There was his private self, so carefully hidden away, and his outer image, just as carefully managed. The mask he presented to the world was as fixed as the face in every portrait of him ever painted or engraved – the official version, as people were supposed to see him, the tireless servant of the monarch, the minister who kept his own counsel, secret and discreet. It was against his will that he spoke publicly, a fact which makes *An Answer to Certain Scandalous Papers* so striking. On that occasion, in early 1606, his enemies had managed to draw him out into the open, against his better judgement. And after that a dignified silence: 'I will henceforth rest in peace in the house of mine own conscience.' Or so he hoped.

There was also Cecil the aesthete, even Cecil the showman. Most certainly he understood the theatre of politics: the trials of Doctor Lopez, the earl of Essex, Father Garnet; he would play to the crowd when he wanted to. He could move in style: as early as 1594 a suite of white horses, imported from Emden, pulled Cecil's coach. Venetian diplomats were dazzled by the sumptuousness of Salisbury's installation in May 1606 into the Order of the Garter, and exactly two years later King James's newly appointed lord treasurer commissioned from Ben Jonson and Inigo Jones a striking entertainment in the impressive library of Salisbury House. A message from Sir Robert Cecil in the 1590s might be carried by Fortunatus, an African servant baptized near Theobalds when Robert had been a boy; the baptismal name was from the first of Paul's New Testament letters to the early Christians of the city of Corinth – Fortunatus was a helper and servant, a comforter of the spirit (1 Corinthians 16:17). This Fortunatus Cuba (as he once called himself in a petition for a Crown wardship) saw his master build one grand house on the Strand (he himself was buried in 1602 not very far from in) but was dead before Lord Salisbury began Hatfield. And it was into these houses that Salisbury packed an outstanding library and put his art, much of it from Italy, bought through the king's ambassador in Venice. One inventory for Hatfield has seventy-nine pictures in 1611 and ninety-two a year later. At Hatfield today is the famous Rainbow Portrait of Queen Elizabeth, attributed to the Flemish artist Marcus Gheeraerts the Younger, inscribed with a motto which celebrated the late, ever-youthful monarch as the bringer of peace and prosperity, *Non sine sole iris* – 'No rainbow without the sun'.[1]

A man as powerful as Robert Cecil was courted by suitors and clients. He received so many gifts from petitioners, colleagues and friends: the usual hawks and falcons (on these he looked with an expert eye), objects from across the seas – a perspective glass, musk from the Indies, or, material in a different way, the book dedications of individuals, such as Richard Hakluyt in his three-volume epic *Principal Navigations of the Voyages, Traffics and Discoveries of the English Nation*, who sought to entice Cecil to support foreign adventures and investments, particularly in America. Here they were pushing at an open door. For Robert Cecil even the staid corridors of Westminster, where he had to spend too much of his life, were scented by spiced Indian air, by the promise of the virgin forests of North America.[2]

In the light of all this, Salisbury's ambition to outshine the Royal Exchange by building and opening 'Britain's Burse' is not so very surprising. This was a luxury Westminster shopping mall more than a trading floor, but as a rival to the Exchange (which was both) it was by summer 1608 causing grumblings amongst London's merchants. John Chamberlain's account of Salisbury's response to their protests is striking: 'that Westminster, being the place where he was born, and of his abode, he sees not but that he may seek to benefit and beautify it by all the means he can'. The site of Britain's Burse was the clearest signal of all: it was next door to Salisbury House on the Strand.[3]

The grand opening of the Burse took place on Tuesday 11 April 1609. The guests of honour were the whole royal family: King James,

Queen Anne, the two princes – fifteen-year-old Henry and eight-year-old Charles (the future Charles I) – and their sister, the twelve-year-old Princess Elizabeth (the future countess palatine of the Rhine and queen of Bohemia, the so-called 'Winter Queen'). Salisbury himself supervised closely the entertainment he had commissioned. Sir Walter Cope was involved too; the poet was Ben Jonson, the set designer Inigo Jones – the by now familiar creative trio behind Salisbury's shows for the court. They celebrated the wonders of the Burse, indeed the wonders of the world: on display were rare luxuries from the Indies and America, all for sale; this was a world of the senses, a world of consumption, which promised to a buyer any object imaginable. In the dramatic entertainment, Jonson's shop boy welcomes the king himself, speaking to his desire to acquire and possess:

> What do you lack? What is't you buy? Very fine China stuffs of all kinds and qualities? China chains, China bracelets, China scarves, China fans, China girdles, China knives, China boxes, China cabinets, caskets, umbrellas, sundials, hourglasses, looking-glasses, burning-glasses, concave glasses, triangular glasses, convex glasses, crystal globes, waxen pictures, ostrich eggs, birds of paradise, musk-cats, Indian mice, China dogs, and China cats? Flowers of silk, mosaic fishes? Waxen fruit and porcelain dishes?'[4]

Luxurious, fantastic, opulent: the earl of Salisbury – connoisseur, showman and salesman – advertised his wares to King James and his family and his Majesty's kingdoms of Great Britain. Power and money, with a look to future investments and opportunities, and service eventually to the king after James. As the master of the shop says to Prince Henry in the final minutes of the entertainment: 'Ye look like a good customer too, and a good paymaster to boot!'[5]

Like all clients Thomas Phelippes had put his faith in patrons, in Lord Burghley, in the earl of Essex, and lastly in Salisbury. Essex and Salisbury were each for a time his protector and paymaster; each had abandoned him. From 1605 Phelippes was caught fast in his own plots and plans, haunted by the real and imaginary characters in his espionage. Sir Francis Walsingham's most secret servant, posted to the embassy in Paris in 1578, the man who had sent Mary of Scotland to the headsman's block, ended up as the most importunate and desperate of suitors. The mathematician and linguist, clever and inventive, the accomplished traveller used to living by his wits, the esquire with a coat of arms, had his world reduced down to a cell and saw his family struggling with poverty.

He knew by 1609 that he had nothing left; this fact he had recognized for many years. Mary Phelippes had been granted the tenancy of her husband's lands, seized by the Crown to pay his debt, but sometime before spring 1608 Lord Treasurer Dorset had taken the tenancy from her and given it to someone else. Phelippes's letter to Secretary Salisbury in response to this deprivation was a howl of pain, urging Salisbury to talk to Dorset about discharging Mary's own heavy debts.

Phelippes's hand moved quickly, urgently, unevenly across the page, scratching out mistakes, correcting himself as he went: 'And I protest before God that I may and shall reckon it as great a grace as your lordship can bestow upon a poor distressed ruined prisoner.'[6]

This was his future: a further sixteen years of living in what he later called the 'doghole' of prison, for ever the destitute petitioner. Now whatever fortune he had had was gone. He was never again trusted, never rehabilitated – all but forgotten.[7]

Seventeen-year-old Viscount Cranborne married Catharine, daughter of the king's lord chamberlain, the earl of Suffolk, in December 1608. It was a quiet ceremony held in the Whitehall apartments of Lady Walsingham, mistress of the robes to Anne of Denmark. The hawk-eyed court observer John Chamberlain tutted that they had not been married in church, which was more usual: 'holy things should be solemnized in holy places.'[8]

A few days later, Cranborne set off for Paris. It was hardly a honeymoon: he travelled with his two new brothers-in-law, Thomas and Henry Howard, whose travels were going to take them into Italy. The three young men braved the stormy December waters of the English Channel. In July 1609 Cranborne was off again, this time on a longer tour of France, the Low Countries, Germany and Italy – like his father before him, he wanted to breathe fresh new air. But now it was the earl of Salisbury who had to risk allowing his only son and heir to journey so far, not knowing what might happen. And the worst almost did: in La Rochelle at the end of August, Will came down with small-pox, and for a week he was confined to bed with a high fever; he was fortunate to escape scarring. For a few days an earldom had hung in the balance.[9]

Salisbury gave his son a critical assessment of the exercise books that Will completed on his travels; these were diligently brought over from France by a servant. These were important now and for the future: 'so visible demonstrations of your respect and care to give me satisfaction in applying yourself and your time to such commendable exercises, whereof yourself alone shall receive the greatest benefit', as Salisbury put it. Cranborne's handwriting had improved, though it still needed a bit more shape and discipline ('not giving your pen so great a liberty'); his exercises of putting English into Latin were good; his translations from the philosopher Seneca sound up to a point ('I find the errors you make not frequent nor gross'). His work on Cicero would improve his English style, and his studies in French would give him models for ordinary forms of speech. However, Will's logic, on which his father wanted him to concentrate, needed more development: 'those notes you have written seem to be somewhat naked'.

Standing out in Salisbury's letter are two particular pieces of advice. He encouraged his son to do what he himself had done in Paris in 1584: excepting with his two brothers-in-law, in France Cranborne should avoid English conversation and immerse himself in French. The second had to do with Cranborne's reading of Seneca, where Robert wanted Will to look beyond the surface for deeper meaning: 'the best use you can make of that author will be to observe his matter rather than his words, for he affected the one much more than the other.' Substance mattered – to read to the heart of things.[10]

Cranborne wrote to his father in a hand which was as disciplined as he could make it – he never quite achieved copybook precision. He looked forward to Salisbury's letters, always ready to take his lord-ship's advice on the next stages of his journeying, the building up piece by piece of his education and experience. But he missed home and said so, as politely as he could, in words which Robert Cecil himself might have used a generation earlier.

> I attended your pleasure concerning my farther courses this summer, to which I will never fail to conform myself with all due obedience: only I beseech you not to be offended if I cannot dissemble [the] desire I have to see your lordship, my wife, and my friends in England.

He signed his letter as his father's most obedient son.[11]

Lord Treasurer Salisbury's ambition was to put the king's finances on a secure and sustainable footing. Inflation had eaten away the resources of the Exchequer, James liked to spend lots of money, parliamentary taxation was sporadic and inadequate, and the ancient practices of revenue-raising for the Crown based on royal prerogative and patronage were both inefficient and corrupt. Here Salisbury had been a beneficiary as much as he was an earnest reformer – the eye-wateringly vast sums of money that built Salisbury House, Britain's Burse and Hatfield were not merely gifts from heaven.

At the Exchequer it was time for retrenchment, for a refoundation of some fundamental principles, for a new beginning. Really there was no alternative, for without reform the royal finances would surely collapse. The burden on the Exchequer was massive; James's debts were estimated at anywhere between £600,000 and £700,000 (perhaps more), and his annual expenditure kept on rising – hardly a surprise given the costs of the new royal family and the king's generosity with patronage. So, the offer was this: a parliamentary endowment would give the Crown £200,000 a year in revenue, in return for the dismantling of the old ramshackle edifices of wardship and patronage. Salisbury and the chancellor of the Exchequer, Sir Julius Caesar, prepared the ground; they wrote papers and did their homework, emphasizing that poverty for James meant insecurity and danger. The lord treasurer counselled the king plainly: 'It is not possible for a king of England, much less of Great Britain ... to be rich or safe, but by frugality.' Salisbury put his 'Great Contract' to parliament between spring and autumn 1610. After weeks of division and deadlock, lobbying by outside interests, speeches, committees and meetings and endless failed compromises, there was a flash of hope and a possible resolution.[12]

It all foundered on politics. The truth was that the Great Contract was more than simply about money or the repair of the king's ruinously leaky finances. Parliaments had long used negotiations over the taxes they authorized to communicate to monarchs their preferences or worries about royal government. And there was always much to worry about: money, religion and Church, war and military commitments of armies and navies, internal and external security, the stresses and strains more generally of surviving in conflict-torn Europe, and royal succession and the future of England. Tax bills were leverage, or at the very least a chance for ordinary gentlemen to be heard – monarchs listened to their subjects when they wanted their subjects' money. Now a parliament was dealing with a new king; they were trying to make sense of him (they worried, for example, that he spoke in elevated terms about his own powers and seemed to like making extra-parliamentary royal proclamations) just as he was getting used to them. King and parliament weren't opponents, but partners – and partners often disagree with one another, and can be plain in saying so.

The summer of 1610 therefore saw protracted financial haggling between parliament (the House of Commons especially) and King James. And on the front line of this robust exchange – in some ways caught between the two – was Salisbury. He certainly felt the weight of it all. Sometimes in speeches he found himself going over the history of Queen Elizabeth's reign, at once point even using the response she had made on Mary Queen of Scots, and he himself had put into print, in 1586: '[I] must answer as the late Queen did . . . for this time I must give you an answer answerless.' He spoke about his physical infirmities; once he asked his hearers to forgive a memory that was not quite once what it had been.[13]

Addressing the king in the Banqueting House at Whitehall Palace on 10 July, Salisbury said:

> I should reckon it for a great grace, that your Majesty inviteth and directeth me (being a servant) to do that which your Majesty (my sovereign lord and master) doth practise yourself. And there cannot be a

greater honour than to move, though in a low and smaller sphere, yet in the same figure and motion that his sovereign doth.

It fell to the servant to be the pragmatist, to secure what could in the real world be achieved. Ten days after his speech to the king Salisbury declared that 'This great contract between the King and the kingdom is concluded but not finished ... I long to hear my master say he approve it.'[14]

But James did not approve it. Losing patience, and against his lord treasurer's advice, the king called time on parliament.

So the old sticking plasters of ad hoc parliamentary revenues continued to be applied to the royal finances. And over the succeeding decades the problems avoided only became worse, the tensions ever greater – as James's son and successor King Charles would find out by the 1640s, to his and his kingdoms' very great cost.

Perhaps the Great Contract would have helped to change history as we know it, or at least to have eased one of the problems that combined with others in the 1630s and early 1640s to precipitate a war between a king and his parliament – it is impossible to know for sure. What is clear, however, is that its failure affected Salisbury deeply.

In the early winter months of 1610, the earl had to make new sense of what he gave deeply of himself to God's anointed, and what he received in return. Letters the king and his lord treasurer exchanged in December reveal some of Salisbury's bruises. They also show that James never doubted for a moment that it was his ministers who were fallible. 'I think fit to give your Majesty an account with the same diligence by which I have endeavoured (in the whole course of my life) to give your Majesty the best course I could, to bear with me my other wants and weaknesses', wrote Salisbury. The king replied a few days later with a letter which had a sting in its tail.

> My little beagle, I wonder what should make you to conceit so the alteration or diminishing of my favour towards you ... your greatest error hath been that ye ever expected to draw honey out of gall, being a little blinded with the self-love of your own counsel in holding together of this parliament.

In other words, this was Salisbury's misjudgement, and James of course knew best.[15]

Salisbury wrote to James that he would open his conscience to the king and make his confession in audience. 'And thus I humbly kiss your Majesty's hands with my prayers that God may make your Majesty both of kings and of men the fullest of days and blessings.'[16]

The same day, Sunday 9 December, the lord treasurer wrote to Sir Thomas Lake, a brilliant administrator now always close to James, who had been critical of Salisbury's judgement, and had told the king so for months: the correspondence between Salisbury and Lake had been tense.

> Now that I have seen this parliament at an end, whereof the many vexations have so overtaken one another as I know not to what to resemble them so well as the plagues of Job, I am so far from meaning to trouble myself with the memory of any of the dregs, as I mean not now to spend my time from his Majesty's service in disputing this matter by my letters, in which no man hath interest but you and I.[17]

It was time to move on, in what time turned out to be left to him.

At Hatfield in July 1611 Salisbury entertained the king for dinner. The house wasn't quite finished: masons, bricklayers, carpenters, joiners, painters, plasterers and smiths were still busy at work on its fabric, and in its east and west gardens, as they would be until the end of the year. The chapel was taking shape, fitted with its pulpit and pews, soon to be grandly furnished and decorated.[18]

Salisbury was by now, after a few years of fragile health, seriously ill. At the beginning of August he was examined by one of the king's physicians, the distinguished Théodore Turquet de Mayerne. Finding a large abdominal tumour in the hypogastrium on the patient's right-hand side, Mayerne recommended for Salisbury moderate exercise and a healthy diet. It was not, of course, enough; Robert's cancer was well advanced. In late summer and autumn there were more symptoms: rheumatism in the right arm, ague, shortness of breath, melancholy. In March 1612 he rallied a little, and there was even hope of a recovery:

'His disease proves nothing so dangerous as was suspected,' John Chamberlain reported, 'being now discovered to be but the scorbut or (as we term it) the scurvy, which is of easy and ordinary cure if it be not too far over passed. His sickness drowned all other news.' But he was not at court. On retreat in rural Kensington he was visited by King James, Queen Anne and Prince Henry.[19]

In the first week of March Salisbury made his will: a first instalment on Tuesday 3rd, a long codicil added to it on Saturday 7th. It was the usual complex business of settling affairs and estates, making bequests to friends and family, professing faith and hope of salvation. On 3 March he dug deeply, acknowledging himself 'to be a most grievous sinner', whose wretchedness could be washed away only by the blood Jesus Christ had shed on the cross. There was something Salisbury had to prove, whether to God, or to the witnesses of the will, or indeed to himself. Some, he said, believed that those men who in 'their calling are employed in matters of state and government under great kings and princes' had little or no religion. He rejected this. Of course, Christian realms were imperfect – he said nothing about imperfect monarchs or ministers – but he was sure in his faith and doctrine. As in the *Answer* of 1606, to which this element of the will's preamble is almost a continuation, the politician turned theologian. He knew he was right.[20]

This self-reckoning was a long way from the theatre of riches and power and display in Westminster or at Hatfield. It was the submission by a son of Adam to the power of his Creator, the beginning of a preparation for the end.

In April he travelled to Bath for a cure in its warm spring waters. With him went old friends, physicians and servants, some of whom had witnessed (and would continue to witness) the various instalments of his last will and testament: Sir Michael Hickes, Sir Walter Cope, Doctor Poe and Doctor Atkyns, and his chaplain John Bowle, who later made a record of what was done and said. In Kensington on 28 April, the day they left, Salisbury told Bowle that they would have a 'long and troublesome journey'. He was speaking about more than geography and itinerary. He had made his audit with God; he did not fear death. He saw burial in Bath Abbey as a sound a way to heaven and resurrection as any other. So great was God's love and charity, he told Bowle, 'that for His part there was never a man in the world, but He could take him by the hand'. The sinner sought forgiveness.[21]

He seemed to rally a little on the journey: on 1 May the earl of Shrewsbury, at Whitehall, was relieved to have heard reports from Poe and Cope that Salisbury had so far eaten well, had slept very well and was enjoying the air. On Sunday 3 May the party arrived in Bath. The following day Salisbury added a schedule to his will: money for the poor of Hatfield, Westminster and Cranborne, and further personal bequests, witnessed and signed by Michael Hickes and Walter Cope.[22]

For a few days the waters seemed to do him good. Bowle recorded that on 8 May his lordship 'was exceedingly revived', for which he gave thanks to God. Salisbury wrote that same day to Lord Cranborne. In his bathing, he explained, he had been following a routine, despite the sharp cold wind. 'This day I go in again, for I desire to neglect no time, and the sun shines. I have no prejudice by sweating, for I sit no higher than the navel. I am already warmed from that part downward, but the swelling in the thighs, in the knees and legs hath yet small vent.' He would try the warmer waters early the following week. When he signed the letter his hand shook slightly.[23]

On Tuesday 12 May livid blue spots appeared on his skin; Bowle also called it the scorbut. He was very ill for three days. Then his mind cleared. He asked Bowle to pray for him. Salisbury announced that he had confessed his sins, professed his faith, forgiven all his enemies, made his peace with God, had the seal of the holy sacrament: 'I doubt not but God will have mercy upon me for his Son Jesus Christ His sake; although great and many have been my sins. For which sins of mine God hath laid this sickness upon me.'

Bowle reminded him of two Gospel parables of mercy, of God's forgiveness and reconciliation: the prodigal son and the lost sheep who had wandered away from the flock. It was to the second that Salisbury responded with passion: 'Oh, that sheep am I! That sheep am I!' He said he wanted to die and to be with Christ. But was it time? Was there still work for him to do? Bowle recalled for Salisbury the death-bed words of St Martin of Tours: *Domine, si populo tuo sum necessarius, non recuso laborem* – 'Lord, if I be needful to thy people, I refuse not to work.'[24]

*

Sometimes he slept, often he prayed. Servants were always close by, comforting, mostly watching. Almost every hour of those few days, 15–17 May, promised something different: treatment, health and recovery, death and a meeting with God. On Saturday 16 May he was up on his crutches, remembering his friends and servants, remembering the king, smiling, weeping, ready and prepared: 'O Lord Jesus, now sweet Jesus! O Jesus, now, O Jesus, let me come unto thee! My audit is made.'

On Sunday it was sleep that took him, not death, a sleep from which he woke clear-headed. He conducted with John Bowle a spiritual review of his children, of his daughters Frances and Catharine, above all of William, Viscount Cranborne: 'I love him more because he is religious than because he is my son.' He made the final addition to his will, just three bequests (to two servants and to a surgeon) signed and sealed, witnessed by Doctor Poe and Master Bowle.[25]

On Monday 18 May he reflected that death was the centre to which we all move: some went to it across the diameter of the circle, some around the circumference. But for Salisbury, forty-eight years old, the human timeframe seemed not to matter. As he expressed it, 'all men must fall down to the centre'. 'And I know that though my sins were of a scarlet or crimson hue, yet they shall be all bathed in the blood of the Lamb, and shall be made whiter than snow. I do not despair of life and I do not fear death: God's will be done, I am prepared for it.' The following day Lord Cranborne arrived in Bath, against his father's express commandment. It was Bowle who brought them together. He spoke to Salisbury. Would it not be a comfort to see his son if God in his providence should arrange it? 'Oh yes,' Salisbury replied, 'the greatest comfort in the world.'

There were words, exhortations to William to live a religious life. But mostly they wept together. Master Bowle gave Salisbury the Eucharist. Then his lordship slept.[26]

On Thursday, 21 May, he began his intended return to London. Twenty-four hours later he was on the edge of consciousness; Bowle heard from him snatches of speech about physic, as well as some sentences from the Book of Common Prayer, one especially: 'and take not thy Spirit from us'. Salisbury was failing, and quickly. On Saturday 23 May they arrived in the village of Marlborough in Wiltshire and went, probably, to the former priory of St Margaret, which they had stopped at on the way to Bath.

After dinner on Sunday afternoon Doctor Poe and Master Bowle went in to see him. Bowle recorded the final minutes of Robert Cecil's life.

He lay with his head on two pillows held in the lap of Roger Townsend, the comptroller of his household. A servant was adjusting the frame which supported the earl. 'So,' he said, 'lift me up but this once.' He wanted Doctor Poe to take his hand: he gripped it: his eyes calmed. He cried out 'Oh Lord', then sank back down; he didn't groan, he didn't struggle. Bowle began to pray with him that God would receive his soul and spirit. Those few words were as far as he got: 'he was clean gone, and no breath nor motion in him.'[27]

Postscript

Retrospective Malice

They buried him at Hatfield on Tuesday, 9 June 1612. His son William, now the 2nd earl of Salisbury, was chief mourner, joined by the earls of Suffolk and Worcester (the two overseers of Robert Cecil's final earthly dispositions), the earls of Pembroke and Montgomery, four barons, a tightly knit band of cousins and kinsmen and senior household staff, three physicians, two chaplains, and the preacher. Of the six gentlemen who carried the pennants of arms three were Sir Francis Bacon, Sir Michael Hickes and Levinus Munck. 'Let me therefore have no more than blacks [suits of mourning clothes] for mine own servants and some few friends and so go without noise and vanity out of this vale of misery', as Salisbury put it in his will; his was to be a Christian burial 'without any extraordinary show or spectacle but only so much respect as may agree with decency and comeliness'.[1]

He had been presented with a model for his tomb as early as 1609; the artist was Maximilian Colt, master sculptor to the king. The materials and cost for the tomb – in black and white marble on two tiers, at each corner the cardinal virtues of Temperance, Justice, Prudence and Fortitude – were assessed by James's surveyor, Simon Basil, in January 1614. 'My will is my executors cause a fair monument to be made for me, the charge thereof not exceeding two hundred pounds.' Basil's calculation of the sum for stone and labour was well more than double that.[2]

On the upper tier of the tomb Robert, earl of Salisbury lies in full robes, the lord treasurer's wand of office held in his right hand. It was an uncompromising design more in tune with earlier times. Underneath Salisbury, represented as he had been in life, is laid out a skeleton, the man stripped of flesh, without office or rank; it is a memento mori, the centre to which we all move. Cecil's two bodies: the power and the man.

'Our great, strange, little lord is gone, and as soon forgotten.' So wrote John Chamberlain on 25 June 1612. The libellers were in their element, even with Robert, 2nd earl of Essex dead for eleven years, for there was something about Cecil and about his family – about his and their power and influence – that provoked still a visceral reaction. So there were more offensive verses about the late Lord Salisbury than ever.

> Backed like a lute-case,
> Bellied like a drum,
> Like Jack Anapes on horseback
> Sits little Robin Thumbe.

> Here lies little Crookback
> Who justly was reckoned
> Richard the Third and Judas the second,
> In life they agreed,
> But in death they did alter
> Great pity the pox prevented the halter.[3]

Francis Bacon had his own long personal history of frustration and envy, remembering cousin Robert's apparently easy rise to power and his own years as a disappointed aspirant for office. Bacon did family duty at Hatfield in June. Months later he published a short piece of writing 'On Deformity'. Everyone knew his target in the essay: the diarist and court watcher John Chamberlain wrote that 'the world takes notice that he [Bacon] paints out his late little cousin to the life'. In deformed persons, so Bacon explained, nature was seen to be twisted out of shape. Bold and ambitious, they saw the weakness in others, and suppressed emulators and rivals: to rulers they were officious, of everyone else envious. They were better spies and whisperers, Bacon wrote, than they were good ministers.[4]

Robert Cecil was hated because he had achieved power beyond his deserving: that was the notion. The caricature of the libels, and of

Francis Bacon's essay, articulated how very much distance there was between the minister who possessed unrivalled influence and the distortion of nature he was in his physical form – a crook-backed aberration, a bear's whelp, a fox or a monkey, a sexual deviant and adulterer, a persecutor, a tyrant; all familiar themes of political libels going back decades. Every charge possible was thrown at him. His enemies – and now there seemed to be so many of them – took to the extreme what Salisbury had himself admitted for form's sake in the preamble to his last will and testament: his honours and offices were 'things wherewith I was laden both beyond my merit and beyond my original desire'. And it wasn't simply the man who was loathed, but the whole Cecil establishment, their vested interests and accumulation of power over decades, the extraordinary ministerial authority of the 1st Lord Burghley, the raising up of Master Robert Cecil to a place in the monarch's government as his father's successor. Enemies and libellers hated the hypocrisy of power, especially when it came with supposedly ill-gotten riches; Salisbury, the benefactor of the poor of Hatfield, had for his own estate enclosed some common land, and even on the day of his funeral there were local protests.[5]

Ben Jonson in conversation in 1618 said that 'Salisbury never cared for any man longer nor he could make use of him'. Perhaps he was right; but perhaps Jonson could have said the same thing of most ministers and courtiers. The court, for all its flatteries and flutterings, was unforgiving, even brutal. To be called a friend was to receive a warning. To stand in the penetrating light of royal favour was to risk being burned to ash. In the same collection of essays as 'On Deformity', Francis Bacon published another short piece, 'Of Cunning', where, without names, he exposed one of his cousin's alleged sleights of hand in disposing of a rival for the principal secretaryship. According to Bacon, the two men had been on good terms and talked together about the challenges of politics in the last, declining years of a reign. One of them (we may identify him as Robert Cecil) said that to be the queen's secretary 'in the declination of a monarchy was a ticklish thing, and that he did not affect it'. The other man repeated this observation to his friends, probably suggesting that it was his own, only to find that his rival had already leaked that conversation to Elizabeth, 'who hearing of a declination of a monarchy took it so ill, as she would never after hear of the other's suit.' Cecil was untouched by the episode.[6]

This thwarted rival may have been the accomplished diplomat Thomas Bodley, who had returned from The Hague in 1596 in the hope of being appointed a secretary, at least eventually. In Salisbury's later years Bodley made his peace with Robert Cecil, with whom (along with the 1st Lord Burghley) he had been on good terms. But the earl of Essex's aggressive lobbying for Bodley had irritated Elizabeth, for every time Essex talked to her on Bodley's behalf he attacked Burghley. Salisbury later told Bodley that it had been impossible for the queen to promote a man pressed on her 'with such violence'. Something similar had happened with Francis Bacon over the office of solicitor general. This was the reality of court: the surface politeness, the deeper currents of ambition and suppressed animosity, the long processes of reconciliation, the grudging acceptance.[7]

What it was that drove Robert Cecil he kept to himself. Does Bacon's essay on deformity get closer than we might at first think? Bacon claimed that deficiency of nature stirred industry. Was this Robert Cecil's effort to prove his ability, his sheer energy in keeping going in spite of constitutional weakness and failing health, the drive that in Dover in the sharp cold February of 1588 had taken him up and down the steep stairs of the castle, which in the Low Countries had kept him on horseback for hours, which kept him at his desk for so many years, one step ahead of friends and rivals?

Undoubtedly Cecil possessed an adamantine core. Perhaps it was ruthlessness, or the passion to prove himself by serving, or to fulfil his parents' expectations – the obedient son, the obedient minister. And those expectations were as clear as they were inescapable: all other potential Robert Cecils contained within him were subordinated to the minister he was always going to become. He was fashioned – and disciplined himself – for that impossible task of achieving in perfect form what the monarch wanted and expected. It was all or nothing: 'if not worthy of trust', then the minister and servant was 'not worthy of life'. How he came to terms with all this we pick up in fragments of his letters and papers. He served and would always serve. He protected queen and king. He was honest in his dealings. He was like anyone else a son of Adam. And so, after so many years, so many events and compromises, blood and pain, those final days of self-reckoning, confession and prayer in Bath, that rawness of the soul which his chaplain heard and saw and set down on paper with all the familiar Christian conventionalities. Everything stripped down to the marble skeleton in Hatfield.

Life carried on; government continued. Salisbury seemed soon forgotten. Courtiers jostled for offices and preferments, as King James enjoyed new favourites and ministers: the Scot Robert Carr had established for himself a close relationship with the king from 1607 and rose in prominence as Viscount Rochester and earl of Somerset. Later there was the greatest of James's favourites, George Villiers, duke of Buckingham.

The Cecils of Hatfield House were after 1612 an established family, but William, 2nd earl of Salisbury never got to the political heights of his father and grandfather, and probably never wanted to. There were good reasons for curbing ambition. The age of the great minister was over: the Stuarts were not the Tudors, the seventeenth century was even more fractured and complex than the sixteenth, and kings' favourites now had a habit of finding their necks on the executioner's block. Will's closeness to James's heir, Prince Henry – a connection that was carefully cultivated by Robert Cecil – might have meant a future career at the court of King Henry IX of Great Britain and Ireland. But we'll never know: Henry died a few months after Robert Cecil, in November 1612.

The London poet Richard Johnson was unique in celebrating and commemorating Salisbury's life publicly. His *Remembrance of the Honours due to the Life and Death of Robert, Earl of Salisbury*, decorated on its title page with a woodcut of the familiar standardized face of Robert Cecil which gave so little away, was on sale in the city in 1612 at John Wright's bookshop. One slim pamphlet against scores of libels and slanders. But Johnson did his best.

Educated by his father, Burghley, from whom he sucked up the milk of deep understanding, Robert Cecil had possessed all the virtues, Johnson argued. By 'a secret instinct of nature', developed by practice, he had been trained for service. An enemy to parasites, whisperers, mutineers, he had swept them away like cobwebs. Self-ruled by reason and wisdom, moved by charity and compassion for the poor, he had protected the kingdom against its enemies, whatever the papist libellers said.[8]

One senses from Johnson's account of Salisbury's last words that the tears and reconciliations of his final days, as reported by John Bowle, had become public property. Johnson used them for sympathy: 'His departing gesture moved sad compassion, his words seasoned with deadly sighs, bathed the hearers' cheeks with distilling tears, making confession of his secret sins, calling for help of prayer . . . So yielding up the ghost, he left this world for a better.'[9]

Less public than Johnson's doomed effort to laud Robert Cecil was Sir Walter Cope's equally passionate paper defence of Salisbury's character and ministerial rectitude. That Cope had to work so hard at rescuing his late master from the total collapse of his reputation is itself eloquent. Cope went into detail, especially on his management of the Crown finances as lord treasurer. But he began with the man, a decade or so younger than himself, he had served: experienced, wise, mild in his manner, full of integrity, possessed of deep powers of penetration and perception, praised by everyone during his life, now denounced posthumously for supposed failings and corruptions which Cope strenuously denied.

Walter Cope said that he had to tell the truth: like an honest servant he would give the facts. 'I held it base to flatter him in his life: I will not now begin to flatter him in his grave. To offer such incense to the dead I account the basest kind of sacrifice.'[10]

Notes

ABBREVIATIONS

Bacon, *Early writings*	Francis Bacon, *Early writings, 1584–1596*, ed. Alan Stewart and Harriet Knight, The Oxford Francis Bacon vol. i (Oxford, 2012).
Bacon, *Essays*	Francis Bacon, *The essayes or counsels, civill and morall*, ed. Michael Kiernan, The Oxford Francis Bacon vol. xv (Oxford, 2000).
Bacon, *Letters*	*The Letters and Life of Francis Bacon*, ed. James Spedding, 2 vols. (London, 1861–2).
Birch	Thomas Birch, *Memoirs of the reign of Queen Elizabeth from the year 1581 till her death from the original papers of . . . Anthony Bacon*, 2 vols. (London, 1754).
BL	British Library, London, Western Manuscripts.
	Add. Additional
	Cott. Cotton
	Harl. Harley
	Lans. Lansdowne
	Yelv. Yelverton
Bruce, *Correspondence*	*Correspondence of King James VI of Scotland with Sir Robert Cecil and others*

	in England, ed. John Bruce, Camden Society, 1st ser. 78 (Westminster, 1861).
Burghley letters	*The letters of Lord Burghley, William Cecil, to his son Sir Robert Cecil, 1593–1608*, ed. William Acres, Camden Society, 5th ser. 53 (Cambridge, 2017).
Cecil letters	*Letters from Sir Robert Cecil to Sir George Carew*, ed. J. Maclean, Camden Society, 1st ser. 88 (Westminster, 1864).
Chamberlain letters	*The letters of John Chamberlain*, ed. N. E. McClure, 2 vols. (Philadelphia, 1939).
CP	Cecil Papers, Maps and Petitions, Hatfield House Archives, Hertfordshire.
CUL	Cambridge University Library.
Devereux	W. B. Devereux, *Lives and Letters of the Devereux, Earls of Essex . . . 1540–1646*, 2 vols. (London, 1853).
E 351/541–543	National Archives, Kew, London, Declared Accounts (Pipe Office), Chamber Accounts.
Elizabeth I, *Compositions*	*Elizabeth I: Autograph Compositions and Foreign Language Originals*, ed. Janel Mueller and Leah S. Marcus (Chicago, 2003).
Elizabeth I, *Works*	*Elizabeth I: The Collected Works*, ed. Leah S. Marcus, Janel Mueller and Mary Beth Rose (Chicago, 2000).
Hartley	*Proceedings in the Parliaments of Elizabeth I*, ed. T. E. Hartley, 3 vols. (Leicester, 1981–95).
Hughes and Larkin	*Tudor Royal Proclamations*, ed. Paul L. Hughes and James F. Larkin, 3 vols. (New Haven, CT, and London, 1964–9).
James VI and I, *Letters*	*Letters of King James VI and I*, ed. G. P. V. Akrigg (Berkeley and Los Angeles, 1984).
Jonson, *Works*	*The Cambridge Edition of the Works of Ben Jonson*, ed. David Bevington, Martin

	Butler and Ian Donaldson, 7 vols. (Cambridge, 2012).
Munck	Howard Vallance, 'The journal of Levinus Munck', *English Historical Review*, 68 (1953), 234–58.
Murdin	William Murdin, *A collection of state papers ... from the year 1571 to 1596* (London, 1759).
Nichols	*John Nichols's* The Progresses and Public Processions of Queen Elizabeth I: *A New Edition of the Early Modern Sources*, ed. Elizabeth Goldring, Faith Eales, Elizabeth Clarke and Jayne Elisabeth Archer, 5 vols. (Oxford, 2014).
ODNB	*Oxford Dictionary of National Biography*, ed. H. C. G. Matthew and Brian Harrison, 60 vols. (Oxford, 2004). See also, for updated biographies, www.oxforddnb.com.
PC 2	National Archives, Kew, London, Privy Council Office, Registers.
PROB 11	National Archives, Kew, London, Prerogative Court of Canterbury and related Probate Jurisdictions: Will Registers.
Salisbury MSS	Historical Manuscripts Commission, *Calendar of the Manuscripts of ... the Marquis of Salisbury*, 24 vols. (London, 1883–1976).
Sidney papers	*Letters and memorials of state ... written and collected by Sir Henry Sydney ... Sir Philip Sydney and his brother Sir Robert Sydney*, ed. Arthur Collins, 2 vols. (London, 1746).
SP	National Archives, Kew, London, State Paper Office.
	12 Domestic, Elizabeth I
	14 Domestic, James I

15   Domestic, Addenda
46   Domestic, Supplementary
52   Scotland, Elizabeth I
53   Mary, Queen of Scots
63   Ireland
70   Foreign, Elizabeth I
75   Denmark
77   Flanders (from 1585)
78   France
83   Holland and Flanders (1577–84)
84   Holland
94   Spain
101 News Letters
106 Ciphers

STC   A. W. Pollard and G. R. Redgrave, *A Short-title Catalogue of Books Printed in England, Scotland, and Ireland and of English Books Printed Abroad, 1475–1640*, ed. W. A. Jackson, F. S. Ferguson and Katharine F. Pantzer, Bibliographical Society, 3 vols. (2nd edn, London, 1986–91). See also the British Library's online English Short Title Catalogue.

Winwood memorials   *Memorials of affairs of state ... from the original papers of ... Sir Ralph Winwood*, ed. Edmund Sawyer, 3 vols. (London, 1725).

TO THE READER

1. Justus Lipsius, *Sixe bookes of politickes or civil doctrine*, trans. William Jones (London, 1594; STC 15701), 56 (sig. G4v).
2. Conyers Read, *Mr Secretary Walsingham and the Policy of Queen Elizabeth*, 3 vols. (Oxford, 1925), i. 437–8.
3. Sir Thomas Smith, *De republica Anglorum*, ed. Mary Dewar (Cambridge, 1982), 78–9.
4. Sir John Harington, *A tract on the succession to the crown*, ed. Clements R. Markham, Roxburghe Club (London, 1880), x–xi.

5. The quotation from Lord Burghley is SP 83/23, no. 28.

PRELUDE

1. Carl van de Velde, *Frans Floris (1519/20–1570): leven en werken*, 2 vols. (Brussels, 1975), i. 209–13; ii. pl. no. 26.
2. *A true report of the yeelding up of the cittie of Antwarpe, unto the Prince of Parma* (Amsterdam, [1585?]; STC 693.3) sig. A1v; Daniel Vervliet, *Articulen, Ende conditien vanden tractate, aenghegaen ende ghesloten tusschen de hoocheyde vanden Prince van Parma* (Antwerp, 1585); John Windet, *An historicall discourse, or rather a tragicall historie of the citie of Antwerpe* (London, 1586; STC 691), sigs. F3–G1v.
3. SP 77/2, f. 240r.
4. SP 77/3, f. 42r; Richard C. Barnett, *Place, Profit, and Power: A Study of the Servants of William Cecil, Elizabethan Statesman* (Chapel Hill, NC, 1969), 89–91.
5. SP 12/208, no. 69; BL, Lans. MS 55, f. 118r.
6. SP 15/30, no. 80.
7. SP 15/30, no. 83; SP 77/2, f. 136r; SP 84/21, f. 243r.
8. SP 84/21, f. 243r; BL, Lans. MS 107, f. 74r.
9. SP 77/2, f. 156r; SP 77/2, f. 209r; BL, Lans. MS 107, f. 74r.
10. SP 106/1, f. 49r–v.
11. SP 77/2, ff. 227v–228v; SP 77/2, f. 281r.
12. SP 77/2, ff. 240r–241r; SP 77/3, f. 76r; Sir Roger Williams, *The Actions of the Low Countries*, ed. D. W. Davies (Ithaca, NY, 1964), 156.
13. SP 77/2, f. 347r–v.
14. SP 77/2, ff. 297r–298v; SP 77/2, ff. 335r–336r.
15. SP 77/3, f. 42r; *Advice to a Son: Precepts of Lord Burghley, Sir Walter Raleigh, and Francis Osborne*, ed. Louis B. Wright (Ithaca, NY, 1962), 6.
16. SP 77/3, ff. 74r, 94r.
17. SP 77/3, ff. 109r, 111r, 134r, 184r, quotation at f. 107v.
18. SP 77/2, f. 347v.
19. SP 77/2, f. 298v.

I. TREES OF PARADISE

1. BL, Lans. MS 6, f. 131r; Psalm 127:4 (Greek numbering) or Psalm 128:4 (Hebrew numbering), with the quoted English translation taken from

the Geneva Bible, 1560. Lord Burghley made a short record of Robert's birth on 'primo Junii' 1563 in a note of family events he compiled *c.*1594, CP 140/13 (*Salisbury MSS*, v. 69).

2. *ODNB*, x. 746; 'Public Baptism' from the Book of Common Prayer (London, 1559; STC 16293.3), sigs. R2v, R4v.

3. CUL, MS Ee.3.56, no. 138; *Burghley letters*, 293.

4. BL, Lans. MS 102 f. 89r–v; BL, Add. MS 33591, f. 102r.

5. CUL, MS Ee.3.56, no. 85; *Burghley letters*, 218; SP 63/25, no. 63.

6. *Advice to a Son: Precepts of Lord Burghley, Sir Walter Raleigh, and Francis Osborne*, ed. Louis B. Wright (Ithaca, NY, 1962), 3; SP 12/51, no. 6.

7. SP 12/51, no. 6.

8. Revelation 18:2 (Geneva Bible, 1560); George Gifford, *Sermons upon the whole booke of the Revelation* (London, 1596; STC 11866).

9. BL, Add. MS 32091, f. 199v.

10. BL, Cott. MS Vespasian C.viii, f. 14r.

11. CUL, MS Ee.3.56; no. 85; *Burghley letters*, 218.

12. BL, Lans. MS 102, ff. 55v–56r, 136r.

13. *Advice to a Son*, ed. Wright, 9. The two early Elizabethan portraits of Mildred Cecil, both attributed to Hans Eworth (d. 1574) and both at Hatfield House, Hertfordshire, are reproduced as pl. II and pl. IV in *Patronage, Culture and Power: The Early Cecils, 1558–1612*, ed. Pauline Croft (New Haven, CT, and London, 2002), in which book see also 286–8.

14. Lisa Jardine and Alan Stewart, *Hostage to Fortune: The Troubled Life of Francis Bacon, 1561–1626* (London, 1998), 35–7.

15. Philip Gaskell, 'Books bought by Whitgift's pupils in the 1570s', *Transactions of the Cambridge Bibliographical Society*, 7 (1977–80), 284–93; David McKitterick, *A History of Cambridge University Press: Printing and the Book Trade in Cambridge, 1534–1698* (Cambridge, 1992), 69–70.

16. SP 78/3, no. 14; Jardine and Stewart, *Hostage to Fortune*, 39–66.

17. *Patronage, Culture and Power*, ed. Croft, 295.

18. CP 226/1 (28 Feb. 1577).

19. SP 12/103, no. 26.

20. BL, Harl. MS 6992, ff. 52r, 54r–v; Murdin, 301–2; Devereux, i. 141–2, 144.

21. BL, Lans. MS 23, f. 190r; BL, Lans. MS 22, f. 200r; Devereux, i. 166.

22. BL, Lans. MS 25 f. 96r; CP 226/1.

23. BL, Harl. MS 6992, f. 52r; Murdin, 301–2; Devereux, i. 144.

24. CP 226/1 (3 and 10 May 1577); BL, Lans. MS 25, ff. 52r, 102r.
25. BL, Lans. MS 25, f. 40r.
26. Henry Lok, *Ecclesiastes, otherwise called the preacher* (London, 1597; STC 6696), sig. X1v.
27. SP 12/262, no. 23.
28. Epistle to Robert, earl of Essex by Edward Waterhouse in Richard Davies, *A funerall sermon preached . . . at the buriall of the right honourable Walter Earle of Essex and Ewe* (London, 1577; STC 6364).

2. THE AMBASSADORS' MEN

1. SP 78/2, no. 23.
2. SP 78/2, nos. 53, 54.
3. SP 70/143, ff. 106r–107r; CP 226/1.
4. BL, Cott. MS Vespasian F.vi, ff. 148r, 149r; SP 78/2, nos. 24, 27.
5. SP 78/2, no. 54.
6. SP 83/7, no. 39; J. M. B. C. Baron Kervyn de Lettenhove and L. Gilliodts van Severen, *Relations politiques des Pays-Bas et de l'Angleterre sous le règne de Philippe II*, 11 vols. (Brussels, 1882–1900), x. 524–5, 545–6.
7. PROB 11/77/101; SP 53/18, no. 75.
8. *Grace Book Δ: Containing the Records of the University of Cambridge for the Years 1542–1589*, ed. John Venn (Cambridge, 1910), 270, 299–301.
9. *Copy-book of Sir Amias Poulet's letters, written during his embassy to France (AD 1577)*, ed. Octavius Ogle, Roxburghe Club (London, 1866), 252.
10. *Copy-book of Sir Amias Poulet's letters*, 55, 108, 181, 261.
11. *The Register of Admissions of Gray's Inn, 1521–1889*, ed. Joseph Foster (London, 1889), 42; BL, Lans. MS 18, f. 170r; BL, Lans. MS 21, f. 27r; BL, Lans. MS 23, f. 172r; SP 70/139, f. 64; SP 70/139; f. 75.
12. SP 70/142, f. 20r.
13. SP 70/143, ff. 47r, 107r; *Copy-book of Sir Amias Poulet's letters*, 224.
14. SP 78/4A, no. 59; E 351/542 (25 Apr. 1580); SP 78/4A, nos. 85, 86, 88.
15. CP 11/101; Murdin, 353; SP 94/1, ff. 201r–206v, 216r–219r, 224r–225v; SP 94/1, ff. 216r–219r.
16. SP 53/11, nos. 50 and 50.1; SP 78/6, no. 26.
17. SP 75/1, ff. 49r–51r; Jacqueline D. Vaughan, 'Secretaries, Statesmen and Spies: The Clerks of the Tudor Privy Council, *c*.1540–*c*.1603', PhD dissertation, University of St Andrews (2007), 38; BL, Add. MS 48018 (Yelv. MS 19), f. 4r.

18. SP 15/27A, no. 99; SP 78/7, no. 141.
19. SP 15/28, no. 8.
20. SP 78/9, no. 101.
21. SP 78/9, no. 105; E 351/542 (20 May 1583).
22. SP 78/4A, no. 63.
23. SP 78/5, no. 33.
24. SP 78/2, no. 70.

3. GATHERING FRUIT

1. SP 12/149, no. 65.
2. *Grace Book Δ: Containing the Records of the University of Cambridge for the Years 1542–1589*, ed. John Venn (Cambridge, 1910), 339–40; Paul E. J. Hammer, *The Polarisation of Elizabethan Politics: The Political Career of Robert Devereux, 2nd Earl of Essex, 1585–1597* (Cambridge, 1999), 30; BL, Lans. MS 36, f. 37r; Devereux, i. 171.
3. Thomas Baker, *History of the College of St John the Evangelist, Cambridge*, ed. John E. B. Mayor, 2 vols. (Cambridge, 1869), ii. 414–16; Richard Rex, 'The sixteenth century', in *St John's College Cambridge: A History*, ed. Peter Linehan (Woodbridge, 2011), 83–4; SP 12/149, no. 65.
4. CP 162/84; *Alumni Cantabrigiensis*, ed. John Venn and J. A. Venn, 10 vols. (Cambridge, 1922–54), pt. 1 (to 1751), iv. 412; *Grace Book Δ*, 278, 308; Fred B. Tromly, 'Lord Burghley's "Ten Precepts" for his son, Robert Cecil: a new date and interpretation', *Historical Research*, 88 (2015), 187–8.
5. Gervase Babington, *A very fruitfull exposition of the commaundements by way of questions and answeres* (London, 1583; STC 1095), 182 (sig. M3v).
6. *The execution of justice in England for maintenance of publique and Christian peace* (London, 1584; STC 4903), sig. E2r.
7. Christopher Haigh, *Reformation and Resistance in Tudor Lancashire* (Cambridge, 1975), 248, 250–51, 260–61; PC 2/13, p. 512; Francis Peck, *Desiderata curiosa*, 2 vols. (London, 1779), i. 134; SP 12/167, no. 40; *Records of the English Province of the Society of Jesus* [ed. Henry Foley] (Roehampton, 1875), 135–6.
8. SP 12/168, no. 28.
9. *Il Perfetto Scrittore di M. Gio. Francesco Cresci Cittadino Melanese* (Rome, 1570); Alfred Fairbank and Berthold Wolpe, *Renaissance Handwriting: An Anthology of Italic Scripts* (London, 1960), 27, 95, pl. 86.

10. SP 12/169, no. 8; Peck, *Desiderata curiosa*, i. 147.
11. SP 78/10, no. 58; BL, Lans. MS 104, f. 168r; SP 15/28, no. 37.
12. SP 52/35, no. 9.
13. SP 52/35, no. 42; SP 78/12, f. 57r.
14. SP 78/12, no. 28.
15. SP 78/12, no. 28.
16. SP 78/12, no. 48; SP 78/12, nos. 39, 42.
17. SP 12/172, no. 118.
18. SP 78/10, no. 58.
19. SP 12/172, no. 118.
20. SP 78/12, no. 72.
21. *Foreign Intelligence and Information in Elizabethan England: Two English Treatises on the State of France, 1580–1584*, ed. David Potter, Camden Society, 5th ser. 25 (Cambridge, 2004), 4–8, 169–97.
22. BL, Cott. MS Galba E.vi, ff. 263r–265v.
23. BL, Lans. MS 107, f. 76r–v; SP 78/12, no. 105.
24. CP 13/63.
25. Hartley, ii. 158.
26. BL, Lans. MS 43, f. 118r.
27. SP 12/177, no. 4; Christopher Barker, *A true and plaine declaration of the horrible treasons, practised by William Parry the traitor, against the Queenes Majestie* (London, [1585]; STC 19342).

4. R. C.

1. *A true, sincere and modest defence, of English Catholiques* ([Rouen, 1584]; STC 373), title page: Psalm 49:19 (Greek numbering, Vulgate) and 50:19 (Hebrew numbering). Richard Topcliffe's copy of Allen's *Defence* now in CUL (shelf-mark F*.14.24(E)) has the following note on the title page: 'To be read and used for the service of God, Queen Eliz[abeth] and the peace of England and for no other cause or purpose.' See Mark Rankin, 'Richard Topcliffe and the book culture of the Elizabethan underground', *Renaissance Quarterly*, 72 (2019), 499–501, 532.
2. SP 78/12, no. 105.
3. SP 53/14, no. 3.
4. SP 53/14, no. 7.
5. BL, Lans. MS 51, f. 9r; Bacon, *Letters*, i. 59–60.
6. BL, Lans. MS 50, ff. 49r, 50v.
7. SP 12/194, no. 60.

8. BL, Cott. MS Caligula C.ix, f. 693r; BL, Add. MS 48027 (Yelv. MS 31), f. 554r.

9. BL, Cott. MS Caligula C.ix, ff. 702r–707r.

10. SP 12/194, no. 40.

11. Hartley, ii. 232.

12. *The copie of a letter to the right honourable the Earle of Leycester* (London, 1586; STC 6052), 11 (sig. B4v).

13. BL, Lans. MS 94, f. 85r; *Copie of a letter*, 16 (sig. C3).

14. BL, Lans. MS 94, ff. 84r–85r (12 Nov. 1586), 86r–88r (response to deputation of 24 Nov. 1586); Elizabeth I, *Compositions*, 67–78; Hartley, ii. 248–61, 266–71.

15. BL, Add. MS 48027 (Yelv. MS 31), f. 484r; SP 84/11, f. 139r–v.

16. *Copie of a letter*, 12 (sig. C1); 'An act for provision to be made for the surety of the Queen's Majesty's most royal person and the continuance of the realm in peace' (27 Eliz. I c. 1), House of Lords Record Office, Parliamentary Archives, London, HL/PO/PU/1/1584/27E1N1, printed by Christopher Barker in *At the parliament begunne and holden at Westminster, the xxiii. day of November, in the xxvii. yeere of the reigne of . . . Elizabeth . . . and there continued, untill the xxix. of March following* (London, 1585; STC 9485), sigs. A2r–A3v.

17. *Copie of a letter*, 29 (sig. E1v).

18. BL, Cott. MS Galba C.x, ff. 19r–20r.

19. *Copie of a letter*, 1 (sig. A3r).

20. *Copie of a letter*, 2 (sig. A3v).

21. BL, Cott. MS Caligula C.ix, f. 616r.

22. SP 78/17, ff. 12r–13r; PC 2/14, p. 247.

23. BL, Add. MS 48027, f. 636r.

24. CP 165/57; BL, Lans. MS 102, f. 10r–v.

25. SP 12/200, no. 20.

26. CP 15/111.

27. Folger Shakespeare Library, Washington DC, MS L.a.39; CP 165/94.

5. ENEMIES AND FRIENDS

1. SP 77/2, no. 86.

2. SP 77/2, f. 347v; BL, Harl. MS 290, ff. 216r–217r.

3. SP 77/3, f. 42r–v.

4. SP 77/2, f. 347v.

5. *Admonition to the nobility and people of England and Ireland* ([Antwerp], 1588; STC 368), esp. pp. lix–lx (sig. D6r–v).

6. SP 12/211, no. 56; Hughes and Larkin, iii. 13–17.

7. Geoffrey Parker, *The Grand Strategy of Philip II* (New Haven, CT, and London, 1998), 200–201.

8. SP 12/213, nos. 68, 86.

9. Historical Manuscripts Commission, *The Manuscripts of . . . the Duke of Rutland*, 4 vols. (London, 1888–1905), i. 253–4.

10. *Manuscripts of . . . the Duke of Rutland*, i. 255.

11. SP 12/213, no. 64.

12. SP 12/213, no. 66.

13. SP 77/4, f. 285r.

14. BL, Lans. MS 57, f. 106r.

15. BL, Lans. MS 107, f. 65r; Miles Coverdale, *Certain most godly, fruitful, and comfortable letters of such true Saintes and holy Martyrs of God* (London, 1564; STC 5886), sig. A2v.

16. BL, Lans. MS 58, f. 89r.

17. BL, Lans. MS 103, f. 167r; Stephen Alford, *Burghley: William Cecil at the Court of Elizabeth I* (New Haven, CT, and London, 2008), 309; *Advice to a Son: Precepts of Lord Burghley, Sir Walter Raleigh, and Francis Osborne*, ed. Louis B. Wright (Ithaca, NY, 1962), 9.

18. SP 12/208, no. 69.

19. CP 18/74; BL, Lans. MS 103, f. 167r.

20. Pauline Croft, 'Mildred, Lady Burghley: the matriarch', in *Patronage, Culture and Power: The Early Cecils, 1558–1612*, ed. Pauline Croft (New Haven, CT, and London, 2002), 294–6; see also Alford, *Burghley*, 310.

21. On Pymmes see *Salisbury MSS*, xxiii. 2, 102; CP Maps Supplementary 27.

22. SP 77/3, f. 126r.

23. CP 91/85.

24. BL, Lans. MS 107, f. 66r.

6. HERMIT, GARDENER, MOLECATCHER

1. PC 2/17 p. 589.

2. Quotation at BL, Lans. MS 102, f. 55r.

3. Privy seals for payments from Michaelmas 1588 to March 1591, CP 223/4.

4. E 351/542 (20 Oct. 1590). On James see *The House of Commons, 1558–1603*, ed. P. W. Hasler, History of Parliament Trust, 3 vols. (London, 1981), ii. 374; and Richard Hakluyt, *The principall*

navigations, voiages and discoveries of the English nation, ed. D. B. Quinn and R. A. Skelton, Hakluyt Society, extra ser. 39, 2 vols. (Cambridge, 1965), i. xx–xxi.

5. BL, Lans. MS 68, f. 16r; Conyers Read, *Mr Secretary Walsingham and the Policy of Queen Elizabeth*, 3 vols. (Oxford, 1925), i. 428.

6. SP 12/233, no. 109.

7. BL, Cott. MS Vespasian C.viii, f. 288r.

8. BL, Harl. MS 290, ff. 240r, 244r.

9. Paul E. J. Hammer, 'Letters from Sir Robert Cecil to Sir Christopher Hatton, 1590–1591' in *Religion, Politics, and Society in Sixteenth-century England*, ed. Ian W. Archer, Camden Society, 5th ser. 22 (Cambridge, 2003), 222–3.

10. Edmund Lodge, *Illustrations of British History*, 3 vols. (London, 1838), ii. 426–7.

11. BL, Lans. MS 107, f. 81r.

12. Hammer, 'Letters from Sir Robert Cecil', 223; Justus Lipsius, *Sixe bookes of politickes or civil doctrine*, trans. William Jones (London, 1594; STC 15701), 56–7.

13. Hammer, 'Letters from Sir Robert Cecil', 224.

14. BL, Lans. MS 107, f. 83r.

15. BL, Lans. MS 66, f. 186r.

16. CP 140/15v; *Salisbury MSS*, v. 71.

17. Hammer, 'Letters from Sir Robert Cecil', 224–6.

18. SP 12/181, no. 42 (f. 159r).

19. CP 143/65.

20. *Salisbury MSS*, v. 70; E. K. Chambers, *The Elizabethan Stage*, 4 vols. (Oxford, 1951 edn), iv. 81; CP 140/33.

21. BL, Lans. MS 31, ff. 116r–v, 118r–121v; *Documents Relating to the Office of Revels in the Time of Queen Elizabeth*, ed. Albert Feuillerat (Louvain, 1908), 345.

22. Nichols, iii. 530–34.

23. Nichols, iii. 540–41.

24. *Sidney papers*, i. 326; Nichols, iii. 539.

7. SPIES

1. PROB 11/75/375; PROB 11/77/101.

2. SP 53/21, no. 26; SP 12/199, no. 86.

3. SP 15/31, nos. 131, 149.

4. SP 12/238, no. 158.

5. E 351/542 (21 May 1591); Stephen Alford, *The Watchers: A Secret History of the Reign of Elizabeth I* (London, 2012), 271–84, 360.
6. Mitchell Leimon and Geoffrey Parker, 'Treason and plot in Elizabethan diplomacy: the "Fame of Sir Edward Stafford" reconsidered', *English Historical Review*, 111 (1996), 1143; CP 167/118.
7. SP 12/238, no. 155.
8. SP 12/238, no. 185.
9. E 351/542 (27 May 1591).
10. SP 12/239, nos. 3, 4; see also CP 168/25.
11. SP 12/239, no. 4.
12. SP 52/47, no. 74.
13. BL, Cott. MS Titus B.vi, f. 34r–v; SP 12/239, nos. 37–9, 57, 57.1, 60; Murdin, 796.
14. SP 12/239, no. 46.
15. SP 12/239, nos. 78, 87.
16. BL, Lans. MS 102, ff. 200r–203v; SP 78/25, ff. 70r–73v; PC 2/18, p. 390.
17. BL, Lans. MS 68, f. 216r.
18. Murdin, 797; BL, Cott. MS Titus B.vi, f. 34r; SP 78/25, f. 121r; *Correspondence of Sir Henry Unton*, ed. Joseph Stevenson, Roxburghe Club (London, 1847), 21–2.
19. BL, Cott. MS Caligula E.viii, f. 310r; *Correspondence of Sir Henry Unton*, ed. Stevenson, 19.
20. SP 78/25, f. 107r.
21. PC 2/18, pp. 471–2.
22. CP 20/9; BL, Cott. MS Caligula E.viii, ff. 128r–129v.

8. PROGRESS

1. Paul E. J. Hammer, 'Letters from Sir Robert Cecil to Sir Christopher Hatton, 1590–1591' in *Religion, Politics, and Society in Sixteenth-century England*, ed. Ian W. Archer, Camden Society, 5th ser. 22 (Cambridge, 2003), 228–30.
2. PC 2/19, p. 1A.
3. SP 78/25, f. 182r; Devereux, i. 223; BL, Cott. MS Caligula E.viii, f. 312r; *Correspondence of Sir Henry Unton*, ed. Joseph Stevenson, Roxburghe Club (London, 1847), 26.
4. Hammer, 'Letters from Sir Robert Cecil', 228–30; BL, Lans. MS 68, f. 220r.
5. BL, Cott. MS Titus C.vii, f. 16r.

6. E 351/542 (6 Aug. 1591); SP 12/239, no. 128.

7. SP 12/239, no. 128.

8. SP 12/239, nos. 148, 153.

9. *The honorable entertainment given to the Queenes Majestie at Cowdrey in Sussex, by Lord Montecute* ([London,] 1591; STC 3907.5), 2–3, 9; Curtis C. Breight, 'Caressing the great: Viscount Montague's entertainment of Elizabeth at Cowdray, 1591', *Sussex Archaeological Collections*, 127 (1989), 160–62.

10. *Correspondence of Sir Henry Unton*, ed. Stevenson, 35–9, 43; BL, Cott. MS Titus B.vi, f. 34v; SP 78/25, f. 346r; Hammer, 'Letters from Sir Robert Cecil', 230.

11. *Correspondence of Sir Henry Unton*, ed. Stevenson, 31–4, 44–5; BL, Cott. MS Caligula E.viii, f. 126r.

12. Hammer, 'Letters from Sir Robert Cecil', 232; BL, Cott. MS Caligula E.viii, f. 126r; Historical Manuscripts Commission, *Calendar of the Manuscripts of the Marquis of Bath*, 3 vols. (London, 1904–8), ii. 37; BL, Lans. MS 68, f. 202r.

13. Hammer, 'Letters from Sir Robert Cecil', 236–7.

14. CP 286, unfoliated.

15. Gary A. Remer, *Ethics and the Orator: The Ciceronian Tradition of Political Morality* (Chicago and London, 2017), 111; John-Mark Philo, 'Elizabeth I's translation of Tacitus: Lambeth Palace Library, MS 683', *Review of English Studies*, new ser. 71 (2019), 46. See also Elizabeth I, *Compositions*, 1–15; and Elizabeth I, *Works*, xviii–xxxii.

16. *The Ende of Nero and Beginning of Galba. Fower Bookes of the Histories of Cornelius Tacitus*, trans. Henry Savile (London, 1591; STC 23642), sig. ¶2r–v; Murdin, 786; CP 139/194–203; Mordechai Feingold, 'Scholarship and politics: Henry Savile's *Tacitus* and the Essex connection', *Review of English Studies*, new ser. 67 (2016), 855–74.

17. CP 139/203v.

18. CP 168/41; Hammer, 'Letters from Sir Robert Cecil', 244–6.

19. Hammer, 'Letters from Sir Robert Cecil', 247.

20. BL, Cott. MS Caligula E.viii, ff. 116r–17v; Hammer, 'Letters from Sir Robert Cecil', 263–4.

21. SP 84/43, f. 86r.

22. CP 20/52–3; CP 20/44.

23. *Correspondence of Sir Henry Unton*, ed. Stevenson, 142; SP 78/26, f. 7r.

24. *Correspondence of Sir Henry Unton*, ed. Stevenson, 145–6; PC 2/19, p. 50.

25. *Correspondence of Sir Henry Unton*, ed. Stevenson, 178.

26. CP 20/88; E 351/542 (24 Nov. 1591).

27. CP 20/99, 100; Murdin, 650; Sir Thomas Coningsby, 'Journal of the siege of Rouen, 1591', ed. J. G. Nichols, Camden Society, *Miscellany* i (London, 1847), 64.

28. SP 78/26, f. 337r; Devereux, i. 272.

9. FOX AND CUB

1. CP 203/124; *Salisbury MSS*, xiii. 456–7.

2. CP 20/38.

3. SP 12/241, no. 109.

4. STC 8207 (Richmond Palace, 18 Oct. 1591); Hughes and Larkin, iii. 86–93, quotation at 90; for the warrant for the commissions drafted by Burghley for Lord Chancellor Hatton, 17 Oct. 1591, see CP 20/57.

5. *A declaration of the true causes of the great troubles, presupposed to be intended against the realme of England* (Antwerp, 1592; STC 10005); CP 142/130–45.

6. *True causes*, 72–3 (sigs. E4r–E5r).

7. SP 78/36, f. 181r; *A Spaniard in Elizabethan England: The Correspondence of Antonio Pérez's Exile*, ed. Gustav Ungerer, 2 vols. (London, 1974–6), i. no. 219; Catherine Loomis, '"Little man, little man": early modern representations of Robert Cecil', *Explorations in Renaissance Culture*, 37 (2011), 137–56.

8. *True causes*, 51 (sig. D2r).

9. CP 21/49; *True causes*, 55–6 (sig. D4r–v); *The Letters and Despatches of Richard Verstegan*, ed. Anthony G. Petti, Catholic Record Society, 52 (London, 1959), 39–40.

10. CP 21/33. See also SP 12/242, no. 25.

11. Sept. 1592 in STC 444.9, the second of four almanacs used by Lord Burghley (John Securis, 1581, STC 512.11; Gabriel Frende, 1592, STC 444.9; John Dade, 1594, STC 434.5; and Gabriel Frende, 1594, STC 444.11) bound in a single unfoliated volume, CP 333.

12. *The sea-mans triumph. Declaring the honorable actions of such ... as were at the takinge of the great Carrick, lately brought to Dartmouth* (London, 1592; STC 22140), quotation at sig. C1v.

13. CP 21/58; Edward Edwards, *The Life of Sir Walter Ralegh ... Together with his Letters*, 2 vols. (Cambridge, 1868), ii. 51–2.

14. Edwards, *Sir Walter Ralegh*, ii. 63.

15. CP 168/136; SP 12/243, no. 14; PC 2/20, p. 36.

16. SP 12/143, no. 16.

17. SP 12/243, no. 17.

18. CP Petitions 2237.
19. CP 98/62.
20. Edwards, *Sir Walter Ralegh*, ii. 72.
21. PC 2/20, p. 65 (10 Oct. 1592); STC 8223, printed in Hughes and Larkin, iii. 111–12 (12 Oct. 1592); Oct. and Nov. 1592 in STC 444.9, CP 333, unfoliated.
22. SP 12/244, nos. 35, 75.
23. CP 21/81; BL, Lans. MS 115, f. 233r.
24. CP 21/81.

10. THE BEAR'S WHELP

1. *St Martin-in-the-Fields: The Accounts of the Churchwardens, 1525–1603*, ed. John V. Kitto (London, 1901), 451.
2. Hartley, iii. 14–22, 62–4, quotation at p. 62; SP 12/242, no. 25.
3. BL, Lans. MS 73, ff. 2r–3r; BL, Lans. MS 104, ff. 78r–82v; Hartley, iii. 11–13, 23–7, quotation at 24.
4. Hartley, iii. 71.
5. Hartley, iii. 71–3.
6. PC 2/20, p. 248.
7. Folger Shakespeare Library, Washington DC, MS L.a.45; Paul E. J. Hammer, *The Polarisation of Elizabethan Politics: The Political Career of Robert Devereux, 2nd Earl of Essex, 1585–1597* (Cambridge, 1999), 31 and n. 107.
8. *The House of Commons, 1558–1603*, ed. P. W. Hasler, History of Parliament Trust, 3 vols. (London, 1981), i. 572.
9. Hartley, iii. 104–10, quotation at 107; Pliny the Elder, *Natural History*, ed. Henry Rackham *et al.*, 9 vols. (London and Cambridge, MA, 1938–62), iii. 90–91; H. W. Seager, *Natural History in Shakespeare's Time* (London, 1896), 29.
10. *A declaration of the true causes of the great troubles, presupposed to be intended against the realme of England* (Antwerp 1592; STC 10005), 71 (sig. E4r).
11. *The Letters and Despatches of Richard Verstegan*, ed. Anthony G. Petti, Catholic Record Society, 52 (London, 1959), 126.
12. CUL, MS Ee.3.56, nos. 2, 3; *Burghley letters*, 91–2; CP 22/96; *Letters and Despatches of Richard Verstegan*, ed. Petti, 115.
13. CUL, MS Ee.3.56, no. 5; *Burghley letters*, 94.
14. CP 19/91.
15. CP 19/54.

16. CP 143/70–72.
17. Curtis C. Breight, 'Entertainments of Elizabeth at Theobalds in the early 1590s', *Records of Early English Drama*, 12 (1987), 7–8.
18. SP 52/52, for Oct. 1593 to June 1597.
19. CP 133/109.
20. *The Consolation of Queen Elizabeth I: The Queen's Translation of Boethius's* De Consolatione Philosophiae, ed. Noel Harold Kaylor, Jr., and Philip Edward Phillips (Tempe, AZ, 2009), 146–7.
21. CUL, MS Ee.3.56, no. 10; *Burghley letters*, 102.

11. DESPERATE TREASON

1. SP 12/246, nos. 39 and 39.i–iii; SP 12/246, no. 45.
2. SP 12/247, no. 13; SP 12/248, no. 20.i; E 351/542 (14 Jan. 1594).
3. BL, Add. MS 48029 (Yelv. MS 33), f. 148r–v; CP 170/1; SP 12/247, no. 13.
4. SP 12/247, no. 19
5. Birch, i. 147; SP 15/33, no. 5; SP 52/52, f. 25r; CUL, Ee.3.56, no. 15; *Burghley letters*, 114–17, quotation at 117; see also Paul E. J. Hammer, *The Polarisation of Elizabethan Politics: The Political Career of Robert Devereux, 2nd Earl of Essex, 1585–1597* (Cambridge, 1999), 161, n. 43.
6. *Leicester's Commonwealth: The Copy of a Letter Written by a Master of Art of Cambridge (1584) and Related Documents*, ed. Dwight C. Peck (Athens, OH, and London, 1985), 116.
7. Birch, i. 149–50; Hammer, *Polarisation*, 138; John Hawarde, *Les reports del cases in camera stellata, 1593–1609*, ed. W. P. Baildon (London, 1894), 1.
8. Stephen Alford, *The Watchers: A Secret History of the Reign of Elizabeth I* (London, 2012), 300.
9. Hawarde, *Camera stellata*, 3–4.
10. BL, Add. MS 48029 (Yelv. MS 33), ff. 163v–164r.
11. Hammer, *Polarisation*, 161 n. 45.
12. SP 12/247, no. 66; STC 8236, Hughes and Larkin, iii. 134–6.
13. SP 12/247, nos. 41, 44, 51, 60.
14. CP 169/34; CP 22/43.
15. CP 169/37.
16. Thomas M. McCoog, *The Society of Jesus in Ireland, Scotland, and England, 1589–1597* (Farnham and Burlington, VT, 2012), 120–30.
17. *A briefe apologie, or defence of the catholike ecclesiastical hierarchie* ([Antwerp,] 1601; STC 19391.5), 38v–39r (sigs. F2v–F3r); *The Letters*

and Memorials of William Cardinal Allen (1532–1594), ed. T. F. Knox (London, 1882), 339.

18. *Calendar of State Papers, Domestic Series, 1591–4*, ed. Mary Anne Everett Green (London, 1867), 255.
19. SP 12/248, no. 22.
20. SP 12/247, nos. 83, 84; *A true report of the sundry horrible conspiracies to have taken away the life of the Queenes Majestie* (London, 1594; STC 7603), 28–30, 31 (sigs. D2v–3v, D4).
21. SP 63/173, no. 51 (f. 140r).
22. SP 12/247, no. 93; CP 169/142.
23. SP 12/247, no. 97.
24. CP 169/43, 44; SP 12/47, no. 97.
25. SP 12/248, no. 33.
26. SP 12/248, no. 22.
27. *True report*, sig. D2r–v.
28. SP 12/248, no. 7; CP 22/54, 56; BL, Add. MS 48029 (Yelv. MS 33), ff. 147r–184v.
29. SP 12/248, nos. 15 (mainly in the hand of Henry Maynard), 16 (fair copy); Bacon, *Early writings*, 431–2.
30. Bacon, *Early writings*, 437–49, quotations at 445.
31. *Henslowe's Diary*, ed. R. A. Foakes (2nd edn, Cambridge, 2002), 30–31; Andrew Gurr, *The Shakespearean Stage, 1547–1642* (4th edn, Cambridge, 2009), 157.
32. CP 26/29, 30.
33. *Henslowe's Diary*, ed. Foakes, 14.

12. *CREDO IN DEUM*

1. Bacon, *Early writings*, 452–3.
2. Bacon, *Letters*, i. 289–94.
3. CP 25/111.
4. Bacon, *Letters*, i. 294–5, quotation at 295.
5. CP 26/56, 58.
6. Bacon, *Letters*, i. 295–6, quotation at 296.
7. Bacon, *Letters*, i. 297.
8. Bacon, *Letters*, i. 297–8; Bacon, *Early writings*, 455.
9. Bacon, *Letters*, i. 298.
10. Entry for 4 May 1594 in Lord Burghley's copy of John Dade's almanac (STC 434.5), CP 133; SP 52/53, no. 53.

NOTES

11. *The Warrender Papers*, ed. Annie I. Cameron, 2 vols., Scottish History Society, 3rd ser. 18–19 (Edinburgh, 1931–2), ii. 43.
12. Paul E. J. Hammer, *The Polarisation of Elizabethan Politics: The Political Career of Robert Devereux, 2nd Earl of Essex, 1585–1597* (Cambridge, 1999), 167; SP 52/52, f. 29r.
13. *Salisbury MSS*, xiii. 507; Elizabeth I, *Works*, 100–103, quotation at 101; Elizabeth I, *Compositions*, 103.
14. SP 52/53, no. 61.
15. CP 133/123; James VI and I, *Letters*, 127–130, quotation at 130.
16. James VI and I, *Letters*, 127–34, quotation at 131.
17. SP 52/53, no. 52.
18. SP 52/53, no. 53.
19. SP 52/52, f. 80r; SP 52/53, no. 54.
20. SP 52/53, nos. 58, 61.
21. SP 12/249, no. 3.
22. John Stow, *The annales of England* (London, 1600; STC 23335), 1278 (sig. Oooo8v).
23. *Salisbury MSS*, xiii. 507; Murdin, 804–5; July 1594 in Burghley's copy of Dade's almanac (STC 434.5), CP 133; CP 140/15v; *Salisbury MSS*, v. 71.
24. SP 12/249, no. 34.
25. CP 28/79; SP 12/250, no. 10; CP 139/41–8.
26. CP 139/41v.
27. CP 139/45r–v.
28. *A true report of the sundry horrible conspiracies to have taken away the life of the Queenes Majestie* (London, 1594; STC 7603), sigs. A4r–B1r.
29. CP 139/43; *True report*, sig. B1v.
30. BL, Lans. MS 77, f. 170r.
31. *True report*, sigs. D2r–D4r.

13. ASSURED FRIENDS

1. CP 25/40.
2. Paul E. J. Hammer, *The Polarisation of Elizabethan Politics: The Political Career of Robert Devereux, 2nd Earl of Essex, 1585–1597* (Cambridge, 1999), 304–5; CP 20/99; Murdin, 650.
3. Alexandra Gajda, 'The State of Christendom: history, political thought and the Essex circle', *Historical Research*, 81 (2008), 423–46.

4. Lisa Jardine and Alan Stewart, *Hostage to Fortune: The Troubled Life of Francis Bacon, 1561–1626* (London, 1998), 168–9; BL, Lans. MS 78, f. 74r; Bacon, *Letters*, i. 358.
5. SP 78/36, f. 181r; *A Spaniard in Elizabethan England: The Correspondence of Antonio Pérez's Exile*, ed. Gustav Ungerer, 2 vols. (London, 1974–6), i. no. 249.
6. SP 12/253, no. 14; SP 63/183, no. 40; *Sidney papers*, i. 348, 353.
7. PC 2/21, pp. 1A–1.
8. *Sidney papers*, i. 348, 350, 358; Bacon, *Early writings*, 681–2.
9. SP 15/33, no. 51.
10. *Sidney papers*, i. 357.
11. *A conference about the next succession to the crowne of Ingland* ([Antwerp, 1595]; STC 19398), sig. *2v.
12. Bacon, *Early writings*, 707–21, quotations at 707, 715.
13. Bacon, *Early writings*, 721.
14. *Sidney papers*, i. 362.
15. Elizabeth I, *Works*, 6; Elizabeth I, *Compositions*, 15.
16. *Sidney papers*, i. 363–4; SP 46/39, f. 279r.
17. BL, Cott. MS Galba D.x, f. 20r.
18. SP 12/256, no. 28.

14. 'BELIEVE CECIL'

1. CUL, MS Ee.3.56, no. 65; *Burghley letters*, 191–2.
2. CUL, MS Ee.3.56, no. 85; *Burghley letters*, 218.
3. CP 39/111.
4. CP 40/6.
5. SP 12/257, no. 30.
6. SP 12/257, no. 31.
7. SP 12/257, no. 34.
8. SP 12/257, no. 32.
9. *A declaration of the causes moving the Queenes Majestie of England, to prepare and send a navy to the seas* (London, 1596; STC 9203), with the foreign language translations STC 9204–9208.
10. CP 40/66.
11. CP 40/67.
12. CP 41/43.
13. CP 41/31.

14. Richard Hakluyt, *Principal navigations, voiages, traffiques and discoveries of the English nation*, 3 vols. (London, 1598–1600; STC 12626), i. 605 (actually 608).
15. Birch, ii. 19.
16. For a narrative account of the Cadiz expedition, see R. B. Wernham, *The Return of the Armadas: The Last Years of the Elizabethan War Against Spain, 1595–1603* (Oxford, 1995), 93–113.
17. Hakluyt, *Principal navigations*, i. 611–12, 616; Anthony Payne, 'Richard Hakluyt and the Earl of Essex: the censorship of the voyage to Cadiz in *Principal navigations*', *Publishing History*, 72 (2012), 7–52.
18. Hakluyt, *Principal navigations*, i. 615.
19. CP 41/99.
20. CP 41/92.
21. Hakluyt, *Principal navigations*, i. 618.

15. MAECENAS

1. PC 2/21, p. 298.
2. Conyers Read, *Mr Secretary Walsingham and the Policy of Queen Elizabeth*, 3 vols. (Oxford, 1925), i. 423–43; Charles Hughes, 'Nicholas Faunt's discourse touching the office of principal secretary, 1592', *English Historical Review*, 20 (1905), 499–508, quotation at 499–500.
3. CP 42/16
4. PC 2/21, pp. 358, 383.
5. SP 12/259, no. 60.
6. CP 42/22; SP 52/59, no. 4.
7. Birch, *Memoirs*, ii. 61. For 'affectionate' as meaning eager, ambitious or earnest see *OED* 2.c.
8. CP 42/103.
9. CP 41/116.
10. BL, Lans. MS 82, f. 178r; Seneca, *Moral Essays*, trans. John W. Basore, 3 vols. (Cambridge, MA, 1928–35), i. 238–9; CP 44/5; SP 12/259, no. 109.
11. PC 2/21, pp. 348–52.
12. BL, Harl. MS 286, f. 260r.
13. Devereux, i. 380; Lambeth Palace Library, London, MS 658, f. 88r–v; Paul E. J. Hammer, 'Myth-making: politics, propaganda and the capture of Cadiz in 1596', *Historical Journal*, 40 (1997), 631–2; Anthony Payne,

'Richard Hakluyt and the Earl of Essex: the censorship of the voyage to Cadiz in *Principal navigations*', *Publishing History*, 72 (2012), 11.

14. Hammer, 'Myth-making', 627.
15. Birch, ii. 131; Hammer, 'Myth-making', 627–8.
16. Devereux, i. 389–90.
17. Bacon, *Early writings*, 723–37, 979; Bacon, *Letters*, ii. 40.
18. *A Spaniard in Elizabethan England: The Correspondence of Antonio Pérez's Exile*, ed. Gustav Ungerer, 2 vols. (London, 1974–6), ii, no. 432; Birch, ii. 227.
19. *St Martin-in-the-Fields: The Accounts of the Churchwardens, 1525–1603*, ed. John V. Kitto (London, 1901), 488; PC 2/21, p. 78.
20. Birch, ii. 241.
21. SP 12/262, no. 24.
22. Henry Lok, *Ecclesiastes, otherwise called the preacher* (London, 1597; STC 16696); James Doelman, 'Seeking "The fruit of favour": the dedicatory sonnets of Henry Lok', *English Literary History*, 60 (1993), 1–15.
23. SP 12/234, no. 6.
24. Lok's is the last of the six pieces of commendatory verse in *His Majesties poeticall exercises at vacant houres* (Edinburgh, 1591; STC 14379); *Original letters of Mr John Colville, 1582–1603*, ed. David Laing, Bannatyne Club, no. 104 (Edinburgh, 1858), 260–61; SP 52/53, no. 24.
25. CP 171/22; BL, Lans. MS 108, f. 1r.
26. CP 173/86.
27. Lok, *Ecclesiastes*, sigs. V7v–V8r.
28. Lok, *Ecclesiastes*, sigs. V7v, X1v.

16. THE BURIAL OF THE DEAD

1. PC 2/22, p. 103; CP 204/50.
2. CP 37/102; CP 37/103.
3. CP 37/97/2.
4. CP 37/105; SP 12/262, nos. 16, 19.
5. SP 12/262, no. 53.
6. PC 2/22, p. 132.
7. *Essayes. Religious meditations. Places of perswasion and disswasion* (London, 1597; STC 1137), sig. A3r–v; Bacon, *Essays*, 145–7.
8. CUL, MS Ee.3.56, no. 115; *Burghley letters*, 256.
9. BL, Lans. MS 85, f. 36r.

10. R. B. Wernham, *The Return of the Armadas: The Last Years of the Eliza-bethan War Against Spain, 1595–1603* (Oxford, 1994), 148–9, 158–6, quotation at 161.
11. CUL, Ee.3.56, no. 117; *Burghley letters*, 258–9. Burghley adapted the Latin of Psalm 31:24 (Psalm 30:25 in the Vulgate: *Viriliter agite, et con-fortetur cor vestrum, omnes qui speratis in Domino*), translated in the Bishops' Bible (1568) as 'All ye that put your trust in God be ye of good courage: and he will comfort your heart.'
12. CP 53/20.
13. CUL, MS Ee.3.56, no. 120; *Burghley letters*, 262.
14. CP 58/21, 22.
15. Birch, ii. 351–2.
16. SP 12/264, nos. 54, 57.
17. SP 12/264, no. 61.
18. CP 54/26; see also CP 54/33.
19. CP 54/75.
20. Munck, 237.
21. Robert Somerville, *History of the Duchy of Lancaster, 1265–1603* (London, 1953), 317–36, 396; Munck, 237.
22. CP 56/4; CP 53/85.

17. WAYS OF SAFETY

1. CP 57/49; CP 57/26; SP 12/265, no. 134; SP 106/2, f. 117r–v; Lawrence Stone, *An Elizabethan: Sir Horatio Palavicino* (Oxford, 1956), 255.
2. Book III, chapter 14 of *Sixe bookes of politickes or civil doctrine*, trans. William Jones (London, 1594; STC 15701), 117 (sig. Q3r); Justus Lip-sius, *Politica: Six Books of Politics or Political Instruction*, trans. and ed. Jans Waszink (Assen, 2004), 517.
3. 'The names of the intelligencers', SP 12/265, no. 134. Though divided up by Victorian archivists into the separate classes of the modern State Papers (mainly SP 94, Spain, and SP 106, Ciphers), some of the contents of the secret file can be reconstructed; hiding behind often two or three nineteenth- or twentieth-century folio or item numbers is the original foliation given to the documents by William Wade or Simon Willis. So we have for folio 5 of the secret file Roger Houghton's note of monies paid to Thomas Honiman in Oct. 1596 (SP 94/5, f. 142r); folio 7, monies paid to Edmund Palmer in Nov. 1596 and May 1597 (SP 94/5, f. 205r); folio 8, Palmer's cipher, Nov. 1596 (SP 106/3, f. 62r); folios 12–13, Mas-sentio Verdiani's cipher and monies paid to him (Brussels), Nov. 1596

(SP 106/2, ff. 133r–134r); folio 16, cipher for Robert Poley and monies for his mission to Flanders, Dec. 1596 to July 1597 (SP 106/2, f. 74r–v); folio 20, monies paid to Francis Bolton (Seville), March to June 1598 (SP 106/1, f. 27r–v); folio 21, cipher for Roger Aston in Scotland (SP 106/1, f. 14r–v); folio 25, monies and cipher for William Resold, July 1597 (SP 106/2, f. 83r–v); folio 28, cipher for More and monies for Brussels, May 1597 (SP 106/2, f. 18r–v); folio 29, cipher and monies for Paolo Teobast, Dec. 1597 (SP 106/2, f. 117r–v); folio 32, cipher for George Nicolson in Scotland, May 1597 (SP 106/2, f. 37r); and folio 33, cipher for Robert Poley in Antwerp (SP 106/2, f. 73r).

4. SP 12/272, no. 3.
5. SP 106/2, f. 117r.
6. SP 12/265, no. 134; SP 94/5, ff. 142, 205; CP 29/15–17; SP 12/269, no. 30; CP 48/70; SP 78/39, f. 111r.
7. *A journal of all that was accomplished by Monsieur de Maisse, ambassador in England from King Henri IV to Queen Elizabeth, 1597*, trans. and ed. G. B. Harrison and R. A. Jones (London, 1931), esp. 4–5, 97–101, 104–17.
8. SP 12/266, no. 3.
9. BL, Cott. MS Caligula D.ii, f. 349r; Munck, 237; CP 48/83.
10. CP 48/77.
11. SP 12/265, no. 133; Stone, *Sir Horatio Palavicino*, 325–30.
12. SP 52/68, no. 82.
13. *Searching for Shakespeare*, ed. Tarnya Cooper (London, 2006), 127; Samuel Schoenbaum, *Shakespeare's Lives* (Oxford, 1991), 132.
14. SP 12/266, nos. 59, 64.
15. SP 12/266, no. 65.
16. SP 12/266, no. 73; CP 48/70.
17. *Salisbury MSS*, xxiii. 40–41.
18. CP 351/1, ff. 30v–31r; *Salisbury MSS*, xxiii. 27, 33.
19. SP 78/41, f. 120r.

18. NO ORDINARY AMBASSADOR

1. 'Master Secretary Cecil, his negotiation into France' (CP 351/1) is a journal of the journey and talks in France, covering the weeks between 31 Jan. and 30 Apr. 1598, as well as a letterbook of the ambassadors' letters home, most of the originals of which are in SP 78/41–2. There is a full and accurate transcript of CP 351/1 in *Salisbury MSS*, xxiii. 10–74.

2. *Salisbury MSS*, xxiii. 38–41.
3. *Salisbury MSS*, xxiii. 42–3.
4. *Salisbury MSS*, xxiii. 43–4.
5. *Salisbury MSS*, xxiii. 44.
6. *Salisbury MSS*, xxiii. 45.
7. Francis Bacon, *Several letters* (London, 1657), 92–3 (sigs. Mmm4v–Nnn1v), printed as a supplement to *Resuscitatio . . . Several pieces of the works . . . of the Right Honourable Francis Bacon*, ed. William Rawley (London, 1661); Bacon, *Letters*, ii. 101–2.
8. Jan den Tex, *Oldenbarnevelt*, trans. R. B. Powell, 2 vols. (Cambridge, 1973), i. 260–63.
9. *Salisbury MSS*, xxiii. 53–5.
10. *Salisbury MSS*, xxiii. 67–71.
11. CP 351/1, ff. 104r–105r; *Salisbury MSS*, xxiii. 74.
12. CP 60/66.
13. *Chamberlain letters*, i. 33.
14. John L. Motley, *History of the United Netherlands*, 4 vols. (London, 1875–6), iii. 456–60, quotation at 460; Tex, *Oldenbarnevelt*, i. 272–3; R. B. Wernham, *The Return of the Armadas: The Last Years of the Elizabethan War Against Spain, 1595–1603* (Oxford, 1994), 234–6, quotation at 236.
15. Motley, *United Netherlands*, iii. 463.
16. Conyers Read, *Lord Burghley and Queen Elizabeth* (London, 1960), 543–4.
17. CP 61/10, 72, 94; CUL, MS Ee.3.56, no. 133; *Burghley letters*, 283–4; CP 62/34, 36; *The Letters and Epigrams of Sir John Harington*, ed. N. E. McClure (Philadelphia, 1930), 68.
18. CUL, MS Ee.3.56, no. 138; *Burghley letters*, 292–3.
19. CP 62/36.
20. BL, Cott. MS Galba D.xii, ff. 181r–182r.
21. CP 213/46.
22. CP 63/4.
23. Munck, 237.

19. ONE HEART, ONE WAY

1. SP 63/202/3, f. 16r.
2. CP 63/26, 27, 29, 34, 38.
3. CP 63/43.
4. PROB 11/92/316, stamped f. 244r.

5. T. S. Eliot, 'Little Gidding' (1942), in *The Complete Poems and Plays of T. S. Eliot* (London, 1969), 192.
6. *Chamberlain letters*, i. 41; Nichols, iv. 62–3; Munck, 238.
7. CP 63/74v, 75.
8. *Chamberlain letters*, i. 41.
9. CP 49/51.
10. SP 52/62, no. 43.
11. BL, Cott. MS Caligula D.ii, f. 358r, with damaged portions of the letter supplied from a copy in BL, Cott. MS Titus C.vii, f. 19r; James VI and I, *Letters*, 157–8, quotation at 157; CP 133/138; James VI and I, *Letters*, 158–9, quotation at 158.
12. SP 52/63, no. 4.
13. *To Maister Anthonie Bacon. An apologie of the earle of Essex* (London, 1600; STC 6787.7), sigs. A1, E1v.
14. *Chamberlain letters*, i. 46.
15. Joel Hurstfield, *The Queen's Wards: Wardship and Marriage under Elizabeth I* (London, 1958), 67–70.
16. Alan G. R. Smith, *Servant of the Cecils: The Life of Sir Michael Hickes, 1543–1612* (London, 1977), 57–60, 72–7; CP 44/47; Hurstfield, *Queen's Wards*, 299. Examples of other approaches to Robert Cecil over the prospective wardships of heirs to gentlemen not yet dead are CP 78/90 and CP 79/18. See also Hurstfield, *Queen's Wards*, 263–4 and Stephen Alford, *Burghley: William Cecil at the Court of Elizabeth I* (New Haven, CT, and London, 2008), 338–40.
17. H. E. Bell, *An Introduction to the History and Records of the Court of Wards and Liveries* (Cambridge, 1953), 17; Hurstfield, *Queen's Wards*, 297–9.
18. CP 65/29.
19. *Apologie of the earle of Essex*, sig. E1v; *Chamberlain letters*, i. 58; SP 52/52, p. 239.
20. SP 52/63, no. 81.
21. SP 52/63, no. 82.
22. CP 133/140; James VI and I, *Letters*, 159–63.
23. CP 58/86.

20. ARMED ON THE BREAST

1. SP 52/64, no. 53.
2. SP 52/64, no. 33.
3. SP 52/64, no. 34.

4. SP 52/52, ff. 244v–245r.
5. Nichols, iv. 71.
6. Nichols, iv. 73–8, quotation at 73–4.
7. Nichols, iv. 71.
8. BL, Cott. MS Caligula D.ii, ff. 391r–397r, quotations at f. 393r–v. Where the text is missing in this manuscript because of fire damage, it is supplied from *Calendar of State Papers Relating to Scotland and Mary, Queen of Scots, 1547–1603*, 13 vols. (London, 1898–1969), xiii. (pt. 1) 455–61.
9. H. E. Bell, *An Introduction to the History and Records of the Court of Wards and Liveries* (Cambridge, 1953), 167–71.
10. Munck, 239.
11. CP 70/47; *Winwood memorials*, i. 41.
12. Libel A9 (with spelling modernized and some punctuation adjusted) from 'Early Stuart Libels: An Edition of Poetry from Manuscript Sources', ed. Alastair Bellany and Andrew McRae, Early Modern Literary Studies Text Series 1 (2005), http://purl.oclc.org/emls/texts/libels/.
13. SP 52/64, no. 75.
14. *Winwood memorials*, i. 57.
15. SP 63/204, ff. 177v–179v, quotation at f. 179r. See also SP 63/205, no. 114.
16. CP 133/182; SP 63/205, nos. 131, 132.
17. Nichols, iv. 83–4; also Devereux, ii. 68.
18. SP 63/205, no. 170; Devereux, ii. 73–5, quotations at 73, 74.
19. *Winwood memorials*, i. 105.

21. SPRIGS OF GOLD

1. The first quotation is from Edmund Howes's edition of John Stowe's *Annals* (1615), quoted in Nichols, iv. 87; *Sidney papers*, ii. 127.
2. *Sidney papers*, ii. 127–9.
3. *Sidney papers*, ii. 131–2.
4. *Sidney papers*, ii. 131.
5. *Sidney papers*, ii. 131.
6. *Winwood memorials*, i. 118.
7. *Sidney papers*, ii. 133.
8. *Sidney papers*, ii. 133–4.
9. *Sidney papers*, ii. 135.
10. SP 12/268, no. 45; SP 12/273, nos. 35–7.
11. SP 63/206, no. 57.

12. SP 63/206, no. 55.
13. CP 75/24; CP 74/79; *Sidney papers*, ii. 152–5; CP 75/37.
14. *Winwood memorials*, i. 139–40.
15. *Sidney papers*, ii. 154.
16. SP 12/273, no. 51.
17. Nichols, iv. 105.
18. *Sidney papers*, ii. 156.
19. *Sidney papers*, ii. 164.
20. *Sidney papers*, ii. 166.
21. SP 12/274, no. 39.
22. *Sidney papers*, ii. 166; SP 12/274, no. 40.
23. SP 12/274, no. 42.
24. SP 12/274, no. 48; *Chamberlain letters*, i. 86; *Sidney papers*, ii. 167.
25. CP 68/66.
26. *Winwood memorials*, i. 156.
27. SP 52/66, no. 19.

22. FEELING THE PULSE

1. CP 79/5; *Winwood memorials*, i. 167; see also Munck, 239; and Nichols, iv. 117.
2. PROB 11/75/375; PROB 11/77/101. On the debt see SP 46/39, f. 141r, which by June 1597 was calculated at £11,683 6s. 5½d. from two whole accounting years, Michaelmas 1593 to Michaelmas 1595: BL, Lans. MS 83, f. 233v.
3. SP 12/274, no. 103.
4. SP 12/274, no. 107.
5. SP 12/240, no. 119, was dated '1591?' by M. A. E. Green in *Calendar of State Papers, Domestic Series, 1591–4* (London, 1867), 153–4. There is another suggestion in pencil on the manuscript of 1596. Apr. 1600, in response to Phelippes's petition, seems to me most likely.
6. CP 83/9; see also Hugh Gazzard, '"Idle papers:" *An Apology of the Earl of Essex*', in *Essex: The Cultural Impact of an Elizabethan Courtier*, ed. Annaliese Connolly and Lisa Hopkins (Manchester, 2013), 179–99.
7. CP 79/40.
8. *To Maister Anthonie Bacon. An apologie of the earle of Essex* ([London, 1600]; STC 6787.7), sig. A2r, 'La. Rich to her Majestie in the behalfe of the Earle of Essex'.
9. CP 79/37; CP 80/2 (see also CP 180/93); SP 12/274, no. 138.
10. Bacon, *Letters*, ii. 174–88, quotation at 179.

11. Lisa Jardine and Alan Stewart, *Hostage to Fortune: The Troubled Life of Francis Bacon, 1561–1626* (London, 1998), 228–32.
12. Bacon, *Letters*, ii. 190–91.
13. Bacon, *Letters*, ii. 192.
14. *Sidney papers*, ii. 167.
15. SP 12/275, no. 8.
16. SP 101/1, f. 257r.
17. SP 52/66, no. 37.
18. Robert Pitcairn, *Criminal Trials in Scotland, 1488–1624*, 3 vols. (Edinburgh, 1829–33), ii. 173.
19. SP 52/66, no. 53. See also 'The true discourse of the late treason', dated by Simon Willis 5 Aug. 1600 but more likely drawn up during the investigations into the conspiracy in Aug. and Sept. 1600, SP 52/66, no. 50.
20. *Cecil letters*, 23.
21. CP 134/3.
22. CP 81/60.
23. SP 12/281, no. 6.

23. INSURRECTION

1. *Chamberlain letters*, i. 105, 107; *Cecil letters*, 8, 23; CP 81/62.
2. SP 12/275, no. 38; SP 12/275, no. 61, in Public Record Office, *Museum Catalogue* (London, 1974), 59; and Public Record Office, *Tudor Royal Letters: Elizabeth I and the Succession*, ed. C. J. Kitching (London, 1972), pl. 8.
3. Nichols, iv. 137; CP 67/37.
4. Historical Manuscripts Commission, *Report on the Manuscripts of the Earl of Mar and Kellie* (London, 1904), 36–7.
5. *Calendar of State Papers Relating to Scotland and Mary, Queen of Scots, 1547–1603*, 13 vols. (London, 1898–1969), xiii. (pt. 2) 755–7.
6. SP 52/67, no. 8.
7. SP 52/67, no. 11; James VI and I, *Letters*, 168–9.
8. James VI and I, *Letters*, 169–70, quotation at 170.
9. Paul E. J. Hammer, 'Shakespeare's *Richard II*, the play of 7 February 1601, and the Essex rising', *Shakespeare Quarterly*, 59 (2008), 1–35; SP 12/278, no. 78.
10. John Hayward, *The life and raigne of King Henrie IIII*, ed. John J. Manning, Camden Society, 4th ser. 42 (London, 1991), 17–34; *Chamberlain letters*, i. 70; Hammer, 'Shakespeare's *Richard II* ', 9.
11. SP 12/278, no. 17; Hayward, *Henrie IIII*, 26–7, 65.

12. *The New Oxford Shakespeare: Authorship Companion*, ed. Gary Taylor and Gabriel Egan (Oxford, 2017), 512–13; CP 36/30; SP 12/278, no. 85; *Searching for Shakespeare*, ed. Tarnya Cooper (London, 2006), 161. On Shakespeare and Phillips and the Lord Chamberlain's Men see Samuel Schoenbaum, *William Shakespeare: A Documentary Life* (New York, 1975), 150–51, 154.
13. CP 84/7.
14. *Cecil letters*, 67–8.
15. *Cecil letters*, 67–8, dated from the execution of Sir Gelly Meyrick and Henry Cuffe on 13 Mar. 1601: *Complete Collection of State Trials*, ed. William Cobbett *et al.*, 33 vols. (London, 1809–26), i. col. 1412.
16. SP 12/278, no. 55.
17. SP 52/67, no. 17.
18. CP 76/89.
19. *State Trials*, cols. 1333–58, quotations at 1351–2.
20. SP 52/67, no. 45.
21. CP 84/11, 12–13, 16, 18; BL, Lans. MS 88, f. 28r.
22. CP 180/30.
23. Richard Davies, *A funerall sermon preached . . . at the buriall of the right honourable Walter Earle of Essex and Ewe* (London, 1577; STC 6364), epistle to Robert, earl of Essex.

24. THIRTY, TEN

1. On libels left at the Royal Exchange, see CP 181/127; libel A13 (with spelling modernized) from 'Early Stuart Libels: An Edition of Poetry from Manuscript Sources', ed. Alastair Bellany and Andrew McRae, Early Modern Literary Studies Text Series 1 (2005), http://purl.oclc.org/emls/texts/libels/; the case of William Buttes is in CP 76/50.
2. CP 76/97.
3. In the quotations from *King Richard II* (3.4.34–53) I have modernized spelling using the *New Oxford Shakespeare* but kept the punctuation from the 1597 text: *The tragoedie of King Richard the Second* (London, 1597; STC 22307), sig. G3r.
4. *Salisbury MSS*, xi. 21.
5. CP 83/99/2.
6. SP 52/67, no. 45; *Cecil letters*, 68.
7. SP 52/67, no. 26.
8. CP 77/77.

9. SP 52/67, no. 29; SP 52/67, no. 31; *Letters of Queen Elizabeth and King James VI of Scotland*, ed. John Bruce, Camden Society, 1st ser. 46 (London, 1849), 134–5; BL, Cott. MS Caligula D.ii, ff. 419r–420v, where the text missing in this manuscript because of fire damage is supplied from *Calendar of State Papers Relating to Scotland and Mary, Queen of Scots, 1547–1603*, 13 vols. (London, 1898–1969), xiii. (pt. 2) 812–13.

10. James VI and I, *Letters*, 173–7, quotation at 175.

11. SP 52/58, no. 58.

12. CP 135/61; Bruce, *Correspondence*, 12.

13. SP 52/67, no. 45.

14. *Sidney papers*, ii. 326.

15. CP 135/54; Bruce, *Correspondence*, 1–3; James VI and I, *Letters*, 178-80.

16. Bruce, *Correspondence*, 8.

17. CP 135/55–8; Bruce, *Correspondence*, 3–8.

18. CP 250/49; SP 12/275, no. 106; SP 78/45, ff. 13r–14v, 62r.

19. SP 52/67, nos. 110, 113.

20. SP 52/67, no. 103; see also SP 52/67, no. 136; and Helen G. Stafford, *James VI of Scotland and the Throne of England* (New York and London, 1940), 256–7.

21. CP 135/5–9; Bruce, *Correspondence*, 9–11; James VI and I, *Letters*, 181–3.

25. FACTIONS AND FANTASIES

1. CP 135/61–2; Bruce, *Correspondence*, 12–13.

2. Hartley, iii. 278–81, 288–97, quotations at 278, 293.

3. *The Secret Correspondence of Sir Robert Cecil with James VI King of Scotland*, ed. Sir David Dalrymple, Lord Hailes (Edinburgh, 1766), 25–6.

4. *Secret Correspondence*, ed. Hailes, 73; CP 184/9.

5. *Cecil letters*, 105; David Crystal and Ben Crystal, *Shakespeare's Words: A Glossary and Language Companion* (London, 2002), 424.

6. *Secret Correspondence*, ed. Hailes, 39, 75–6.

7. SP 52/68, no. 5; CP 84/74/2.

8. SP 52/68, no. 6; see also SP 52/68, nos. 33, 39, 46, 55, 62, 66.

9. CP 135/63–4; Bruce, *Correspondence*, 15–16.

10. CP 135/85; Bruce, *Correspondence*, 42.

11. Lord Henry Howard's abstract of George Nicolson's letter was printed by Lord Hailes after Howard's letter to King James VI of 24 Aug. [1602], *Secret Correspondence*, ed. Hailes, 195–8. Nicolson's letter was perhaps the one he wrote to Sir Robert Cecil on 3 Aug. 1602, which Cecil referred to in his reply (24 Aug. 1602, SP 52/68, no. 92) to Nicolson's packets of 3 and 14 Aug. 1602.

12. *Secret Correspondence*, ed. Hailes, 202–3; Helen G. Stafford, *James VI of Scotland and the Throne of England* (New York and London, 1940), 257; CP 135/65–v; Bruce, *Correspondence*, 17–18.

13. CP 184/54; CP 96/109; *Chamberlain letters*, i. 163.

14. *Sidney papers*, ii. 326.

15. *Cecil letters*, 144, 149; *Chamberlain letters*, i. 171; CP 213/120.

16. John Stow, *A Survey of London*, ed. C. L. Kingsford, 2 vols. (Oxford, 1908), ii. 95; Manolo Guerci, 'Salisbury House in London, 1599–1694: the Strand Palace of Sir Robert Cecil', *Architectural History*, 52 (2009), 31–78, esp. 37–40; *The Letters and Epigrams of Sir John Harington*, ed. N. E. McClure (Philadelphia, 1930), 93.

17. Sir John Harington, *A tract on the succession to the crown*, ed. Clements R. Markham, Roxburghe Club (London, 1880), quotations at 40, 46, 51, 85.

18. *Letters and Epigrams of Sir John Harington*, 96–8.

19. Nichols, iv. 204–8, quotation at 205–6.

20. CP 96/09; CP 101/101.

21. CP 204/145.

22. Sir Thomas Craig, *Concerning the Right of Succession to the Kingdom of England*, trans. James Gatherer (London, 1703), quotations at 399, 410.

23. SP 52/69, no. 58.

26. ACCESSION

1. Nichols, iv. 218–20, quotation at 219; *The Memoirs of Robert Carey*, ed. F. H. Mares (Oxford, 1972), 59.

2. *Diary of John Manningham, of the Middle Temple ... 1602–1603*, ed. John Bruce, Camden Society, 1st ser. 99 (Westminster, 1868), 146–7.

3. CP 96/170; CP 92/18/2–3.

4. CP 92/22, 28 47 (2), 57.

5. CP 92/65.

6. CP 134/28; James VI and I, *Letters*, 208.

7. SP 14/1, no. 2.

8. SP 14/1, no. 2.
9. CP 135/63 (James VI and I, *Letters*, 192–4, quotations at 193); CP 135/101 (James VI and I, *Letters*, 194–5. See also Alexander Courtney, 'The Scottish king and the English Court: the secret correspondence of James VI, 1601–3', in *Doubtful and Dangerous: The Question of Succession in late Elizabethan England*, ed. Susan Doran and Paulina Kewes (Manchester, 2014), 134–51.
10. *Memoirs of Robert Carey*, 60–61; *Salisbury MSS*, xv. 1; STC 8297–8299.
11. *Salisbury MSS*, xv. 1.
12. Munck, 243.
13. [Robert Cecil, earl of Salisbury,] *The state and dignity of a secretary's place* (London, 1642), 3.
14. CP 135/69; Bruce, *Correspondence*, 24–5; James VI and I, *Letters*, 199.
15. CP 135/76; Bruce, *Correspondence*, 30–32; James VI and I, *Letters*, 200–202, quotations at 201; Hughes and Larkin, iii. 250–55.
16. CP 135/78; Bruce, *Correspondence*, 33; Robert Graves, *The Greek Myths*, 2 vols. (Harmondsworth, 1960), i. 30.
17. CP 135/78–9; Bruce, *Correspondence*, 33–5.
18. CP 135/80; Bruce, *Correspondence*, 36–8; James VI and I, *Letters*, 204–5.
19. *Chamberlain letters*, i. 190.
20. James VI and I, *Letters*, 208–9.
21. CP 204/137–8; CP 206/3–4; SP 14/1, no. 2.
22. CP 134/31, misdated 1 Apr. 1603 in *Salisbury MSS*, xv. 25.
23. CP 187/23.
24. James VI and I, *Letters*, 209–10, 212–13.
25. CP 99/118, 125.
26. CP 99/135; *The Letters and Epigrams of Sir John Harington*, ed. N. E. McClure (Philadelphia, 1930), 320.
27. CP 187/30.
28. CP 100/74.
29. SP 12/283, no. 21; CP 92/4.
30. CP 100/96.
31. CUL, MS Ee.3.56, no. 138; *Burghley letters*, 292–3; SP 12/176, no. 29.
32. *State and dignity of a secretary's place*, 2; see also Pauline Croft, 'Can a bureaucrat be a favourite? Robert Cecil and the strategies of power', in *The World of the Favourite*, ed. J. H. Elliott and L. W. B. Brockliss (New Haven, CT, and London, 1999), 83–4 and n. 13.
33. CP 100/133.

27. LITTLE BEAGLE

1. CP 87/50.
2. CP 187/91.
3. SP 14/19, no. 41 (f. 89r).
4. CP 100/143, 144; CP 101/7.
5. CP 101/80, 84.
6. CP 101/85.
7. CP 102/32.
8. CP 103/42.
9. CP 101/170 (of which the draft is CP 187/120); Historical Manuscripts Commission, *Calendar of the Manuscripts of the Marquis of Bath*, 3 vols. (London, 1904–8), ii. 51.
10. CP 134/59; James VI and I, *Letters*, 227–8.
11. CP 134/50v; James VI and I, *Letters*, 260.
12. 'The Somerset House Conference, 1604', National Portrait Gallery, London, NPG 665; Roy Strong, *Tudor and Jacobean Portraits*, 2 vols. (London, 1969), ii. 351–2.
13. CP 103/151.
14. SP 14/12, no. 37.
15. SP 14/12, no. 38.
16. SP 14/12, no. 42; see also SP 14/12, no. 44; and CP 104/5.

28. THE VARIABLE MOTIONS OF MEN

1. Jonson, *Works*, v. 141.
2. Ian Donaldson, *Ben Jonson: A Life* (Oxford, 2011), 17, 136; CP 114/58; Jonson, *Works*, ii. 641–7, quotation at 645.
3. Ben Jonson, *Sejanus, His Fall* (London, 1605; STC 14782). The estimate of the length of a performance from the printed book is Gregory Doran's in his 'Director's Note' to the Royal Shakespeare Company's play text of *Sejanus: His Fall* (London, 2005), where Martin Butler's introduction is invaluable in understanding the play in its context. On Shakespeare and *Sejanus*, as possible collaborator as well as actor, see *The New Oxford Shakespeare: Authorship Companion*, ed. Gary Taylor and Gabriel Egan (Oxford, 2017), 538–42; and Samuel Schoenbaum, *William Shakespeare: A Documentary Life* (New York, 1975), 150.
4. 2.442–9 and 1.64–9 in Jonson, *Works*, ii. 239–40, 287, on which see Donaldson, *Ben Jonson*, 186–92.

5. Munck, 258.
6. CP Patent 215/18; *Salisbury MSS*, xxiii. 222.
7. CP 199/106, 111.
8. CP 134/72; James VI and I, *Letters*, 270–71.
9. Jonson, *Works*, v. 132–3.
10. SP 14/216, no. 101; Public Record Office, *Museum Catalogue* (London, 1974), 60.
11. Donaldson, *Ben Jonson*, 216–17.
12. George Blacker Morgan, *The Identification of the Writer of the Anonymous Letter to Lord Monteagle in 1605* (London, 1916), 1. See also Mark Nicholls's biography of Francis Tresham in *ODNB*. The conspirators and the Crown's case and evidence against them are summarized in *A true and perfect relation of the proceedings at the severall arraignments of the late most barbarous traitors* (London, 1606; STC 11168), sigs. C3r–D1v.
13. SP 14/216, no. 2; Mark Nicholls, *Investigating the Gunpowder Plot* (Manchester, 1991), 6; Morgan, *Anonymous Letter*, 6–7.
14. SP 14/216/2, no. 129; *His majesties speach in this last session of parliament* (London, 1605; STC 14392), quotations at sigs. F1v–F2r.
15. Nicholls, *Gunpowder Plot*, 7–8; 'The reports of William Udall, informer, 1605–1612', ed. P. R. Harris, *Recusant History*, 8 (1966), 200.
16. *His majesties speach*, sigs. F1v–F2r.
17. CP 134/133; James VI and I, *Letters*, 273.
18. SP 14/216/2, f. 36v.
19. *His majesties speach*, sigs. G1v–G2r; Nicholls, *Gunpowder Plot*, 8–9.
20. SP 14/216/1, no. 17; James VI and I, *Letters*, 274–5.
21. SP 14/16, nos. 6, 70.
22. Jonson, *Works*, ii. 655–6; Donaldson, *Ben Jonson*, 220–22; Frances Teague, 'Jonson and the Gunpowder Plot', *The Ben Jonson Journal*, 5 (1998), 249–52.
23. SP 14/17, no. 2.
24. William, 2nd Earl of Salisbury's copy of the paper 'cast into the Lord of Salisbury's court, December 4 1605' is CP 113/76, reproduced in *An answere to certaine scandalous papers* (London, 1606; STC 4895), sigs. B2v–C1v.
25. *Answere*, sigs. A3r–v, C3v. On *Macbeth* in the context of 1606 see *The New Oxford Shakespeare: Authorship Companion*, ed. Gary Taylor and Gabriel Egan (Oxford, 2017), 564, with the quoted lines from the play at 2.3.6–9.
26. *Answere*, sig. C4v.

27. *Answere*, sigs. D4v, E4r.
28. *Answere*, sig. F2r.
29. John Day, *The ile of guls* (London, 1606; STC 6412), sigs. A2v, C3r; Blair Worden, *The Sound of Virtue: Philip Sidney's* Arcadia *and Elizabethan Politics* (New Haven, CT, and London, 1996), 218, 219, 244.
30. Day, *Ile of guls*, sig. E1r.
31. Andrew Gurr, *The Shakespearean Stage, 1547–1642* (4th edn, Cambridge, 2009), 69–70.

29. EQUIVOCATIONS

1. Albert J. Loomie, *The Spanish Elizabethans* (London, 1963), 83–90.
2. SP 101/1, ff. 302r–303v, 316r–317v.
3. CP 113/106; CP 109/141, 142.
4. CP 190/37.
5. SP 14/18, no. 124.
6. SP 14/73, ff. 70r–71r, which is *A book of proclamations* for 1603–9 (London, 1609; STC 7759), 120–22, quotation at 122.
7. Henry Garnet, *A Treatise of Equivocation*, ed. David Jardine (London, 1851), quotation at 3.
8. SP 14/18, ff. 129r–130r, 131r–132r. See also Philip Caraman, *Henry Garnet, 1555–1606, and the Gunpowder Plot* (London, 1964), 348–53; *ODNB*, xxi. 494–5.
9. CP 110/33; 'Two declarations of Garnet relating to the Gunpowder Plot', ed. S. R. Gardiner, *English Historical Review*, 3 (1888), 515; SP 14/19, no. 41.
10. CP 115/19–20; *Salisbury MSS*, xviii. 75–7.
11. SP 14/19, no. 27. Philip Caraman's quotations from this letter (Levinus Munck's draft minute of the earl of Salisbury to the earl of Mar, 9 Mar. 1606) are seriously awry and should not be trusted: Caraman, *Henry Garnet*, 376.
12. *Chamberlain letters*, i. 220.
13. *A true and perfect relation of the proceedings at the severall arraignments of the late most barbarous traitors* (London, 1606; STC 11618), sig. Y1r; Caraman, *Henry Garnet*, 396–420.
14. *True and perfect relation*, sigs. Y1v–Y2v.
15. *True and perfect relation*, sig. Y4r–v.
16. CP 114/118.
17. *True and perfect relation*, sigs. Bb3v–Bb4r.
18. *True and perfect relation*, sigs. Cc3v–Cc4r.

19. *Chamberlain letters*, i. 221–2.
20. *Chamberlain letters*, i. 222.
21. SP 14/20, no. 51.
22. Caraman, *Henry Garnet*, 430–32.

30. YIELDING THE KEYS

1. CP 228/8. Thomas Nashe's scholarship verse from 1585 is SP 15/29, f. 130r; see Richard Rex, 'The sixteenth century', in *St John's College Cambridge: A History*, ed. Peter Linehan (Woodbridge, 2011), 83–4.
2. CP 111/113.
3. CP 115/164.
4. CP 119/162–3; Jonson, *Works*, iii. 195–9, quotation at 198.
5. CP 117/82.
6. CP 117/115; Pauline Croft, 'Can a bureaucrat be a favourite? Robert Cecil and the strategies of power', in *The World of the Favourite*, ed. J. H. Elliott and L. W. B. Brockliss (New Haven, CT, and London, 1999), 86.
7. CP 117/123, 130.
8. CP 143/112.
9. Claire Gapper, John Newman and Annabel Ricketts, 'Hatfield: a house for a Lord Treasurer', in *Patronage, Culture and Power: The Early Cecils, 1558–1612*, ed. Pauline Croft (New Haven, CT, and London, 2002), 67–87.
10. Jonson, *Works*, iii. 203–15, quotations at 214; CP 144/271; James M. Sutton, 'Jonson's Genius at Theobalds: the poetics of estrangement', *Ben Jonson Journal*, 7 (2000), 297–323.
11. CP 228/16, 19
12. CP 228/14.
13. CP 191/128.
14. The quotation by Sir Walter Cope is from BL, Add. MS 11600, f. 37r; John Gutch, *Collectanea curiosa*, 2 vols. (Oxford, 1781), i. 122.

31. THE PLAGUES OF JOB

1. Susan Bracken, 'Robert Cecil as art collector', in *Patronage, Culture and Power: The Early Cecils, 1558–1612*, ed. Pauline Croft (New Haven, CT, and London, 2002), 121–32; CP 26/85 (horses, 1594); Jonson, *Works*, iii. 277–9 (entertainment at Salisbury House, 1608); CP 169/140

(Fortunatus, 1593); Miranda Kauffman, *Black Tudors* (London, 2017), 164, 223–4, and CP Petitions 1220 (Fortunatus Cuba, 1601).

2. CP 28/21 ('muscat', or musk, 1594); CP 26/57 (perspective glass, 1594); Richard Hakluyt, *Principal navigations, voiages, traffiques and discoveries of the English nation*, 3 vols. (London, 1598–1600; STC 12626), ii. sigs. *2r–*4v (1599); iii. sigs. (A2)r–(A3)v (1600).

3. *Chamberlain letters*, i. 259.

4. Jonson, *Works*, iii. 353–68, quotation at 359.

5. Jonson, *Works*, iii. 368.

6. CP 197/42.

7. SP 14/184, no. 34.

8. *Chamberlain letters*, i. 259, 273.

9. CP 195/63; *Salisbury MSS*, xxi. 104–13, 127, 146; *Chamberlain letters*, i. 259, 273.

10. CP 228/28.

11. CP 228/27.

12. John Cramsie, *Kingship and Crown Finance under James VI and I, 1603–1625* (London, 2002), 78–9, 89–101; 'A collection of the several treatises and speeches of the late Lord Treasurer Cecil', ed. Pauline Croft, Camden Society, *Miscellany* xxix (London, 1987), 278–317, quotation at 285.

13. *The House of Commons, 1558–1603*, ed. P. W. Hasler, History of Parliament Trust, 3 vols. (London, 1981), i. 579.

14. *Parliamentary Debates in 1610*, ed. S. R. Gardiner, Camden Society, 1st ser. 81 (London, 1862), 154–5; *Proceedings in Parliament, 1610*, ed. Elizabeth Read Foster, 2 vols. (New Haven, CT, and London, 1966), i. 130; Cramsie, *Kingship and Crown Finance*, 101.

15. CP 134/142; *Salisbury MSS*, xxi. 263–4; CP 134/143–4; James VI and I, *Letters*, 316–17.

16. CP 134/117–18; *Salisbury MSS*, xxi. 267–8.

17. CP 128/172.

18. CP 140/38; Claire Gapper, John Newman and Annabel Ricketts, 'Hatfield: a house for a Lord Treasurer', in *Patronage, Culture and Power: The Early Cecils, 1558–1612*, ed. Pauline Croft (New Haven, CT, and London, 2002), 69.

19. *Theo. Turquet Mayernii equitus aurati medici et philosophi suo ævo perplurime celeberrimi opera medica* (London, 1701), 78–90; *Chamberlain letters*, i. 338; Algernon Cecil, *A Life of Robert Cecil, 1st Earl of Salisbury* (London, 1915), 332–3.

20. PROB 11/119/598, stamped f. 289v.

21. Francis Peck, *Desiderata curiosa*, 2 vols. (London, 1779), i. 205–6.
22. BL, Lans. MS 92, f. 165r; PROB 11/119/598, stamped ff. 392v–393r.
23. CP 129/106.
24. Peck, *Desiderata curiosa*, i. 206–7.
25. PROB 11/119/598, stamped f. 393r; Peck, *Desiderata curiosa*, i. 208.
26. Peck, *Desiderata curiosa*, i. 209.
27. Peck, *Desiderata curiosa*, i. 210.

POSTSCRIPT

1. CP 206/1; *Chamberlain letters*, i. 353–4; PROB 11/119/580, stamped f. 390r; CP 206/60.
2. Susan Bracken, 'Robert Cecil as art collector', in *Patronage, Culture and Power: The Early Cecils, 1558–1612*, ed. Pauline Croft (New Haven, CT, and London, 2002), 132–3; PROB 11/119/598, stamped f. 390r; CP 206/62.
3. SP 14/69, no. 75; *Chamberlain letters*, i. 362; Bacon, *Essays*, 274.
4. Bacon, *Essays*, 133–4.
5. PROB 11/119/598, stamped f. 390r.
6. Jonson, *Works*, v. 377; Bacon, *Essays*, 71–2, 222.
7. *Reliquiæ Bodleianæ: or some genuine remains of Sir Thomas Bodley* (London, 1703), 8–10.
8. Richard Johnson, *A remembrance of the honors due to the life and death of Robert Earl of Salisbury* (London, 1612; STC 14691), quotation at sig. B2r.
9. Johnson, *Remembrance*, sigs. B4v–C1r. For libels on his treatment by Doctor Atkyns and Doctor Poe, which also suggest wider reports of his final illness, see Pauline Croft, 'The reputation of Robert Cecil: libels, political opinion and popular awareness in the early seventeenth century', *Transactions of the Royal Historical Society*, 6th ser. 1 (1991), 58–9.
10. BL, Add. MS 11600, f. 35v, punctuation from John Gutch, *Collectanea curiosa*, 2 vols. (Oxford, 1781), i. 119–20.

Acknowledgements

Every book has its own story, and each its unique journey. This one began with the happy find of a cache of volumes for sale in Oxford – it felt like a sign – and a resolution to write a book that had been tapping me on the shoulder for some time. The route proceeded by way of scribbled notebooks, great accumulations of primary sources, and many, many drafts written and corrected in tea rooms, coffee shops, college guest rooms and a Benedictine monastery, on trains and in some buses, and in 2020 and 2021 exclusively at home in the time available between online lectures and tutorials. In writing the book's proposal, Peter Robinson, set me the cunning challenge of not using the word 'biography' or writing one. Natasha Fairweather has steered the book from contract to publication and, with Simon Winder at Penguin, helped me to lick the bear's whelp of a too hefty first typescript into readable shape. No book turns out in quite the way I expect it to; this one, like all the others, has written me as much as I've written it. 'A portrait of RC as rich and as textured as I can make it' is what I wrote in my first rough manifesto for the book in January 2018. If I've got close to that ambition, I have Peter, Natasha and Simon to thank profoundly for it, along with the teams at RCW Literary Agency and Penguin, Matthew Marland, Eva Hodgkin, Richard Duguid and Pen Vogler especially. Charlotte Ridings has copy-edited the book expertly, handling my syntactical and grammatical eccentricities with equanimity. Howard Davies and Alex Macqueen were kind and generous enough to read the first draft of the typescript, and I am hugely grateful to them.

This book is built upon primary sources, though many of them are hidden below the waterline of research: the endnotes tell a small part of the story. Thirty years ago, as a PhD student studying at St Andrews, I would spend a few summer weeks happily scampering between the Students' Room of the British Library in the British Museum and the old Public Record Office on Chancery Lane with my notebooks and pencil. These days I can read and compare archives in a few hours thanks to electronic resources like State Papers Online (Gale) and the Cecil Papers (ProQuest). Without their riches, I would have found it impossible to do any serious work on the book during the pandemic lockdown: a computer groaning under the weight of PDFs is proof of that. Any serious student who wants to get to know the Cecils should explore these databases, as well as the twenty-four volumes of the Historical Manuscripts Commission's *Calendar* of the Cecil and Salisbury papers. It was the final ten volumes of this series missing from my bookshelves that I discovered in an Oxford bookshop in a cold January 2018, all neat in their orange dust jackets – the final nudge for me to write about Robert Cecil. And, in taking the plunge, I have been sustained by teaching three years of my special subject on 'The Later Elizabethan Age', where I have learned so much from exploring the sources and scholarship with some wonderful final-year History students.

There are some final salutes it is a pleasure to be able to give. To John Cramsie, an old and dear friend as well as a superb historian, in our adventures together and continued and earnest meetings at the Clytemnestra Arms. To Kissy, Sarah and Snowy, who survey human affairs present and past with a serene hauteur, bringing to Robert Cecil a critical eye: to adapt a very old proverb, a cat may look upon a minister. And above all – yet another superlative – to Max and Tilly, whose love and support are beyond all measure, incalculable and joyous, who make life worth living.

At St Andrews, John Guy taught me my trade and made me feel – as I still feel now – the exhilaration and challenge of working, thinking and writing as a historian, the thrill of the archive and all its possibilities. For a few years we were colleagues, working within hailing distance of each other across the lawn between Gibbs' Building, King's Chapel and Clare Old Court. He has been to me an inspiration and always will be: would that I could keep up with his energy and insight. This book, at long last, is dedicated to him.

Index

Bacon, Francis – *cont'd.*
'think tank', 149, 170; lobbies for
solicitorship, 137–9, 149, 151;
need for patronage/preferment,
44, 137–9, 149, 151, 348; new
king promotes, 296; in Paris with
Paulet, 14–15, 19, 22–3; presents
case against Essex (5 June 1600),
243, 244, 254; at Salisbury's
funeral, 347, 348
Bacon, Nicholas, 14, 94
Bancroft, Richard, 292, 293–5, 305
Barker, Christopher, 48–9, 51
Barker, Robert, 312
Barnes, Thomas, 80–81, 106,
317, 318
Basil, Simon, 330, 347
Beale, Robert, 151, 166
Beaufort, Lady Margaret, 325
Bellièvre, Monsieur de, 51
Bellot, Thomas, 16, 76
Bellyn, Randoll, 68
Bergen op Zoom, 6, 56, 92
Berkeley, Sir Richard, 240
Blackfriars playhouse, 314–15
Blount, Sir Michael, 136
Bodley, Thomas, 154, 350
Boleyn, Anne, xxx, xxxi
Bothwell, Francis Stewart, earl of,
140–41, 172
Bowes, Robert, 142, 143
Bowes, Sir William, 224–5,
227–8
Bowle, John, 342–3, 344, 345,
351, 352
Brielle, 205
Bright, Lawrence, 194
Bromley, Sir Thomas, 53
Brooke, George, 294, 295
Brouncker, Sir Henry, 250

Browning, Robert, 'Bishop
Blougram's Apology', xxix
Bruce, Edward, 139–40, 141–2,
252–3, 262–6, 268, 270,
271, 273
Bruges, 5, 59–60
Brussels, 193, 299, 316–17
Buchanan, George, 246
Buckhurst, Lord (Thomas Sackville,
earl of Dorset), 165, 170, 232,
235, 237, 244, 287, 291, 336;
death of (April 1608), 331–2; and
Lopez Plot, 125–6; made lord
treasurer, 225, 226; and peace
with Spain (August 1604), 298–9;
and Spanish peace overtures
(1598), 190–91
Buckingham, George Villiers, duke
of, 351
Burghley, Mildred Cecil, Lady
(mother of Salisbury, née Cooke),
13–14, 15, 16, 18, 30, 32, 53–4,
209; death of (1589), 13, 64–5,
177, 210; worries over Salisbury's
weak constitution, 2–3, 55, 64–5
Burghley, William Cecil, Lord, xxiv,
xxvii; and Allen's *Admonition*,
58–60, 82; appointed lord
treasurer (1572), 69; appointed to
Privy Council (1558), 14; and
Bacon's career, 44; as both
secretary and lord treasurer,
68–79, 88, 90–94, 165; and Cadiz
expedition, 169–70; and
Cambridge University, 29, 30,
325; censors Parry plot story, 39;
and Lord Cobham, 7, 38; Lady
Cobham's support for, 53, 66; as
controller of court patronage, 10,
45–6, 172–3, 183–4; and Court

of Wards corruption, 184, 215;
court's loathing of the Cecil
establishment, 349; cuts number
of spies on payroll, 187; death of
(4 August 1598), 206–7, 208–11;
death of daughters, 64, 177;
death of wife Mildred (1589), 13,
64–5, 177, 210; and earl of Essex,
16, 17–18, 29–30, 54, 153–4,
168, 170, 180; and earl of
Leicester, 50, 52; and earl of
Oxford, 44–5; Elizabeth's fury at
over Mary's death warrant, 52–4;
The Execution of Justice, 31–2,
36, 40; and expeditionary force to
France (1591), 85–6, 87–8, 90,
92–3, 96–7, 99–100, 115; and
fate of Mary Queen of Scots, 45,
46, 47–8, 49, 50, 51–4, 140, 262;
financial cost of high influence,
xxiv, 30, 74–6, 327; Fixer and
Cecil as prisoners of, 81–2, 83,
84–5, 86, 130–31; funeral and
burial of, 211, 212; gardens of,
57, 75; handwriting, 33; Hatton's
support for, 53–4; ill health of,
93, 99, 111, 112, 118–20, 128,
132, 145, 150, 152, 155, 166,
204, 205–7; and James VI of
Scotland, 140–43; last will and
testament, 210–11; and Lopez
Plot, 125, 126, 127, 128, 132,
133, 134–5, 145–7; as master of
the Court of Wards, 15, 183–4,
195, 215–16, 258; meeting with
Oldenbarnevelt, 205; monarch's
principal secretary role, xxvi,
9–10, 68–79, 88, 90–91, 93–4;
and Michael Moody, 82–4, 91,
98, 101–3, 106; Paget as model

and mentor, xxvi; pitch for
Salisbury's promotion (Theobalds,
May 1591), 77–9, 83, 90, 153,
326–7; political longevity, xxiii,
12–13; portfolio of work shared
with Salisbury, 123, 165, 188,
208; and Portuguese plot
allegations, 125; Protestantism of,
10–11, 12, 21, 31–2; pursuit of
Phelippes over debts, 241; and
queen's visit to Theobalds (May
1591), 74–6, 77–9, 81, 83, 153,
326–7; remains as lord treasurer
(1596), 166; Salisbury as his voice
at court, 122, 150, 165, 195–6,
208; Salisbury as understudy to,
78–9, 90–91, 93–4, 96, 111, 120;
and Salisbury's embassy to
France, 195–7; and the
secretaryship (1590), 68–73, 88,
90–91, 93–4; sense of vocation as
fixed/unyielding, 12, 19, 37, 69,
156; service to God as service to
the queen for, 10–11, 156–7, 205,
206, 290; signs letter to Essex and
Howard (August 1596), 168; and
Spanish Armada, 60, 62; and
Spanish peace overtures (1598),
189–92; speech to the Lords
(February 1593), 113–14; and
Stanley's Irish Catholic soldiers,
129, 145; as target of *True Causes*
(1592), 103–6, 117; team of
private secretaries, 4; at
Theobalds (summer 1597), 179,
180–81; trains Salisbury for rule,
4, 7, 8, 12, 15, 19, 54, 94, 96,
208–9, 350; and William Wade,
23–4; and war against Spain,
xxxi, 156, 158, 159, 180; and

Henslowe, Philip, 135–6
Herbert, John, 197, 198–9, 201–2
Herle, William, 45–6
Hickes, Sir Michael, 4, 38, 63–4,
  66–7, 72, 73, 76, 90–91, 93, 94,
  175, 296; with Burghley (July
  1597), 179, 180–81; as
  moneylender, 173, 241; with
  Salisbury in Bath, 342, 343; at
  Salisbury's funeral, 347
Hoby, Sir Edward, 38, 161, 163,
  164, 167, 175, 176, 254–5
Holbein the Younger, Hans, xxi
Holstein, Ulric, duke of, 305
Holy Roman Empire, xxx
Home, Sir George, 256
Honiman, Thomas, 188–9, 193
Hooper, Humphrey, 177–8
Houghton, Roger, 2, 3, 185, 187,
  189, 204, 207
Howard, Lord Henry (earl of
  Northampton), 265–6, 270, 271,
  272, 273, 298–9, 302, 303, 308,
  319, 321, 322–3
Howard, Lord Thomas, 179, 195
Howland, Richard, 30
Hudson, James, 239
Hunsdon, Lord, 62, 173, 190, 231
Huntingdon, earls of, 283

Ireland, 191, 193, 200, 206; battle
  of the Yellow Ford (August 1598),
  212, 217, 218; Catholicism in,
  xxviii, 217–18, 235; colonizing of
  Ulster, 16–17, 217; Essex as lord
  lieutenant, 218, 219–20, 223–4,
  228–30, 231–3, 234–5, 243–5,
  255; Essex's expedition to (1599),
  223–4, 228–30, 231–3, 234–5,
  243–5, 255; Fenton and Ormond

meet Tyrone (November 1599),
  234–5; Gaelic resistance in 1590s,
  217–18; the Pale (anglicized
  territory around Dublin), xxviii;
  Protestant settler outposts, xxviii;
  rebellion (1593), xxviii; Scottish
  aid to rebels, 221; Spanish army
  in (1601–2), 269–70; Stanley's
  Catholic soldiers, 128–9, 145;
  Watson-Markham plot in (1603),
  293–6
Isabella, Infanta of Spain, 252,
  257–8, 262–3, 265, 266–7, 283,
  298

James, John, 69–70
James I, king (James VI of Scotland):
  accession to English throne (24
  March 1603), 282–4, 286–7;
  ambassadors' mission to Elizabeth
  (1594), 139–43; ambassadors'
  mission to Elizabeth (1601),
  252–3, 262–7; annual pension
  from Elizabeth, 140, 141, 142;
  atmosphere/tone of new court,
  296–7; *Basilikon Doron*, 286;
  Bowes as ambassador to, 224–5,
  227–8; as boy king of Scotland,
  43; Catholic revolts against, 113,
  120–21, 139–40, 141, 142, 143–4;
  desire for full union, 305; Duchy
  House meeting, 264–5; Dutch
  support for claim to throne, 246;
  and earl of Essex, 141–2, 143–4,
  252–3, 262–3, 265–6; Elphinstone
  in government of, 221–3, 224,
  249, 253, 256; embassy to
  Germany, 227–8; and Essex
  rebellion (8 February 1601),
  256–7, 262; exchanges Hatfield

James I, king – *cont'd.*
for Theobalds, 329–30; finances
of, 305–6, 338–41; fondness for
hunting, 288, 297, 305, 309; as
generous with patronage, 290,
296–7, 338; Gowrie murder plot
(1600), 247–50; at grand opening
of the Burse, 334–5; intellectual/
cultural interests, 288–9; links
succession with religion, 285; Lok
at court of, 172; makes peace with
Spain (August 1604), 298–9, 316;
marries Anne of Denmark (1589),
222; new favourites after
Salisbury, 351; as prisoner at
Ruthven Castle (1582–3), 239;
royal minority of, xxxii; at
Theobalds (July 1606), 327–8;
Valentine Thomas allegations,
212–14, 218–19, 222–3, 263,
289; travels south to London
(April 1603), 287–9; views on
Catholicism, 285, 286; visits
Salisbury at Salisbury House (May
1605), 305; watches Garnet trial,
321 *see also* succession, English
James IV, king of Scotland, 41
James V, king of Scotland, xxx, 41–2
Jesuits, 104, 124–5, 130, 145, 285,
286, 292, 293–4, 316, 320–23;
Fixer and Cecil as prisoners of
Burghley, 81–2, 83, 84–5, 86,
130–31; Jesuits bill (1584), 38–9
Johnson, Richard, 351–2
Jones, Inigo, 328, 333, 335
Jonson, Ben, 302–4, 306, 307, 311,
328, 330, 333, 335, 349

Katherine of Aragon, xxx
Killigrew, William, 52, 108

Knollys, Sir William, 182, 231,
257–8

Lake, Sir Thomas, 155, 341
Lancaster, chancellor of Duchy of,
xxv, 68, 184, 226, 264
Lancaster, John of Gaunt, duke of,
151, 184, 283
Latymer, Edward, 216
Leicester, Robert Dudley, earl of, 21,
23, 48–9, 50, 52, 126, 298
Lennox, duke of, 247, 248, 256
Lindley, Henry, 181–2
Lipsius, Justus, xxii, xxix, 73, 95,
185–6
Lisbon, 180, 193
Lok, Henry, 19, 171–4
Lopez, Ruy (or Roderigo), 123, 124,
125–8, 132–6, 144–7
Loseley Park, Surrey, 90
Luther, Martin, xxx
Lyminge, Robert, 330

Machiavelli, Niccolo, 117
Madre de Deus (Portuguese
galleon), 107–11
Maecenas, Gaius, 172, 174
Maisse, André Hurault, sieur de,
189–91, 192
Mar, John Erskine, earl of, 246–7,
248, 252–3, 262–6, 268, 270,
271, 273
Marbeck, Roger, 162, 163
Marchaumont, Henri Clausse, sieur
de, 35, 76
Margaret Tudor, 41, 42, 276
Markham, Sir Griffin, 293–6
Marlowe, Christopher, 116, 187;
The Jew of Malta, 117, 135–6
Mary I, Queen, 121

Nottingham – *cont'd.*
and peace with Spain (August
1604), 298–9; Privy Council letter
to (August 1596), 168, 169; and
queen's last days, 280; and
Salisbury's embassy to France,
195, 196; and Spanish Armada,
60–62, 75, 77; and Spanish peace
overtures (1598), 190–91
Nowell, Alexander, 32–4

Oatlands Palace, Surrey, 97
Oldenbarnevelt, Johan van, 197,
201–2, 204–5
Orange, House of, 34, 36, 37,
38, 201
Ormond, Thomas, earl of, 208,
234–5
Ostend, 1, 3–4, 6–7
Owen, Hugh, 194, 299, 300–301,
308, 316
Owter, Hans, 193
Oxford, Anne, countess of (née
Cecil, sister of Salisbury), 13, 15,
16, 18, 63, 64, 66; daughters of,
63, 64, 65; death of (June 1588),
64, 65, 177
Oxford, Edward de Vere, earl of, 15,
16, 44–5, 64, 66, 172

Paget, Charles, 83
Paget, William, xxvi
Palatino, Giambattista, 33
Palavicino, Sir Horatio, 185, 186,
187, 193, 209
Palmer, Edmund, 188, 189, 193
Paris, 26–7, 34–8, 40–41; Francis
Bacon in with Paulet, 14–15, 19,
22–3; English Catholic émigré
dissidents, 27–8, 31, 36–7, 40–41,

82–4; Phelippes in, 22–5, 26–7,
336; Salisbury visits (1584), 34–8,
40; scholarly life, 35–6; size of in
sixteenth-century, 35; Wade in,
22–5
parliament, xxvi–xxvii; Elizabeth's
tenth (autumn 1601), 269–70;
failure of 'Great Contract'
(1610), 338–41; and fate of
Mary Queen of Scots, 47–8,
49–50; and financing of war,
113, 114, 115; House of
Commons, xxvi, xxvii, 112–13,
114, 115–17, 118, 139, 339;
House of Lords, xxvi, xxvii,
112–14, 118, 307; James' first
(1605), 306; James I's
relationship with, 338–41;
post-Gunpowder Plot security
legislation, 317; Salisbury as
member for Westminster, xxvii,
38, 47; Salisbury's 'Great
Contract' put to (1610), 338–41;
security bills (1584–5), xxvii,
38–9, 49, 214; as summoned by
the monarch, xxvii, 38, 112; tiny
electorate of property- holders,
xxvii
Parma, duke of, 2, 56–7, 59–60,
91–2; audience with Salisbury
(1588), 4–6, 55, 58, 209; peace
talks with Derby's delegation
(1588), 6–7, 58, 62–3, 298;
Salisbury obtains English dogs
for, 57–8; and Spanish Armada, 7,
58, 60, 61, 62–3
Parry, William, 36, 38–9, 40, 49, 94
Patrick, William, 306
patronage, xxii, xxiv–xxv, 137–9,
149–50, 171–4, 183–4, 215,

225, 350; Francis Bacon's need for, 44, 137–9, 149, 151, 348; Burghley as controller of, 10, 45–6, 172–3, 183–4; and Essex, 70–71, 115, 138–9, 149, 151, 181, 183, 215, 350; James I as generous with, 290, 296–7, 338; lobbying and petitioning, xxv, 70–71, 137–9, 149, 151, 172, 350; Salisbury as controller of, 19, 45–6, 63, 172, 183–4, 274, 278
Paulet, Sir Amias, 14–15, 20–24, 28, 31, 43
Peele, George, 94
Pembroke, earl of, 347
Penne, Juliana, 64
Percival, Richard, 187
Percy, Thomas, 306, 307, 310–11, 318
Pérez, Antonio, 149–50, 171
Perne, Doctor, 29, 30
Persons, Robert, 104, 130, 131, 151, 156, 257–8, 278, 285, 293
Peyton, Sir John, 281
Phelippes, John, 192
Phelippes, Stephen, 318
Phelippes, Thomas, 22–3, 28, 31; Thomas Barnes as agent of, 80–81, 106, 317, 318; and Catholicism, 43, 51, 57, 80–81, 82, 240–41, 245–6, 253, 289, 299–301, 309, 316–17; as codes and ciphers expert, 23, 25, 26, 43, 51, 188, 240; as collector of revenue on exports, 80, 111, 241; crushing debt problems, 241, 250, 289; and fate of Mary Stuart, 43, 51, 289, 300, 336; and Gunpowder Plot, 318;

'imaginary intelligencer' called Vincent, 299–300; imprisonment of (1605), 299, 300, 301, 316–17; Salisbury's suspicions of, 299–301, 316–18, 323–4; sent to the Tower, 318, 320, 323–4, 328, 335–6; spy work for Salisbury, 242, 245–6, 250, 268, 289–90, 299–301, 309; unauthorized communications with Owen, 299–301, 309, 316–17, 323–4; Walsingham as patron, 24, 25, 26–7, 43, 57, 336; works for Essex, 240–41, 299, 300, 301
Philip, Sir David, 318
Philip II, King of Spain, xxiii, xxvii, xxxi, 25, 85, 113, 162, 163; costs of Dutch War, 56; failing health of, 190; and Lopez Plot, 124–5, 126, 132, 133, 134, 146; and Mary Queen of Scots, 42; and Persons's *Conference*, 151–2, 156, 257–8, 278; and Portugal, 123–5, 126
Phillips, Augustine, 255
Pius V, Pope, 11
plague, 110–11
Poe, Doctor, 342, 343, 344, 345
Poley, Robert, 187
Popham, Sir John, 225, 237, 254, 295–6, 319, 320
Portugal, xxxi, 123–8, 129–30, 132–6
privateering, 107–11
Privy Council: and the accession of James I (24 March 1603), 282–4, 286–7; and death of Elizabeth I, 280, 281–2; Essex appointed to (1593), 114–15; Essex's aggressive play for pre-eminence,

Salisbury, Robert – *cont'd.*
new king, 287–8; and Howard's
anger at Essex, 158–9; inherits
Burghley's enormous working
archive, 210–11; Richard
Johnson celebrates, 351–2; as
Ben Jonson's patron, 302–3, 304,
306, 311; knighted at Theobalds
(May 1591), 79, 80; as landed
gentleman, 65–6, 67, 78; last
will and testament, 342, 343,
344, 349; leads James'
provisional government, 287–8;
learns trade of espionage, 80,
84–5, 86; Leicester as godfather
of, 50; lobbies for Francis Bacon,
137, 138; Lok's sonnet on, 174;
and Lopez Plot, 123, 124–7,
132–3, 136, 146, 147; as Lord
Treasurer, 338–44; and *Madre
de Deus* problem (1592),
107–11; marries Bess, 66–7;
meets Dutch embassy in France
(1598), 201–2; meets new king
in York, 287–8, 289; mission to
the Low Countries (1588), xxiii,
1–8, 55–7, 64–5; and Michael
Moody, 83–4, 91–2, 101–3,
105–6, 123; as MP for
Westminster, xxvii, 38, 47; as
new king's 'little beagle', 297,
305; official narrative of
Gunpowder Plot, 308–10, 311;
opens communications with
James VI (1601), 264–7; and
Owen and Garnet's role in
Gunpowder Plot, 316–23; and
peace with Spain (August 1604),
298–9; Phelippes as spy for, 242,
245–6, 250, 268, 289–90,

299–301, 309; portfolio of work
shared with Burghley, 123, 165,
188, 208; portrayed in Somerset
House painting, 298–9;
posthumous libels, 348–50;
pragmatism of, 290; presides
over Gunpowder Plot inquiry,
310–12; as principal secretary to
king, 290–91; private secretariat
of, 187, 192, 332; Protestantism
of, 12; public disquiet at riches
and dominance of, xxii, 226–7,
237; queen visits (early 1593),
112; and queen's last days,
280–81, 284, 286; and queen's
visit to Theobalds (May 1591),
77–9, 81, 83; raising and
shaping of son William, 325–6,
327, 330–31, 336–8, 351;
reading of queen's mood and
mind, 98–9, 154–5, 165;
relations with Essex, 54, 100,
153–4, 171, 181–2, 218, 226,
234, 235, 237, 238, 267; role in
choreographing the accession
(24 March 1603), xxii, 281,
282–4, 286–7, 290; and
Scotland, 123, 140–44, 221–3,
227–8, 246–9, 253, 256–7,
262–7; and Scottish embassy
(1601), 262–7; secret
correspondence with James VI,
267–8, 269, 270–74, 281,
284–6; sense of vocation as
fixed/unyielding, 350–51;
seriously ill health (autumn
1602), 274–5; service to God as
service to the queen for, 290;
signature, 33, 89, 150; signs
letter to Essex and Howard